Second Language Research

In this second edition of the best-selling *Second Language Research*, Alison Mackey and Susan M. Gass continue to guide students step by step through conducting the second language research process with a clear and comprehensive overview of the core issues in second language research. Supported by a wealth of data examples from published studies, the book examines questions of what is meant by research and what defines good research questions, covering such topics as basic research principles and data collection methods, designing a quantitative research study, and concluding and reporting research findings. Supplementary materials, including an extensive glossary and appendices with helpful materials that students can use in conducting their own studies, serve as useful reference tools, with suggestions on how to get research published re-emphasizing the book's practical how-to approach. The second edition of *Second Language Research* is the ideal resource for understanding the second language research process for advanced undergraduates, graduate students, and professionals in Second Language Acquisition and Applied Linguistics.

Alison Mackey is Professor in the Department of Linguistics at Georgetown University.

Susan M. Gass is University Distinguished Professor in the Department of Linguistics and Germanic, Slavic, Asian and African Languages at Michigan State University.

Second Language Research

Methodology and Design

Second Edition

Alison Mackey and Susan M. Gass

Georgetown University and
Michigan State University

 Routledge
Taylor & Francis Group

NEW YORK AND LONDON

This edition published 2016
by Routledge
711 Third Avenue, New York, NY 10017

and by Routledge
2 Park Square, Milton Park, Abingdon, Oxon OX14 4RN

Routledge is an imprint of the Taylor & Francis Group, an informa business

First edition published by Lawrence Erlbaum Associates, Inc. 2005

Library of Congress Cataloging in Publication Data
Mackey, Alison, author
  Second language research: methodology and design/Alison Mackey and
  Susan M. Gass, Georgetown University and Michigan State University.—
  Second Edition.
  pages cm
  Previous edition: Second language research/Alison Mackey, 1st ed.,
  2005.
  Includes bibliographical references and index.
  1. Second language acquisition. 2. Second language acquisition—
  Research—Methodology. I. Gass, Susan M., author II. Title.
  P118.2.M23 2015
  418.0072—dc23
  2015006149

ISBN: 978-1-138-80855-3 (hbk)
ISBN: 978-1-138-80856-0 (pbk)
ISBN: 978-1-315-75060-6 (ebk)

Typeset in Helvetica Neue and Optima
by Florence Production Ltd, Stoodleigh, Devon, UK

MIX
Paper from
responsible sources
FSC www.fsc.org **FSC® C014174**

Printed and bound in the United States of America by Sheridan Books, Inc. (a Sheridan Group Company).

Contents

Preface

This book is designed to be used as a text for introductory courses on research methodology and design, as well as for other courses in second language studies, where there is an emphasis on research. It can also be used as a general resource book by people carrying out second language research.

The first edition was published a decade ago. This new edition provides updates to reflect changes and developments in the field, together with some internal reorganization, and a new chapter on mixed-methods research, reflecting the current state of the art in the field. We have also included some new features to improve its pedagogically friendly nature, including boxed "time to think" and "time to do" suggestions throughout each chapter, to supplement the exercises at the end of each chapter. Throughout the revisions, we retained our primary goal of providing an introductory text for novice researchers. We explain key concepts and provide concrete examples wherever possible for those with little or no research experience. Exercises are provided throughout the text to allow students to think about the concepts introduced and to get hands-on practice at doing the various activities involved in research. We assume that our readers will have some background in the general topic of second language learning. The discussion and data-based questions throughout each chapter and the activities at the end of each chapter are aimed to promote better understanding of the concepts as readers work through the book. We also include a detailed and updated glossary to aid researchers who prefer to use the book more as a resource than a text.

We take a broad and inclusive view of "second language" research. For this reason, our examples reflect concepts from a variety of perspectives in the second language field. The book is designed to address issues important for research in both second and foreign language settings, for child as well as adult second language learning, for research on bilingual and multilingual language learning, as well as the acquisition of third and subsequent languages. We have attempted to cast a similarly wide net in our coverage of topics; for example, we include research design issues that range from the use of highly experimental data elicitation tools, to qualitative concerns, as well as teacher-initiated research in classrooms. We also include topics of recent interest in the field, such as dealing with university, institutional, and school review boards that grant permission for data gathering from human subjects, including recent concerns about the replication of research. Although our goal is to acquaint readers with the basic issues, problems, and solutions involved in conducting second language research, we believe that some of the content of the book is also relevant to a wider applied linguistics context. In other words, some issues of design are common to many areas of applied linguistics research, even though the examples may not always be. We also recognize that some chapters might not be relevant to all courses on second language research. The book is designed so that chapters or parts of chapters can be skipped. The most obvious example is Chapter 2, which deals with obtaining consent and obtaining permission from institutional review boards. Not all countries or research contexts require stringent procedures, and sections of this chapter, while important for research in some parts of the world, are less relevant for research in other countries.

Although the book focuses specifically on issues of research design and methodology, we have included one chapter that focuses on introductory statistics. Because the field of statistics is so broad and has its own special-ized texts and courses, we provide only a simple overview of some of the basic concepts in this area. For those who intend to conduct detailed statistical analyses, we recommend coursework, expert consultations, and other com-parable means of learning about advanced statistics, including statistics textbooks. We do not include specific recommendations about particular statistics texts because the selection of the text depends on the focus of the research problem. Second language research can focus on educational or pedagogical practice or on theory building; it can address issues from a variety of perspectives, including psychology, sociology, linguistics, and bilingualism. We suggest that users of this book consult one of the many appropriate statistics books available.

It is always difficult to decide on the order in which to present information. One researcher's ordering of material and chapters might not coincide with the preferences of another researcher or reader. We have placed information on data gathering at the beginning of the book due to the fact that our experience in teaching research methods courses over the years has led us to believe that researchers need to think about where data come from at the outset of a project, and to think about how data are gathered before becoming immersed in some of the more technical issues of design. In this book, then, issues of data gathering serve as an anchor for later chapters. Of course, when using the book as a text, we imagine that instructors will adapt the book and reorder chapters to match their particular syllabus and preference for presentation. For this reason, we have made sure, where possible, that each chapter can work as a stand-alone introduction to the area it covers.

We are grateful to many individuals for their support in this project that ended up, like most projects of this sort, having a longer history than we had originally anticipated. For both editions, we first thank the many students we have had in different classes over the years who have not hesitated to provide feedback on our various syllabi and our sequencing of materials, as well as the designs of our own research. The following individuals provided various kinds of invaluable assistance and feedback on the first edition, and we recognize them here: Rebekha Abbuhl, Rebecca Adams, Zoltán Dörnyei, Rod Ellis, Seon Jeon, Kendall King, Patsy Lightbown, Kimberly McDonough, Kara Morgan-Short, Jenefer Philp, Charlene Polio, Rebecca Sachs, Ildikó Svetics, Ian Thornton, and Harriet Wood. In this second edition, we were fortunate, once again, to have the invaluable input and help of our research assistants: Lara Bryfonski and Alex Marsters at Georgetown University, and Lorena Valmori at Michigan State University. Ina Choi of Michigan State University helped with NVivo examples. Luke Plonsky also helped with many parts of this revised edition. His input was essential in helping us to see how to present material better and even to help us better understand particular concepts. After many years of using this book in our own courses and hearing from students (and faculty) around the world, we have made adjustments to this edition based on their comments. Four external reviews of the first edition were commissioned, with extensive comments on the book, some dealing with ways to update the manuscript, some with ways to make things clearer, and some with ordering of material. You know who you are (we do not), and we thank you sincerely for your input. You will undoubtedly see your many helpful suggestions reflected in this edition.

Finally, Leah Babb-Rosenfeld and Elysse Preposi of Routledge have been unwavering in their support of this book and enormously patient awaiting this revised edition. We are grateful for the general support and encouragement we consistently receive from everyone at Routledge.

Alison Mackey
Georgetown, Washington, DC
Susan Gass
Williamston, Michigan

CHAPTER ONE

Introduction to Research

How do we identify good research questions? How do we answer them? What do we mean by research? These sorts of questions are not always easy to answer, but we anticipate that by the end of this book, you will be in a better position to think about them. The book is practical in nature, aimed at those who are involved in second language studies, second/foreign language instruction and researcher training, and in it, we aim to demystify the research process.

Oxford Dictionaries defines research as *"the systematic investigation into and study of materials and sources in order to establish facts and reach new conclusions"* (www.oxforddictionaries.com/us/definition/american_english/research?searchDictCode=all, retrieved January 17, 2015). Thus, in its most basic and simplest form, research is a way of finding out answers to questions.

We are all involved in research every day. Let's think about what probably occurs as part of many of our lives—being stuck in a traffic jam. As we find ourselves not moving on a freeway, we ask why this has happened and come up with a hypothesis (because there is an accident ahead, for example, or because it is 5:00 p.m. on a Friday afternoon). We then seek verification of our hypothesis by waiting patiently (or impatiently) until the traffic starts moving again. If we see an accident, hear a radio report, look at live traffic on our GPS, or if we see the flashing lights of an emergency vehicle, we might be able to confirm or reject our hypothesis. In the absence of an accident, we might conclude that it must be typical rush hour traffic. In other words, every day we ask questions, come up with hypotheses, and seek confirmation of those hypotheses. Research, then, is not something to be wary of; it is not something that is done only in laboratories or controlled conditions. It is something that we do on a small or large scale every day. We can pose and (hopefully) answer questions of deep theoretical significance and we can also pose questions that assist us in our daily lives. As teachers, research helps us think through problems that intrigue us with regard to our students and, as a consequence, helps us be more effective.

TIME TO THINK ...

Come up with two to three questions about language learning and/or language teaching that you have been puzzled about. Keep these in mind (or develop new ideas) as you continue to use this book.

In this chapter, we discuss the process of generating research questions and formulating hypotheses, and we outline what readers can expect from a typical research report. We conclude by discussing issues of feasibility and the importance of confirming findings, a process known as replication, in second language research.

1.1 RESEARCH METHODS

Research is not monolithic. That is, there is no single way to go about doing research. The way we approach our understanding of language learning will guide us in how we go about collecting information (data) to answer our questions. For example, there are numerous ways to think about second language learning (for example, there are a number of textbooks that cover the wide field of second language acquisition, such as Gass with Behney and Plonsky, 2013). Some researchers conceptualize language as consisting of a set of linguistic abstractions (mental representations). Learning a second language, then, involves learning a new set of mental representations with the focus being on language forms. These are often called formal approaches. Others view language as a sociocultural phenomenon with language learning based not only on internal linguistic factors, as in formal approaches, but on how language forms interact with external factors (contexts for learning). Still others are concerned with how second languages are processed. Are the mechanisms used when processing a first language the same as those used when processing a second? Each of these approaches (and others) will require different data sets to answer the questions posed. For example, in approaches where the social setting is important, context must be provided. In approaches where only grammatical forms are of concern, context is not a consideration. These general orientations influence the methodologies that are used. In the following section, we outline two broad approaches to research that have received attention in the second language literature: quantitative and qualitative, and we also discuss mixed-methods studies, which use both. We believe that there is no perfect approach; there are strengths and weaknesses to all. What is important to recognize is that choices (and typically trade-offs) have to be made when conducting research. What is equally important to recognize is that whatever research method we choose, we need to justify using that particular methodology in light of our research question. In other words, the process of conducting research involves theoretical conceptualizations as well as practical considerations. These interrelated notions guide decision-making at all stages of the research process, as will become apparent throughout this book.

TIME TO THINK ...

If you have taken a course on second language acquisition (SLA), what theoretical approach do you align with to the greatest extent?

If you have taught language, what learning approach is most helpful to you in understanding how your students are learning?

1.2 DIFFERENT TYPES OF RESEARCH

As mentioned above, there are many approaches to dealing with research. Two of the most common are known as quantitative and qualitative, although this distinction is somewhat simplistic as the relationship is best thought of as a continuum of research types, and mixed-methods research involves elements of both. Quantitative research generally starts with an experimental design in which a specific hypothesis precedes the quantification of data with follow-up numerical analyses (e.g., a study comparing student test results before and after an instructional treatment). Qualitative studies, on the other hand, generally are not set up as experiments; the data cannot be easily quantified (e.g., a diary study in which a student keeps track of his or her attitudes during a year-long Japanese language course), and the analysis is interpretive rather than statistical. As mentioned above, this is rather a simplistic view because one can imagine a number of variations on this theme. In general, though, quantitative and qualitative research can be characterized as in Table 1.1 (see Reichardt & Cook, 1979).

In this book, we attempt to be as inclusive as possible and cover a variety of research orientations. In particular, we show in Chapter 9 how the types

TABLE 1.1 Characteristics of quantitative and qualitative research

Quantitative Research	Qualitative Research
• obtrusive, involving controlled measurement	• naturalistic and controlled observation
• objective and removed from the data	• subjective
• verification-oriented, confirmatory	• discovery-oriented
• outcome-oriented	• process-oriented
• reliable, involving "hard" and replicable data	• "soft" data
• generalizable	• ungeneralizable, single case studies
• assuming a stable reality	• assuming a dynamic reality
	• close to the data

represented in Table 1.1 are combined; in other words, these represent "pure" forms of these two research types.

Grotjahn (1987) points out that there are many parameters that can be used to distinguish between research types, including the type of data (quantitative or qualitative), the method of analysis (interpretative or statistical), and the manner of data collection (experimental or non-experimental [naturalistic]). He outlines six "mixed" forms (see Table 1.2).

TABLE 1.2 Six mixed forms of research

Type of Research	Form of Data		Method of Analysis		Manner of Data Collection	
	Quantitative	Qualitative	Statistical	Interpretative	Experimental/ Quasi-Experimental	Non-Experimental
Experimental-qualitative-interpretative		✔		✔	✔	
Experimental-qualitative-statistical		✔	✔		✔	
Experimental-quantitative-interpretative	✔			✔	✔	
Exploratory-qualitative-statistical		✔	✔			✔
Exploratory-quantitative-statistical	✔		✔			✔
Exploratory-quantitative-interpretative	✔			✔		✔

TIME TO DO ...

Part 1
Read the following abstract from Philp (2003, p. 99).

Interaction has been argued to promote noticing of L2 form in a context crucial to learning—when there is a mismatch between the input and the learner's interlanguage (IL) grammar (Gass & Varonis, 1994; Long, 1996; Pica, 1994). This paper investigates the extent to which learners may notice native speakers' reformulations of their IL grammar in the context of dyadic interaction. Thirty-three adult ESL learners worked on oral communication tasks in NS-NNS pairs. During each of the five sessions of dyadic task-based interaction, learners received recasts of their nontargetlike question forms. Accurate immediate recall of recasts was taken as evidence of noticing of recasts by learners. Results indicate that learners noticed over 60–70 percent of recasts. However, accurate recall was constrained by the level of the learner and by the length and number of changes in the recast. The effect of these variables on noticing is discussed in terms of processing biases. It is suggested that attentional resources and processing biases of the learner may modulate the extent to which learners "notice the gap" between their nontargetlike utterances and recasts.

Does this abstract seem more part of a quantitative or a qualitative study? In thinking about this, consider the following:

* Does the study have quantitative data?
* How are data analyzed?
* Were data collected experimentally?

Part 2
Read the following abstract from Willett (1995, p. 473).

This ethnographic report "thickly describes" (Geertz, 1973) the participation of ESL children in the daily classroom events of a mainstream first-grade classroom. Data for this paper come from a year-long study of one classroom in an international school on a college campus in the U.S. Using a language socialization and micropolitical orientation, the report describes how, through socially significant interactional routines, the children and other members of the classroom jointly constructed the ESL children's identities, social relations, and ideologies as well as their communicative competence in that setting. The sociocultural ecology of the community, school, and classroom shaped the kinds of microinteractions that occurred and thus the nature of their language learning over the course of the year.

Does this abstract seem to describe a quantitative or a qualitative study? Consider the following:

- Does the study use naturalistic data?
- If so, of what sort?
- Does it provide an interpretative or a statistical analysis?
- Is there an experimental design?

Part 3
Look at a recent issue of one of the journals listed below. Consider the abstracts for two to three of the articles and determine whether they seem to be more quantitative or qualitative.

- *Studies in Second Language Acquisition*
- *TESOL Quarterly*
- *Language Learning*

What led you to that conclusion?

1.3 WHAT IS A RESEARCH REPORT?

In this section, we provide a guide for readers as to what to expect in a typical article in the field of SLA, focusing primarily on quantitatively oriented research articles. Unlike quantitative research reports where there is a relatively standard format for reporting, qualitative research articles are more wide-ranging in terms of organization (see Chapter 7, where we discuss qualitative research). Our goal is to give an idea of what to expect in a research report. To that end, below we present a basic skeleton of a research paper. Chapter 11 provides detailed information for researchers concerning the *writing* and *reporting* of their own research based on all of the areas covered in this book.

We now consider in more detail what might be included in each of these parts.

Typical research paper format

TITLE PAGE
ABSTRACT
BODY

I. Introduction
    A. Statement of topic area
    B. Statement of general issues
    C. General goal of paper
    D. Literature review
        1. Historical overview
        2. Major contributions to this research area
        3. Statement of purpose including identification of gaps
        4. Hypotheses

II. Method
    A. Participants
        1. How many?
        2. Characteristics (male/female, proficiency level, native language, etc.)
    B. Materials
        1. What instruments?
        2. What sort of test? What sort of task?
    C. Procedures
        1. How is the treatment to be administered?
        2. How/when is the testing to be done?
    D. Analysis
    How will the results be analyzed?

III. Results
Charts, tables, and/or figures accompanied by verbal descriptions

IV. Discussion/Conclusion (often two separate sections)
Common features:
- Restatement of the main idea of the study
- Summary of the findings
- Interpretation of the findings in light of the research questions
- Proposed explanation of the findings, usually including information about any findings that were contrary to expectations
- Limitations of the study
- Suggestions for future research

NOTES
REFERENCES
APPENDICES

TIME TO DO ...

There are many journals where research in SLA is published. Conduct a library or online search and come up with a list of five journals focusing on some area (general or specific) of second language research.

1.3.1 Title Page

- Name of author(s)
- Title of paper
- Contact information

1.3.2 Abstract

The abstract presents a summary of the topic of the paper and the major findings of the research. Abstracts are very often printed through abstracting services and are generally the primary source in finding out about a paper. They are usually 100–150 words in length, although there is variation depending on where the article is published. In the box below is an example of an abstract (Williams, 1999, p. 583).

Abstract

Recent studies have suggested that the incorporation of some attention to form into meaning-centered instruction can lead to improved performance in processing input and increased accuracy in production. Most have examined attention to form delivered by instructors or instructional materials. This study examines the production of 8 classroom learners at 4 levels of proficiency to determine the extent to which learners can and do spontaneously attend to form in their interaction with other learners. Results suggest that the degree and type of learner-generated attention to form is related to proficiency level and the nature of the activity in which the learners are engaged. They also indicate that learners overwhelmingly choose to focus on lexical rather than grammatical issues. (118 words)

In this short abstract, two sentences are devoted to past research, with the third sentence informing the reader what this study is about and how it fills a gap in the literature. The final two sentences provide information about what the reader can expect from the results.

TIME TO DO ...

Find abstracts from two different articles in two different journals.
Analyze each in the way that we did above.

1.3.3 Introduction

The introduction sets the scene and provides the reader with background material (statement of topic area and general issues), as well as an outline of the purpose of the research. This is generally followed by a literature review. Some possibilities for literature reviews include the following:

- Historical overview

Example:

In earlier views of the relationship between x and y . . .

- Major players in this research area, including questions, past findings, and controversies

Example:

In 1994, Smith claimed that the relationship between x and y was an important one and went on to show that . . .

However, in a more recent paper, Jones (1995) argued that this relationship could not be valid because . . .

- General goal of the paper

Example:

In this paper, I will argue that Jones's interpretation of Smith's data is incorrect and that when one looks at variable *z* in the context of *x* and *y*, the relationship is indeed valid. I will present data that support Ellis's original interpretation of *abc*.

- Research questions/hypotheses

In Williams' (1999) article abstracted above, the following research questions are provided after the introduction (p. 591):

Example:

1. Do learners in learner-centered, communicative classrooms spontaneously attend to form?
2. Is proficiency level related to the extent to which they do so?
3. How do learners draw attention to form?
4. When do learners draw attention to form, that is, during what types of activities?
5. What kinds of forms do they attend to?

As can be seen, these questions build on one another. They are not, however, formulated as predictions. Below are specific hypotheses from a different study (Gass & Alvarez-Torres, 2005):

Example:

1. Given that interaction is said to be an attention-drawing device, we predict that the three experimental groups with interaction will perform better than the group with no interaction.
2. Because input and interaction serve different important functions, when there is a combination of conditions (input followed by interaction and interaction followed by input), performance will be better than when only one type of presentation is available.

---

3.   Given Gass's (1997) assumption that interaction serves as a priming device that "readies" learners to utilize follow-up input, the best performance will take place in the group with interaction followed by input.

The amount of detail needed in a literature review will depend on the purpose of the report. For example, a Ph.D. dissertation will generally be as exhaustive as possible. On the other hand, the literature review for a journal article or for a chapter in a book will only address previous research that directly relates to the specific purpose of the research report and might only be about 5–10 pages.

1.3.4 Methods Section

In the methods section, the reader can expect to be informed about all aspects of the study. One reason for this is the later possibility of replication (see section 1.4.3). Another reason is that in order for a reader to come to an informed opinion about the research, he or she needs to have as much detail as possible about what was done.

1.3.4.1 Participants

This section includes information about the participants[1] in a study. For example, how many participants were there? What are their characteristics (e.g., male/female, native language, age, proficiency level, length of residence, amount and type of instruction, handedness)? The characteristics that researchers describe will depend, in part, on the experiment itself. For example, handedness was listed above as a possible characteristic. This would probably be relevant in a study that required participants to press a button on a computer as a response to some stimulus. Most such studies are set up for right-handed individuals, so it might be important to know if the particular setup favored those individuals.

1.3.4.2 Materials

The materials used to conduct the study are usually presented in detail and where there is insufficient space, a new trend in our field, supported by all the major journals, is to encourage the upload of the original materials to the free, online, up- and downloadable, searchable database IRIS (www.iris-database.org). Below is an example of a materials section from an article on deriving meaning from

11

written context by Dutch children (grades 2, 4, and 6) in their L1 (Fukkink, Blok, & de Glopper, 2001, p. 481).

Target words were selected from a primary-school dictionary (Verburg & Huijgen, 1994), to warrant that relevant concepts would be selected, representative of the words young readers encounter during reading. An initial sample of words with a frequency below 10 per million (Celex, Centre for Lexical Information, 1990) was selected from this dictionary to ensure that no words were used that students were already familiar with. Three judges evaluated the concreteness of the target words, defined as a dichotomy, and words were excluded if the judges did not arrive at a unanimous agreement. A final sample of 12 words was selected, evenly divided into concrete and abstract words. The average word frequency of the words in the sample is 4.4 per million (ranging from 1 to 10 per million). Only morphologically nontransparent words were included, to promote deriving word meaning from (external) context.

Short texts of approximately a hundred words were constructed for each target word. The difficulty level of each text was adjusted to an appropriate level for average readers at the end of grade 2 on the basis of a reading difficulty index (Staphorsius & Verhelst, 1997). The narrative texts contained no explicit clues (e.g., synonyms, antonyms, or description clues). Target words were not placed in the first sentences of the text.

A version of the twelve texts was presented to three adults with target words deleted. They were instructed to fill each cloze with an answer that was as specific as possible and fitted the context. Only four out of the 36 answers, each concerning a different target word, did not match the concept of the deleted word. The other answers, however, were identical or synonymous with the deleted target word (58 percent) or closely related hypernyms (31 percent) ("to break" was filled in for the deleted target word "to shatter," for example). The texts were therefore considered to provide sufficient contextual support.

As can be seen, there is sufficient information provided for the reader to understand the nature of the task that these learners were being asked to do.

In addition to treatment materials, assessment materials may also appear in this section or, alternatively, this section may be divided into two sections, one dealing with treatment materials and another with testing/assessment materials. An example of assessment materials from a study on think-alouds and reactivity is found below. The authors measured comprehension, intake, and written production following a think-aloud task. Only a portion of the description for each measure is provided (Leow & Morgan-Short, 2004, p. 45). In all three instances, the actual tool is provided in the appendix:

> To measure participants' comprehension, an 11-item comprehension task was designed to elicit 17 pieces of information based exclusively on the advice, tips, or recommendations provided through the imperatives found in the text. The information was elicited predominantly via short and multiple-choice answers . . .
>
> To measure participants' intake of the targeted forms, a multiple-choice recognition task was prepared. The 17 items on this task were also based exclusively on the advice, tips, or recommendations provided through the imperatives found in the text . . .
>
> To measure participants' controlled written production of the targeted forms, a fill-in-the-blank task comprising 17 items that provided a list of advice for leading a healthy life was prepared . . .

The materials section presents a description of the actual materials used, but does not specify how they were used. The procedures section provides that information.

1.3.4.3 Procedures

The next questions that a reader can expect to be informed of include logistical issues related to what was actually done. How exactly was the task carried out? How was the treatment administered? How and when was testing done? The following is the procedures section from the study discussed above (Fukkink, Blok, & de Glopper, 2001, p. 482):

> Participants were tested individually. Sessions started with a standardized explanation of directions to the students. It was decided that each text would first be read orally by the student, because reading aloud first appeared to encourage giving oral definitions in a pilot study and a previous study (Van Daalen-Kapteijns, Elshout-Mohr, & de Glopper, 2001). Students tried to decipher the meaning of the target

word thereafter in response to the question, "Which explanation does the dictionary give for this word?" Students were permitted to reread the text.

A warming-up task was introduced first, using materials that were similar to the experimental task. The experimental items were introduced only if students demonstrated adequate understanding of the procedure. The order of items was randomized for each participant. The sessions were tape recorded and transcribed for coding.

The Fukkink, Blok, and de Glopper (2001) study contained a separate section for scoring, in which detail was provided as to how responses were scored. A subsequent analysis section presented information about the statistical procedures used to analyze the data.

In some studies, authors present a visual image of the procedures followed, as in Figure 1.1.

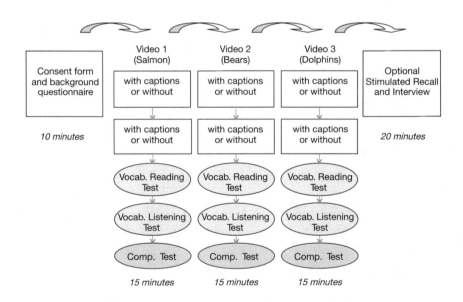

FIGURE 1.1 Example of graphic image of procedures

Source: Winke, P., Gass, S., & Sydorenko, T. (2010). The effects of captioning videos used for foreign language listening activities. *Language Learning & Technology*, *14*(1), 65–86, p. 71. Reprinted with permission of authors.

In other words, there are many ways to ensure that the reader understands what was done, how it was done, and the order in which various parts of an experiment were carried out.

1.3.4.4 Analysis

In some research reports, the mode of analysis may be a separate section or may be included in the results section. We present two examples of what might be included in a discussion of how one will analyze the results. The first, from Leow and Morgan-Short (2004, p. 46), provides information about the scoring procedure, and the second, a study on planning and narrative writing, from Ellis and Yuan (2004, p. 72), presents information about the statistical procedures to be used. In the first case, the section is called "Scoring Procedure" and in the second, the section is titled "Data Analysis."

Scoring Procedure

For the recognition and controlled written production tasks, one point was awarded to each correct answer, and no points for incorrect answers, for a total of 17 points. The comprehension task was scored in the following manner: For all items except item 1, one point was awarded for each correct answer and zero for an incorrect one. For item 1, five out of seven correct responses were required before one point was awarded. For item 11, answers could have been provided in either English or Spanish.

Data Analysis

The normal distribution of the three groups' scores on all variables was tested in terms of skewness and kurtosis. A series of one-way ANOVAs were subsequently performed followed by post hoc Scheffé tests where appropriate (i.e., if the F score was statistically significant). In the one variable where normal distribution was not evident . . . , a Kruskal-Wallis Test was run, followed by independent t-tests to compare the pairs of groups. The alpha for achieving statistical significance was set at .05. Additionally, effect sizes were calculated . . . to examine the size of the effect of the different kinds of planning on performance of the task . . .

It is not always the case that all of these categories appear in every research report. Some may be combined, and others may not be relevant. The precise organization of the report will depend on the design of the study and the authors' preference for presentation of the data.

1.3.5 Results

In this section of a research article, the results are presented with verbal descriptions of data, which are also often displayed in charts, figures, or tables. Results sections usually provide objective descriptions presented without interpretation. The excerpt below is a small part of a results section from Philp (2003, p. 110).

The provision of recasts depended entirely on the production of nontargetlike forms by each learner. Generally, as illustrated in Table 2, each learner received 44–55 recasts of question forms over five sessions with those in the Low group generally receiving higher numbers of recasts. Of these recasts, all groups received over 60 percent of recasts of stage 4 questions.

TABLE 2 Recasts provided to each group

Group	n	Recasts N	M	Percentage of question forms in recasts Stage 3	Stage 4	Stage 5
High	15	659	43.93	7 (44)	65 (415)	28 (179)
Intermediate	11	531	48.93	8 (42)	62 (316)	30 (155)
Low	7	379	54.14	6 (15)	63 (237)	33 (122)

As shown in Table 3, the High group was presented more frequently with long recasts (62 percent), whereas the Low group received more short recasts (67 percent). Similar numbers of recasts with one, two, or three or more changes to the learner's trigger utterance were received by all groups, although the Low group received slightly more of the latter. A comparison between groups is shown in Figure 1.

TABLE 3 Length of recasts and changes to learners' utterances in recasts: Percentages by group

Group	n	Length of recast Short	Long	Number of changes 1 change	2 changes	≥ 3 changes
High	15	38	62	39	30	31
Intermediate	11	52	48	37	31	32
Low	7	67	33	30	30	40

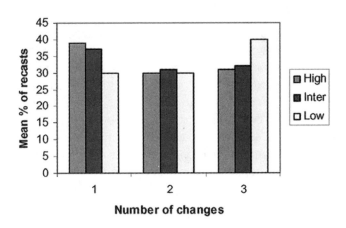

FIGURE 1 Comparison by group of proportion of number of changes in recasts

Philp, J. (2003). Constraints on "noticing the gap": Nonnative speakers' noticing of recasts in NS-NNS interaction. *Studies in Second Language Acquisition*, *25*, 110. Copyright © 2003 by Cambridge University Press. Reprinted with the permission of Cambridge University Press and with the permission of J. Philp.

Additional information about statistical results is also presented in the results section, as seen below (Philp, 2003, p. 111).

Results

To test hypothesis 1, which predicted that recall of recasts would be more accurate the higher the level of the learner, the High, Intermediate, and Low groups were compared. The results of a one-way ANOVA, provided in Table 4, show a significant effect for learner level on recall of recasts. With an alpha level of .05, the effect of learner level on recall of recasts was statistically significant, $F(2,30) = 4.1695$, $p < .05$. A priori contrasts, tested by the *statistic*, were computed to establish the source of difference between groups. A significant difference was found between the High and Intermediate groups on the one hand and the Low group on the other ($p < .05$). The High and Intermediate groups were not significantly different in performance on recall ($p = .814$) . . .

1.3.6 Discussion/Conclusion

The discussion and conclusion are often two separate sections and are primarily interpretive and explanatory in nature. The main idea of the study may be restated and the findings summarized. Then, the findings are interpreted in light of the research questions and an explanation is attempted (perhaps with regard to findings that were contrary to expectations). Below is an example from a discussion section on form-meaning mapping by native and nonnative speakers (Jiang, 2002, p. 624) where the author, in three separate paragraphs, provides a summary, an interpretation (along with problems), and a possible explanation. Below are the first sentences from each paragraph.

Summary statement
The results of experiment 1 show that whether an L2 word pair shares a single L1 translation does not affect native speakers' performance in the rating task . . .

Interpretation and problems
Although the findings of experiment 1 are consistent with the L1 lemma mediation hypothesis, there are two potential problems that have to be resolved before one can interpret the findings as evidence in support of it . . .

Explanation
One explanation for this discrepancy may lie in the possible involvement of conscious knowledge about L2 words in the rating task on the part of the nonnative speakers . . .

Finally, many studies include a section on the limitations of the study and suggest ways of remediating the limitations. Possible topics for future research may also be included. Typical contents of discussion, conclusion, and limitations sections are also discussed at length in Chapter 11, where we provide tips on writing and reporting research.

1.3.7 Notes

In some journals, any parenthetical material in an article is placed in footnotes at the bottom of the relevant page. In other journals, this material may appear as endnotes, where all the notes are collected together at the end of the article. In addition, there is generally an author's note, often including contact information,

information concerning prior presentations based on the research presented in the paper, and acknowledgments.

1.3.8 References

In most journals in the second language research field, everything cited in the paper appears in the reference list, and all sources listed in the reference list are cited in the paper. There is no single style used by all journals in the field; different journals have different styles for references. The use of style manuals is further discussed in Chapter 11.

1.3.9 Appendices

The appendices to a research article may include examples of the actual materials used in the study, along with any other information that, while necessary for the interpretation of the study, might interrupt the flow of the paper if included in the body of the article.

Now that we have provided a brief description of what can be expected in a typical quantitatively oriented article in the field of second language research, we move on to the main focus of this book, namely how to do second language research. We begin by considering the identification of research questions.

1.4 IDENTIFYING RESEARCH QUESTIONS

The first issue, and perhaps one of the most difficult aspects of any research undertaking, is the identification of appropriate research questions. Research questions are an integral part of quantitative research. The identification process for qualitative research, discussed in Chapter 7, is often quite different than it is for quantitative research. For example, in qualitative studies, in keeping with the goals of research, questions are often not as narrowly constrained.

Questions need to be interesting in the sense that they address current issues; at the same time, they need to be sufficiently narrow and constrained so that they can be answered. Broad questions can be difficult, if not impossible, to address without breaking them down into smaller answerable questions. For example, a general research question such as "What is the effect of the native language on the learning of a second or foreign language?" cannot be answered as formulated. This is because it represents a research area, but not a specific research question. To address the research area, a researcher might investigate the effect of a native language on specific aspects of a target language (e.g., phonology, syntax). One way to begin to reduce the general question would be to consider the learning of a language that has a linguistic category not present in the native language. Again, this is somewhat broad, so the researcher might want to further reduce this to a specific question: "How do learners of a non-tonal language learn to make lexical distinctions using tone?" This is a reasonable starting point for the investigation of this question. The researcher could then examine the interlanguages of native speakers of English learning Chinese. Of course, the researcher would have to determine whether he or she wanted to examine production or comprehension in order to come up with specific hypotheses and a design. We return to the issue of hypotheses in section 1.4.2 of this chapter.

Where do research ideas come from? We mentioned earlier that research investigations need to be current, which of course entails that the questions have not already been answered in the literature, or have only partially been answered, and therefore require further or additional investigation. Research questions also need to be theoretically interesting; otherwise, we run into a "so what?" response to our research. Most reasoned research questions come from a reading of the literature and an understanding of the history of current issues. The conclusion sections of many articles suggest questions for future research. Some are quite specific, while others are merely suggestive.

TIME TO DO ...

Below are examples from three journals in which the authors refer to future research. Consider one or two of them: What research question could you develop from these suggestions?

1. A study of lexical repetition as a function of topic, cultural background, and development of writing ability by learners of English who are native speakers of Arabic, Japanese, Korean, and Spanish.
    Future studies may wish to examine other possible topic-related variations, including distinctions between personal and nonpersonal writing and among different writing purposes. A second question is whether the time limitation imposed on these essays encouraged the use of repetition as a cohesion strategy (Reynolds, 2001, p. 472).
2. A study on the acquisition of English causatives by native speakers of Hindi-Urdu and Vietnamese.
    There is, nonetheless, a need for further research in this area, involving a larger repertoire of verb classes, as well as a wider

range of proficiency levels . . . Similarly, further research could be undertaken on the influence of L1 verb serialization in languages like Vietnamese on the acquisition of the argument structure of verbs in nonserializing languages like English . . . Further research could also include studies on the acquisition of semantic classes relevant to various syntactic phenomena, involving a variety of languages (both as L1s and L2s), with different morphologies, classes of verbs and selectional restrictions on verbs (Helms-Park, 2001, p. 94).

3. A study of the relationship between speech and reading in a group of ESL learners who are native speakers of Japanese, Chinese, Korean, and Persian.

[F]urther exploration of the alphabet group differences on the figure pairs might prove productive. This should include a more detailed analysis of three groups (Roman alphabet, non-Roman alphabet, and Ideographic) instead of two groups as in the present study. In addition, the students might be presented with the decision tasks in their native language as a further control against the test effects . . . (Muchisky, 1983, pp. 94–95).

Another way to develop research questions is through the extensive reading and analysis of existing research. This can lead to the identification of gaps that may strike a reader as important. Often in reading an article, one might recognize that something has not been controlled for or that different languages might function differently on a certain important dimension. Alternatively, some controversy may have been left unresolved. This information may turn out to form the basis of a follow-up study, but a researcher must first make sure that others have not conducted such studies. A first step in this process is to consult a citation index (see your university librarian) to locate work that has cited the paper that you will be basing your study on. Another way of locating relevant information is through Web-based searches, which often yield studies published in a range of venues.

On other occasions, ideas for research might stem from observing learners either in or out of a classroom context or through some general feeling of curiosity having observed nonnative speaker linguistic behavior. These ideas may or may not develop into research studies, but in any case the first task is to do a literature search to see what has been done. There are many databases available for this purpose. Again, university librarians can assist with this process, and Web-based searches can often yield fruitful results.

TIME TO THINK ...

Return to the first "time to think" box in this chapter, in which you were asked to think about two to three questions about language learning and/or language teaching that you have been puzzled about.

Can you now take one or two of them and turn them into a research question?

1.4.1 Feasibility

The feasibility of a study may depend on a number of factors, some of which we have already mentioned (e.g., the breadth of the study in relation to its research questions' scope and answerability). Another factor to take into account when considering feasibility is whether or not it will be possible to obtain the data necessary to answer the question. Consider a study in which one wants to conduct a survey of the attitudes of heritage learners (i.e., students who are learning the language of their parents, grandparents, etc.). In order to do this, the researcher first has to define exactly what constitutes a heritage learner. One question might be whether someone can be considered a heritage learner if he or she has distant relatives in Uzbekistan, for example, but has only very rarely heard the language spoken. Or, is a heritage learner limited to a family where the language was regularly spoken in the home while the language of the environment was the language of schooling and all outside of the home transactions? Following this step, the researcher needs to go about identifying individuals who would qualify under the definition chosen. In many settings, it would be difficult to find a reasonable number of participants to make the study interesting. Thus, pertinent data sources need to be identified as a part of determining the feasibility of the study.

Another study might seek to compare performance on different communication task types. As we discuss in Chapter 3, there are many important dimensions on which communicative tasks can differ. However, it might not be feasible to require participants to do 15 different tasks. Exhaustion and boredom might set in, and the researcher would not know how to interpret the results. This is not to say that such a study could not be conducted; it is just that the design of the study might entail large numbers of participants who may or may not be available for the many rounds of data collection that such a study would necessitate.

Thus, any study should be designed with a full understanding of the fact that the limitations of the setting and the population might constrain the research.

1.4.2 Research Questions and Hypotheses

Research problems are generally expressed in terms of research questions and/or hypotheses. Research questions are the questions for which answers are being sought, while research hypotheses can be used to express what the researcher expects the results of an investigation to be. The hypotheses are based on observations or on what the literature suggests the answers might be. There may be times when, because of a lack of relevant literature, hypotheses cannot be generated because the researcher is dealing with new and/or unexplored areas.

The literature review that leads up to the hypotheses should report all sides of an issue. In other words, fair and complete reporting is essential in any research study. We return to the issue of hypotheses in Chapter 5.

To see examples of both research questions and hypotheses, consider the following from Lakshmanan (1989, pp. 84–86). This was a study that investigated the acquisition of verb inflection and the use of pronouns by children learning English (native speakers of Spanish, French, and Japanese). The data, collected by other researchers, are from longitudinal studies of these three children. Below are five research questions from this study.

RQ#1. Do null subjects in the interlanguage (IL) of these child L2 learners decrease with time?[2]

RQ#2. Is there a developmental relation between null subjects and verb inflections in the IL of these child L2 learners? In other words, is increase in verb inflections accompanied by a corresponding decrease in the use of null subjects?

RQ#3. Are obligatory verb inflections acquired at the same time for all the categories of verb morphology or does the acquisition of verb inflections depend on the specific category of verb morphology (e.g., be copula, auxiliaries be, do, have, present 3rd singular regular, past regular etc.)?

RQ#4. Is there a developmental relation between null subjects in is constructions (is copula and auxiliary utterances) and is constructions? In other words, does the proportion of null subjects present in is contexts increase with the increase in the proportion of is constructions?

RQ#5. Are there any differences between the distribution of null subjects and subjects in is constructions and non-is constructions in these child L2 learners' IL?

As can be seen, these research questions are expressed as explorations of relationships. Lakshmanan also formulated them as hypotheses. Examples of hypotheses stemming from the above research questions are given below.

Hypothesis 1. Null subjects in the four subjects' IL will decrease with time.

Hypothesis 2. There is a negative relation between the development of verb inflections and the use of null subjects; in other words, null subjects will decrease with the increase in verb inflections.

Hypothesis 3. The acquisition of obligatory verb inflections depends on the specific category of verb morphology.

Hypothesis 4. There is a positive relationship between the use of null subjects in is constructions and the development of is constructions.

Hypothesis 5. There are significant differences between the distribution of null subjects and lexically realized subjects in is constructions and non-is constructions. The frequency of occurrence of null subjects will be greater than the frequency of occurrence of lexically realized subjects in is contexts; the frequency of occurrence of null subjects in non-is contexts will be less than the frequency of occurrence of lexically realized subjects in non-is contexts.

In other instances, the research questions are expressed as one item, as in Révész, Sachs, and Hama (2014, p. 623), and with different degrees of elaboration. In the third of their questions, the results of previous research were mixed and, in the last of their research questions, there was no previous research to base any prediction on.

1) Do different intended levels of task complexity result in different levels of cognitive load during task performance, as measured by expert judgments, performance on a secondary task, and eye tracking?

It was hypothesized that the task version designed to be more complex would impose greater cognitive load.

2) What is the effect of task complexity on the acquisition of the English past counterfactual construction under task conditions where recasts are provided?

Based on the Cognition Hypothesis, which drove our operationalization of task complexity along resource-directing dimensions, it was hypothesized that learners who received recasts during tasks with greater reasoning demands would show more development.

3) What is the effect of manipulating the input frequencies of verbs (skewed vs. balanced) on the acquisition of the English past counterfactual construction under task conditions where recasts are provided?

To date empirical results have been mixed regarding the effects of input frequency manipulations; thus, the null hypothesis was assumed.

4) Is there an interaction between the effects of task complexity and input frequency in the acquisition of the past counterfactual construction under task conditions where recasts are provided?

To our knowledge, this is the first empirical study to address this question. Thus, the null hypothesis was assumed.

The above examples have been expressed in terms of yes/no questions, or as questions that have a dichotomous possibility as an outcome, but as research areas become more nuanced, it is often the case that we need to dig deeper. In other words, we know whether something has an effect on something else; what we need to explore is how great the effect is. For example, Dale, Harlaar, and Plomin (2012), in a study of early development of twins, point out that because of previous research, they are able to address a wider range of questions. These are posed as "to what extent" questions rather than "yes/no" questions, as is seen below (p. 32), particularly in questions 1, 4, and 5:

(1) How well do measures of early and adolescent L1 learning, and adolescent reading, predict SLA, both individually and collectively?
(2) How does the etiology of L2 achievement compare with that of early and adolescent L1 and adolescent reading?
(3) Is there evidence for differential etiology of poor or exceptionally capable L2 achievement relative to the rest of the normal distribution of L2 achievement?
(4) To what extent do the same genes account for variability in L1 and L2 achievement?
(5) To what extent do the same environmental influences account for variability in L1 and L2 achievement?

Nassaji (2012), in his study investigating teachers' perceptions of the relationship between SLA and language teaching, asked the following questions (p. 344):

(1) To what extent are teachers familiar with SLA research?
(2) How easily can they access SLA research, and what sources do they consult?

(3) To what extent do they read research articles and, if they do not read them, what are their reasons?

(4) How do they judge the relevance and usefulness of SLA research for classroom teaching?

(5) How do they perceive the relationship between researchers and teachers?

(6) What are their expectations of SLA research?

The important point to remember is that defining research questions requires an understanding of previous research. This is so because we need to know what an interesting question is in relation to what we already know and we need to further previous knowledge by extending that knowledge with questions that suggest a more continuous answer (to what extent) rather than just a *yes* or a *no* answer.

TIME TO THINK ...

Given the questions in Nassaji's study, what type of data do you think would be appropriate to answer his questions (e.g., questionnaires, observations, experimental)?

1.4.3 Replication

Replication is a central part of the development of any field of inquiry. If one cannot repeat the results of a particular study, the validity of the results of the original study might be called into question.[3] In fact, the *Publication Manual of the American Psychological Association, Sixth Edition* states, "The essence of the scientific method involves observations that can be repeated and verified by others" (American Psychological Association, 2010, p. 12). Similarly, Albert Valdman, the then editor of the journal *Studies in Second Language Acquisition*, has asserted that "the way to more valid and reliable SLA research is through replication" (1993, p. 505). As Porte (2002) further notes, without critical replication studies, "it will be extremely difficult ever to discover the definitive response to a research question or hypothesis found in one particular study . . . which then permits us to generalize those findings to fit exactly another context of language learning" (p. 35). Porte (2012) defines a replication study (p. 3) as one that "attempts to discover whether the same findings are obtained by another research in another context, and whether the outcome appears to reflect knowledge which can therefore be separated from the context in which it was originally found." It is thus crucial that researchers report in enough detail to allow others to determine with precision what has been done. Unfortunately, since much research in the field of second language learning is published in journals, space constraints often preclude full and complete reporting. To this end, Polio and Gass (1997) recommend that researchers submit detailed appendices for publishers to keep either online or as hard copies if journal space is limited, although publishers have not yet fully embraced this idea. More specifically, Polio and Gass suggest that these appendices include information about any guidelines used for coding the data, measures of proficiency or development, instruments for data elicitation (including pre- and post-tests), experimental protocols, and biodata on the participants. Generally speaking, there are two primary reasons for replication: verification and generalizability. We return to the issue of replication in Chapter 11.

1.5 CONCLUSION

In this chapter, we have dealt with some of the basics of L2 research, including the range of different types of research that exist, what to expect from a typical research report, and how to identify research questions, generate hypotheses, and consider issues such as feasibility and the role of replication in second language research. In Chapter 2, we deal with the question of research ethics, focusing on the important issue of informed consent.

POINTS TO REMEMBER

- Research is a systematic approach to finding answers to a question.

- There are many approaches to conducting research.

- Two main orientations are quantitative and qualitative.

- There are standard components to a quantitatively oriented research report.

- A first step in conducting research is to identify a research question.

- Some considerations in developing a research question include ensuring that it addresses current research and that it is feasible to conduct research to answer the question.

- Replication and full reporting are important parts of the research process.

MORE TO DO AND MORE TO THINK ABOUT ...

1. Consider the journals you found from your search in section 1.1. Can you determine the scope of each journal? What kinds of topics do they deal with? Some journals are quite explicit; others might require a look through the tables of contents and abstracts.

2. Select three of these journals and consider the extent to which the articles follow the framework set up in this chapter. If they do not, in what way(s) do they deviate?

3. Consider these same journals. Do the journals give guidelines for submission (e.g., length, style guidelines, number of copies to submit, mode of submission)? List the guidelines you have found.

4. Find three articles and consider the end of the discussion section or perhaps the beginning of the conclusion section to determine if the authors acknowledge limitations of the study. What do they say?

5. Consider the following research questions that are expressed as yes/no questions:

    a. Is motivation important for second language learning?
    b. Is it important to like your teacher to be successful at learning a second language?
    c. Is learning a language by living in the second language environment as effective as learning a language in the classroom?

    Assume that previous research has already answered them in the affirmative. Change them into questions that provide more detailed information by asking them not as dichotomous yes/no questions, but ones that suggest a more continuous nature of the response.

6. Read the conclusion sections from three different articles in three different journals. Do the authors point to future research possibilities? If not, do they do this elsewhere (perhaps shortly before the conclusion)? What do they say, and are there any issues that are of interest to you?

7. How can the following research topics be turned into researchable questions?

    Example:
    Gender differences in language classes
    Do males perform differently than females on a grammar test following treatment in which negative feedback is given?

a. Motivation
b. Task effectiveness
c. Novice teacher performance
d. Attention
e. Final grades

NOTES

1. According to the *Publication Manual of the American Psychological Association*, *Sixth Edition*, the word *participant* is more appropriate than words such as *subject*. In a section titled "Guidelines for reducing bias," they state, "although descript terms such as *college students, children*, or *respondents* provide precise information about the individuals taking part in a research project, the more general terms *participants* and *subjects* are also in common usage" (American Psychological Association, 2010, p. 73). They go on to say that when discussing statistical results, the word *subjects* is appropriate (e.g., *between subjects* design).

2. Null subjects refer to expressions in languages such as Italian or Spanish that have verbs with no overt subjects. In Italian, for example, to say *I speak Italian*, one can say *Parlo italiano*, where the first word means *I speak*. The overt word for *I* (*io*) is not used.

3. Along with the issue of replication comes the important issue of data reporting. How much should be reported? How much detail? The simple answer is: enough so that someone can replicate the study.

CHAPTER TWO

Issues Related to Data Gathering

In this chapter, we introduce an increasingly important issue related to gathering data from second language learners. We focus our discussion on ethical issues in research involving humans, including the process of obtaining informed consent and the institutional review of research together with the steps to be taken in preparing a research protocol.

2.1 ETHICAL ISSUES IN RESEARCH INVOLVING HUMAN SUBJECTS[1]

Second language researchers often have questions about why approval from institutions and informed consent from individuals is necessary to collect data from human subjects, given that second language research usually poses minimal to no risks and often provides added benefits, such as language practice. To address these questions, in the next few sections we provide a brief review of the development of guidelines in the U.S.[2]

Ethical considerations for research involving human subjects are outlined in various publicly available international and U.S. government documents. These have become a standard since our first edition. Most institutions now require that faculty and students undergo human subjects training, which includes information about the history of the development of these guidelines. The historical records include the Declaration of Helsinki (World Medical Association, 1964), the Belmont Report (1979), and the Nuremberg Code (1949), all available online. In the U.S., the Office for Human Research Protections (OHRP) of the U.S. Department of Health and Human Services (DHHS) and the Office of Human Subjects Research (OHSR) of the U.S. National Institutes of Health (NIH) provide online documentation concerning ethical principles and guidelines for the protection of human subjects. For the pertinent websites, please consult the reference list at the end of the book as well as the URLs provided in this chapter. Much of the information we provide in this chapter is based on these documents, together with the online training module offered by the U.S. NIH (n.d., available online at www.hhs.gov/ohrp). These free and publicly available resources provide a careful review of historical events that have shaped current U.S. ethical regulations governing scientific research with human subjects. While we summarize some of that information here, we also recommend that researchers visit some of the websites and online documents that have been designed to promote understanding of the processes of human subjects research. Indeed, many funding bodies require that online training modules be completed before research grants are awarded. It should be noted that following the proliferation of regulations, there has also been debate about how necessary or helpful they are. For more information, we refer the reader to Schneider's (2015) new book *The Censor's Handbook*.

TIME TO THINK ...

Is it ethical . . .

. . . for teachers to conduct research with their own students as participants?

. . . to offer extra credit in a course for participating in research?

. . . to teach language learners nonnative-like forms in a study?

Consider these questions as you read this chapter.

2.1.1 Obtaining Informed Consent from Second Language Learners

Beginning with the Nuremberg Code (1949), the notion of informed consent has become a cornerstone of ethical practice in research involving human subjects. A number of helpful sources outline in detail the essentials of informed consent, in particular the responsibilities of the researcher, as well as typical elements of a written informed consent document. These include information provided by the U.S. Office for Human Research Protections (OHRP) in their Investigator Responsibilities and Informed Consent training module (n.d., available online at www.hhs.gov/ohrp/education/training/introduction.html), which also provides details about other government guidelines and information on human subjects.

The institutional review boards (IRBs) of various universities also provide guidelines for writing informed consent documents. IRBs are also sometimes known as human subjects committees, informed consent committees, or research ethics committees, among other possibilities. In this chapter, we consistently use the term IRBs.

According to the Belmont Report (1979), which was important in the development of informed consent and will be discussed further below, informed consent requires that human subjects, to the degree that they are capable, be provided with the opportunity to choose what shall or shall not happen to them. This can happen only when at least the following three conditions are fulfilled:

---

1. Suppliance of sufficient information (i.e., full disclosure about the experiment by the researcher).
2. Comprehension on the part of the participant.
3. Voluntary participation, where the participant is free from undue pressure or coercion.

Thus, consent implies voluntary agreement to participate in a study where the potential participant has enough information and understands enough to make an informed decision. Let's examine each of these in detail.

2.1.1.1 Sufficient Information

What constitutes sufficient information? This depends to some extent on what source on human subjects is consulted. Different institutions (including different universities and government bodies) may have different interpretations of "complete disclosure." Core elements include the idea that potential participants should receive information that describes the procedures and purposes of the research, as well as the potential risks and benefits. This may sometimes be interpreted as including details, such as the method by which participants will be assigned to any groups in the study (e.g., treatment groups or control group). Some institutions also agree that potential participants should receive information about whom to contact if questions arise regarding the study or the participants' rights. Sometimes the researchers' contact information may be supplied on the consent form; sometimes the review board details are made available; and occasionally both are supplied. Typically, information is also provided about the steps the researcher will take to ensure that any identifying aspects of the data will be held confidential.

These points are all applicable to second language research. For example, many review boards or human subjects committees will require that learners be informed about the procedures, purposes, and potential risks and benefits of the studies. Second language research usually does not lead to risks in the same way that some medical or psychologically-based research can. However, in research on the effect of second language instruction, there might be a control group that will not receive equal instructional time as that of the experimental groups. Depending on the regulations of the body approving the research, learners might need to be informed that they could be assigned to a group that, theoretically, could benefit less than a treatment group. In the same study, if intact classes are used and group assignment is made on this basis, learners might need to be informed about this method of assignment—even if it leads them to ask questions or wish to change classes.

TIME TO THINK ...

Do researchers need to make sure that all participants, even those in a control group, benefit from the research? How can a researcher compensate for differing benefits between groups? Brainstorm the answers to these questions based on a study you know or plan to conduct in the future, or simply imagine a situation where this might occur.

Also, second language researchers are often required to include their contact information on informed consent documents, even if it results in their students (if they are classroom researchers, for example) calling them to discuss class work outside the experiment. Finally, confidentiality of data is important in second language research. As Duff and Early (1996) note in their discussion of confidentiality: "although it is common practice to change the names of research subjects, this in itself does not guarantee subject anonymity. In reports of school-based research, prominent individuals or focal subjects tend to be more vulnerable than others" (p. 21).

If the researcher uses quotations in the final write-up or presentation, certain individuals may be recognizable to others (perhaps because of what they say, for example in terms of their position on a topic or if the data are played audibly, perhaps by the sound of their voice). This may be less likely to apply to learners, but can certainly apply in school settings. If teachers are identified, even unintentionally, this could have ramifications for future promotions, contract renewals, or class assignments; for students, identification might have implications for how other teachers perceive them, and consequently their grades and letters of recommendation could be impacted. Immigrant and refugee populations may also fear that sensitive information may be intentionally or inadvertently disclosed to the authorities. Neufeld et al. (2001), for example, note that "in Middle Eastern immigrant populations, individuals were distrustful of research and of the university, which they associated with the government" (p. 586).

To alleviate these concerns, we advise researchers to make it clear from the beginning that all information will remain confidential and anonymous *wherever possible,* and to explain the various steps that will be taken to protect the learners' anonymity (e.g., using numbers instead of names to refer to participants, not revealing identifying information, and discussing the location of records and who will have access to them). In particularly sensitive situations, such as those involving refugees, second language researchers might even volunteer to check with the participants before using any potentially identifying information in transcripts, data, reports, papers, or presentations, even when numbers are assigned instead of names. Some review boards or committees might even ask where the data are to be stored and with whom they are to be shared. For example, the use of learner corpora is growing in the field of second language research, and many corpora are freely available over the Internet. Corpora can be an excellent way to avoid duplication of effort in the extremely time-consuming practice of data elicitation, collection, and transcription. However, this practice of sharing data may lead researchers to forget that sharing transcripts or data from their research may require permission from the IRB and must be covered under the informed consent documents the learners signed. Not all universities and schools in all countries require consent and, even when they do, requirements may differ. It is therefore important to verify IRB requirements before embarking on a research project.

Checklist for obtaining informed consent

Overall goal: To ensure that participants are supplied with enough information to make informed voluntary decisions about participating. This can include information about:

- The procedures and purposes of the research
- The potential risks and benefits of the research
- The methods by which participants will be assigned to groups and what those group assignments might entail in terms of treatment
- Whom to contact with questions regarding the study or their rights as participants
- The specific steps that will be taken to ensure confidentiality and anonymity, for example:
  - Using numbers instead of names
  - Not revealing identifying information
  - Safeguarding the location of and access to records

Researchers need to remember to:

- Consider the special implications the research (and confidentiality/anonymity issues) may have for any teachers, students, or immigrant/refugee populations involved
- Make sure any subsequent sharing of data is permissible by institutional regulations and the informed consent that was obtained from participants

TIME TO DO ...

Think of a potential study that might be relevant for second language research. Answer the following questions for your context:

- What are the procedures and purposes of the research?
- What are the possible risks and how will you explain them to your participants?
- How do you plan to ensure the confidentiality of your participants?
- Are any of your participants from special populations, such as minors? If so, what safeguards will you use to protect these populations?

2.1.1.2 Is Withholding Information Ever Necessary?

In general, researchers are advised to provide as much information as possible to participants because failure to disclose information may constitute deception. In second language research, however, it may occasionally be necessary not to fully disclose information. We discuss this throughout the book as "giving away the goals of the study." As Rounds (1996) explains, in second language research, "sometimes . . . a research design requires that the researcher conceal her real interests, and perhaps use small deceptions to deal with the classic 'observer's paradox'" (p. 53).

For example, if the researcher is studying a teacher's use of questions in the L2 classroom, informing the teacher about the goals of the research may bias his or her use of questions and thus lead to an unrepresentative sample of data. In this case, withholding information may be acceptable and allowed by the human subjects committee, but three conditions will often need to be met:

1. Incomplete disclosure is essential to the aims of the research
2. No risks are undisclosed
3. All participants will be given an opportunity to be debriefed after the study

Researchers need to think carefully about how much deception is ethical. For example, while telling a teacher that the study is about her language use (and not specifically about her use of questions) is not fully disclosing the purposes of the study, and is therefore not ideal, it might be a better route than deceiving the teacher by telling her that the research is focusing on her use of the whiteboard. In some studies, it may be appropriate to advise the participants ahead of time that the study is about second language learning and that the exact features of it will be described to them after the study. This is a practice also used in some psychology-based research (Baumrind, 1990 provides helpful discussion of ethical issues and deception in applied psychology research).

TIME TO DO ...

University students enrolled in an intensive summer language program in the U.S. are asked to participate in a study. In the study, one group of learners will be taught a nonnative-like form of the target language and in the other group, they will be taught the target-like version.

Draft a plan for informing the nonnative-like form group that they will be learning some incorrect forms during the study and come up with a way to offer this group compensatory instruction. Consider the following questions in your plan: Are there any aspects of the research that require keeping participants naïve? How do researchers plan to avoid giving away the goals of the study? How much concealment is ethical?

In summary, incomplete disclosure may be acceptable in some cases, and seems to be a common practice in some areas of second language research. In these cases, it may be sufficient to indicate to participants that they are being invited to participate in research about which some features will not be revealed until the research is concluded. In those instances, the purpose of the study is presented in general terms only. However, in all cases, and based on current guidelines, such second language research can be justified only if the three conditions above are met.

2.1.1.3 Participant Comprehension in Informed Consent

In addition to supplying sufficient information to potential participants to allow them to make informed decisions, researchers are also responsible for ensuring participants understand. So, the way in which information is conveyed might be as important as the information itself. This implies: (1) that the potential participants have the opportunity to discuss concerns and get any questions answered; and (2) that the informed consent document is given to them in a language that is understandable for them, respecting factors such as learners' ages and reading levels, educational background, mental capacity, and language proficiency, including, importantly, literacy (Belmont Report, 1979).

The Language of Informed Consent

Second language learners are frequently asked to read and sign consent forms that are not written in their native languages. OHRP suggests writing the consent documents so that they are understandable to people who have not graduated from high school. However, for low-proficiency language learners, it may be necessary to provide a translation of the consent document in the learners' first language. Alternatively, the document can be presented orally in the first language, along with a short form of the consent document attesting to the oral presentation in the first language containing a summary of the information presented orally. Using research assistants who speak the participants' L1 may be especially valuable in this respect. Sometimes, though, using the L1 is not possible or practical, for example when the researcher is studying a large population with multiple L1s. In these cases, the document should be written (or orally provided) in the L2 at a level understandable to the potential subjects as recommended in the OHRP training. Below, we provide some guidelines that are based on government recommendations.

Consent form guidelines for nonnative speakers

Wherever possible, informed consent information should be presented in a language that is understandable to the subject. For example, for ESL speakers, that should be their native language or a language in which they are highly proficient.

(Best Option) The written consent form is translated into the native language(s) of the learner unless the learners are clearly proficient enough to understand the form. Both the English consent forms and the translations should be approved by the review board or human subjects committees. Translated forms are often presented on the reverse side of the sheet.

(Backup Option) A translator can explain the consent form to the learner. This option might be best if the learner is not literate in his or her L1, if the L1 has no written form, or if a written translation has proved very difficult to obtain. If the consent form is explained orally, researchers need: (a) a bilingual translator (who also serves as a witness); (b) a short consent form in a language understandable to the speaker; and (c) a review board- or human subjects committee-approved L1 version of the consent form. The following process can be followed: (a) the translator explains the consent form to the participant; (b) both the participant and the translator sign the short form; and (c) the researcher and the translator sign the English version.

In Appendices A–D, we provide examples of informed consent forms. The first (Appendix A) is an example of an abbreviated informed consent form that might be used, together with the services of a translator, for learners whose native language is not English. Appendix B provides an example of a complete informed consent form that might be used with learners whose native language is not English, but who are deemed proficient enough to understand the form. Appendix C is a sample consent form for a study in a foreign language context, and Appendix D is a sample consent form for a classroom study. However, we urge researchers to check with their own institutional review board for guidelines and sample consent forms.

TIME TO DO ...

Using the outline provided above, draft an informed consent document to be used in a study you plan to conduct. Consider the age, educational background, language proficiency, and literacy of your proposed participants.

Child Second Language Learners

When collecting data from children for second language research purposes, there are several important things to consider. As Thompson and Jackson (1998) note, "second language researchers must keep in mind that children cannot be treated just like adults as research subjects. Because their capabilities, perspectives, and needs are different, children approach the research context uniquely and encounter a different constellation of research risks and benefits from their participation" (p. 223).

Because of this, the researcher needs to explain the research in language that is comprehensible and meaningful to the child; in addition, the researcher needs to inform the child's parents about the nature and consequences of the study, as well as obtain a signed consent form (active parental consent) from them. Researchers will also need to assure school boards and parents that the procedures used in the research will not negatively impact the second language learning process, or pose any more than a "minimal risk" to the physical and psychological well-being of the child. As defined by the U.S. Department of Health and Human Services (2003), "minimal risk" is a risk of harm not greater than that "ordinarily encountered in daily life or during the performance of routine physical or psychological examinations or tests" (p. 113). With respect to potentially vulnerable research subjects such as children, the institutional review board at the University of Pennsylvania stipulates the following:

> [R]esearch in children requires that the IRB carefully consider consent, beneficence, and justice . . . Children may be subjects of research only if informed consent is obtained from the parents or legal guardian. Children over the age of 7 must agree to participate in the research and provide written assent and separate assent forms should be provided based on reasonable age ranges for comprehension.
>
> (n.d., pp. 3–4, www.upenn.edu/IRB, retrieved April 19, 2015)

TIME TO THINK ...

Consider the following situation: a researcher plans to conduct a classroom-based study on whether or not elementary school-aged ESL students provide each other with corrective feedback on their nontarget-like forms. Who does the researcher need to obtain consent from? What kinds of provisions will be made for students whose parents decide that they should not participate? What should be included on an informed consent document?

2.1.1.4 Voluntary Participation and Informed Consent

As should be clear by now, invitations to participate in research must involve neither threats of harm nor offers of inappropriate rewards. Undue influence may be exercised, even unwittingly, where persons of authority urge or suggest a particular course of action.

For second language research, care must be taken, for example, when classroom teachers invite their students to participate in a study. Even when it is clear that there will be no extra points or higher grades for participation, and no penalty for declining to participate, the simple fact that the teacher is the person requesting the students' participation may constitute undue influence. For this reason, it can often be best for teachers to distance themselves from the process and leave the room while a third party explains the research and distributes the forms. Even when the teacher is the researcher, this course of action may be preferable so as to avoid potentially influencing the students. Some universities may go as far as prohibiting researchers from carrying out research with their own students, although it should be noted that even those universities that have a stated policy along these lines may allow some flexibility. For example, Indiana University's institutional review board guidelines in this respect are as follows:

> The Committee has long taken the position that teachers should not use their own students as subjects in their research if it can be avoided. This general policy is in accord with that of other institutional review boards. The Committee recognizes, however, that in some research situations, use of one's own students is integral to the research. This is particularly true of research into teaching methods, curricula and other areas related to the scholarship of teaching and learning.
>
> (1999–2003, http://archive-edu-2012.com/edu/i/
> 2012-11-17_683373_120/Human-Subjects-Committee,
> retrieved January 22, 2015)

Issues Involved in Collecting Data Online

Avoiding coercion during the recruitment process is integral to ensuring participation in a study is voluntary. One way to avoid coercion during recruitment of participants is to recruit through general announcements or advertisements online, rather than through individual solicitations. Social media sites such as Facebook and Twitter allow researchers to access large amounts of participants with little cost. Another method is to utilize crowdsourcing websites to recruit participants.

There are numerous crowd-work platforms available (e.g. CrowdFlower, Clickworker, and CloudSource), but currently a popular one is Amazon's Mechanical Turk. Formally introduced in 2005 by Amazon after researchers in the computational linguistics community developed the innovative idea of using readily available humans for natural language processing tasks in 2004, the name derives from an eighteenth-century chess-playing robot called the Turk, which was eventually revealed to have a chess-master hiding inside, controlling the moves of the robot. Like the Turk, though the Mechanical Turk can appear to be an automated piece of technology, it is actually human—powered by thousands of people—sometimes called "Turkers." There is a pool of more than

10,000 of these active "workers," though the population of Turkers is estimated to be close to 500,000. Despite the service's popularity, particularly among the academic community, the platform is still technically in beta testing on Amazon, and has undergone very few changes since it first came online, much to the disappointment of those who work with it, who have sometimes lobbied for a better interface and conditions.

At its core, Mechanical Turk provides a platform for requesters to post Human Intelligence Tasks (HITs), which Turkers complete. These tasks can range very widely, including, for instance, taking a survey for academic research, transcribing audio, or validating information on a website, and can take a few seconds or much longer. The workers receive compensation for these tasks. Though Turkers come from all over the globe, the majority of them live in the United States and India, the only two countries where they are paid actual money for their work, as opposed to Amazon credit. Turkers in other countries are compensated only in Amazon gift cards. Amazon recommends that workers be paid 10 cents per minute—$6 per hour—but Amazon does not mandate any minimum amount.

Obviously, the compensation rate is an ethical issue that arises out of the use of Mechanical Turk or any crowd-work platform, but it is not the only ethical issue. There is little regulation on the part of Amazon. Currently, a requester can reject the work of a Turker for no apparent (or obvious) reason—leaving the Turkers with no pay for their time, and potentially hurting their rating and therefore their prospects for additional work. In this circumstance, Amazon refuses to get involved, and there is no channel through which a Turker can resolve a dispute with a requester. Additionally, there is no oversight in terms of the kinds of task or surveys requesters can propose. Some Turkers report unpleasant or uncomfortable surveys. As noted in Schneider's (2015) article in the *Chronicle of Higher Education*, because Turkers work individually and in a piecemeal fashion, they might not know what their work is being used for. Nor would they automatically care. Because crowd-work platforms are relatively new, institutional review boards often do not have standard regulations regarding their use. In 2013, the U.S. Department of Health and Human Services acknowledged, "Current [IRB] human subjects regulations, originally written over thirty years ago, do not address many issues raised by the unique characteristics of Internet research" (www.hhs.gov/ohrp/sachrp/mtgings/2013%20March%20Mtg/internet_research.pdf, retrieved January 22, 2015).

Besides ethics, another concern for academic uses of crowd-work platforms is reliability. Because workers complete tasks in their own homes, there is no way for researchers to standardize the survey environment or guarantee participants' full attention. Dedicated Turkers report that they frequently multitask, meaning they could be chatting with peers, in a Facebook group or forum— possibly even talking to co-Turkers taking the same survey. Because surveys are the most popular kind of task completed by U.S.-based Turkers, they may see the same or similar questions repeatedly, which may affect reliability. Because Turkers are paid by the minute, they may also quickly breeze through surveys without deeply considering the questions or their responses.

All that being said, academic researchers are still among the chief requesters on Mechanical Turk, especially in sociology, economics, and psychology departments. Though crowd-work platforms are not conducive to longitudinal studies, research that depends on physical measurement or requires the participation of a protected class, the low cost and accessibility make them very attractive.

There are also concerns about validity. Do Turkers respond to surveys as honestly and thoroughly as traditionally surveyed populations? Concerns about non-naïveté are also being addressed by academics. In 2012, the journal *Behavior Research Methods* published a paper making suggestions for avoiding this, which it described as a "common problem" (Mason & Suri, 2012, p. 1).

There are also the concerns of the Turkers to consider. Some websites (e.g. mturkgrind) have been created to allow collaboration between Turkers and facilitate the sharing of information about particularly lucrative jobs or unreliable requesters. There are ways to rate requesters. Turkers have also drafted Guidelines for Academic Requesters, which ask academic researchers to agree to basic rules of crowd-work use—so far, only approximately 50 scholars have agreed to abide by these guidelines. The guidelines were inspired by a researcher who posted fake reviews of requesters on a Turker website, in order to study the Turker community as noted in Schneider (2015). The guidelines prohibit this kind of deception and encourage researchers to pay at least the minimum wage, provide honest and reliable information about themselves and their tasks, be responsive to Turkers' questions and concerns, and reject a Turker's work only with good reason.

There are many potential solutions to the ethical issues raised by digital labor, including the guidelines proposed by the Turker community and the University of Oxford's ethically minded crowd-work website called Prolific Academic. Options exist for the continued, ethical development of these platforms. Second language researchers can benefit from these sorts of platforms with quick, easy, and relatively inexpensive subject pools that are much larger than is typically the case in applied linguistics research. We recommend, naturally, that researchers understand this as an emerging technology and pay particular attention to the potential ethical issues involved.

Finally, we emphasize the need to check with local authorities regarding standard procedures. For example, in some countries, there is suspicion concerning consent forms, the idea being: "Why is a consent form needed? It might be an indication that something bad can happen." In other words, consent is a common part of the research process in some parts of the world, but not in others. This can create a dilemma when researchers must have signed consent given the regulations of their universities, but are conducting research in an environment where signed consent is a foreign concept and looked upon with suspicion. It is important to verify the research climate in the setting where the research will be conducted; if a conflict is likely to exist, it must be dealt with before beginning data collection, to avoid serious problems after data have been collected.

2.1.1.5 The Informed Consent Document

Guidelines for creating informed consent documents for research appear in government publications (e.g., OHRP) as well as in the IRB guidelines of various universities. These documents tend to be quite similar. The following checklist may be helpful in drawing up informed consent documents:

- ☐ Does your informed consent document explain the general procedure of the research?
- ☐ Does it explain the purpose of the study?
- ☐ Does it include information about the risks (and benefits) that participants may be exposed to, as well as steps you will take to minimize any risks?
- ☐ Does it provide information about how the participants' identities will be kept anonymous and confidential as far as possible?
- ☐ Does it provide contact information so that the participants can contact you or you and/or your human subjects committee if they have questions or concerns?
- ☐ Does it make it clear that participation is purely voluntary and that the participants have the right to withdraw at any time?
- ☐ Have you checked to make sure the document does not contain any language suggesting that the participants are giving up any rights or are releasing the investigators from any liability?
- ☐ Is the document written in language understandable to the participants (in the participants' L1 or, alternatively, in basic English that avoids technical jargon)?
- ☐ Have you considered how you will provide the participants with ample time to review the document before making their decision?
- ☐ If the potential participants do agree to participate, have you checked to make sure the documents are dated on the same day they are signed?
- ☐ Have you considered that multiple consents may need to be obtained for one study, for example from parents, teachers, child learners, school administrators and so on?
- ☐ Have you given a copy of the signed consent form to all those who agreed to participate and kept an original signed copy for your own records?

2.1.2 History of Institutional Review of Human Subjects Research, Compliance, and Problem-Solving

2.1.2.1 Purpose of Reviews and IRB Responsibilities

As noted at the beginning of this chapter, some second language researchers wonder why it is necessary to adhere to human subjects guidelines for research areas where no risk is involved (for example, judging sentences as to their correctness). To try to explain why this is important, it is worthwhile looking at some history of research with human subjects. This provides context for today's regulations. In the U.S. in 1974, the National Research Act, which created the U.S. National Commission for the Protection of Human Subjects of Biomedical and Behavioral Research, also required the establishment of institutional review boards (IRBs) to review all research funded by the Department of Health and Human Services. Requirements for IRBs have been periodically revised and widely adopted. Thus, most major universities in the U.S. have institutional review boards that review all research involving human subjects, including all second language research. As noted previously, not all are termed IRBs; the term human subjects committee is often used interchangeably with institutional review board.

IRB reviews are designed to ensure the protection of human research subjects. In general, the job of the IRB is to ascertain that the investigator is in compliance with federal standards for ethics and is taking adequate steps to protect the rights and well-being of research participants. This includes equitable selection of subjects, adequate communication of information and risks in informed consent documents, and clear statements about the confidentiality of data. It is also the responsibility of the IRB to investigate any alleged or suspected violations of approved plans. IRBs usually have the right to suspend or require modifications to research protocols if they deem it necessary.

The IRB review may also entail, to some degree, assurance of the scientific merit of the research, although U.S. federal regulations leave IRBs without clear direction on this point. According to the OHRP Guidebook for IRBs (n.d., www.hhs.gov/ohrp/archive/irb/irb_guidebook.htm, retrieved April 19, 2015), many IRBs appear to take the following approach: If the investigator is seeking external funding for the research, review of the scientific quality of the research involved is left to the agency but, if no such funding is being sought, the IRB may take more care in reviewing the research design.

In relation to second language research, it is important to note that full IRB reviews can be time-consuming when they are carried out. However, second language (and other linguistically oriented) research often qualifies for either exempt status (no IRB review required) or expedited review, depending upon the policy of the institution's IRB. For example, observational studies (such as the observation of adult behavior in public places, with no manipulation of the environment) are generally exempt from IRB review as they are considered low-risk. Expedited reviews also apply to certain kinds of low-risk research, such as minor changes in previously approved research during the authorized approval period. Sometimes classroom observational research is considered low-risk, as is the examination of data collected from regular classroom tests. In an expedited review, all of the requirements for IRB approval of research are in effect. However, in expedited reviews, approval may be granted by the chair of the IRB alone or by one or more members of the IRB, instead of requiring a full review by the entire board. Expedited reviews are processed more quickly, but the full protocol for an application for a complete review is usually required in addition to the application for expedited review. As in all instances of human subjects research, researchers are urged to check with their local IRB for specific requirements.

2.1.2.2 Why Guidelines to Protect Human Subjects Were Developed

Various troubling practices of the past have raised questions about the ethical treatment of human subjects in research. Although the detail that follows on medical experimentation may seem at first glance to be some distance from second language research, it is important to understand that the various principles developed out of the statements and reports have direct consequences for guidelines involved in carrying out all research involving human subjects. This includes research involving second language learners.

Perhaps the most notorious violation of human rights, with a substantial number of people affected and a significantly high degree of harm caused, is the case of the Nazi "medical experiments" carried out in concentration camps during the Second World War. In the Nuremberg Military Tribunals, where 23 physicians and administrators were indicted for their participation in these experiments, the judges provided a section in their written verdict entitled "Permissible Medical Experiments," which has become known as the Nuremberg Code (1949). A number of aspects of this important code inform current research practices.

Another disturbing example of the prolonged and deliberate violation of the rights of a vulnerable population is the well-known U.S. Tuskegee Syphilis Study (1930–1972). The course of untreated syphilis was studied in a group of 399 infected black airmen. These men were not only recruited for the study without their informed consent, but were also misinformed because researchers implied that they were receiving treatment. Even when penicillin was confirmed as an effective treatment for syphilis in the 1940s, the men were neither informed nor treated. Press coverage of this study began to appear in 1972. This, together with other biomedical abuses, led to public outrage in the U.S. and eventually to the U.S. Congress establishing a permanent body to regulate all federally-supported research involving human subjects; this body is now known as the National Commission for the Protection of Human Subjects of Biomedical and Behavioral Research. Many other violations of the rights of human subjects can be found in the literature. Collectively, these disturbing events helped to shape the course of the development of an ethical code for research practices.

2.1.2.3 Development of Research Codes of Ethics

The Nuremberg Code (1949), which has served as the basis for many later ethical codes governing research involving human subjects, outlines 10 directives for human experimentation, the first of which is that voluntary, fully informed consent to participate in experiments is essential. Also, the experiment should be necessary and fruitful for the good of society, should avoid unnecessary physical and mental suffering and injury, and should be based on prior animal research where applicable. Human subjects should be protected against possibilities of injury or death and be allowed to withdraw from the experiment; moreover, the degree of risk should not outweigh the experiment's humanitarian importance. This code was, in effect, the first international code of research ethics.

The Declaration of Helsinki, first adopted in 1964, was developed by the World Medical Association (2000, www.wma.net/en/30publications/10policies/ b3, retrieved January 22, 2015) to serve as a statement of ethical principles providing guidance to physicians and other investigators in medical research involving human subjects. It was the medical community's first major attempt at self-regulation, and it periodically undergoes revisions and updates. Like the Nuremberg Code, it emphasizes the importance of the voluntary consent and protection of the subject, the subject's freedom to withdraw from the research, and the idea that potential benefits should outweigh foreseeable risks. It also requires special protections for vulnerable research populations.

The Belmont Report (1979) in the U.S., based on the work of the National Commission for the Protection of Human Subjects of Biomedical and Behavioral Research, identifies three major ethical principles that should guide individual and institutional considerations in human research: (1) respect for persons; (2) beneficence; and (3) justice. These basic principles appear in the NIH online training module mentioned above. Respect for persons entails that all people should be treated as autonomous agents and that those with diminished autonomy are entitled to special protections. Beneficence involves respecting people's decisions and protecting them from harm, as well as making efforts to ensure their well-being. It has been taken to imply two general rules: (1) do no harm; and (2) maximize possible benefits and minimize possible risks. Justice means fairness in the distribution of the risks and benefits of research.

TIME TO THINK ...

In the domain of second language acquisition research, what kinds of populations may have the "diminished autonomy" described by the Belmont Report? What kinds of special protections should they be offered?

2.1.2.4 Preparing a Protocol for the IRB

A protocol is essentially an application to an IRB for approval to carry out research. IRBs generally provide an application form that solicits the information they need for their review. This often includes a template for an informed consent document.

The protocol to be submitted generally requires the following sections, although different institutions may name or organize these sections differently. In the Précis (also known as the abstract), the researcher provides a short overview of the study's objectives, population, design, and potential results of interest. In the Introduction, background information is provided along with a review of the relevant literature. In the Objectives section, the researcher states the objectives of the study and, whenever possible, the hypotheses. Next, in the Study Design and Methods section, the researcher describes how the participants will be chosen and how treatment is to be administered. In the Data Analysis section, the researcher explains how the outcomes will be measured and statistically analyzed. After this, in the Human Subjects Protection section, the researcher usually provides:

1. Information about any strategies or procedures for recruitment (including advertising, if applicable).
2. A description of the potential benefits that may reasonably be expected from the research.
3. An explanation of the potential risks (physical, psychological, social, legal, or other), their likelihood, and what steps the researcher will take to minimize those risks.
4. A description of the consent procedures to be followed.

A section on the qualifications of the researcher to carry out the study is also often required. Finally, in the References section, the researcher provides a list of studies that were cited in the protocol (OHSR, Information Sheet #5, 2000).

General Use of Protocols in Research

In addition to being an essential step in obtaining IRB approval, protocols are also useful in that they can be used to provide a "roadmap" for researchers. Since method and design in second language research can often be complex, a detailed protocol "helps the researcher to anticipate problems in advance while also acting as a checklist for the many variables and factors the researcher needs to consider and balance while carrying out the procedure" (Gass & Mackey, 2000, p. 57). A detailed protocol also ensures that if multiple individuals are responsible for administering a test or collecting data, they will do so in a uniform fashion. Preparation of a detailed research protocol often goes hand in hand with a pilot study (see Chapter 3) as part of the preparatory steps in carrying out second language research. Thus, even if researchers feel constrained by the requirements to make applications to IRBs, human subjects committees, or ethics boards, they should feel encouraged that the preparation of a protocol can be a helpful step in thinking through and planning out the steps involved in the research.

2.2 CONCLUSION

Ethical issues in the use of human subjects in second language research, including informed consent, IRBs, and protocol preparation, have been covered. After reading this chapter, you should understand how to ensure that participants are adequately informed about research and their rights as participants. This will foster confidence between the research community and the public. Gaining expertise in writing research protocols and knowledge about them can lead to legal confidence for IRBs and researchers. Finally, awareness of ethical issues is likely to lead to more thoughtful and ethical research practices, which has benefits for scientific research as well as society. Thus, a broad understanding of the issues reviewed here should benefit all researchers, both novice and experienced. In Chapter 3, we turn to a discussion of eliciting data.

POINTS TO REMEMBER

- Institutional review boards review and approve of human subject research activities. IRB approval provides a significant affirmation of the scientific and ethical quality of the research, and therefore offers important validation to the research investigator and the research institution.

- The goal of informed consent is to ensure that participants are supplied with enough information to make informed voluntary decisions about participating.

- Informed consent requires the following conditions are met: suppliance of sufficient information (i.e., full disclosure about the experiment by the researcher), comprehension on the part of the subject, and voluntary participation, where the subject is free from undue pressure or coercion.

- Withholding (necessary) information from participants may be acceptable and allowed by the human subjects committee, but three conditions will often need to be met: incomplete disclosure is essential to the aims of the research, no risks are undisclosed, and all participants will be given an opportunity to be debriefed after the study.

- Social media sites such as Facebook and Twitter allow researchers to access large amounts of participants with little cost. Another method is to utilize crowdsourcing websites to recruit participants. Online workforces such as Amazon's Mechanical Turk provide low-cost, valid alternatives to traditional human subject pools.

- The IRB determines whether research is exempt from IRB review, qualifies for expedited review, or requires full-board approval before research can be conducted.

- Ethical considerations for research involving human subjects are outlined in the Declaration of Helsinki (World Medical Association, 1964), the Belmont Report (1979), and the Nuremberg Code (1949). These documents serve as the basis for ethical principles in scientific research.

- A protocol is an application to an IRB for approval to carry out research that delineates the design, methodology, recruitment, benefits and risks to participants, and informed consent procedures of a given research study.

MORE TO DO AND MORE TO THINK ABOUT ...

1. Why is informed consent important for research involving second language learners?

2. When planning a classroom study of 30 ESL learners aged 11–12 years old, discuss how you would resolve the following issues:

   a. The children are not required by the school to give their consent, but you wish to supplement your parental consent form by giving the children the opportunity to opt out. Indicate the principles by which you would modify the parental consent form for the children.

   b. Two children and their parents decline to consent. What steps can you take to avoid collecting data from these children on your videotapes? (Obviously, you will not *use* any data collected in this way, but there are also steps you might take to avoid collecting them.)

   c. Halfway through the study, one child's parents withdraw him, and a second child says she will be absent for the next five classes. How do you deal with each data set?

   d. The potential participants for your research tend to be suspicious about researchers and are hesitant to participate for fear that sensitive information may be revealed about them upon completion of the research. What sort of information could you provide to reassure them?

3. What is an IRB protocol?

4. Explain the difference between an expedited and an exempt IRB review.

5. Why is it important to provide as much detail as possible in a research report?

NOTES

1. As noted in Chapter 1, wherever possible throughout this book we refer to *learners* or *participants* in research since this is most common. However, the nature of the current chapter requires that we use the term *subjects* in the sections on human subjects.

2. Guidelines for research involving human subjects are available in a number of countries, although formal regulations seem to be most specific in the U.S. and Canada. This chapter is based mostly on U.S. sources. In Canada, there is a tri-council policy statement on the ethical conduct for research involving humans

developed by the Canadian Medical Research Council, Natural Sciences and Engineering Research Council, and Social Sciences and Humanities Research Councils. Individuals and institutions are required to comply with the policy in order to qualify for funding. The policy is fully described at www.pre.ethics.gc.ca/ english/policystatement/introduction.cfm (retrieved April 19, 2015). In the U.K., the British Association of Applied Linguistics publishes general practice guidelines at www.baal.org.uk/public_docs.html (retrieved April 19, 2015). In Australia, an article by Chalmers (2003) suggests that the *National Statement* on research will ensure a very high standard of protection for human subjects. It is beyond the scope of this chapter to discuss specific global informed consent practices, but other countries will have varying (and evolving) approaches to the protection of human subjects.

CHAPTER THREE

Common Data Collection Measures

Data collection in second language research is multidimensional. In this chapter, we provide details about many of the measures that second language researchers commonly use to collect data. We have divided the chapter into sections according to research area, providing a sample of methods used in each area. However, this does not imply that methods used commonly in one area are not also used in other areas. For a more complete discussion of elicitation methods, our book focused exclusively on this topic can be consulted (Gass & Mackey, 2007). We include methods used with formal models, processing-based research, interaction-based research, research on strategies and cognitive processes, sociolinguistic and pragmatics-based research, and questionnaire and survey-based research. Finally, we discuss the use of databases in the second language research field. We begin with a discussion of the importance of pilot testing.

3.1 PILOT TESTING

A pilot study is a small-scale trial of the proposed procedures, materials, and methods, and sometimes also includes coding sheets and analytic choices. The point of carrying out a pilot study is to test, and often to revise, and then finalize the materials and the methods. Pilot testing is carried out to uncover any problems, and to address them before the main study is carried out. A pilot study is an important, if not essential, means of assessing the feasibility and usefulness of the data collection methods and making any necessary revisions before they are used with the research participants.

In general, it is crucial for researchers to allocate time for conducting pilot tests. While it might seem that careful advance planning and preparation might allow the researcher to skip pilot testing, such testing is in fact critical, as it often reveals subtle flaws in the design or implementation of the study that are not readily apparent from the research plan itself. As Gass and Mackey (2000) explain, pilot testing "can help avoid costly and time-consuming problems during the data collection procedure . . . [as well as] the loss of valuable, potentially useful, and often irreplaceable data" (p. 57). We will return to the importance of pilot testing in several of the following chapters as we consider issues such as data coding and classroom research.

Sometimes pilot studies result in data that might be useable for the main study. Some researchers choose to seek permission from their human subjects committees or institutional review boards to carry out an experiment in such a way that if they do not encounter problems with their pilot testing, they can use the data for their main study as long as it is collected in exactly the same way. However, not all institutions will give permission for this, and many do not have a process for the retroactive use of data. It is worthwhile to investigate these issues while also keeping in mind that it is a rare pilot study that does not result in some sort of revision of materials or methods.

3.2 THE SIGNIFICANCE OF DATA COLLECTION MEASURES

Findings in second language research are highly dependent on the data collection (often known as "data elicitation") measures used. One goal of research is to uncover information about learner behavior or learner knowledge independent of the context of data collection. There is no single prescribed elicitation measure, nor is there a "right" or "wrong" elicitation measure, although many research paradigms have common measures associated with them. Saying that there are numerous elicitation measures that have been used in second language research does not, however, imply that measures are random or that one is as good as another. The choice of one measure over another is highly dependent on the research question asked and may also be related to the theoretical framework within which research is conducted. It is the purpose of this chapter to present some common elicitation measures. While we have organized this chapter by research paradigms, the reader should be aware that, as we noted earlier, this is in some sense for the sake of convenience, and there is often crossover from method to paradigm. For example, stimulated recall, which is discussed in this chapter as part of strategies-based research, is actually used in many types of research as well, for example studies of noticing and interaction, and studies of L2 writing products. The measures that we have chosen to describe here do not represent an exhaustive list; in fact, a complete list would be impossible because elicitation measures are constrained only by the limits of researchers' imaginations.

We mentioned above that research questions, to a certain extent, dictate a particular method. We now turn to asking what this means by looking at some hypothetical examples.

a. Syntax: Japanese passives

After an extensive literature review and after years of teaching Japanese, you recognize that English-speaking learners of Japanese have great difficulty with passives. You do some reading and realize that there are theoretical reasons for this, so you decide to investigate. The task in front of you is to gather data from learners of Japanese to determine exactly what faulty generalizations they may be making. In other words, what are the learner-language forms that are being used at various stages of Japanese proficiency? Once you have determined what data you need to elicit (i.e., samples of Japanese passives), your next task is to determine how to elicit appropriate data.

Your first thought is to have learners describe pictures that depict various actions (e.g., a man being hit by a ball, a dog being kissed by a boy). Unfortunately, the learners, who are experts at avoidance, produce very few examples of the structure in question and instead produce sentences such as "The ball hits the man." You then modify the task and tell the learners to start with the patient, that is, with the object of the action. You even point to "a man" and to "a dog." This doesn't work very well because the learners do not do what is being asked; they still begin with "ball" and "dog." You are thus left with the question: Did they fail to produce the requisite passive because: (1) they don't have the linguistic knowledge; (2) the active sentence is easier to formulate; or (3) they didn't understand how to carry out the task? There are too many possibilities as you attempt to interpret the data. Only the first interpretation will help you in dealing with your research questions. It is therefore necessary to question the value of this research elicitation method.

You then realize that you have to force the issue and make learners behave in a way that allows you to be confident that you are obtaining information that reflects their actual knowledge about passives. There are a few ways that this is commonly done in second language research. One way is to use what are known as "acceptability judgments" (see section 3.3.1), where a list of grammatical and ungrammatical sentences is presented to learners who are then asked to indicate whether they consider them acceptable Japanese sentences or not. This is followed by a request to the learners to correct those sentences they have judged to be incorrect. This method ensures that at least the sample of sentences that you are interested in (passives) is the target of investigation. Another way to gather information about passives is through "elicited imitation" (see section 3.3.2). In this method, sentences are read to the learners (usually tape-recorded to ensure that everyone hears the same sentences at the identical rate and with identical intonation), and the learners are asked to repeat them; the assumption being that if a given sentence is part of one's grammar, it will be relatively easy to repeat. As with acceptability judgments, the researcher can control all aspects of the sample sentences. A third possibility for eliciting information about passives is known as "truth-value judgments" (see section 3.3.4). With truth-value judgments, learners are given short contextualized passages with relevant sentences embedded in them. Following each passage is a question that ascertains whether or not a learner can correctly interpret the meaning of the sentence. These might be particularly useful in the case of Japanese passives because some of the differences between sentences involve subtle meaning differences.

Thus, the investigation of a particular grammatical structure offers a number of possibilities for data elicitation measures, the choice of which will depend on the questions being asked (e.g., truth-value for subtle meaning differences, or acceptability judgments or elicited imitation to gather information about grammatical knowledge). In any event, the specific research question can be used to narrow the choice of data collection measures.

TIME TO THINK ...

Suppose your research interest is to find out whether recasts or negotiation will lead to faster development of relative clauses in a second language. A recast is usually defined as a nontarget-like NNS utterance that has been rephrased in a more target-like way while maintaining the original meaning. You find groups of English learners of Italian who are at four different stages of development in their knowledge of relative clauses. How might you design this study? What elicitation method would you choose?

Now, suppose you've gathered and analyzed the data and found no difference between groups. Upon reading the transcripts from the research, you realize this is probably due to a lack of relative clause examples in the data. How could you redesign the study to ensure that relative clauses are elicited?

b. Pragmatics research

Assume that you want to conduct research on pragmatic problems that a particular group of students might have (e.g., English speakers learning Chinese). You have further limited your research to interactions between English learners of Mandarin and their Mandarin-speaking professors. You obtain permission to observe interactions between these two groups of people in order to determine what sorts of pragmatic errors may occur, but after five days of observations you have little in the way of consistent results. Why might that be the case? One reason might be that you have not narrowed down your research question sufficiently (see Chapter 1 for more information on research questions). For example, you might be looking for too many pragmatic areas (e.g., complaining, apologizing, requesting, inviting) rather than constraining the data. A second reason is that waiting for a language event to occur may be dependent on luck. You might end up with some interesting examples that could be fodder for insightful qualitative analyses, but if you are looking for sufficient examples to be able to make quantitative generalizations, you may need to force the issue, for example by using discourse completion tests (see section 3.7.3), well-designed role plays (see section 3.7.4), or by asking about the participants' perceptions in relation to videos of speech acts. In their simplest form, discourse completion tests present learners with a context in which a response is required. Role plays involve acting situations and are also useful for establishing specific contexts. Data could be set up so that a learner and another person are sitting at a table when the second person accidentally knocks over the water. What the learner actually says to accept the apology could then be recorded.

As can be seen through the examples above, the research questions will help guide you to more or less appropriate elicitation measures. In the remainder of this chapter, we present some common methods used in a variety of research paradigms. As we noted earlier, this list is neither exclusive nor exhaustive, and may even cross categories.

TIME TO DO ...

You want to investigate the acquisition of past time reference by English language learners. What data elicitation method would you choose? Outline a design for this study.

3.3 RESEARCHING FORMAL MODELS OF LANGUAGE

The first paradigm that we consider in this chapter on elicitation methods is Universal Grammar (UG), arguably the most common paradigm within the general category of formal models. The UG approach to second language acquisition begins from the perspective of learnability. The assumption is that there are innate universal language properties; innateness is invoked to explain the uniformly successful and speedy acquisition of first language by normal children despite incomplete (impoverished) input. In UG theory, universal principles form part of the mental representation of language, and properties of the human mind are what make language universals the way they are. As Chomsky (1997) noted, "The theory of a particular language is its *grammar*. The theory of languages and the expressions they generate is *Universal Grammar* (UG); UG is a theory of the initial state S_o of the relevant component of the language faculty" (p. 167, emphasis in original). The assumption that UG is the guiding force of child language acquisition has long been maintained by some researchers. The question for second language research concerns the extent to which UG may be available to second language learners. Or, to put it differently, they ask, to what extent does UG constrain the kinds of second language grammars that learners can come up with?

3.3.1 Acceptability Judgments

The theory underlying UG assumes that language is constrained by a set of abstract principles that characterize core grammars of all natural languages. In addition to principles that are invariant (i.e., characteristic of all languages) are parameters that vary across languages. UG-based second language research seeks to determine the extent to which second language learners have the same abstract representations as native speakers. One needs to determine, then, what learners believe to be grammatical in the language being learned and what they consider ungrammatical. Importantly, second language input alone does not provide learners with this information (see Gass with Behney & Plonsky, 2013, Chapter 11, for further details). Because UG researchers need to understand the nature of abstract representations and because abstractness is only inferable from surface phenomena, researchers are often in a position of needing to force learners into stating what is possible and what is not possible in their second language. Acceptability judgments, a common elicitation tool in linguistics, are often used for this purpose. It is often the case that the term *acceptability* judgment is used interchangeably with *grammaticality* judgment. This is technically not correct. We make inferences about grammaticality based on judgments of acceptability, but since grammar is abstract we cannot ask about it directly.

In an acceptability judgment task, learners are asked whether a particular sentence is acceptable in the second language. As mentioned above, some sort of forced elicitation may be necessary in cases when researchers want to investigate a particular grammatical structure because otherwise they might have to wait a considerable amount of time for enough instances to occur in natural production to draw reasonable conclusions, and with time, of course, changes can occur in second language grammars. Moreover, part of understanding what someone knows about language is understanding what they include in their grammar and what they exclude. This cannot be inferred from natural production alone, as the following example demonstrates.

Research question: Do learners know the third-person singular –s in English?

Typical production: The man walks down the street.

If learners consistently produce sentences such as the one above, we might be able to conclude that they have knowledge of third-person singular. However, that is a conclusion based on insufficient evidence. It is a valid conclusion only if we also know what the learners exclude—that is, if we know that they rule out as a possible English sentence *The boys walks down the street. In other words, do they recognize that –s is limited to third-person singular as opposed to being a generalized present-tense marker?

In addition, if learners do not use a form at all, we cannot assume that they cannot use the form unless they consistently do not use it in a required context.

TIME TO DO ...

Conduct a library search for a study that utilizes acceptability judgments. First, determine the research question, such as: Does length of exposure in a foreign language setting influence target-like performance of grammatical judgments? What method of data elicitation did the authors use? Why do you think the researchers chose this method of data elicitation? Would another method have been more suitable?

Over the years, there have been numerous challenges and controversies surrounding the use of acceptability judgments. Among them are questions relating to what individuals are doing when they make judgments. In other words, what sort of knowledge is being tapped? For example, particularly with second language learners, we can ask whether their responses to sentences are truly representative of their knowledge of the second language or whether they are trying to remember what some teacher said should be the case. In fact, learners will often judge that a particular sentence is not possible (as in *The boys walks down the street*), but will still continue to produce similar sentences. How does one reconcile their apparent knowledge with their practice? It is important to remember that native speaker judgments are tapping a system that the individual has command over. This is not the case with nonnative speakers, who are being asked about the second language while inferences are being made about another system: their interlanguage.

The general procedure for using acceptability judgments is to give a list of target language sentences to be judged and to ask for corrections of any sentences judged incorrect. There are numerous practical considerations when dealing with collecting judgment data, some of which we address below (see also Schütze, 1996).

3.3.1.1 Materials

Order of Presentation

Counterbalance so that order of presentation does not affect results (see Gass, 1994 for a study in which each participant received a different sentence ordering). No two participants should receive the same order of sentences. This reduces the possible interpretation that the ordering affected the results.

Number of Sentences

Balance grammatical and ungrammatical sentences. Judging sentences can become tiresome and judgments may become unreliable. One way of countering this is to make sure that participants have different orders (see above). Another way is to limit the number of sentences given. Although studies have been carried out with as many as 101 (Hawkins & Chan, 1997) and 282 (Johnson & Newport, 1989), we recommend no more than approximately 50 sentences. If more are necessary, it would be advisable to follow Johnson and Newport's practice of presenting them in blocks with a break in between and letting the participants know that they can rest if they are tired.

It is also important to make sure that there are sufficient numbers of filler or distracter sentences so that participants in a study cannot easily guess what the study is about. As we will see in Chapter 5, this would be a threat to internal validity. If a researcher is investigating a number of structures in one study, it may be possible for the structures to serve as distracters for one another.

Timing

With tests given orally or on the computer, the timing between sentences can be controlled. Questions about how much time should elapse have not been seriously addressed in the literature, but could potentially affect the results (see Murphy, 1997). Another related question to consider is whether participants should be allowed to go back and change their answers. Given that one is attempting to gain knowledge about a learner's grammar and not about formal rule knowledge, it is advisable to get quick responses without a great deal of thinking time. With an orally administered test or with a computer-based test, this is relatively easy to control; with a paper and pencil test, one could, for example, give everyone a pen with non-erasable ink so that answers cannot be changed. Exact times are sometimes recorded, in milliseconds, so that speed can provide researchers with additional information as they assess the data. Likewise, confidence judgments (how convinced a learner is about his or her answer, often measured on a scale of "very confident to not sure") can provide additional information.

Context

Sentences can be embedded in a situational context (see below under truth-value judgments) to ensure consistency.

Comparisons

At times, one wants to have sophisticated judgments of acceptability involving subtleties in language. In such instances, it might be advisable to ask participants to judge sentences as they relate to one another (e.g., *We didn't dare to answer him back* versus *We didn't dare answer him back*—which is better?). This technique is not often used in second language research (see also section 3.3.3 on magnitude estimation below).

Modality

Are sentences given orally, on paper, or on a computer? Examples abound of each type although computer administration is most common these days. The least common is oral administration (although see Ionin & Wexler, 2002 for an example of this, or review article by Murphy, 1997 on the effects of modality on outcomes). While not actual judgments of acceptability, a slight variation on acceptability involves the use of pictures. In these situations, learners might have to match up a sentence with a picture (see Bley-Vroman & Joo, 2001 for examples) or provide a judgment about a sentence in relation to an accompanying picture, as in Montrul (2001) and in Juffs (2001). Information from these tasks may lead to inferences regarding grammaticality.

3.3.1.2 Procedures

Corrections

Certain assumptions that are often made with native speaker judgments cannot always be made with nonnative speaker judgments. For instance, one can reasonably assume with native speakers that the area targeted by the researcher will also be the one targeted by the native speaker judge. With nonnative speakers, this is not the case since their grammars can be nonnative-like in many ways. Thus, in order to ensure that the research focus is the same as the nonnative speakers' focus, it is necessary to ask learners to correct those sentences they judge to be unacceptable. For example, given the sentence *She knows the woman whom is the sister of my friend*, learners might judge this as incorrect. But without correction, we do not know what they think is incorrect about it. If our target is relative pronouns (*whom*) and they change the sentence to *She knows the woman whom is my sister's friend*, we can make the assumption that they believe that *whom* is correct. This is an important consideration when contemplating scoring.

When do participants make corrections? This is generally done immediately following the judgment. In other words, participants judge a sentence as correct or incorrect and make corrections to the sentences that were judged incorrect. The instructions (see below) should generally include information about corrections as part of what participants are expected to do. In Gass and Alvarez-Torres (2005), judgments were collected on a computer. At the end of the session, the computer printed out all sentences for which the participant had given a judgment of incorrect. At that point, the participant was asked to make corrections. This has the potential of reducing the possibility that respondents are responding "good" due to their desire not to have to do the additional work of having to correct.

Instructions

The idea of rating sentences for grammaticality/acceptability is novel to many participants. Participants often confuse "making sense" with judgments of grammaticality. For example, the sentence *The table bit the dog* is grammatical in the pure sense; there is a noun phrase and a transitive verb followed by another noun phrase. However, because the first noun is inanimate and the second is animate, the sentence doesn't make sense; tables can't bite dogs. Instructions, therefore, and the examples provided need to be carefully crafted. For example, Ionin and Wexler (2002) provided explanation orally: "The investigator talked the practice items over with the child and ensured that the child was responding to the grammaticality and not to the meaning of the sentences" (p. 121).

Birdsong (1989, pp. 114–115) gives examples of some unsuccessful instructions:

- Do the following sentences sound right?
  This does not eliminate the problem of confounding grammaticality with sentences that are semantically anomalous.
- Tell me if for you this makes a sentence.
  A "sentence" such as "When will your grandmother arrive?" may be rejected because it is a *question* and not a *sentence*.

One of the most thorough sets of instructions comes from Bley-Vroman, Felix, and Ioup (1988, p. 32) in their investigation of accessibility to UG with a specific focus on *wh*-movement by Korean learners of English.

Sentence intuitions

Speakers of a language seem to develop a "feel" for what is a possible sentence, even in the many cases where they have never been taught any particular rule.

For example, in Korean you may feel that sentences 1–3 below sound like possible Korean sentences, while sentence 4 doesn't. [The sentences below were actually presented in Korean.]

1) Young Hee's eyes are big.
2) Young Hee has big eyes.

---

3) Young Hee's book is big.

4) Young Hee has a big book.

Although sentences 2 and 4 are of the same structure, one can judge without depending on any rule that sentence 4 is impossible in Korean.

Likewise, in English, you might feel that the first sentence below sounds like it is a possible English sentence, while the second one does not.

1) John is likely to win the race.

2) John is probably to win the race.

On the following pages is a list of sentences. We want you to tell us for each one whether you think it sounds possible in English. Even native speakers have different intuitions about what is possible. Therefore, these sentences cannot serve the purpose of establishing one's level of proficiency in English. We want you to concentrate on how you feel about these sentences.

For the following sentences, please tell us whether you feel they sound like *possible* sentences of English for you, or whether they sound like *impossible* English sentences for you. Perhaps you have no clear feeling for whether they are possible or not. In this case mark *not sure*.

Read each sentence carefully before you answer. Concentrate on the structure of the sentence. Ignore any problems with spelling, punctuation, etc. Please mark only one answer for each sentence. Make sure you have answered all 32 questions.

It is often beneficial if instructions can be translated into the native languages of the participants. The above instructions would, of course, need to be modified according to the specific circumstances.

Scoring

Scoring will depend on how the task is set up. For example, you can provide options for a dichotomous choice (the sentence is either good or not good), or an indication of relative "goodness" on a Likert scale. There is little uniformity in the second language literature on this issue. We took a single issue of the journal *Studies in Second Language Acquisition* (2001, vol. 23, 2) with relevant studies. There are two articles that use a Likert scale. Inagaki (2001), in an article on the acquisition of motion verbs, uses a five-point Likert scale (–2 = completely unnatural, 0 = not sure, +2 = completely natural), while Montrul, in an article on agentive verbs, uses a seven-point Likert scale (–3 = very unnatural, 0 = cannot decide, 3 = very natural).

Some researchers eliminate the "not sure" option or the middle of the road option and instead have a four-point scale (see Hawkins & Chan, 1997). Juffs (2001) points out that without a standard in the field, it is difficult to compare the results of studies. He also points out that having a positive and negative scale with a zero midpoint makes it difficult to interpret a zero response as a "don't know" or as a midpoint. His suggestion is to use a completely positive scale (e.g., from 1 to 7). Another possibility is to put no numerical value on the scale itself and to use a scale with only descriptors, as below.

X . . . . X . . . . X . . . . X . . . . X . . . . X X
very natural   don't know   very unnatural

When doing the actual scoring, one needs to separate the grammatical from the ungrammatical sentences in order to determine learners' knowledge of what is correct (i.e., grammatical) and knowledge of what is ungrammatical (i.e., excluded by their second language grammar). If one is using a five-point Likert scale, the following is a possible scoring scheme:

Grammatical sentences	Ungrammatical sentences
Definitely correct = 4	Definitely incorrect = 4
Probably correct = 3	Probably incorrect = 3
Don't know = 2	Don't know = 2
Probably incorrect = 1	Probably correct = 1
Definitely incorrect = 0	Definitely correct = 0

One might also give partial credit for recognizing where the error is, even though the correction may not be accurate. Before doing the actual scoring, it is important to consider the corrections that have been made. For example, assume that you are studying the acquisition of morphological endings and the following sentence appears: *The man walk to the subway.* If the learner marks this "Incorrect" and then changes the second definite article on the test sheet to *a*, one would want to ignore the correction and count the sentence as if the learner had said "Correct" because the object of inquiry, morphological endings, was deemed to be correct.

While acceptability judgments had their origins within formal linguistic approaches to language and are most commonly used within the UG paradigm, like other elicitation techniques, they are not limited to that paradigm. Whatever the research question, they are difficult to use and interpret and must be used with caution and careful thought, as well as with awareness of the advantages and difficulties.

Recommendations and considerations for the use of acceptability judgments

1. Counterbalance presentation order.
2. Carefully determine appropriate number of sentences.
3. Include filler/distracter sentences.
4. For computer administration, determine if you want time pressure or not. If so, how much time for each sentence (based, in part, on level of proficiency).
5. Do you want sentences in isolation or embedded in context?
6. How will you ensure that the targeted structure is the one being judged? If done via corrections, how will corrections be requested? After each sentence? At the end of the task?
7. Make sure that instructions are clear.
8. Carefully consider the scale to be used for judging:

   a. How many points?
   b. What is the wording for the scale?
   c. Do you want a "not sure" option?

9. How will scoring be done?

3.3.2 Elicited Imitation

Elicited imitation, like acceptability judgments, is used to determine grammaticality. The basic assumption underlying elicited imitation is that if a given sentence is part of one's grammar, it will be relatively easy to repeat; it is as if sentences are "filtered" through one's grammatical system. In elicited imitation tasks, sentences are presented to participants auditorily (i.e., either prerecorded or orally by the researcher), and the participants are then asked to repeat them. The sentences are typically designed to manipulate certain grammatical structures, and a person's ability to repeat the sentences accurately is a reflection of his or her internal grammatical system. A crucial factor in designing suitable test sentences is to keep the length at an appropriate level, generally a level that exceeds short-term memory. Thus, sentences that might be appropriate for a more advanced level might be inappropriate for early-level learners. Sometimes researchers ask participants to count to three before beginning to speak to ensure that "echoic" memory, or the short-term memory of auditory information, is not being used. This ensures that participants are not simply parroting the sentences without any processing. Elicited imitation, then, elicits an actual prompted utterance. This is unlike acceptability judgments, which elicit learners' beliefs about the language being learned.

Recommendations for elicited imitation tasks

1. Ensure an appropriate length in terms of words and syllables for all sentences. For example, a length between 12 and 17 syllables might be appropriate, depending on proficiency level.
2. Prerecord sentences for uniformity.
3. Randomize all sentences.
4. Include enough tokens of each grammatical structure so that you can make reasonable conclusions. This will depend on how many structures you are dealing with. As with other methodologies, one has to balance the need to have an appropriate number of tokens with the necessity of not tiring the participants to the point that their responses are not reliable. Different randomizations for different learners can help guard against this latter possibility.
5. Ensure that there is enough time between the end of the prompt and the time that a learner begins to speak.
6. Pilot test everything.

3.3.3 Magnitude Estimation

Magnitude estimation is a well-established research tool used in a variety of disciplines (see Bard, Robertson, & Sorace, 1996 for a detailed description and history). It is useful when one wants not only to rank items in relation to one another, but also to know how much better X is than Y. It has recently been used when eliciting grammatical knowledge not as an absolute (yes or no), but as a matter of gradations (i.e., which sentence is more acceptable than another?). We can easily rank a list of things into an order of 1–9, but magnitude estimation allows us to determine whether each of the rankings is equidistant from the others, and if not, the magnitude of the ranking differences. Two of the positive aspects of this method, as noted by Bard et al. (1996), are:

- Researchers do not set the number of values that are used to measure the particular property of concern. Thus, the research does not impose a preset number of categories. The end result is a set of data that is more informative because the participant establishes both the range and the distribution of responses.
- One can observe meaningful differences that directly reflect differences in impressions of the property being investigated. This is so because magnitude estimation allows researchers to subtract the score on one sentence from that of another and be confident about the magnitude of difference.

As mentioned above, magnitude estimation is a ranking procedure. The scale that one uses is not imposed by the researcher, but rather is determined by each participant him or herself. A stimulus is presented (orally or visually) and each participant assigns a numerical value. Each subsequent stimulus is rated according to the basis established from the previous stimulus. Thus, if a rater gives a value of 20 for an initial stimulus, and the second stimulus is perceived as being twice as good, he or she would give it a 40. It is common to train raters on the physical stimulus of line length. To do this, one shows raters a line and asks them to assign a numerical value to it. Following this, they are shown another line and are asked to assign a number to it in comparison to the length of the previous line. To make sure that raters understand the task, this can be repeated. It is best to tell raters to begin with a scale larger than 10 so that subsequent ratings do not end up with small numbers that might be difficult to work with. In other words, because ratings are multiples of a previous rating, if one were to start with 2, and the second were given half that value, the second one would have a value of 1. The next one, if smaller, would end up being a fraction, which, of course, could soon be an unwieldy number.

Below is a description of magnitude estimation in a second language study concerned with the effects of task repetition on language development (Gass et al., 1999). The purpose of the judging was to rank excerpts of second language speech. The data were from English-speaking learners of Spanish who had repeated a narration of a film. The question was whether a later narration was better than an earlier one, and if so, by how much.

Description

After working with line length and before listening to the actual tapes, raters listened to a training tape. They heard three samples of one minute each which they rated using the magnitude estimation methodology. For the actual rating, raters listened to the first 2.5 minutes of each participant's tape. For purposes of analysis, to compare the magnitude of improvement judged by each rater it is necessary to convert the unique scales created by individual raters into a logarithmic scale. Conversion to a logarithmic scale is standard procedure when using magnitude estimation. Because the methodology allows for unique scales to be created by each rater, there must be a way to standardize the scales across raters to obtain a meaningful comparison (Gass et al., 1999, p. 560).

As with all procedures, instructions are important. Below are the instructions provided to the raters of the magnitude estimation test in the above study.

Instructions

You will hear nine tapes of different nonnative speakers of Spanish doing an online description in Spanish of a video they were watching. Your task is to rate their Spanish. Assign any number that seems appropriate to you to the first speech sample. This number will be your "base." Then assign successive numbers in such a way that they reflect your subjective impression (use a range wider than 10). For example, if a speech sample seems 20 times as good, assign a number 20 times as large as the first. If it seems one-fifth as good, assign a number one-fifth as large, and so forth. Use fractions, whole numbers, or decimals, but make each assignment proportional to how good you perceive the person's Spanish to be (Gass et al., 1999, p. 581).

TIME TO DO ...

Suppose you are designing a study where French teachers rate the native-likeness of recordings of French language learners describing their favorite recipe. Generate a list of pros and cons for implementing magnitude estimation judgment methodology as opposed to a Likert scale rating system.

3.3.4 Truth-Value Judgments and Other Interpretation Tasks

Truth-value judgments are a way of understanding how people interpret sentences. These have been used extensively in the study of reflexives by L2 learners. An example of a truth-value token is given below from Glew (1998):

Bill was sick and in the hospital. Nobody knew what was wrong with Bill. The hospital did a lot of tests on Bill to find out what was wrong. Bill had to wait a long time in his hospital room. Finally, a doctor came in to tell Bill why he was sick.

After the medical tests, the doctor informed Bill about himself.

True False

Provided with sufficient contextual information, participants are able to consider all possible referents for *himself* (Bill or the doctor). In other words, appropriateness is determined by the context of the story.

Creating stories of this sort is a difficult process, and all such stories should be piloted. To underscore the importance of pilot studies, below we give another example that was created for a study on reflexives, but ruled out after preliminary testing because there were multiple interpretations.

Sally drove Jane to a party. They had a good time, but Sally had too much to drink. Jane didn't want her to drive home so Jane offered to drive.

Sally was happy that Jane drove herself home.

(True)   (False)

This example was intended to elicit "False," because Jane drove Sally home (not herself), but it is clear that the story could be interpreted either way. Needless to say, this example was not included in the final set of materials. Over the years, there have been other means of obtaining information about reflexives. This is a particularly difficult structure to investigate because many sentences are only grammatical given a particular context. Other than the truth-value paradigm discussed above, researchers have used multiple-choice formats.

Example: John said that Bill hit himself.

Who does *himself* refer to?

a. John
b. Bill
c. Either John or Bill
d. Another person
e. Don't know

Lakshmanan and Teranishi (1994) point out that this is not an acceptable task because we gain information about who *himself* can refer to, but not about who *himself* cannot refer to. They offer the following revision (see original article for their interpretation of results):

John said that Bill saw himself in the mirror.

a. 'Himself' cannot be John.	agree	disagree
b. 'Himself' cannot be Bill.	agree	disagree

For further discussion of many of the methodological points with regard to the study of reflexives, see Akiyama (2002).

3.3.5 Sentence Matching

Sentence matching is a procedure that, like acceptability judgments, has its origins in another discipline, in this case psycholinguistics. Sentence matching tasks are usually performed on a computer. Participants are seated in front of a computer and are presented with a sentence that is either grammatical or ungrammatical. After a short delay, a second sentence appears on the screen, with the first sentence remaining in place. Participants are asked to decide as quickly as possible if the sentences are identical or are not identical (i.e., if they match or do not match), entering their decision by pressing specific keys. The time from the appearance of the second sentence to the participant's pressing the key is recorded and forms the database for analysis. Research with native speakers has shown that participants in a matching task respond faster to matched grammatical sentences than they do to matched ungrammatical ones (see Gass, 2001 for possible explanations for this phenomenon). In other words, it would be expected that the reaction time would be less for the following two sentences:

John stated his plan to steal the car.
John stated his plan to steal the car.

than for the following:

John stated his plan for steal his car.
John stated his plan for steal his car.

Things to consider in designing sentence matching tasks

- How long the two sentences remain on the screen
- Delay time between the two sentences
- Whether or not the two sentences remain on the screen until the participant has responded
- Whether or not the screen goes blank after a pre-determined time
- Whether standard orthography or upper-case letters are used
- The physical placement of the second sentence relative to the first
- Whether participants are provided with feedback after each response
- How the keys are labeled (same, different; different, same)
- The number of items included
- The number of practice items included
- Whether participants control the onset of each pair of sentences

---

With regard to general design, there are many issues that have to be decided when doing a sentence matching task, and researchers are not in agreement as to the "best solution." We list above some of the variables that need to be weighed when designing a study using a sentence matching task.

Another consideration when using sentence matching tasks relates to which data are kept in the final data pool. For example, a participant might just press the "same" key with no variation. Given that this individual's data are probably not reflective of anything other than his or her not being on task, a researcher might decide to eliminate these data. We discuss these issues in greater detail in Chapter 5 (see also Beck, 1998; Bley-Vroman & Masterson, 1989; Duffield, Prévost, & White, 1997; Eubank, 1993 for further information on scoring).

3.4 PROCESSING RESEARCH

Processing research has its basis in psycholinguistic processing rather than in the structure of linguistic forms. As discussed earlier in this chapter, research on formal models of language emphasizes constraints on grammar formation, whereas in psycholinguistics, the emphasis is on the actual mechanisms involved in learning. Clearly, there is overlap in the interests of both areas, but each paradigm (formal models and processing) has its own particular approach.

3.4.1 Sentence Interpretation

One model dealing with sentence interpretation is known as the Competition Model (Bates & MacWhinney, 1982). The Competition Model has spurred a great deal of research that focuses on how learners process information. The major concern is what information people use in coming to an understanding of the relationships of words in a sentence. For example, when we see or read a sentence such as *Sally kissed John*, how do we come to an interpretation of who kissed whom? In English, we rely on word order (the first noun is typically the subject), meaning and animacy status of lexical items (if the sentence were *The pencil kissed John*, we would be confused as to the relationship), and morphological agreement. Some languages use case markings as the dominant cue with word order being less important. Not all languages use these same criteria (called *cues*), and not all languages assign the same degree of importance or strength to each criterion.

The methodology in the second language research literature based on the Competition Model utilizes sentences with various cues. Learners whose native language uses cues and cue strengths that differ from those of the target language are presented with sentences designed to contain conflicting cues and are asked to determine what the subjects or agents of those sentences are. As with many elicitation methods, there is a great deal of variation in the procedures. Some issues to consider are listed below:

Things to consider in designing sentence interpretation tasks

- Are sentences read or tape-recorded? There is a lack of consistency when sentences are read as it is often difficult to neutralize natural intonational biases. This is particularly important when using unusual sentences such as *The pencil the cat saw.*
- How many sentences? As with all other methods, in order to eliminate fatigue and avoid compromising the reliability of the study, it is usually necessary to limit the number of sentences. A study by Sasaki (1997) used 144 sentences, although most studies have used between 27 and 54.
- What is the pause time between sentences? There appears to be no widely accepted standard.
- What are the instructions? A typical set of instructions is presented in Harrington (1987, p. 360):

  "You are going to hear a tape with a series of very simple sentences. After each sentence is read you will have to interpret it: you should say which one of the two nouns in the sentence is *the subject of the sentence,* that is, *the one who does the action."*

  In the Harrington study, half of the participants were given the "syntactic bias" instruction first (the subject of the sentence), while the other half were given the "semantic bias" instruction first (the one who does the action).

- In what format are the responses given: oral or written?

All of these areas are important to consider when designing a study in which sentence interpretation is being used as an elicitation technique. The advantage of sentence interpretation is that researchers can learn what cues learners use in comprehending second language sentences and how those cues might be related to first language knowledge.

3.4.2 Reaction Time

Reaction time is considered here because it is believed to shed light on how people process certain parts of language. It is assumed that the more time it takes to respond to a sentence, the more processing "energy" is required. For example, if someone is asked about the acceptability of sentences in English, it would be predicted that a sentence such as *I saw a big beautiful cat today* (seven words) would take less time to respond to than a sentence such as *Who did Ann say likes her friend?* (seven words) because the second sentence represents a more complex syntactic structure (and, hence, a greater processing load) than the first. Reaction time measures are often used in conjunction with other kinds of research already discussed. For example, they can be an integral part of sentence matching experiments because the framework underlying sentence matching relies on comparing reaction times between grammatical matched sentences and ungrammatical matched sentences. Times are generally measured in milliseconds. In addition to self-made programs, there are commercially available programs for measuring reaction times as well as for doing psycholinguistic research in general such as E-Prime and PsyScope.

TIME TO DO ...

You want to conduct a study focused on *wh-* questions with two groups of Chinese students learning English (as in White & Juffs, 1998). The two groups of students have had different amounts of exposure to English. Design a methodology using a reaction time task. Then, compare your design to the one actually utilized by White and Juffs.

3.4.3 Moving Window

The moving window technique is another elicitation measure that is typically carried out on a computer. Like other data collection methodologies in second language research, it also has its roots in the discipline of psycholinguistics (Just, Carpenter, & Wooley, 1982). In a moving window experiment, words are presented on a screen one at a time, with each successive word appearing after a participant indicates that he or she is ready. In other words, the participant controls the reading speed. Once a new word appears on the screen, the previous word disappears. After the entire sentence has appeared, the participant presses a button to indicate whether the sentence is grammatical or ungrammatical. Juffs and Harrington (1995) used a moving window technique to investigate differences between long-distance object extraction (*Who did Jane say her friend likes?*) and subject extraction (*Who did Ann say likes her friend?*). Their main concern was to investigate the source of any differences, focusing on both processing time and linguistic knowledge (acceptability judgments were also used in their experiment).

Moving window techniques can provide information about processing times for various parts of the sentence. Instructions for these tools are similar to those exemplified earlier for acceptability judgments. An example follows from Juffs and Harrington (1995, p. 515) (see also the instructions from Bley-Vroman et al., 1988 in section 3.3.1.2). This is an acceptability judgment task, but with a focus on processing time. Because the participant indicates readiness to move to each subsequent word, researchers can determine which parts of a sentence require additional processing time.

Essential components of the instructions, as for acceptability judgments, include an explanation of what "intuition" means, together with the fact that there are no right or wrong answers.

Instructions

Speakers of a language seem to develop a "feel" for what is a possible sentence, even when they have never been taught any particular rules. For example, in English, you might feel that sentences (a) and (c) sound like possible sentences, whereas (b) and (d) do not.

a. Mary is likely to win the race.
b. Mary is probable to win the race.
c. It seems that John is late.
d. John seems that he is late.

In this experiment, you will read sentences word by word on a computer screen. Concentrate on how you feel about these sentences. Native speakers of English often have different intuitions about such sentences, and there are no right or wrong answers. Tell us for each one whether you think it sounds possible or impossible in English.

Read each sentence carefully before you answer. Think of the sentences as spoken English and judge them accordingly. Work as quickly and accurately as you can.

3.4.4 Eye-Tracking

A relatively recent entry onto the scene of second language processing is eye-tracking. It involves relatively expensive and specialized equipment and particular expertise in using that equipment, but also provides a unique perspective into the cognitive processes of the second language user (for more information, see the 2014 special issue of *Studies in Second Language Acquisition* (volume 36, issue 2)). The benefits of eye-tracking are reflected in its name: It provides documentation on eye gaze and/or duration while reading/watching something on a screen. As such, through a precise record of eye gaze/duration, it provides evidence of where a learner is focusing attention. The assumption behind eye-tracking is the eye-mind link (Reichle, Pollatsek, & Rayner 2006, 2012), which assumes that where one focuses one's eyes is a reflection of thought processing:

Longer durations assume some sort of difficulty. "The point of gaze serves as an index of overt attention (Wright & Ward, 2008) that can be used to make inferences about participants' corresponding covert attentional processing, or mental focus" (Godfroid et al., 2015).

Many uses have been made of eye-trackers including interpretation, grammaticality, and caption use, to give only a small sample. In general, following calibration, individuals see something (e.g., a text, a sentence, a picture) on the screen to which they may respond in some way (e.g., a judgment of acceptability) or may simply read. During reading, precise measures are taken of where their eyes land and for how long. When individuals spend longer on certain parts of a sentence, for example, or go back and reread something, the assumption is that there is sensitivity to that particular word/phrase. For example, if a native speaker of Spanish/Italian encountered a lack of noun–adjective agreement in a sentence, she would presumably hesitate and perhaps go back and relook at the first word (generally the noun) of the pair, suggesting sensitivity to gender agreement. If a learner of Spanish/Italian read over the noun–adjective pair without stopping, one could assume lack of knowledge of this part of the language.

3.5 INTERACTION-BASED RESEARCH

The above two research areas (formal models and processing research) have methodologies that stem from other disciplines (for the most part formal linguistics and psycholinguistics, respectively). We now turn to interaction-based research, where the focus is learners' conversational interactions with others (e.g., other learners, native speakers, and teachers) and the developmental benefits of such interactions.

TIME TO DO ...

Find a research study that uses a formal or processing approach to language learning and another study that takes an interaction-based perspective. Compare and contrast the research questions and elicitation strategies in the two studies.

Within interaction-based research, the goal is usually to manipulate the kinds of interactions that learners are involved in, the kind of feedback they receive during interaction, and the kind of output they produce in order to determine the relationship between the various components of interaction and second language learning. The most common way of gathering data is to involve learners in a range of carefully planned tasks.

There are a variety of ways of categorizing task types (see Pica, Kanagy, & Falodun, 1993 for task categorization suggestions). For example, a common distinction is to classify tasks as one-way and two-way tasks. In a one-way task, the information flows from one person to the other, as when a learner describes a picture to his or her partner. In other words, the information that is being conveyed is held by one person. In a two-way task, there is an information exchange whereby both parties (or however many participants there are in a task) hold information that is vital to the resolution of the task. For example, in a story completion task, each learner may hold a portion of the information and must convey it to the other learner(s) before the task can be successfully completed.

Another way to classify tasks is to consider the resolution of the task. Is there one correct outcome, as in a closed task (e.g., when two learners need to identify exactly five differences between two pictures), or do the participants need to agree on a common outcome or conclusion, as in an open task such as a discussion activity?

Considering these dimensions, researchers need to be creative in eliciting interactive data. Frequently, one is interested in eliciting certain grammatical structures, with the idea that interactive feedback on nontarget-like forms might be associated with learning, possibly reflected through changes in the learners' output on the particular structures about which they have received feedback. Thus, it is always important to pilot whatever instrument is selected to make sure that opportunities for the production of appropriate forms and feedback are being provided. Before turning to general ways of eliciting interactive data, a word is necessary about recording data.

When recording data, the most important piece of equipment is a good microphone for a tape recorder. Clip-on microphones allow voices to be easily heard on the tape. Omnidirectional microphones may work if the research is being carried out in a laboratory (i.e., research with only the participants in a room); however, if the research is classroom-based, it may be essential to use clip-ons. Ideally, tape recorders should have two inputs for microphones or, alternatively, an adapter can be used. Having two inputs makes later transcription easier. More detailed information about the recording and transcribing of oral data can be found in Chapter 4. In the current section, we describe commonly used data collection techniques within the interaction paradigm. In each case, for purposes of exposition, we categorized tasks. This is an unavoidable oversimplification; in many instances, there is overlap between or among the task types.

3.5.1 Picture Description Tasks

Many picture description tasks are information-gap tasks. Successful task completion usually depends on learners sharing information. In many such tasks, it is important to ensure that if someone is describing a picture to another, the describer's picture cannot be seen. When this is the case, individuals (usually two, although these tasks can also be carried out in small groups) are separated by a barrier. This barrier can be made of cardboard or can even be a simple file folder. Whatever is used, the idea is to ensure that none of the picture can be seen through the back. In some versions of picture description tasks, one person is given a picture with instructions to describe the picture so that another person can draw it. Instructions must also indicate that the person with the picture cannot show the picture to the other person. In some instances, such as when one wants to manipulate different types of input, recorded instructions and descriptions may be appropriate. There are experimental contexts in which one might want standardized input, that is, input that is the same for all participants, for instance modified input, or the modification of speech so that a learner can more easily understand (e.g., Gass & Varonis, 1994). In this situation, researchers can prepare a recording or a transcript and then use that recording or transcript in the actual experiment. Other kinds of picture description tasks are collaborative and do not involve a gap in information. An example of this type of task is a dictogloss task, described below in section 3.5.4.

3.5.2 Spot the Difference

Spot the difference tasks utilize pictures that are different in pre-determined ways (see Iwashita, 2003, where they are used in an interaction experiment). Participants are asked to find the differences, and the number of differences can be pre-specified so that the participants have a goal to work towards. As with picture description tasks, it is important to ensure that the pictures are appropriate in terms of vocabulary for the level of the participants. In terms of format, it is crucial that participants not see their partners' pictures. An example of a setup is seen in the photograph below (this setup can also be used for picture description tasks, or any sorts of tasks where participants should not view each other's pictures).

Figures 3.1a and 3.1b below show examples of pictures that can be used for spot the difference tasks between two or three participants. Figure 3.1a depicts a park scene. These pictures can be used to elicit locatives, plurals, and, as with most spot the difference tasks, questions. The vocabulary is some-what difficult (e.g., slide, swing), but this can work with advanced learners or by using pre-taught vocabulary. The picture is somewhat busy but can be modified to meet the needs of an appropriate pair or group of participants.

Figure 3.1b shows a kitchen scene that can be used with three participants (or two, if one uses two of the three pictures).[1] Again, question forms, locative constructions, plural forms, and (easier) household vocabulary would be produced.

The photograph (reprinted with permission of participants) shows a simple barrier placed between the participants.

Guidelines for spot the difference and picture description tasks

1. Find a picture that contains items that can easily be described, but that includes vocabulary that are likely to cause some lack of understanding, and hence, some negotiation. This might involve physical objects or the placement of objects (*above, on top of*).
2. Separate individuals by a barrier or at least ensure that the picture is not visible to the other person in the pair.
3. Ensure that the picture contains appropriate items for description and/or appropriate location of items in the picture. For example, a picture with a car on top of a house would add another element of difficulty to the task.
4. If relevant, make sure that the task elicits the linguistic structures or forms of interest.
5. Ensure that there are sufficient opportunities for interactional modifications, feedback, and output based on the research question.
6. For picture description:
   Make sure the participants understand that the person drawing should not see the picture until the task is completed.
   For spot the difference:
   Make sure that no participant shows his or her picture to the other(s). Inform participants about the number of differences if necessary.
7. As usual, carefully pilot test the task.

FIGURE 3.1a Spot the difference aliens task

Source: Reprinted with permission of the National Languages and Literacy Institute of Australia.

FIGURE 3.1b Spot the difference kitchen task

Source: Designed by and printed with permission of Jane Ozanich.

3.5.3 Jigsaw Tasks

In a jigsaw task, which is a two-way task, individuals have different pieces of information. In order to solve the task, they must orally interact to put the pieces together. One example of a jigsaw task is a map task (see Pica et al., 1993 for an example) in which participants are given a map of a section of a city. Each participant is provided with different information about street closings, and they must explain to each other about which streets are closed and when. Once this portion is completed, they have to work together to determine a route from Point A to Point B by car, keeping in mind that certain streets are closed. The example in Figure 3.2 below shows a map of a city with locations in Spanish. Examples of sets of street closings are also included, along with an English translation. Alternatively, each person can be given a map with pre-blocked-off streets. In this instance, they would be given a separate blank map in order to draw the route, with instructions not to show the original map to each other.

Another example of a jigsaw task is a story completion, or a story sequencing task, in which different individuals are given parts of a story (written or pictorial) with instructions to make a complete story. Figure 3.3 provides an example of this sort of task.[2]

The important point about jigsaw tasks is that, because they involve an information exchange, they require participants to interact as they complete the task.

TIME TO THINK ...

Look at Figure 3.3. What kinds of interactions might you expect learners to produce as they negotiate a solution to this jigsaw task?

3.5.4 Consensus Tasks

Consensus tasks generally involve pairs or groups of learners who must come to an agreement on a certain issue. For example, 10 individuals are stranded on an island, but only five can fit into a boat to get to the mainland. Characteristics are provided for each individual, and the pair or group must come to an agreement about which five should get into the boat. This task allows for a less guided discussion than others, but it does not guarantee that there will be interaction. One individual might not participate, or, if the task is not engaging, they might take only a few minutes to pick five individuals without giving elaborate justifications. As with other methods, instructions are important to ensure that the participants understand the need to participate. For example, each participant can be assigned a role of an individual and argue for that person's suitability for the boat.

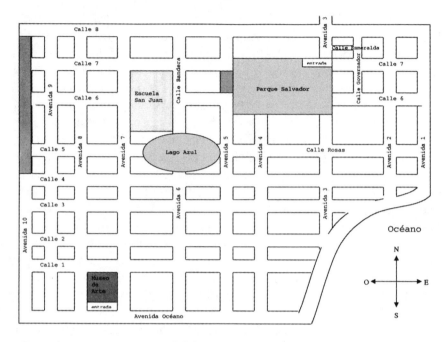

Example of instructions — Map task

Participante 1

- La avenida 10 está cerrada entre la calle 4 y la calle 8.
  Avenue 10 is closed between Street 4 and Street 8.

- La calle 5 está cerrada desde el Lago Azul hasta la avenida 10.
  Street 5 is closed from the Blue Lake to Avenue 10.

- La avenida Oceano va en una sola dirección hacia el oeste.
  Ocean Avenue goes in a single direction towards the west.

Participante 2

- La avenida 5 está cerrada entre la calle 6 y la calle 7.
  Avenue 5 is closed between Street 6 and Street 7.

- La avenida 8 va en una sola dirección hacia el sur.
  Avenue 8 goes in a single direction towards the south.

- La avenida 2 estará cerrada todo el día.
  Avenue 2 will be closed all day.

FIGURE 3.2 Map task

FIGURE 3.3 Story sequencing task

Source: Designed by and printed with permission of Jenefer Philp.

Another type of consensus task is a dictogloss task (see Swain & Lapkin, 2001). In this type of task, learners work together to reconstruct a text that has been read to them. It is possible to choose a text based on content, vocabulary, or particular grammatical structures. In its normal mode of delivery (although this could be modified for the purposes of research), the text is read aloud twice at normal speed. Participants can take notes on the second reading. This will depend on the researcher's goals. Because the text is read at normal speed (unlike a typical dictation), the participants cannot write down everything. Following the readings, participants can work in dyads or small groups to reconstruct the text maintaining the meaning of the original.

3.5.5 Consciousness-Raising Tasks

As the name implies, consciousness-raising tasks are intended to facilitate learners' cognitive processes in terms of awareness of some language area or linguistic structure. In these tasks, learners are often required to verbalize their thoughts about language on their way to a solution. An example of such a task is provided by Fotos and Ellis (1991). The linguistic object of study was dative alternation (*I gave books to my friends* versus *I gave my friends books* and *I suggested a plan for her* but not **I suggested her a plan*). Each student in a group of four was given a sentence (some were correct and some not). Their task was to talk and determine the "rules" for dative alternation in English. Each student read his or her sentence aloud to the others and then using a worksheet, the students determined which verbs could and could not use the alternating structure.

3.5.6 Computer-Mediated Research

Computer-mediated communication (CMC) involves learners in communicative exchanges using the computer. CMC is a text-based medium that may amplify opportunities for students to pay attention to linguistic form as well as providing a less stressful environment for second language practice and production. Thus, it may be that CMC can provide richer data than face-to-face oral exchanges for second language learners. CMC software generally allows users to engage in both simultaneous (chat-based) and asynchronous (forum-based) communication. What is typed is stored, and users, teachers, and researchers can then retrieve prior conversations if desired. The forums generally include open, moderated, closed, and restricted formats, and some have support for distance learning.

Computer-based research can also utilize the various tracking possibilities that technology allows—for example, to see the extent to which learners do and do not use look-up sources such as dictionaries, and when they do, how and how often. This can then be examined in the context of measures of learning. Since computer-based data allow learners more anonymity than face-to-face data, they may also be less restricted in what they say and how they say it. Again, this can be examined in the context of learning.

There are various computer programs that can be used in second language research. As one attempts research using computers, it is important to be informed about advances in technology that will best match one's research question.

One concern about task-based research is that different activities and different interactive treatments might involve more or less time on task, or more or less input and output of linguistic form and interactional modification. It is useful to keep this in mind when planning research, and again, pilot testing is crucial in this respect.

3.6 STRATEGIES AND COGNITIVE PROCESSES

Strategy-based research is aimed at determining the strategies used when learning a second language together with the variables that determine the selection of strategies. Macaro (2001, p. 37) lists the following ways of gaining access to that information:

- Asking learners (directly or through a questionnaire) which strategies they use in general, or which strategies they use when attempting a particular task.
- Observing learners while they work at their language learning tasks.
- Asking learners to give a *retrospective commentary* on how they learn (e.g., through keeping diaries or through dialogue journals).
- Asking learners to provide a *synchronic commentary* on how they accomplished a task (i.e., to talk about their thoughts to an interviewer while they were doing the task).
- Tracking learners (through the use of a computer) on a variety of measures.

In the following sections, we elaborate on some of the resources that researchers have to elicit strategy information, including observations and introspective methods such as think-alouds and stimulated and immediate recalls.

3.6.1 Observations

Observations, discussed in greater detail in Chapters 7 and 8, frequently take place within a classroom context. Macaro (2001, p. 66) provides ways we may consider conducting research on strategies used within the classroom, although there are clearly limits to the conclusions that can be arrived at on the basis of observational data. In terms of strategies-based research, we might observe:

- when students are moving their lips, which might be an indication that they are preparing themselves to speak by practicing under their breath;
- to what extent and which students are "buying processing time" by using such markers as "uh" or "well" or other discourse markers designed to show that they wish to keep their turn;
- to what extent students are employing the compensation strategy of circumlocution (finding alternative ways of saying something they don't know how to say);
- which students are asking a friend for help when they don't understand;
- which students are sounding out words before saying them;
- which students are reasoning by deduction ("it must mean this because of this");
- which students are focusing on every word rather than the gist, perhaps by observing them as they move their finger from word to word;
- which students plunge straight into [an] activity and which students spend some time planning their work; and
- which students use the dictionary and with what frequency.

3.6.2 Introspective Measures

Like other methods discussed thus far, introspective methods, which tap participants' reflections on mental processes, originated in the fields of philosophy and psychology (see Gass & Mackey, 2000; Bowles, 2010 for more information about the origin and use of introspective methods in second language research). The use of introspection assumes that what takes place in consciousness can be observed in much the same way that one can observe events in the external world.

Verbal reporting is a special type of introspection and consists of gathering protocols, or reports, by asking individuals to say what is going through their minds as they are solving a problem. Cohen (1998) outlines three primary types of verbal reporting used in second language research:

1. Self-report. With self-report data, one can gain information about general approaches to something. For example, a statement such as "I am a systematic learner when it comes to learning a second language" might be found on a typical second language learning questionnaire. Such statements are removed from the event in question and are less of a concern here than other types of verbal reporting.

2. Self-observation. Self-observation data can be introspective (within a short period of the event) or retrospective. In self-observation, a learner reports on what he or she has done. An example from Cohen (1998) is the following: "What I just did was to skim through the incoming oral text as I listened, picking out key words and phrases" (p. 34). Such self-observations refer to specific events and are not as generalized as self-report data.

3. Self-revelation, also known as "think-aloud." A participant provides an ongoing report of his or her thought processes while performing some task (see section 3.6.2.2 for further details).

In general, we can think of introspective reports as differing along a number of dimensions: (1) currency (time frame); (2) form (oral or written); (3) task type (think-aloud, talk-aloud, or retrospective); and (4) amount of support for the task.

TIME TO THINK ...

Consider the three types of verbal reporting outlined above. How do the types differ according to time frame, form, task type, and amount of support? What kinds of research questions could be investigated with each type?

The major advantage to the use of verbal reports is that one can often gain access to processes that are unavailable by other means. However, it is also possible to question the extent to which verbal report data are valid and reliable.

The major disadvantage to the use of verbal reports as data has to do with the accuracy of the reporting. This is particularly the case in self-report and self-observational data. With self-report and self-observational data, when the time between the event being reported and the reporting itself is short, there is a greater likelihood that the reporting will be accurate. This particular issue is discussed in relation to stimulated recall below. We further discuss introspective measures in Chapter 8 on second language classrooms.

3.6.2.1 Stimulated Recall

Stimulated recall is usually viewed as a subset of introspective measures. It is a means by which a researcher, in an effort to explore a learner's thought processes or strategies, can prompt the learner to recall and report thoughts that he or she had while performing a task or participating in an event. Gass and Mackey (2000) provide an extensive description of stimulated recall, together with examples of its use (see Mackey, Gass, & McDonough, 2000 for an example of stimulated recall in an experimental context). Stimulated recalls are conducted with some degree of support, known as the stimulus; for example, learners may be shown a videotape so that they can watch themselves carrying out the task, or they may be given their second language written product so that they can follow the changes they made, commenting on their motivations and thought processes along the way.

One thing that is clear from the proliferation of studies using stimulated recalls, and from the corresponding number of critiques of verbal report methodologies, is that stimulated recall is a methodology that, like many others, must be used with care. Many potential problems relate to issues of memory and retrieval, timing, and instructions. Thus, studies that utilize stimulated recall methodology require carefully structured research designs to avoid pitfalls.

Recommendations for stimulated recall research

1. Data should be collected as soon as possible after the event that is the focus of the recall. This is to increase the likelihood that the data structures being accessed are from short-term memory. Retrieval from long-term memory may result in recall interference, and as the event becomes more distant in memory, there is a greater chance that participants will say what they think the researcher wants them to say because the event is not sharply focused in their memories.

2. The stimulus should be as strong as possible to activate memory structures. For example, in a stimulated recall of oral interaction, participants can watch a video if the recall is immediately after the event. If it is more delayed, they can watch a video and possibly even read a transcript of the relevant episodes as well.

3. The participants should be minimally trained; that is, they should be able to carry out the procedure, but should not be cued into any aspects that are extra or unnecessary knowledge. This can be achieved through the use of pilots. Often, simple instructions and a direct model will be enough in a stimulated recall procedure. Sometimes, even instructions are not necessary; the collection instrumentation will be sufficient (e.g., in the case of a questionnaire or a Q&A interview).

4. How much structure is involved in the recall procedure is strongly related to the research question. Generally, if participants are not led or focused, their recalls will be less susceptible to researcher interference. Also, if learners participate in the selection and control of stimulus episodes and are allowed to initiate recalls themselves, there will again be less likelihood of researcher interference in the data. However, unstructured situations do not always result in useful data.

Adapted from Gass and Mackey (2000)

3.6.2.2 Think-Alouds or On-Line Tasks

In think-aloud tasks, also known as on-line tasks, individuals are asked what is going through their minds as they are solving a problem. Through this procedure, a researcher can gather information about the way people approach a problem-solving activity. The following protocols illustrate two very different thought processes during the solving of a mathematical problem (from van Someren, Barnard, & Sandberg, 1994, pp. 5–6). A comparison of these two protocols reveals the way that two individuals can solve the same problem correctly, but in two vastly different ways. By looking only at the starting point and the end product (the solution), it would be difficult to fully understand the two different approaches that can be observed by comparing the complete protocols.

Problem to be solved: A father, a mother, and their son are 80 years old together. The father is twice as old as the son. The mother has the same age as the father. How old is the son?

Student 1	Student 2
1. a father, a mother, and their son are together 80 years old	1. father, mother, and son are together 80 years old
2. the father is twice as old as the son	2. how is that possible?
3. the mother is as old as the father	3. if such a father is 30 and mother too
4. how old is the son?	4. then the son is 20
5. well, that sounds complicated	5. no, that is not possible
6. let's have a look	6. if you are 30, you cannot have a son of 20
7. I just call them F, M, and S	7. so they should be older
8. F plus M plus S is 80	8. about 35, more or less
9. F is 2 times S	9. let's have a look
10. and M equals F	10. the father is twice as old as the son
11. what do we have now?	11. so if he is 35 and the son 17
12. three equations and three unknowns	12. no, that is not possible
13. so S . . .	13. 36 and 18
14. 2 times F plus S is 80	14. then the mother is
15. so 4 times S plus S is 80	15. 36 plus 18 is 54
16. so 5 times S is 80	16. 26 . . .
17. S is 16	17. well, it might be possible
18. yes, that is possible	18. no, then she would have had a child when she was 9
19. so father and mother are 80 minus 16	19. oh, no

89

20. 64	20. no the father should, the mother should be older
21. er . . . 32	21. for example 30
	22. but then I will not have 80
	23. 80 minus 30, 50
	24. then the father should be nearly 35 and the son nearly 18
	25. something like that
	26. let's have a look, where am I?
	27. the father is twice . . .
	28. the mother is as old as the father
	29. oh dear
	30. my mother, well not my mother
	31. but my mother was 30 and my father nearly 35
	32. that is not possible
	33. if I make them both 33
	34. then I have together 66
	35. then there is for the son . . . 24
	36. no, that is impossible
	37. I don't understand it anymore
	38. 66, 80
	39. no, wait, the son is 14
	40. almost, the parents are too old
	41. 32, 32, 64, 16, yes
	42. the son is 16 and the parents 32, together 80

Even though both participants arrive at the correct answer, different problem-solving approaches are revealed: one algebraic and one "hit or miss" combined with logic (how old a mother or father was likely to have been when the child was born). Considering only the outcome reveals nothing of the complexities involved in the means of getting there.

In second language research, an example of a think-aloud task can be seen in research by Leow (1998), who investigated issues of attention in second language learning. Leow used crossword puzzles as the task that learners had to perform. Below are the instructions he gave to his university-level learners of Spanish (p. 137).

The kind of data that can be elicited through this method can be quite rich, as can be seen in the excerpt below from Leow (1998). The boldface print indicates words in Spanish.

Instructions for think-alouds

Here is a crossword puzzle similar to the ones you have done in class
. . . Use the clues provided and see if you can successfully complete this
crossword. As you do the crossword, try to speak aloud into the
microphone your thoughts WHILE you perform the task for each word,
NOT AFTER. Include the numbers of the clues also while you are
thinking aloud. Please try to speak in a clear voice.

Vertical now . . . 2 down, OK I have an *o* here but I don't know why because in
1 across I have *se morio* but I guess it has to be **murio** because 2 down has to be
un [changes *o* to *u*] . . . OK I have to but it must be *tu* so it means that 7 across
for the past tense of *dormirse* must be **durmio** instead of *dormio* [changes *o* to *u*]
. . . OK third person plural form of the verb *pedir* they asked for, 5 down . . .
pedieron [pause] OK I am wondering whether because I have **pidieron** [spells
out] and I am thinking it should be *pe-* but that would make it *dormeo* with an *e*
instead of *i* . . . I guess I will see how the other ones go and take a look at that
one again . . . OK, the opposite of *no* is *si* which means that for 1 across I have
mentieron but it should be **mintieron** for the third person plural past tense of
mentir, mintieron [changes *e* to *i*] which makes me now realize that **pidieron**
with an *i* is probably right since the *e* in *mentir* changes to an *i* so the *e* in *pedir*
is also going to change to an *i* as well . . . OK 12 down, the opposite of *no* is *s*,
which means that where I have *corregio* it becomes **corrigio corrigio** so the third
person singular of past tense *corregir* is **corrigio** [changes *e* to *i*] . . . looks like all
the *e's* are becoming *i's* in the stems . . . OK, third person singular form of
descubrir discovered OK it is *descubrio*, OK 17 down possessive adjective in
Spanish OK now here yet again I have *to* because I have *se dormieron* and that
must become *tu* so it becomes *se durmieron* [changes *o* to *u*] OK third person
singular form of *preferir* preferred, OK now here yet again *prefe-* [spells out] is
going to change to **prefi-** [spells out] **prefirio** [changes *e* to *i*] . . . OK 25 down,
the verb to go in Spanish which is *ir* and I have *er* [spells out] because with 24
across I have *repetieron* but I guess now that *e* becomes an *i* becomes **repitieron**
. . . [changes *e* to *i*] . . . and 25 down is *ir*, so now I am going to go back and
change any other ones where I have *e* in the stem that should become an *i*, like
1 down, I believe would become *se divirtieron*, it becomes an *i* and everything
else looks OK so I guess that's it. [9 Minutes]

The example from Leow shows how an individual thinks about a grammar problem. The following example from Morrison (1996) demonstrates a different use of think-alouds, this time focusing on talk between two individuals. Morrison's study was concerned with inferencing strategies used by L2 French learners when encountering unknown vocabulary words in an authentic reading passage. Learner A and Learner B read the text individually, and were asked to think aloud together about the meanings of the underlined words. The following excerpt is based on their discussion of *piétons*, "pedestrians."

A2	OK, '*piétons*.'
B3	I think that's *pedestrian*.
A4	OK . . .
B5	I had no idea when I was writing . . .
A6	Me either, but I have to admit, unfortunately *pedestrian* didn't—that's good. I didn't think of that—it's so obvious. But for some reason I thought it had to do with something like . . . just because it said modern urban city, so I thought of just like, sort of like *businessman*.
B7	Mmm. (oh)
A8	I thought there was some sort of French word for like modern *city dweller*.
B9	Right.
A10	I didn't think of *pedestrian*. But that's right. I think it's *pedestrian*.
B11	I think even, because you see 'pied' and you think foot.
A12	I didn't think of that. But, definitely.
B13	And so, I think it has something to with that. But, again, in there, I had absolutely no idea. I think it's even, when you read the rest of this, this . . .
A14	thing, that's when you understand. That's why now it makes sense.
B15	Exactly
A16	But I should have figured it out.
B17	You . . . different perspectives, you know think, because, you know they talk about being on the road on the street, and the way, you know, they carry themselves on the street and stuff, and right away you think, you know, *pedestrians*. Right?
A18	Yeah.
B19	Like, that's who you'd find on the street.
A20	Uh-huh. Yeah
B21	So
A22	Yeah, I think you're right
B23	I think it has something to do with that. So '*piétons*' (writing) *pedestrian*

A24 And I think also, you're right, the 'pied' and then even just 'pied' *pedestrian,* for the . . .

B25 Yeah, like 'pied,' 'pied,' that's what—

A26 Yeah, OK

B27 . . . so *pedestrian* . . .

A28 And I guess also because you don't have *pedestrians* in the country, countryside. Like you wouldn't call it a pedestrian . . . as in roads, as in . . .

B29 Yeah, when you think *pedestrians,* you think . . .

A30 . . . modern cities

B31 the city, city life . . .

This example illustrates the process of learners reporting their earlier thoughts, together with the new inferencing strategies they use to refine their understanding. These include using their L2 French knowledge (B11, A24) as well as various contextual clues from further on in the passage (A6, B13, B17) and their real-world knowledge (B19, A28). The example shows the development of their comprehension of this word through the integration of these strategies.

The following basic recommendations for think-aloud protocols are adapted from Macaro (2001).

Recommendations for think-aloud protocols

- Give participants a specific task to perform (reading and writing tasks work best).
- Make sure that they understand what they have to do and that they are comfortable with the task. In general, they should be told that you want to know what they are thinking when they are performing the task.
- Find a similar task and demonstrate how a think-aloud works. An alternative is to ask them to practice with a different task. This is often preferable because if the researcher models the task, it is possible that the learner will use the particular strategy that the researcher has used.
- Have the tape recorder ready and start it.
- Students may need to be encouraged when there is insufficient talk-aloud data. Avoid using phrases like "Are you sure?" and "That's good." Instead, use only phrases like: "What makes you say that?"; "What made you do that?" (if, for example, they are looking up a

---

word in a dictionary); "What are you thinking at this moment?";
"Please keep talking."

- Listen to the recording of the think-aloud process (after the session)
  and make a list of all the strategies used by the student, using a pre-
  developed coding system.

As we noted above, in all research that relies on participants giving
information on their thought processes (whether stimulated recall or verbal think-
alouds), one needs to be aware that participants may not be aware of their
processes and/or they may not wish to reveal them. Gass and Mackey (2000,
Chapter 8) provide more detailed information on the dos and don'ts of recalls,
particularly stimulated recalls.

3.6.2.3 *Immediate Recalls*

Immediate recall is a technique used to elicit data immediately after the
completion of the event to be recalled. It can be distinguished from stimulated
recall in that it must occur immediately after the event (whereas stimulated recall
may or may not occur immediately following the event and it does not involve
a stimulus to talk from—e.g., videotape, audiotape, written product), and it can
be distinguished from on-line recall in that it does not occur simultaneously with
the event. For example, in an experiment involving interaction data, immediate
recall can take place after one conversational turn (10–15 seconds in length, for
example) during a conversational session. A stimulated recall would take place
after the entire conversation, using a tape of the conversation as stimulus. Online recall is difficult to implement in interaction research, but immediate recalls
have been used by Philp (2003) and Egi (2003) in explorations of what learners
notice about conversational feedback. In Philp's study, learners were instructed
to verbalize thoughts they had during a conversational turn immediately after a
recall prompt, which consisted of two knocking sounds. The knocking sounds
occurred in three contexts: (1) immediately after recasts of nontarget-like
production of the linguistic items targeted in her study; (2) after other errors; and
(3) after correct responses. As with all recalls, immediate recall can be conducted
in the learners' L1 to allow them to fully express their thoughts, or in the L2.
Either way, training in immediate recall is often essential to help learners get
used to the technique. Immediate recalls may suffer from fewer of the problems
of memory decay that can be a problem with stimulated recalls, yet immediate
recall is arguably a more artificial task and may also interfere with subsequent
task performance. As with all techniques, one must pilot test the technique to
ensure not only that it works with the particular group of learners that will be
used, but also that it elicits the type of data needed.

TIME TO DO ...

Imagine you want to investigate how learners interpret corrective feedback during interactions. You have 40 English language learners from a variety of L1 backgrounds as participants. What introspective measure might you employ? What are the advantages to using an introspective method in this case? What are the potential drawbacks to your chosen method?

3.7 SOCIOLINGUISTIC/PRAGMATICS-BASED RESEARCH

Both sociolinguistics and pragmatics are the study of language in context. Thus, they emphasize social and contextual variables as they affect the learning and production of a second language. The underlying assumption is that second language data do not represent a static phenomenon; rather, second language production is affected by such external variables as the specific task required of a learner, the social status of the interlocutor, and gender differences, among others. The resultant claim is that learners may produce different forms that are dependent on external variables. Pragmatically based second language research deals with both the acquisition and use of second language pragmatic knowledge.

Sociolinguistic and pragmatics-based research studies (see Kasper & Rose, 2002) are difficult to conduct using forced-elicitation devices, given that both consider language in context, and yet, like many other areas, it is often necessary to require examples if one is to collect sufficient data to draw conclusions. If, for example, one wanted to gather data on rudeness, either in terms of production or interpretation, it might be difficult to collect enough tokens from which one could draw reasonable generalizations. Researchers must therefore create contexts that require the necessary tokens. There are certain commonly used methods for doing this, and we discuss them in the following sections.

3.7.1 Naturalistic Settings

Researchers can, of course, attempt to set up situations in which certain language events will recur. Two examples come from research on advising sessions and one from a teaching context. Fiksdal (1990) investigated high-stakes interviews (where the issue was the visa status of international students in the United States), analyzing university-based immigration counseling to both native speakers and nonnative speakers. She was able to obtain the cooperation of the immigration counselor and the students to videotape the sessions. The context was constant (the counselor's office), and thus the author was able to make comparisons between the language used by the advisor to the native speakers and to the nonnative speakers and comparisons of the responses by native speakers and nonnative speakers. Another example is a study by Bardovi-Harlig and Hartford (1996) on advising sessions for graduate students in an applied linguistics graduate program. The sessions were audiotaped, and again, because the context was the same, comparisons could be made between native and nonnative speakers on such areas as suggestions or disagreements. Tyler (1992) also collected data for a qualitative discourse analysis of the spoken English discourse of a nonnative English-speaking international teaching assist-ant, comparing it with the discourse of a teaching assistant who was a native English speaker. She asked native speakers to judge the comprehensibility of the discourse based on hearing transcriptions read by a native speaker. This methodology allowed for comparability of the discourse.

3.7.2 Elicited Narratives

For a variety of different purposes, second language researchers can benefit from eliciting narratives from learners. There are a number of ways to do this. One can, of course, ask participants to tell a story about some past event or future plans in order to elicit these tenses. For example, one could ask:

- Tell me what you did yesterday.
- Tell me about a typical day.
- Tell me how you like to spend your free time.
- Tell me about the town you live in.
- Tell me your plans for the summer vacation.

One problem with this approach is that despite the prompt, learners may opt for a different form than the intended one. The following example comes from research designed to elicit past tense forms in Spanish (English L1). Participants viewed a picture for one minute, then turned the picture over and read the instructions as a prompt for the narration of events. Below is the Spanish prompt with the English translation.

Prompt in Spanish: Anoche el señor Gonzalez estaba leyendo un libro en su casa. Había una lámpara de lectura detrás de él. Aún tenía puesto el traje porque acababa de llegar del trabajo, pero no tenía puesto los zapatos. [Last night Mr. Gonzalez was reading a book in his house. There was a reading lamp behind him. He was still wearing his suit because he had just returned from work, but he had taken off his shoes.]

Below is a response from one participant; this response was typical in that despite the efforts of the researcher, past tense was not used.

> Bueno, mientras el señor Gonzalez está leyendo se ve [eh] que en el otro lado de la pared va caminando su esposa, pues se supone que es su esposa con un regalo muy grande, una caja muy grande que obviamente es un regalo . . . [the story continues] [Good, while Mr. Gonzalez is reading, you see [eh] that on the other side of the wall his wife is walking, well you assume that it is his wife with a very big gift, a very big box that is obviously a gift . . .]

Another point to consider when eliciting narratives is planning time (see Ellis, 2003 for a review; Ellis, 2005, 2009; Tavakoli, 2012). Does one elicit a narrative immediately after providing the learner with a stimulus? Or does one allow the learner time to think about what she or he will say? Planning can impact the quantity and quality of what is produced. Below, we suggest some dimensions that researchers need to consider when eliciting narratives.

Considerations when eliciting narratives

- Should learners have time to plan?
- If so, how much time?
- If planning time is allowed, should learners be allowed to make notes for themselves?
- If so, can these notes be used during the retelling?
- If relevant, how can the use of a particular linguistic form be elicited?

In the next sections, we briefly describe other common ways of eliciting stories and extended stretches of speech.

3.7.2.1 Silent Film

One way to elicit data is through the retelling of a silent film. The idea is to give learners a uniform prompt from which to speak. Usually, these film clips are relatively short (about 2–4 minutes) and allow the researcher to keep all information constant. There are a few areas to be wary of:

- Films must be as culturally neutral as possible if one is to use them for learners of different languages.
- Films cannot be too long or too short. If they are too short, there will not be a sufficient quantity of data. If they are too long, the learner might get embroiled in the recall of events.
- Learners may need to believe that they are telling it to a person who has never seen the film.

There are also variations to consider in the administration of a task like this.

- Do participants tell the story as the film is playing, or do they tell it after the entire film has been shown?
- Do they write their response?
- Do they tell the story orally?
- If they tell the story orally, do they tell it to a tape-recorder or to someone who has not seen the film?

3.7.2.2 Film Strips with Minimal Sound

There are some films that have minimal dialogue (see Gass et al., 1999 and Skehan & Foster, 1999 for examples). These can be used in the same way as silent films by turning the sound off. It is important that learners not be influenced by the speech of either their native language or the target language. On the other hand, it is important that no essential dialogue be removed that would prevent participants from fully understanding the story.

TIME TO DO ...

Find a video clip online that has limited dialogue and answer the following questions: How could you use the video clip as a potential data elicitation activity? What constructs or variables would you measure through the elicitation activity you proposed? What kinds of linguistic targets would you try to elicit with the video?

3.7.2.3 Picture Tasks

In section 3.5.4, we discussed a type of consensus task that involved telling a story. This type of task can also be used with a single individual whose task it is to put the story together on his or her own. There are variations on this theme depending on one's research question. If, for example, one wanted to investigate unplanned speech, one could give participants the picture sequence and have them tell the story immediately. Alternatively, one could give participants time to think about the story and gather their thoughts. This would be appropriate if one were concerned with elements of planned speech.

3.7.3 Discourse Completion Test (DCT)

Perhaps the most common method of doing pragmatics-based research has been through the use of a DCT. This is particularly useful if one wants to investigate speech acts such as apologies, invitations, refusals, and so forth. One can easily manipulate such factors as age differences or status differences between interlocutors. DCTs are implemented most frequently in writing with the participants being given a description of a situation in which the speech act occurs. After the description, there is usually blank space where the response is required. The following example (Beebe & Takahashi, 1989, p. 109) illustrates a situation in which a status difference may be a factor when trying to provide embarrassing information to someone.

You are a corporate executive talking to your assistant. Your assistant, who will be greeting some important guests arriving soon, has some spinach in his/her teeth.

_____

_____

There are other instances when one needs to force a response. One way to do this is not only to provide space for the response, but to sandwich that space between the stimulus and the response to the response. For example, Beebe, Takahashi, and Uliss-Weltz (1990, p. 69) provide the following discourse to elicit refusals:

Worker: As you know, I've been here just a little over a year now, and I know you've been pleased with my work. I really enjoy working here, but to be quite honest, I really need an increase in pay.

_____

_____

Worker: Then I guess I'll have to look for another job.

One can also ask for judgments of appropriateness following a description of scene-setting information, as in the following example.

Yesterday everything went badly. You were flying from Dayton, Ohio to New York for a job interview. You were pleased because you were one of the final candidates. On your way to the airport, there was a water main break and the highway was flooded, which caused a closure of the highway. You had to take back roads to the airport (an area of town you were not familiar with), but arrived too late for your flight. You were going to call the personnel manager to tell her of your predicament, but you couldn't find a phone. Just then you realized that there was another plane to NY that would still get you there in time. You boarded the plane, but because of storms in the NY area, your plane circled and circled, and when you landed, you were late for your appointment. The office is closed and you have to wait until the next morning to talk to the personnel manager.

What would you say?

1. I would like to take this opportunity to apologize for missing the scheduled meeting. I'm sure I'll never let you down again.
   ☐ yes   ☐ no
2. I would like you to give me another chance.
   ☐ yes   ☐ no
3. I'm sorry that I didn't call earlier, but I was tired and so I slept late.
   ☐ yes   ☐ no
4. I really, really want to work in your company. I want to make good use of my studies.
   ☐ yes   ☐ no
5. I sincerely apologize for not making the interview. Because of the storms, my plane circled for over an hour and I couldn't call you. We didn't land until after 5. I would appreciate it if I could reschedule my interview.
   ☐ yes   ☐ no

Judgments can be dichotomous as in the example above, or they could be scalar. Alternatively, the situation could be presented with instructions to the nonnative speaker to say what he or she would say to the personnel manager. A word of caution is in order. The responses represent what a learner believes he or she would say in a particular context. This may or may not correspond to what would actually be said. Thus, results such as these need to be interpreted cautiously or at least verified against real situations whenever possible.

3.7.4 Role Play

In general, there are two types of role plays: open and closed. Closed role plays are similar to discourse completion tasks but in an oral mode. Participants are presented with a situation and are asked to give a one-turn oral response. Open role plays, on the other hand, involve interaction played out by two or more individuals in response to a particular situation. The limits that are given in closed role plays are not present to any significant degree in open role plays. Closed role plays suffer from the possibility of not being a reflection of naturally occurring data. Open role plays reflect natural data more exactly although one must recognize that they are still collected in a non-natural environment and so are subject to the same difficulties as closed role plays (see Gass & Houck, 1999 for an example of a study using an open role play).

3.7.5 Video Playback for Interpretation

In pragmatics research, we might be interested in how people react to pragmatic infelicities. For example, how might the native speaker professor have reacted in the following situation (from Goldschmidt, 1996, p. 255) and why?

NNS: I have a favor to ask you.
NS: Sure, what can I do for you?
NNS: You need to write a recommendation for me.

In this particular case, a researcher might have asked the professor how she interpreted this somewhat abrupt request for a letter of recommendation. It might also be interesting to investigate this issue further by varying the context (a nonnative speaker professor, a native speaker professor, etc.). One way to accomplish this would be to stage scenarios according to variables of interest, videotape them, and prepare specific questions for observers. Bardovi-Harlig and Dörnyei (1998) attempted to determine reactions to pragmatic and grammatical errors by videotaping staged clips of nonnative speakers making them. Listeners (ESL and EFL learners and teachers) were given the following questionnaire and asked to rate each episode (p. 244).

Stimulus from video: I'm really sorry but I was in such a rush this morning and I didn't brought it today.

Was the last part appropriate/correct?   Yes   No

If there was a problem, how bad do you think it was?

Not bad at all ____:____:____:____:____:____Very bad

3.8 QUESTIONNAIRES AND SURVEYS

Brown (2001) defines questionnaires (a subset of survey research) as "any written instruments that present respondents with a series of questions or statements to which they are to react either by writing out their answers or selecting them among existing answers" (p. 6).

The survey, typically in the form of a questionnaire, is one of the most common methods of collecting data on attitudes and opinions from a large group of participants; as such, it has been used to investigate a wide variety of questions in second language research. Questionnaires allow researchers to gather information that learners are able to report about themselves, such as their beliefs and motivations about learning or their reactions to learning and classroom instruction and activities—information that is typically not available from production data alone.

Specialized types of questionnaires have also been developed to address specific research areas or questions. For example, as noted above, discourse completion questionnaires have been used to investigate interlanguage pragmatics.

In addition to different varieties of questionnaires, two types of questionnaire items may be identified: closed and open-ended. A closed item question is one in which the researcher determines the possible answers, whereas an open-ended question allows respondents to answer in any manner they see fit. Closed item questions typically involve a greater uniformity of measurement and therefore greater reliability. They also lead to answers that can be easily quantified and analyzed. Open-ended items, on the other hand, allow respondents to express their own thoughts and ideas in their own manner, and thus may result in more unexpected and insightful data. An example of a closed item question is, "How many hours a week did you study to pass this test? Circle one: 3, 4, 5, or 6 or more." An example of a more open-ended question is, "What ways have you found to be successful in learning a second language?"

The type of questions asked on a questionnaire naturally depends on the research questions being addressed in the study. For example, in relatively unstructured research, it may be more appropriate to ask open-ended questions and allow participant responses to guide hypothesis formation. Once hypotheses are formulated, researchers can ask closed item questions to focus in on important concepts. Of course, questionnaires need not be solely closed or open-ended, but can blend different question types depending on the purpose of the research and on what has previously been learned about the research phenomenon. For a more in-depth discussion of these considerations, as well as a practical guide for the use of questionnaires in second language research, see Dörnyei (with Taguchi)'s text (2010), which provides a helpful list of published questionnaires illustrating the sheer range of research that has been carried out using this approach, as noted below.

Dörnyei (with Taguchi)'s text (2010, pp. 173–178) on questionnaires includes published second language questionnaires on the following topics:

- language attitudes
- computer familiarity
- immigrant settlement
- language course evaluation
- language learning strategies
- needs analysis
- teacher beliefs
- teacher self-evaluation

- biographic background
- feedback
- language anxiety
- language learner beliefs
- language learning styles
- self-evaluation
- teacher evaluation
- preferences for instructional activities

- grammar instruction
- group cohesiveness
- language contact
- language learning motivation
- linguistic self-confidence
- teacher anxiety
- teacher motivation
- willingness to communicate
- self-identity change

Questionnaires can also be customized. An example of a highly customized elicitation procedure of this nature is a grid-based scheme. A researcher creates a grid following analysis of a completed questionnaire, and/or carrying out an in-depth interview with the participant. The grid is designed to both reflect the participant's input as well as to uncover further information, including their perceptions about the patterns and relationships in the data collected to date. For example, drawing on work based on teachers of mathematics and sciences, Breen et al. (2001) created grids to uncover information about teachers' principles and classroom practices. An example of one of their grids appears in Table 3.1.

As Breen et al. note, "prior to the second interview, the researcher drew up a grid for each individual teacher, transcribing the teacher's descriptions of practices and their reasons for them from the cards. The teacher's practices were listed on the vertical axis and their reasons listed on the horizontal axis . . . at this second interview the researcher worked with the teacher on the grid eliciting information as to whether the teacher saw a relationship between each action in turn, and all the reasons on the vertical axis" (pp. 478–479).

One of the primary advantages of using questionnaires is that, in addition to being more economical and practical than individual interviews, questionnaires can in many cases elicit longitudinal information from learners in a short period

TABLE 3.1 Sample grid (part of Kate's grid)

Reasons for Actions

	Quieter students should have a chance to speak/use the language	Students should do things they like doing if they think it's useful for learning	Students' contributions are important for confidence and motivation	Need to simplify or break down the task and give a sense of progress	Build on what students already know
Actions					
Begins the lesson by reviewing work from previous lesson	2	2	2	1	1
Accepts and encourages students' spontaneous suggestions	1	1	1	3	1
Encourages students to write down new items of language	3	3	3	1	3
Gets students to highlight words on the handout	3	3	3	1	3
Expects students to speak in English in the pair work	1	3	3	1	1
Gets some students to sound out individual words that are new	1	1	3	1	1

Note: For Kate, 1 indicates a strong relationship, 2 a weak relationship, and 3 no relationship between an action and a reason. Kate's full grid had 15 reasons on the horizontsl axis and 11 actions on the vertical axis.

Source: Breen, M. P., Hird, B., Milton, M., Oliver, R., & Thwaite, A. (2001). Making sense of language teaching: Teachers' principles and classroom practices. *Applied Linguistics*, 22(4), 479. Copyright © 2001 by Oxford University Press. Reprinted with the permission of Oxford University Press.

of time. Questionnaires can also elicit comparable information from a number of respondents. In addition, questionnaires can be administered in many forms, including over email, by phone, through mail-in forms, and in person, allowing the researcher a greater degree of flexibility in the data-gathering process. Depending on how they are structured, questionnaires can provide both qualitative insights and quantifiable data, so are flexible enough to be used in a range of research. Dörnyei and Csizer (2012) provide a useful account of how to design and analyze surveys in second language research.

There are potential problems related to the analysis of questionnaire data. One concern is that responses may be inaccurate or incomplete because of the difficulty involved in describing learner-internal phenomena such as perceptions and attitudes, for example. This may be the case if the questionnaire is completed in the L2, where lower proficiency in the L2 may constrain the answers. Both learners and native speakers might be able to provide salient details, but they may not be able to paint a complete picture of the research phenomenon. This being so, questionnaires usually do not provide a complete picture of the complexities of individual contexts. This is especially important to remember when using open-ended written questionnaires, since participants may be uncomfortable expressing themselves in writing and may choose to provide abbreviated, rather than elaborative, responses. Hence, whenever possible, questionnaires should be administered in the learners' native language, learners should be given ample time to specify their answers, and learners with limited literacy should be given the option of providing oral answers to the questionnaire (which can be recorded).

Another concern is that even though it is often assumed that researchers can control or eliminate bias by using questionnaires, it is also possible, as with any type of elicitation device, that the data elicited will be an artifact of the device. Thus, for example, if a study utilizes a discourse completion questionnaire, the researcher should take particular caution when interpreting the results, as the situations depicted are usually hypothetical. In this type of questionnaire, learners are only indicating how they think they would respond; this may or may not correspond to how they would actually respond in real life.

To maximize the effectiveness of the questionnaire, researchers should try to achieve the following:

- simple, uncluttered formats
- unambiguous, answerable questions
- review by several researchers
- piloting among a representative sample of the research population

This should be done before undertaking the main bulk of data collection to ensure that the format is user-friendly and the questions are clear.

3.9 EXISTING DATABASES

In addition to the many elicitation techniques we have discussed in this chapter, there are existing databases as well, consisting of data that have already been collected, transcribed, and often analyzed. If the research questions allow it, using an existing database can save considerable amounts of time and effort. The main database for language acquisition research is CHILDES (MacWhinney, 2000), which focuses on spoken language. Other databases include corpora dealing with various aspects of performance (e.g., writing), while still others are available only in languages other than English and serve very specific purposes. We are unable to deal with these here, but encourage those who want to do second language research in a specific language to learn about them. Web-based searches are a good place to start, using particular parameters of relevance to your research. Additionally, IRIS (www.iris-database.org, retrieved April 19, 2015) is a digital repository of materials and stimuli that can be used for eliciting data. Searching for elicitation methods on IRIS allows researchers to adapt preexisting materials to suit particular research goals, rather than starting from scratch. We now turn to a short description of CHILDES.

3.9.1 CHILDES

The CHILDES database was designed to facilitate language acquisition research. It allows researchers to study conversational interactions among child and adult first and second language learners, and includes a variety of languages and situations/contexts of acquisition, including bilingual and disordered acquisition, as well as cross-linguistic samples of narratives. It consists of three main components: (1) CHILDES, a database of transcribed data; (2) CHAT, guidelines for transcription and methods of linguistic coding in a format in which users can create "dependent tiers" (in addition to a main tier containing speakers' utterances) to record their notes on context, semantics, morphology, and syntax; and (3) CLAN, software programs for analyzing the transcripts through, for example, searches and frequency counts. It is also possible in CHILDES to link transcripts to digital audio and video recordings.

3.9.2 Other Corpora

Granger (2002) provides a review of the ways in which corpora can be used in second language research along with numerous references to existing corpora. In general, according to Granger:

> [C]omputer learner corpora are electronic collections of authentic FL/SL textual data assembled according to explicit design criteria for a particular

SLA/FLT purpose. They are encoded in a standardized and homogeneous way and documented as to their origin and provenance.

(p. 7)

In addition, Granger (2012) provides an excellent overview of how to use second and foreign language databases. An important consideration in using corpora is to understand where the data come from and how the data are organized. For example, if one is using a corpus based on written essays, one must have access to basic information such as the prompt that was used to elicit the essay. This is necessary if one plans to make any sort of comparison across languages or across times.

Corpora can be organized in different ways. For example, some might be used to study idioms or collocations, and the database might be tagged for that purpose. Others may be tagged for errors and/or parts of speech. This could be useful if one were looking at German word order acquisition, for example, and wanted to know how many instances could be found of verbs in second position in sentences whose first word is not a noun or pronoun. The following website (http://calper.la.psu.edu/corpus.php, retrieved April 19, 2015) provides resources on learner corpora from a wide variety of languages.

As noted above, corpora can be useful, but a clear understanding of what is and what is not included is essential to an understanding of how they can be used appropriately.

3.9.3 IRIS

IRIS (Instruments for Research into Second Languages) is a free, sustainable digital repository of instruments used to investigate second language learning. IRIS currently provides a wide range of materials used to collect data such as: questionnaires, grammaticality judgment tests, observation and interview protocols, word lists, sound and video files, language tests, picture tasks, and experimental teaching methods, to name a few. All materials held in IRIS are up- and downloadable as well as searchable by instrument type, research area, participant characteristics, L1, L2, language feature, and proficiency level. Quality is assured by only allowing instruments that have been published in peer-reviewed journal articles, books/chapters, conference proceedings, or an approved PhD thesis. IRIS is both free to use as well as independent of any institutions, countries, journals, publishers, or funders.

As of 2015, IRIS included 350+ different data collection instruments spanning 24 languages, 68 research areas, nearly 900 unique materials, such as pictures, questionnaires, and pieces of instruments, and 36 linguistic features, as well as a large array of theoretical frameworks. More than 50 journals and over 500 authors are cited on IRIS, which had received 16,000+ visits by January 2015. About one-third of the visitors downloaded materials from IRIS. IRIS has garnered wide international support with many major journals now encouraging accepted authors to upload their data elicitation materials. Utilizing data elicitation materials available on IRIS saves valuable time in material development as well as contributing to reliability and replicability of research in second language acquisition.

3.10 CONCLUSION

This chapter has provided some preliminary information on some of the more common methodological tools used for eliciting data in second language research. This is by no means an exhaustive list, but was intended to acquaint the reader with some of the issues surrounding each instrument. As we have repeatedly said, with materials and methods, one must pilot test the instruments to ensure that they elicit what one intends and to ensure their appropriateness for the study. In the next chapter, we focus on coding data.

POINTS TO REMEMBER

- A pilot study is a small-scale trial of the proposed procedures, materials, and methods of a study used to uncover any problems and to address them before the main study is carried out.

- Formal approaches to language learning such as Universal Grammar use a variety of methods to investigate language learning:
  - Acceptability judgment tasks ask learners what is possible and what is not possible in their second language by having learners judge whether a particular sentence is grammatically acceptable.
  - An elicited imitation task presents sentences to participants auditorily and the participants are then asked to repeat them.
  - Truth-value judgments are a way of understanding how people interpret sentences by asking them to deem a statement true or false.
  - In sentence matching tasks, participants are asked to decide as quickly as possible if grammatical and ungrammatical sentences are identical or not.

- Processing research investigates the mechanisms involved in learning using methods such as sentence interpretation, reaction time, moving window and eye-tracking.

- Interaction-based research is concerned with learners' conversational interactions with others and the developmental benefits of such interactions. Methodologies include:

  - Picture description tasks: a type of information gap task where learners share information.
  - Spot the difference tasks: learners have to interact to find differences in two pictures.
  - Jigsaw tasks: a two-way task where individuals have different pieces of information and must orally interact to solve the task.
  - Consensus tasks: groups of learners who must come to an agreement on a certain issue.
  - Consciousness-raising tasks: participants verbalize their thoughts about language on their way to a solution.
  - Computer-mediated tasks: learners interact through communicative exchanges using the computer.

- Strategy-based research is aimed at determining the strategies used when learning a second language together with the variables that determine the selection of strategies. Resources that researchers have to elicit strategy information include observations and introspective methods such as think-alouds and stimulated and immediate recalls.

- Sociolinguistic and pragmatics-based research emphasize social and contextual variables as they affect the learning and production of a second language. Common methodologies are naturalistic conversations, elicited narratives, discourse completion tests, role play, and video playback for interpretation.

MORE TO DO AND MORE TO THINK ABOUT ...

1. Take a research question that you came up with from Chapter 1 (or another that you are interested in). What elicitation tool(s) would you use to investigate it and why? Are there any alternatives? If so, which would you choose and why?

2. Conduct a library search. Find three articles that investigate *similar* topics. Do they use the same elicitation tool? If so, why do you think this is the case (e.g., it is the only possibility)? Do you think that there

could have been an alternative? If so, describe the alternative and how it might be better or worse than the one originally used.

3. Conduct a library search. Find three articles that investigate *different* topics. Do they use different elicitation tools? Could they have used other elicitation tools? If not, why not? If so, come up with some other means for eliciting the type of data that they need in order to answer the research questions that they have set out.

4. Find two recent articles in a second language journal that could also have dealt with unanswered questions through a recall procedure. Describe how you would have conducted a recall portion for the study that you have selected.

5. You want to determine the extent to which learners understand aspects of complex syntax, focusing in particular on what the noun phrases refer to. You have decided to use sentences like the following and have decided to use elicited imitation. What factors do you need to take into account? Come up with six test sentences and describe what you will do. Besides elicited imitation, how could you elicit information regarding the appropriate meaning of the pronoun?

   a. When he entered the office, the janitor questioned the man.
   b. As she walked to the blue door, Anne wondered about Joan's father.

6. You want to elicit speech samples containing:

   a. subjunctive (I request that everyone be here by 5.)
   b. embedded questions (The teacher asked why she was late.)

   How might you go about doing this?

7. Assume that you want to investigate how native speakers react to requests by a second language speaker. Further assume that you believe that it is not so much the words people use that affect different native speaker reactions, but the stereotypes that native speakers have formed about particular groups of nonnative speakers. How would you go about investigating this?

8. You want to study agreement in English (e.g., subject-verb agreement). How would you go about collecting data?

9. Describe the major benefits of conducting a pilot test on materials.

NOTES

1. Below is a list of the differences that participants can be asked to identify in the kitchen task (Figure 3.1b):

    1. shades (2 are striped / 1 is black)
    2. picture (2 are landscapes / 1 is a floral arrangement)
    3. table centerpiece (2 are flowers / 1 is candles)
    4. electrical outlet (2 have one / 1 does not)
    5. bottle in cabinet (1 has two on second shelf / 2 have only 1)
    6. plates in cabinet (2 have plates on bottom shelf / 1 has no plates)
    7. drawers in cabinet (2 have three drawers / 1 has two drawers)
    8. oven window (2 have windows / 1 does not)
    9. pot on stove (2 have a pot on the stove / 1 has a tea kettle)
    10. dog food dish (1 has one on the floor / 2 have no dog dish)

2. Answer key to the story sequencing task (Figure 3.3):

    A robber stole a wallet while two students were away playing tennis. The robber was chased by the dog and dropped the wallet. The student found the wallet while gardening a year later—he didn't know that the dog had buried it.

CHAPTER FOUR

Coding

Once data are collected, it is necessary to organize them into a manageable, easily understandable, and analyzable format. In this chapter, we discuss some of the main ways of accomplishing this task. We provide an overview of the various processes involved in data coding, including transcription and the preparation of raw data for coding, the modification or creation of appropriate coding systems (depending on the type of data and the research questions), the issue of reliability measures for coding, and the implementation of coding. We also present examples of some common models and custom-made coding systems, taking both quantitative and qualitative research concerns into account. Finally, we discuss questions related to how and when to decide how much and what to code.

4.1 PREPARING DATA FOR CODING

Some types of data can be considered ready for analysis immediately after collection, for example language test scores such as those from the TOEFL or other standardized language tests. However, for other types of data, after they are collected, they need to be prepared for coding. This chapter focuses primarily on coding of natural data. Coding involves making decisions about how to classify or categorize particular pieces or parts of data. It is helpful to bear in mind Orwin's (1994) comment when preparing to code data: "Coding represents an attempt to reduce a complex, messy, context-laden and quantification resistant reality to a matrix of numbers" (p. 140).

There is a wide range of different types of data in second language research. For example, raw data may be oral and audio and/or video recorded; they may be written, in the form of essays, test scores, diaries, or even check marks on observation schemes; they may appear in electronic format, such as responses to a computer-assisted accent modification program; or they may be visual, in the form of eye movements made while reading text at a computer or gestures made by a teacher in a classroom. They may include learners talking to one another, to native speakers, to teachers, or to themselves in monologues (e.g., narratives). In short, it is important to recognize that a wide variety of data can be collected for L2 studies.

A common type of second language data is oral. Oral data may come from a range of sources, including, for example, native speaker-learner interviews, learners in pairs carrying out communicative tasks in a laboratory setting, or learners in small groups and their teacher in a noisy L2 classroom setting. Oral data usually need to be transcribed in some way for coding and analysis.

4.1.1 Transcribing Oral Data

4.1.1.1 Transcription Conventions

The process of transcription varies depending on the research goals. As will be discussed in more detail below, it is not always the case that every utterance of each learner (and/or teacher or native speaker) on a tape will need to be transcribed. In some cases, only the features of interest for the study are transcribed. In other cases, researchers may decide it is sufficient simply to listen to the data and mark features as present or absent on a coding sheet or schedule. In either of these cases, interesting examples and exceptions to patterns are usually transcribed for later use in illustrating trends. In still other instances, everything is transcribed in great detail.

Depending on the level of detail required, the time necessary for transcription can vary dramatically. In cases where partial transcriptions are made, the process can proceed quite quickly, taking only about one to two hours of researcher time per hour of data. However, in other cases, such as the careful and detailed transcription required for conversation analysis of second language data, countless minute aspects of the conversation must be transcribed, leading to as much as 20 hours of researcher time for the transcription of one hour of straightforward dyadic conversation and up to 40 hours for a one-hour recording of overlapping small-group work and conversation (Markee, 2000). Transcriptions are often referred to as broad, including less detail, or narrow, meaning that they are very finely detailed. Transcriptions can be made more easily in second language research by utilizing two tools. The first is an appropriate set of transcription conventions, and the second is a transcription machine.

Simply put, transcription conventions are used to facilitate the representation of oral data in a written format. Conventions can be useful both for coding and for providing examples from the data when writing up the results of the research. While there are no generally agreed-upon conventions common to all studies, researchers may recognize certain symbols; for instance, the use of dots to convey pauses or silence is quite common. When using transcription conventions, it is important to bear three things in mind. First, the conventions should match the object of inquiry in the study. For example, if emphasis (or stress) is being investigated as part of a teacher's feedback techniques in the classroom, it will be important to mark emphasis very transparently and distinctly in the transcription and the coding system. Some researchers use boldface type for this purpose, as in "You **have** the ball in your picture." Others might put the emphasized word in all capitals, as in "You HAVE the ball," or they might underline it, as in "You <u>have</u> the ball." It might also be necessary for the study to judge and mark the degree of emphasis; for example, a very strongly emphasized item might be both boldfaced and underlined, as in "You **<u>have</u>** the ball," while a less strongly emphasized word would be either bolded or underlined. Regardless of the system chosen, the conventions should be explained in the written report. This is often done at the end of the report, possibly in an appendix. An example of a transcription convention used in a study of scaffolding in L2 peer revision by De Guerrero and Villamil (2000, p. 56) is shown below.

•	*italics*	Italics are employed to cite a letter, word, or phrase as a linguistic example, including Spanish words
•	[brackets]	Brackets enclose actual Spanish words said by students
•	(parentheses)	Explanation by authors
•	a sequence of dots . . .	A sequence of dots indicates a pause
•	**boldface**	Words were said in English (text which is not in English was said in Spanish)
•	"quotation marks"	Quotation marks indicate participants are reading from the text

An example of transcription conventions that provide guidelines and notation for different levels of detail appears in Figure 4.1. Appendices E and F provide two other examples of transcription conventions, including one developed specifically for use in second language classrooms.

Spelling

Normal spelling is used for the NNSs and, with a few exceptions ("y'd" for "you'd"; "c'n" for "can"), for the NS.

Intonation/Punctuation

Utterances do not begin with capital letters; normal punctuation conventions are not followed; instead, intonation (usually at the end of a clause or a phrase) is indicated as follows:

At the end of a word, phrase, or clause

? Rising Intonation
. Falling Intonation
, "Nonfinal Intonation" (usually a slight rise)

No punctuation at clause end indicates transcriber uncertainty

Other

(?) or ( )	incomprehensible word or phrase
(all right)	a word or phrase within parentheses indicates that the transcriber is not certain that s/he has heard the word or phrase correctly
[	indicates overlapping speech; it begins at the point at which the overlap occurs
=	means that the utterance on one line continues without pause where the next = sign picks it up (latches)
y-	a hyphen after an initial sound indicates a false start
(.)	a dot within parentheses indicates a brief pause
((laugh))	nonlinguistic occurrences such as laughter, sighs, that are not essential to the analysis are enclosed within double parentheses
CAPITALS	capital letters are used for nonverbal information important to the analysis (e.g., nods, gestures, shifts in posture or position)
LH	left hand
RH	right hand
sNOD	refers to one nod
NODS	refers to more than one nod
NODS---	refers to nodding accompanying speech, with hyphens indicating how long the nodding (or other behavior) continues
HS	refers to one head shake
HSs	refers to more than one head shake
HSs_ _ _	refers to head shakes accompanying speech, with hyphens indicating how long the head shaking continues

NOTE: If a nod or head shake does not accompany speech, it is indicated before or after the speech that it precedes or follows; if it accompanies speech, it is represented on a separate line beneath the speech it accompanies. Other nonverbal information is positioned below the speech with which it co-occurs.

FIGURE 4.1 Example transcription conventions

Source: Gass, S., & Houck, N. (1999). *Interlanguage Refusals* (p. 209). Berlin: Mouton de Gruyter.

TIME TO DO ...

Record a conversation involving at least one nonnative speaker of a language (only one or two minutes are needed). Transcribe this conversation writing down only the words heard and long pauses.

4.1.1.2 Transcription Machines

Although declining in use owing to free software and apps, transcription machines make the process of transcribing data significantly easier. Transcription machines usually have: (1) a foot pedal so that both hands are free for typing; (2) headphones so that others in the room are not disturbed and so that the transcriber is not disturbed by other distractions; and (3) controls that can be used to adjust the rate of the speech, make typing proceed more quickly, and make it easier to distinguish individual voices. Transcription machines usually have a feature that allows researchers to rewind tapes automatically by a set number of seconds in order to check what they have heard and typed. One can also automate the process through the use of software systems such as NVivo (see section 4.6), allowing one to put in timestamps on the transcriptions and providing the possibility of slowing down the recording to make transcription more manageable.

4.1.1.3 Technology and Transcription

Technology is also changing the process and product of transcriptions. Digital recording equipment is now the standard, and online controls and free software for playback can be customized to make transcription of digital data easier. For cases where native speaker data need to be transcribed, automatic speech recognition software is improving and could eventually automate the bulk of the transcription task. Another way in which technology is changing transcription is the increasing use of online journals where text can be easily and inexpensively manipulated. For example, different colors can be used to represent different speakers or overlap, and multimedia, such as short audio or video clips where readers can actually hear what a learner has said while reading the transcript, can be presented together with the native speaker or teacher prompts— assuming, of course, that the appropriate permissions have been obtained from all individuals whose voices or images appear in the multimedia clips (see also section 4.6 for information regarding NVivo).

4.2 DATA CODING

Transcriptions of oral data can yield rich and extensive second language data, but in order to make sense of them, they must be coded in a principled manner. Data coding, simply defined, entails looking for and marking patterns in data regardless of modality. In this section, we will discuss some of the standard ways to present and summarize data, together with some examples of coding schemes. It is important to note that there is a range of measurement scales that a researcher might employ in second language research. Naturally, the way the data are coded depends in part on the scales used to measure the variables. These scales include nominal (often used for classifying categorical data, such as nationality, gender, and first language), ordinal (often used for ranking data, such as proficiency scores), and interval scales (often used for simultaneously ranking data and indicating the distance, or intervals, between data points).

4.2.1 Scales of Measurement

The three most commonly used scales are nominal, ordinal, and interval. Ratio scales, a type of interval scale, will not be included here as they are not used as frequently in the type of research that is carried out in second language studies.[1]

Nominal scales are used for attributes or categories and allow researchers to categorize variables into two or more groups. With nominal scales, different categories can be assigned numerical values. For example, in a study of gender, (1) may be assigned to male and (2) to female. The numbers indicate only category membership; there is no indication of order or magnitude of differences. Consequently, in a nominal scale, the concept of average does not apply.

An ordinal scale is one in which ordering is implied. For example, student test scores are often ordered from best to worst or worst to best, with the result that there is a 1st ranked student, a 2nd ranked student, a 10th ranked student, and so forth. While the scores are ordered, there is no implication of an equal distance between each rank order. Thus, the difference between student numbers 1 and 2 may not be the same as the difference between students 2 and 3. It is also often the case that researchers need to give holistic judgments to student work. This might be the case, for example, with second language writing scores. If we gave writing scores on a scale from 1 to 100, we might not be able to say that someone who received an 80 is twice as good a writer as someone who received a 40 without having precise information about what 40 and 80 meant on the scale. An ordinal scale might be useful in ordering students for placement into a writing program, but we cannot make judgments about exactly how much better one student is than another.

An interval scale represents the order of a variable's values, but unlike an ordinal scale, it also reflects the interval or distance between points in the ranking. If a test represents an interval scale, then one can assume that the distance between a score of 70 and 80 is the same as the distance between 80 and 90. Thus, we could say, for example, that someone who received a score of 10 on a vocabulary test knew twice as many of the words that were tested as someone who received a 5. As this example shows, an interval scale implies measurable units, such as number of correct answers, years of residence in the target language country, or age.

TIME TO DO ...

To which does each of the following refer: nominal scale, ordinal scale, interval scale, ratio scale?

a. A scale where equal differences are truly equal differences of the variable being measured.
b. A scale that can't measure quantitative variables.
c. A scale with a true zero point.
d. A scale that indicates relative rankings.

4.2.2 Coding Nominal Data

Nominal data include cases where

> entities may be the same or different but not 'more' or 'less' . . . as an example, the part of speech of a given word in a particular sentence, or interpretation of a sentence, is a nominal variable: a word either can be classified as an adjective or it cannot.
>
> (Butler, 1985, p. 11)

In general, there are two ways nominal data can be coded, depending on whether the research involves a dichotomous variable (i.e., a variable with only two values, such as +/− native speaker) or a variable with several values. When dealing with dichotomous variables, researchers may choose to employ signs such as + or −. Alternatively, and particularly when working with a computer-based statistical program such as SPSS, SAS, or R (see Chapter 10), researchers may wish to use numerical values (e.g., 1 and 2). For example, in the small database illustrated in Table 4.1, the data have been coded with numbers to show which participants are native speakers of English, the target language for this hypothetical study. The number "1" is used to indicate native speakers, and the number "2" is used to indicate speakers whose native language is not English.

If the data are not dichotomous and the researcher has a variable with several values to deal with, additional numbers can be used to represent membership in particular categories. For instance, to code the native languages of each of these fictional study participants, a numerical value could be assigned to each of the languages spoken (e.g., Arabic = 1, English = 2, German = 3, Spanish = 4, etc.), as in Table 4.2, which shows, for example, that M.B.'s native language is German.

TABLE 4.1 Sample nominal coding: Dichotomous variables

Code for participant identity	Native speaker status 1 = native speaker 2 = nonnative speaker
A. B. (1)	1
C. P. (2)	2
D. U. (3)	2
Y. O. (4)	2
J. K. (5)	2
H. A. (6)	1
M. B. (7)	1

TABLE 4.2 Sample nominal coding: Non-dichotomous variables

Code for participant identity	Native language
A. B. (1)	2
C. P. (2)	4
D. U. (3)	4
Y. O. (4)	1
J. K. (5)	3
H. A. (6)	1
M. B. (7)	3

119

4.2.3 Coding Ordinal Data

Ordinal data are usually coded in terms of a ranking. For example, with a data set consisting of test scores from a group of 100 students, one way to code these data would be to rank them in terms of highest to lowest scores. The student with the highest score would be ranked "1," while the student with the lowest would be ranked "100." In this scenario, when multiple students have identical scores, ranks are typically split. For example, if two learners each received the fourth highest score on the test, they would both be ranked as "3.5." Or, both could receive a 4 with the person after them receiving a 6.

Alternatively, instead of using a 100-item list, the scores could be divided into groups (e.g., the top 25 percent) and each group assigned a number. For example, in the database in Table 4.3 below, a "1" would signify that the individual scored within the top 25 percent, while a "4" would show that the participant scored in the bottom 25 percent.

Dividing learners into ranked groups can be particularly useful when using a test without having full confidence in the fine details of the scoring. For instance, a researcher may not believe that a student who scores 88 is very much "better" than a student who scores only 83. In this case, dividing participants into groups could be the appropriate way of indicating that certain students are close together, and better than the other groups, without making claims about differences between those students. Ordinal scales can also be used to "roughly" separate learners from each other. For example, in a study using a battery of L2 working memory tests, the researcher might be interested in examining the data from learners with "high" and "low" working memory scores more closely, but might wish to discount the data from learners in the middle range scores on the basis that they are not differentiated clearly enough from each other.

TABLE 4.3 Sample ordinal coding

Student rank	Code for participant identity	Rank group
1	A. B.	1
2	C. P.	1
3	D. U.	1
30	Y. O.	2
67	J. K.	3
99	H. A.	4
100	M. B.	4

In this case, the middle 50 percent of learners from Table 4.3 above could be assigned as "middle" scorers, and only data from students in the top and bottom 25 percent would be used. There could also be several other cut-off points besides the exact test scores used for the ranking, including points based on measures of central tendency, discussed in Chapter 10.

4.2.4 Coding Interval Data

Interval scales, like ordinal scales, also represent a rank ordering. However, in addition, they show the interval, or distance, between points in the ranking. Thus, instead of simply ordering the scores of the test, we could present the actual scores in a table. This would allow us to see not only which scores are higher or lower (as in the ordinal scale), but also the degree to which they differ. For example, in Table 4.4 below, participant M.B. scored 4 points on the test and was ranked 100th (in last place) of the students who took the test.

Other data that are typically coded in this way include age, number of years of schooling, and years of language study. It should be kept in mind, however, that the impact on learning may be different at different intervals. For example, the difference between scores 1 and 10 may have the same interval as those between 90 and 100 on a test, but the impact is quite different. Similarly, the difference between two and three years of instruction may be the same interval as the difference between nine and 10 years. In each case, the difference is only one year, but that year might be very different in terms of the impact on language production for a learner who is at the advanced, near-native stage, as compared to a learner who is in the early stages of acquisition. These are issues that merit careful consideration in the coding stages of a research study.

TABLE 4.4 Sample interval coding

Student rank	Code for participant identity	Test score (X/100)
1	A. B.	98
2	C. P.	96
3	D. U.	95
30	Y. O.	68
67	J. K.	42
99	H. A.	8
100	M. B.	4

4.3 CODING SYSTEMS

The measures presented so far represent some of the common first steps in coding data. Bernard (1995) suggests that "the general principle in research is always use the highest level of measurement that you can" (p. 32). By this, he means if you wish to know about the amount of prior instruction in a particular language, you should ask the learners a question such as, "How many years of prior instruction in X-language have you had?" rather than, "Have you had one to two years, two to five years, or more than five years of prior instruction?" This is the case because at a later point, that researcher might want to distinguish between those who had two to three years and those who had four to five years. Basically, if researchers code data using as finely grained a measurement as possible, the data can always be collapsed into a broader level of coding later if necessary, but finely grained categories are harder, if not impossible, to reconstruct after the data are coded. Another way to put this is that in coding, the categories should always be as narrow as possible. For example, in a study where "interactional feedback" is to be coded, both recasts and negotiation could be considered as feedback. However, it would be much more judicious to code them separately at first and later decide that these two categories could be collapsed into one "feedback" category than it would be to code them both into one "feedback" category and later decide the research question needed to be addressed by separating them, thus necessitating a recoding of the data.

TIME TO THINK ...

If you are interested in differences in learning a second language based on prior education level, is it better to ask a specific question about their level of education, or is it better to ask if they have graduated from high school or if they have a university degree? Why?

A range of different coding practices can be used with second language data to allow researchers to gain a deeper understanding of the information they have collected. Usually in the coding process, patterns in the data are indicated in separate records as one examines the data. However, coding is sometimes recorded directly onto the data source, as in the case of interview transcripts or essays, for example. Coding systems are often referred to as sheets, charts, techniques, schemes, and so on. In any case, they should be as clear and as straightforward to use as possible, as we discuss below. Many researchers develop a coding scheme based on their specific research questions, unless they are carrying out a replication study, in which case they usually use coding instruments identical to those of the original study. In some cases, existing schemes require refinements to capture new knowledge, and sometimes new schemes are required depending on the research question. Coding systems range from those based on standard measures, which have the advantage of increasing the generalizability of the research because they are used by a range of researchers, to highly customized systems developed simply for the study at hand. Many different schemes have been developed for coding all sorts of second language data, and in this chapter we provide examples of some of them, recognizing, however, that it would be impossible to cover the whole range of existing schemes.

4.3.1 Common Coding Systems and Categories

A number of coding units or categories for oral and written data have been proposed over the years. These include such units as the following:

* T-units
* suppliance in obligatory context (SOC) counts
* CHAT convention
* turns
* utterances
* sentences
* communication units
* tone units
* analysis of speech units
* idea units
* clauses
* S-nodes per sentence
* type-token ratios
* target-like usage counts

Three of the most common of these—T-units, SOC, and CHAT—will be discussed in more detail below, together with information about counting different types and different tokens of coding units.

4.3.1.1 T-Units

A T-unit is generally defined as "one main clause with all subordinate clauses attached to it" (Hunt, 1965, p. 20). They were originally used to measure syntactic development in children's L1 writing. However, they have become a common measurement in second language research as well, and have served as the basis for several ratio units, such as number of words per T-unit, words per error-free T-unit, and clauses per T-unit. An example of a T-unit is the utterance:

"After she had eaten, Sally went to the park."

This T-unit is error-free; that is, it contains no nontarget-like language. An alternative T-unit:

"After eat, Peter went to bed"

would be coded as a T-unit containing errors. To code using T-units, a researcher may, for example, go through an essay or a transcription and count the total number of T-units; from this number, the researcher could count all the T-units not containing any errors and then present a ratio. For instance, the researcher could say that of 100 T-units used by a learner, 33 contained no errors. T-units have been used as a measure of linguistic complexity as well as accuracy.

Though commonly employed and sometimes held up as useful because of comparability between studies, the use of T-units has also attracted criticism (e.g., Bardovi-Harlig, 1992; Gaies, 1980). For example, it has been argued that the error-free T-unit measure is not always able to take into account the linguistic complexity of the writing or speech or the severity of the errors (Polio, 1997). In addition, the definitions and types of "error" and the methods of counting errors have varied considerably from one researcher to the next. Nevertheless, T-units remain popular in second language research in part because they are easy to identify and relatively low inference categories.

TIME TO DO ...

Consider the following two essays. Try to divide them into T-units. Are any of them error-free?

1. It is happy for everyone to have a family.
    I think family is very important all over the world.
    I have five members.
    My parents (father, mother), younger sister, younger brother, and me.
    I love so much them and I'm missing now.
    Now I troudure my family.

2. Most people who are parents worry about their child's teacher.
    As you know, we spend the time with our teachers in schools.

> We learned a lot from our teachers, so it is important to meet a good teacher. I have experiences to meet a good teacher and bad teacher in my life.
>
> Which do you think is the more advanced speaker of English? Why?

4.3.1.2 Suppliance in Obligatory Contexts (SOC)

Some second language studies have focused on grammatical accuracy with respect to specified linguistic features. A researcher may be interested in whether a learner has acquired a particular grammatical form such as the simple past tense, the progressive –ing, or the third-person singular s. The learner's level of acquisition can be measured in terms of how often these features are supplied where they are required. This is commonly known as Suppliance in Obligatory Contexts (or SOC). For example, in the sentence "He is singing right now," the –ing is required because this is a context in which the progressive form is obligatory. SOC was first used in early studies of the acquisition of grammatical morphemes by children acquiring English as their first language (e.g., Brown, 1973), but it has also been applied in second language studies.

For instance, SOC was employed as a measure in a two-year study of 16 adult learners of English reported in Bardovi-Harlig (2000). The focus of the research was the emergence of tense-aspect morphology related to past-time contexts. Two researchers independently coded every verb supplied in a past-time context with respect to its verbal morphology. A computer sorting program was then used to analyze the data, coding the verbs into types and tokens and counting them. Whereas a count of tokens would tally repetitions of the same form as separate instances and might therefore artificially inflate the rates of appropriate use by including multiple occurrences of common verbs such as was and went, the counting of types would enable the researchers to provide a conservative view of the acquisition of tense-aspect morphology. Thus, to calculate the rates of appropriate use of the past tense in this study, the researchers used the ratio of the number of past tense forms supplied to the number of obligatory environments, expressing the rates as percentages of appropriate use.

While SOC is a useful measure of morpheme use in required contexts, Pica's (1984) study of the acquisition of morphemes brings up a common criticism of SOC: namely, it does not account for learners' use of morphemes in inappropriate contexts. To address this, Pica used Target-Like Usage (TLU) as an additional measure. This takes into account both appropriate and inappropriate contexts.

125

TIME TO DO ...

Let's assume that you want to look at tense usage by learners of English. Consider the following essays and code them using the SOC method discussed here.

1. Have you been met good teachers? During we have been educated in school, we have met many teachers. Sometimes they are good and gentle but are bad by your category. Look at requested things for good teachers such as skills about teaching, leadership, and love to students.

2. I want to describe about high-school which I attended. I cannot forget my high school time. My high school is located in the middle top of mountain. There are not transportation to get there. So we have to work 20 minutes every morning. It was really good for training and health. We could breath fresh air and see downtown from school. Also we can see the stadium from the top of building in high school. During the baseball season, we were able to watch the game. It was exciting to sly our teacher for watching baseball. We brought our lunch everyday. I ate all lunch before lunch time and then I jumped our from school wall to buy some food. It was illegal to go out of school during class. After eating lunch, I played basketball or soccer in the ground. In the afternoon, most of class were boring. Sometime I feel tired, I slept. In Korea, Most of students have to take a extra class until 10 p.m. It was came from wrong educational system that is just for examination.

Which of these do you think is the more advanced writer of English? Why?

4.3.1.3 CHAT

Whereas T-units and SOC tend to focus primarily on linguistic accuracy, the CHAT system is aimed at discourse. CHAT was developed as a tool for the study of first and second language acquisition as part of the CHILDES (Child Language Data Exchange System) database (see Chapter 3 for more on the CHILDES database). It has become an increasingly common system for the coding of conversational interactions and employs detailed conventions for the marking of such conversational features as interruptions, errors, overlaps, and false starts (MacWhinney, 1999, 2000). A standard but detailed coding scheme such as CHAT is particularly useful in qualitative research. For example, in conversation analysis, researchers typically eschew a focus on quantifying data and concentrate instead on portraying a rich and detailed picture of the interaction, including its sequencing, turn-taking, and repair strategies among participants in a conversation (Markee, 2000). Thus, while a researcher conducting a quantitative study might code a transcript for errors in past tense formation, another researcher undertaking conversation analysis might mark the same transcript with a much more detailed coding system, marking units such as length of pauses and silences, stress, lengthening of vowels, overlaps, laughter, and in-drawn breaths. It is important to realize that many researchers working in qualitative paradigms, including those working on conversation analysis, have argued that quantification of coding does not adequately represent their data. For example, Schegloff (1993) points out that laughter is responsive and its positioning is reactive to conversational structure, leading him to conclude that a quantified measure such as "laughs per minute" would be inadequate to describe the dynamic nature of laughter during conversation.[1]

It is important for researchers to keep in mind that regardless of the potential utility of standard coding systems in increasing the generalizability of findings, the goal is always to ascertain how best to investigate one's own research questions. In much second language research, preexisting coding systems and categories are the exception rather than the rule, with many researchers often developing their own systems. In the next section, we provide examples of custom-made coding systems based on five different research areas: (1) grammatical development (question formation); (2) negative feedback; (3) classroom interaction; (4) L2 writing instruction; and (5) task planning.

4.3.2 Custom-Made Coding Systems

4.3.2.1 Question Formation

An example of a custom-made scheme was used by Mackey and Philp (1998) in their exploration of the relationship between interactional feedback in the form of recasts and the development of question formation by learners of English as a Second Language. They collected data from learners carrying out communicative tasks at four intervals in a pre-test/post-test design. Since their focus was on whether or not the learners' questions developed, the researchers needed a coding scheme that would allow them to identify how the learners' question formation changed over time. They based their coding system on the custom-made six-stage sequence of questions in the morpho-syntactic sequence adapted for ESL by Pienemann and Johnston (1986). Pienemann and Johnston's sequence has been used in a wide range of studies, including Spada and Lightbown's (1993) study of the effects of instruction on question formation and interaction studies carried out by Mackey (1999), Philp (2003), and Silver (1999).

To code the data, Mackey and Philp first designated the questions produced by their child learners as belonging to one of the six stages based on the Pienemann-Johnston hierarchy. A modified version of the stage descriptions used by Mackey and Philp and by a number of other researchers (as noted above) appears in Figure 4.2 below. It is important to note that in coding according to these descriptions, not every question produced by the learners is codable because some questions do not fit into the scheme, given that not all question types are included.

Another important point is that grammaticality is not coded using this scheme; since it was designed by Pienemann and his associates in an attempt to capture processing capabilities and linguistic complexity, linguistic accuracy is not the primary focus. The goal of the description of learners' developmental stages is to capture processing capabilities and developing linguistic complexity.

Following the assignment of each question to a particular stage, the next step in carrying out coding based on this hierarchy was to determine the highest-level stage that the learners reached. Pienemann and Johnston's (1986) model suggests that learners can be assigned to a stage. Assignment to a stage is generally determined by the use of two different forms. A more conservative version of this criterion was adopted by later research, with the result that Mackey and Philp determined that two productive usages of two different question forms on at least two different tasks were required for learners to be said to have reached a given stage. Thus, the second step of the coding involved the assignment of an overall stage to each learner, based on the two highest-level question forms asked in two different tests. It was then possible to examine whether the learners had improved over time. Table 4.5, based on constructed data, shows the second level of the coding, where each learner has been assigned to a particular stage.

As can be seen in Table 4.5, learner AB continued throughout the study at the third stage. If learner AB were in a control group, this would generally be an expected outcome. Learner AA began the study at stage 3 and then continued

TABLE 4.5 Coding for question stage

ID	Pre-test				Immediate Post-test				Delayed Post-test			
	Task 1	Task 2	Task 3	Final Stage	Task 1	Task 2	Task 3	Final Stage	Task 1	Task 2	Task 3	Final Stage
AB	3	3	2	3	3	3	3	3	3	3	2	3
AA	3	3	3	3	5	5	4	5	5	5	4	5
AC	3	4	3	3	2	2	3	2	3	3	3	3
AD	3	3	4	3	3	5	5	5	5	3	3	3

Tentative Stages for Question Formation

Stage 1   *Single words or sentence fragments*
One astronaut outside the spaceship?

Stage 2   *Canonical word order*
It's a monster in the right corner?
The boys throw the shoe?
He have two house in the front?

Stage 3   *Wh-fronting and Do-fronting*
How many planets are in this picture?
Where the little children are?
What the dog do?
What color the dog?
Do you have a shoes on your picture?
Does in this picture there is four astronauts?

Stage 4   *Pseudo inversion*
a. Inversion in wh-questions with copula
Where is the sun?
b. Inversion in yes/no questions with auxiliaries other than do
The ball is it in the grass or in the sky?

Stage 5   *Do-second: Inversion with do in wh-questions*
How many astronauts do you have?
Aux second: inversion with other auxiliaries in wh-questions
What's the boy doing?

Stage 6   *Question tag*
You live here, don't you?
Negative question
Doesn't your wife speak English?
Subordinate clause
Can you tell me where the station is?

FIGURE 4.2 Coding for questions

Note: Adapted from the developmental stages described in Pienemann and Johnston (1986).

Source: Spada, N., & Lightbown, P. (1993). Instruction and the development of questions in the L2 classrooms. *Studies in Second Language Acquisition*, 15(2), 222. Copyright © 1993 by Cambridge University Press. Reprinted with the permission of Cambridge University Press and with the permission of Nina Spada and Patsy Lightbown.

through the next three post-tests at stage 5. Once this sort of coding has been carried out, the researcher can make decisions about the analysis, such as whether to carry out statistical tests on learning outcomes by comparing each test. These sorts of decisions are discussed in Chapter 10 on data analysis.

TIME TO DO ...

In a study on relative clauses, a researcher wanted to determine whether learners could produce a range of English relative clause types. The relative clause types she was interested in were:

Subject: The driver is the man **who married my sister**. (who is the subject of the relative clause)

Direct Object: The pilot is the man **whom my sister married**. (whom is the direct object in the relative clause)

Indirect Object: The nurse is the man **to whom I gave a book**. (to whom is the indirect object in the relative clause)

Object of Prep: The professor is the woman **about whom** I was talking (about whom is the object of the preposition in the relative clause)

Genitive: The janitor is the woman **whose sister he married**. (whose sister is a genitive in the relative clause)

Object of Comparative: The shopkeeper is the man **that my brother is taller than**. (the relative clause expresses a comparative)

She gave a sentence combining task where she asked them to combine the following sentence pairs into one sentence beginning with the first sentence:

The driver is the man. He married my sister.
The pilot is the man. My sister married the pilot.
The nurse is the man. I gave a book to the man.
The professor is the woman. I was talking about the professor.
The janitor is the woman. She married the janitor's sister.
The shopkeeper is the man. My brother is taller than the shopkeeper.

Student responses were either correct, incorrect, or directions weren't followed.

When directions weren't followed, responses were of the following type:

Example:
Correct: The shopkeeper is the man that my brother is taller than.
Incorrect Alternatives: My brother is taller than the shopkeeper.
I was talking about the woman who is a professor.

Create a coding chart that will capture these various response types.

4.3.2.2 Negative Feedback

Oliver (2000) examined whether the provision and use of negative feedback were affected by the age of the learners (adult or child) and the context of the interaction (classroom or pair work). In order to do this, she developed a hierarchical coding system for analysis which first divided all teacher-student and NS-NNS conversations into three parts: (1) the NNS's initial turn; (2) the response given by the teacher or NS partner; and (3) the NNS's reaction. Each part then was subjected to further coding. First, the NNS's initial turn was rated as *correct*, *nontarget-like*, or *incomplete*. Next, the teacher's/NS's response was coded as *ignore*, *negative feedback*, or *continue*. Finally, the NNS's reaction was coded as *respond* (e.g., by incorporating the negative feedback into a subsequent utterance), *ignore*, or *no chance* to react to it. As with many schemes, this one is top-down, sometimes known as hierarchical, and the categories are mutually exclusive, meaning that it is possible to code each piece of data in only one way. Figure 4.3 below represents this scheme graphically.

4.3.2.3 Classroom Interaction

Lyster and Ranta (1997) studied the use of linguistic feedback by adolescent students in second language immersion schools. They were particularly interested in which types of feedback were most commonly employed by the teachers and

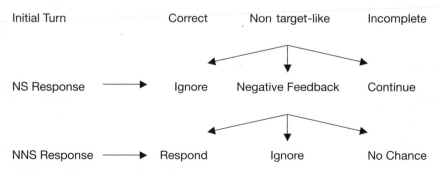

FIGURE 4.3 Three-turn coding scheme

whether certain types of feedback were more likely to be used by the learners, defining use in terms of third-turn uptake. To this end, they examined classroom transcripts for learner errors. When an error occurred, the next turn was examined to determine whether the error was corrected, or whether it was ignored and the topic continued by the teacher or the learner. If the error was corrected, the following turn was examined and coded according to whether the learner produced uptake or whether the topic was continued. Finally, the talk following uptake was examined with regard to whether the uptake was reinforced or the topic continued. The coding categories are illustrated below in Figure 4.4 (from Lyster & Mori, 2006).

TIME TO DO ...

Using the model in Figure 4.4, how would you characterize the following:

1. T = Teacher; S = Student
    S: He finally success.
    T: What?
    S: He finally succeed.
    T: Succeeds.
    S: Yes.

2. T = Teacher; K and C = students (from Ohta, 2001)
    T: Kon shumatsu hima desu ka? Kylie-san.
    "This weekend are you free? Kylie."
    K: Um (..) iie (.) um (.) uh:: (.) hima- (.) hima: (.) hima nai.
    "Um, no, um, uh, not, not, not free." (Error: wrong negator)
    T: Hima ja arimasen?
    "You're not free?" (T corrects form)
    K: Oh ja arim[asen
    C: [hima ja arimasen
    "Not free." (C repeats correct form)

3. St. Le ... le giraffe? (wrong gender 'le') (from Lyster & Ranta, 1997)
    T: Le giraffe?

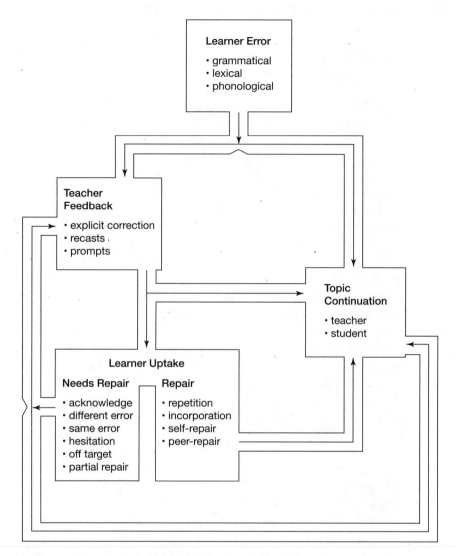

FIGURE 4.4 Classroom interaction coding scheme

Source: Lyster, R., & Mori, H. (2006). Interactional feedback and instructional counterbalance. *Studies in Second Language Acquisition*, *28*, p. 281. Adapted from Lyster, R., & Ranta, L. (1997). Corrective feedback and learner uptake: Negotiation of form in communicative classrooms. *Studies in Second Language Acquisition*, *19*, 37–66. Copyright © 2006 by Cambridge University Press. Reproduced with the permission of Cambridge University Press.

4.3.2.4 Second Language Writing Instruction

The following two studies used coding categories that differ from generally form-oriented coding schemes in that the focus was not on the learners' overall knowledge of forms, but on evidence of development following an intervention.

Adams (2003) investigated the effects of written error correction on learners' subsequent second language writing. In a pre-test/post-test experimental design, university-level Spanish learners wrote short stories based on a set of pictures. During treatment, the learners' stories were rewritten with each form grammatically corrected, and the experimental group was provided with the opportunity to compare their original stories with the reformulated versions. For the post-test, the learners were asked to write their stories again, using the pictures. Adams wanted to determine whether the final versions of the stories would show evidence of learning following the reformulations. The forms in the final essays were coded and compared with those in the pre-test as being: (a) *more target-like*; (b) *not more target-like*; or (c) *not attempted* (avoided).

In a similar study also examining changes in linguistic accuracy following written feedback, Sachs and Polio (2007) compared three feedback conditions (plus a control group). Having written stories based on pictures, the university-level ESL learners in the three experimental groups were provided with the opportunity to compare their original stories with either reformulated or explicitly corrected versions. One of the groups receiving reformulations performed the comparisons while simultaneously producing verbal protocols. A few days later, all four groups were asked to rewrite their stories. Sachs and Polio first coded all of the learners' errors individually. They then segmented the stories and revisions into T-units, examined them side by side, and coded each T-unit as being: (a) at least partially changed in a way related to the original error(s) (+); (b) completely corrected (0); (c) completely unchanged (–); or (d) not applicable (n/a) because there had been no errors in the original T-unit.

It is interesting to note that although the studies by Adams (2003) and Sachs and Polio (2007) focused on changes in linguistic accuracy in L2 writing, the researchers used different coding schemes to fit with the correspondingly different focus of their research questions that involved the comparison of the four feedback conditions with each other. Whereas Adams coded individual forms as more target-like, not more target-like, or not attempted, Sachs and Polio considered T-unit codings of "at least partially changed" (+) to indicate possible evidence of noticing even when the forms were not completely more target-like. An additional part of their study was think-aloud protocols gathered from participants. These were used to determine the level of awareness of language regarding the changes they made in their revisions.

TIME TO DO ...

Below are categories from the think-aloud data in the Sachs and Polio article (2007, p. 80).

Code	Category	Example
M	Mentioned only or read again with special emphasis	Oh, looked *at*, I missed "at."
SP	Misspelling	And they threat, threated, I know this is wrong spell, so, yeah, change it. Mmm . . . threatened people in the bank with their guns.
ML	Use of metalanguage without an explanatory reason	The women were upset, upset, ah, *with* him. Upset with him. I also confused, um, what kind of preposition I have to choose.
O	Oversight	The women were upset with him because they were right! They were worried! [laughs] Why I put "worry"—yeah, right! Worried. They were worried about hurting her, her dog.
RE	Reason	Oh, right, *and*. Yeah, I had to put "and" because I want, I want to connect two sentences, so I have to . . . use a connecting word.
LN	New lexical item	Oh, I learned a new vocabulary: "make out." Make out, make out means about maybe, mm, determine?
LO	Old lexical item	Um, sometimes in my, in my worksheet, uh, I wrote down "delightfully," but the, the closer meaning is "cheerfully," so I . . . I change, I have to change "delightfully" to "cheerfully."
NR	Lack of reason	Unfortunately . . . unfortunately, it started to rain. Here I don't know why put the comma. [laughs] Actually, I, yeah, I don't know where I have to put comma or semicolon. Actually, I'm, I'm every day confused.
RJ	Rejection of change	No examples available, but this would have been something like "No, that's not what I meant to say."
WR	Wrong reason	I think the verb "let" and verb "make" is, uh, similar, so I . . . I wrote the "let." "Let" and "make" is, uh, si-same meanings sometimes, has a same meanings, but . . . uh, this situation, maybe "make" is, uh, acceptable.
RD	Reading the correction aloud	No example provided.

Consider the following think-aloud comments from their participants (Sachs, personal communication, July 2014).

1. (pause) mm . . . I didn't, I didn't know this verb (word?)-endeavor. I'm just, uh, refer to, uh, all kind of physical exercise, I just wrote job, but endeavor, this endeavor, uh, more . . . more appropriate because, uh the middle-aged man trying to lose his, uh, too, too, too much weight. Endeavor means, I think more good, uh, noun.

2. I felt so hard . . . couch potato . . . (pause) In the correction, just, uh, maybe you correct this. I mean, the, I meant a couch potato. But I mean, I, I, I was going to mean, uh, kind of vegetables, just lazy person to do anything . . . I don't know. I just, I just thought that kind of couch potato, that term is used to describe a person who watching the tube all day long. I mean, I don't know. Is it? Can, can it be a symbol of the person who is lazy all the time?

3. To start . . . he read, he read in a book that jogging could be the first step. OK. I put, to start, jogging is the basic step, he read in his book. Oh, I just changed . . . I have some problem with this. Preposition, what is good to, to ca-come before and after, and here, this is a good example, the mess I made sometimes. So to start, to start, he read in a book that jogging could be the first step.

4. Vocabulary. The rope, it should be the leash.

5. Oh, ok. First, the difference is like the wrong vocabulary. I wrote reflection with "x," and in fact it's like reflection with "c." And I made mistakes about the preposition. Though the mirror, and actually it's in the mirror. I don't know why.

6. Never, oh, yeah. Never do jogging and never go jogging. (pause) Ended up. I think the closing of the sentence that you gave me, it's like more flow and connected, like the sentence order, it's like very properly used, uh, good vocab, he ended up, and what he got for the result, it's like very . . . because, like, fore me, I do this writing, I don't think the story in English. I think it, most of the international students think the story that she or he want to write, it's like in his or her own language. Then it's translated into English. When sometimes the, after the translation, it's not fit. And the meaning, it's like, totally different (laughs) I think that's why I make the mistake. And I guess that my weak points, it's like I'm using not good vocab. There is a special vocab to explain the special things like rope and it's . . . should be leash. I think that's all about the mistakes that I made.

Given the Polio and Sachs coding scheme, how would you code these examples? Give your reasons for coding. Keep in mind that some of these examples contain more than one category.

4.3.2.5 Task Planning

Research on the effects of planning on task performance has often utilized measures of fluency, accuracy, and complexity (Norris & Ortega, 2009). Skehan (1996, 1998) argues that fluency is often achieved through memorized and integrated language elements. Accuracy is achieved when learners try to use an interlanguage system of a particular level to produce correct but possibly limited language. Complexity involves a willingness to take risks, and try out new forms even though they may not be completely accurate. He further claims that these three aspects of performance are somewhat independent of one another. A range of different measurements of fluency, accuracy, and complexity have been used in the second language literature. In research on tasks and planning, for example, Yuan and Ellis (2003) investigated the effects of both pre-task and on-line planning on L2 oral production, using multiple measures of complexity, accuracy, and fluency. They operationalized fluency as: (a) number of syllables per minute; and (b) number of meaningful syllables per minute, where repeated or reformulated syllables were not counted. This measure of fluency was chosen because it "takes into account both the amount of speech and the length of pauses" (p. 13). They operationalized complexity as: (a) syntactic complexity, the ratio of clauses to t-units; (b) syntactic variety, the total number of different grammatical verb forms used; and (c) mean segmental type-token ratio; this procedure was followed to take into account the effect of text length. They operationalized accuracy as: (a) the percentage of error-free clauses; and (b) correct verb forms, the percentage of accurately used verb forms. Their study illustrates the benefits of a coding system that is similar enough to those used in previous studies that results are comparable, while also finely grained enough to capture new information.

4.3.3 Coding Qualitative Data

Just as with quantitative research, qualitative researchers code data by identifying patterns. However, in qualitative research, coding is usually grounded in the data. In other words, the schemes for qualitative coding generally emerge from the data rather than being decided upon and pre-imposed prior to the data being collected or coded. This process, where initial categories are based on a first pass through the data, is sometimes known as "open coding." Qualitative researchers explore the shape and scope of the emerging categories and investigate potential connections among categories. As more data are coded, researchers also consider aspects such as the range of variation within individual categories. These processes can assist in the procedure of adapting and finalizing the coding system, with the goal of closely reflecting and representing the data.

For example, one way of coding qualitative data can involve examining the data for emergent patterns and themes, by looking for anything pertinent to the research question or problem, also bearing in mind that new insights and observations not derived from the research question or literature review may be important. Paraphrases, questions, headings, labels, or overviews can be assigned to chunks of the data. These labels or indicators are usually not precise at the early stages. The data should drive the coding, rather than the theory or framework. Many researchers try to code the data by reminding themselves that they will need to explain how they arrived at their coding system, keeping track of the data-based origins of each of their insights. Interesting data that are extra to the goals of the study are not discarded; they are kept in mind, and possibly also coded. Themes and topics should emerge from the first round of insights into the data, where the researcher begins to consider what chunks of data fit together, and which, if any, are independent categories. Finally, a conceptual schema or organizational system should emerge, where researchers consider their contribution to the field. At this stage, researchers often ask themselves if they can tell an interesting narrative based on the themes in the data. At this stage, they are often ready to talk through their data and the patterns with others, so that input can help them in the stages before they write up their research. This is just one method by which qualitative researchers can code and analyze their data. Denzin and Lincoln (1994) present a comprehensive picture of the many alternatives. Baralt (2012) gives a detailed account of coding qualitative data.

One problem with developing highly specific coding schemes is that it can be problematic to compare qualitative coding and results across studies and contexts. However, as Watson-Gegeo (1988) points out, while it may not be possible to compare coding between settings on a surface level, it may still be possible to do so on an abstract level. While a particular event may not occur in two settings, the same communicative need can exist in both. For example, in examining the relationship between second language learning and attitudes of immigrant children, while one study may focus on the school context, and another on the home context, and each may examine different types of events in the data, the overall questions and answers may be comparable. We return to a discussion of coding qualitative data in our discussion of NVivo in section 4.6.

TIME TO THINK ...

Once you have a coding scheme, do all your data need to be coded under that same scheme? Why or why not?

4.4 INTER-RATER RELIABILITY

Regardless of the choice researchers make from the wide range of different types of data coding that are possible, establishing coding reliability is a crucial part of the process. The choice of which coding system to adopt, adapt, or devise ultimately depends on the researcher's goals and the type of study being carried out. However, it is common to ensure that the coding scheme can be used consistently or reliably across multiple coders wherever possible. We do this because humans are notoriously inconsistent for many reasons (e.g., don't understand the task or our mind wanders). This is known as inter-rater reliability, a concept to be discussed in Chapter 5. It is akin to getting a second opinion for a medical issue or to having multiple judges evaluate a figure skating competition.

Because coding involves making decisions about how to classify or categorize particular pieces of data, if a study employs only one coder and no intracoder reliability measures are reported, the reader's confidence in the conclusions of the study may be undermined. To increase confidence, it is important not only to have more than one rater code the data wherever possible, but also to carefully select and train the raters. It may be desirable to keep coders selectively blind about what part of the data (e.g., pre-test or post-test) or for which group (experimental or control) they are coding in order to reduce the possibility of inadvertent coder biases. In some cases, researchers act as their own raters; however, if, for example, a study involves using a rating scale to evaluate essays from second language writers, researchers may decide to conduct training sessions for other raters in which they explain something about the goals of the study and how to use the scale, provide sample coded essays, and provide opportunities and sample data for the raters to practice rating before they judge the actual data. Another way to increase rater reliability is to schedule coding in rounds or trials to reduce boredom or drift, as recommended by Norris and Ortega (2003). One question that is often raised is how much data should be coded by second or third raters. The usual answer is, as much as is feasible given the time and resources available for the study. If 100 percent of the data can be coded by two or more people, the confidence of readers in the reliability of the coding categories will be enhanced, assuming the reliability scores are high. However, researchers should also consider the nature of the coding scheme in determining how much data should be coded by a second rater. With highly objective, low inference coding schemes, it is possible to establish confidence in rater reliability with as little as 10 percent of the data. We now turn to a discussion of those scores.

4.4.1 Calculating Inter-Rater Reliability

In addition to training the raters and having as much data as possible scored by more than one rater, it is also crucial to report inter-rater reliability statistics and to explain the process and reliability estimate used to obtain these statistics.

4.4.1.1 Simple Percentage Agreement

Although there are many ways of calculating inter-rater reliability, one of the easiest ways is through a simple percentage. This is the ratio of all coding agreements over the total number of coding decisions made by the coders. For example, in Mackey and Oliver's (2002) study of children's ESL development, both researchers and one research assistant coded all of the data. This process yielded an inter-rater reliability percentage of 98.89 percent, meaning that there was disagreement in only 1.11 percent of the data. Simple percentages such as these are easy to calculate and are appropriate for continuous data (i.e., data where the units can theoretically have any value in their possible range, limited in precision only by one's ability to measure them—as opposed to discrete data, whose units might be limited to integer values). The drawback is that they have a tendency to ignore the possibility that some of the agreement may have occurred by chance. To correct for this, another calculation is commonly employed—Cohen's kappa (Cohen, 1960).

4.4.1.2 Cohen's Kappa

This statistic represents the average rate of agreement for an entire set of scores, accounting for the frequency of both agreements and disagreements by category. In a dichotomous coding scheme (e.g., coding forms as target-like or nontarget-like), Cohen's kappa requires that the researcher determine how many forms both raters coded as target-like, how many were coded as target-like by the first rater and nontarget-like by the second, how many were coded as nontarget-like by the first and target-like by the second, and so on. The final calculation of kappa therefore involves more detail on agreement and disagreement than simple percentage systems, and it also accounts for chance.

4.4.1.3 Additional Measures of Reliability

Other measures, such as Pearson's Product Movement or Spearman Rank Correlation Coefficients, may also be used. These latter two are based on measures of correlation and reflect the degree of association between the ratings provided by two raters. They are further discussed in Chapter 10, where we focus on analysis.

4.4.1.4 Good Practice Guidelines for Inter-Rater Reliability

In most scientific fields, including second language research and associated fields such as education, "there is no well-developed framework for choosing appropriate reliability measures" (Rust & Cooil, 1994, p. 2). While a detailed examination and comparison of the many different types of inter-rater reliability measures is beyond the scope of this chapter (see Carmines & Zeller, 1979; Chaudron, Crookes, & Long, 1988; Gwet, 2001; Pedhazur & Schmelkin, 1991 for more comprehensive reviews), general good practice guidelines suggest that regardless of which measurement is chosen, researchers should state which measure was used to calculate inter-rater reliability, what the score was, and, if there is space in the report, briefly explain why that particular measure was chosen. Some researchers also explain how data about which disagreements arose were dealt with, for example how agreement was eventually reached and the data were included, or if they were discarded.

There are also no clear guidelines in the field of second language research as to what constitutes an acceptable level of inter-rater reliability. The choices and decisions we make clearly have lower stakes than in the medical or so-called hard science fields. However, the following rough guidelines based on rigorous standards in some of the clinical science research may be of some assistance (Portney & Watkins, 1993):

- For simple percentages, anything above 75 percent may be considered "good," although percentages over 90 are ideal.
- For Cohen's kappa, 0.81 to 1.00 is considered "excellent." In general, a reader should be concerned with a percentage of less than 80, as this may indicate that the coding instrument needs revision.

4.4.1.5 How Data Are Selected for Inter-Rater Reliability Tests

As noted above, in some second language studies, the researchers code all of the data and calculate reliability across 100 percent of the data set. However, an alternative is to have the second or third rater code only a portion of the data. For instance, in some studies the researcher may randomly or semi-randomly select a portion of the data (say 25 percent) and have it coded by a second rater (and sometimes by a third or fourth rater as well depending on the size of the data set and the resources of the researcher). If this approach is taken, it is usually advisable to create comprehensive data sets for random selection of the 25 percent from different parts of the main data set. For example, if a pre-test and three post-tests are used, data from each of them should be included in the 25 percent. Likewise, if carrying out an inter-rater reliability check in an L2 writing study, essays from a range of participants at a range of times in the study should be selected.

It is often necessary to check intra-rater reliability as opposed to inter-rater reliability. In Philp's (2003) study, she coded all of the data. She then recoded 15 percent of the data herself six months later to check for intra-rater reliability. Intra-rater reliability refers to whether a rater will assign the same score after a set time period. Philp used this system together with a standard check for inter-rater reliability, also having one-third of her treatment transcripts double-coded by six assistants.

4.4.1.6 *When to Carry out Coding Reliability Checks*

It is important to realize that if a researcher codes 100 percent of a data set him or herself, and then realizes that the coding system is unreliable, a great deal of unnecessary effort will have been expended, since the coding system may need to be revised and the data recoded. For this reason, many researchers decide to use a sample data set (perhaps a subset of the data, or data from the pilot test) to train themselves and their other coders, and test out their coding scheme early on in the coding process. Following this initial coding and training, coders may then code the rest of the data set independently, calculating inter-rater reliability at the end of the coding process on the data used for the research, rather than for the training.

When space permits, we recommend the following reporting on coding:

What to Report

- What measure was used.
- The amount of data coded.
- Number of raters employed.
- Rationale for choosing the measurement used.
- Inter-rater reliability statistics.
- What happened to data about which there was disagreement (e.g., recoded, not included?).

Complete reporting will help the researcher provide a solid foundation for the claims made in the study and will also facilitate the process of replicating studies. If a low inter-rater reliability statistic is reported, this may be an indication that future studies will need to revise the coding system.

4.5 THE MECHANICS OF CODING

After selecting or devising an appropriate coding system, the researcher must determine how to go about coding the data. Implementations of systems vary between researchers according to personal preferences. Some researchers, for example, may prefer a system of using highlighting pens, working directly on transcripts, and marking such things as syntactic errors in one color pen and lexical errors in another, with a tally on each page and a final tally on the first page of the transcript. Other researchers, depending on their particular questions, may decide to listen to tapes or watch videotapes without transcribing everything; they may simply mark coding sheets when the phenomena they are interested in occur and may decide to transcribe only interesting examples for their discussions. This system may also be used for written data, where coding sheets are marked directly without marking up the original data. Still other researchers may prefer to use computer programs to code data if their research questions allow it. For example, if a researcher is interested in counting the number of words in different sections of an essay or selecting the central portion of a transcript for analysis, it would be much more appropriate to use a word processor than it would be to do this exercise by hand. If the research questions relate to computer-assisted language learning, many CALL programs auto- matically record each keystroke a learner makes, and this data can easily be sorted and coded. Likewise, if the researcher wishes to focus on such things as reaction times to certain presentations on a computer screen, or eye movements as learners read and write text, reaction time software such as DMDX would be a possible choice.

4.5.1 How Much to Code?

As suggested above, not all research questions and coding systems require that an entire data set be coded. When selecting and discussing the data to code, researchers first need to consider and justify why they are not coding all their data. A second important step is determining how much of the data to code. This process is sometimes known as data sampling or data segmentation. Some researchers may decide it is important to code all of the data, whereas others may decide their questions can be answered by examining a portion of the data. In making decisions about how much (and which portions) of data to code, another point to take into consideration is that the data to be analyzed must always be representative of the data set as a whole and should also be appropriate for comparisons if these are being made. Thus, for example, if a researcher chooses to code the first two minutes of oral data from a communicative task carried out by one group of students and the last two minutes from another group of students, the data might not be comparable because the learners could be engaged in different sorts of speech even though the overall task is the same. In the first two minutes, they might be identifying and negotiating the problem or activity, whereas in the final two minutes, they might be making choices about how to complete the activity, or even how to communicate the outcomes to others. Another possibility is that the learners may begin to lose interest or feel fatigued by the end. In view of these concerns, the researcher could instead choose to take the middle section of the data— for example, the central 50 exchanges. Wherever possible, if only a portion of the data is being coded, researchers should check that the portion of data is representative of a data set as a whole. Of course, as with everything else about research design, the research questions should ultimately drive the decisions made, and researchers need to specify principled reasons for selecting data to code.

In much of Oliver's work (1998, 2000, 2002), she makes a general practice of coding only the first 100 utterances of each of her extended interactions. For example, in Oliver (2000) she coded the first 100 utterances of each teacher-fronted lesson and of each of the pair-work tasks in her study. Oliver made this decision because in some cases, the interactions were only a little more than 100 utterances, and she needed a minimum comparable number of units to code. Depending on the research questions and the data set, different segmentation procedures may be appropriate.

TIME TO DO ...

Assume you have collected data from 20 NS-NNS pairs (learners of English) and you are interested in the use of the plural morpheme –s. Each pair recorded seven to eight minutes of free conversation. Your time to do your analysis is limited. What will go into your decision about how much to transcribe and analyze?

4.5.2 When to Make Coding Decisions?

Wherever possible, it is best to make decisions concerning how to code and how much to code prior to the data collection process—that is, when planning the study and preparing the protocol. By addressing coding concerns at the beginning, hopefully through a detailed pilot study, the actual collection of data can be fine-tuned. For instance, if clear coding sheets are designed ahead of time based on research questions and variables, it may become obvious that the proposed data collection procedures cannot provide clear answers to the research questions. This may lead researchers to rework their plans for gathering data so that they can gather more information or different types of information from other sources. The best way to uncover and address such issues is by carrying out an adequate pilot study. This will allow for piloting not only of materials and methods, but also of coding and analysis. Designing coding sheets ahead of data collection and then testing them out in a pilot study is the most effective way to avoid potential problems with the data for the study.

4.6 SOFTWARE FOR CODING

This chapter has dealt extensively with coding without regard to computer programs that can assist in this process. One such program, NVivo (www.qsrinternational.com, retrieved April 19, 2015), is a robust and versatile tool that can organize and analyze data. Its versatility allows it to extract data from transcripts (written), from PDFs, from audio/video data, Web sources, and photos (e.g., handwritten data), and survey data, including open-ended responses transcribed in Excel. It can create visualizations of various types from the data for display in research papers. NVivo allows one to look at data from a variety of perspectives and through its various presentation modes can present data in visual formats such as two- or three-dimensional formats, charts, or various diagrams.

NVivo is particularly useful for qualitative research, with numerous features that can be used to organize and synthesize data. In NVivo, one can import data, code data, and create various queries. One such feature is its sophisticated word search query system. If one is concerned with word frequency and collocational information, NVivo allows one to search a data set for word frequencies (the length of words can be specified—e.g., words of four characters or more—to eliminate articles and some frequent prepositions). It can create a word cloud in which individual "clouds" represent more frequent words by giving them prominence (e.g., in size). An example of this visual representation of word frequency is given in Figure 4.5 with the raw data displayed in Figure 4.6. These (and Figure 4.7) are based on an article (Gass, 2015) that has as its title "Comprehensible input and output in classroom interaction." From these data, one can create a word tree (Figure 4.7), which shows collocations and distributions. In this figure, the word *input* is targeted and all of its distributions of words preceding and following the target word are visually apparent.

NVivo further allows one to link qualitative and quantitative data. One useful tool is the ability to calculate a kappa coefficient and percentage agreement between/among raters (this can also be done using other software programs such as R, Excel, and SPSS). In NVivo, one can also click on the individual ratings and determine where the discrepancy lies.

FIGURE 4.5 Word cloud

Word	Length	Count	Weighted Percentage (%) ▽	Similar Words
learner	7	91	2.31	learner, learners, learners'
feedback	8	52	1.32	feedback
language	8	52	1.32	language
input	5	45	1.14	input
output	6	45	1.14	output
learned	7	43	1.09	learn, learned, learning
teacher	7	43	1.09	teacher, teachers, teachers'
working	7	38	0.97	work, working, works
one	3	35	0.89	one, ones
different	9	34	0.86	differ, difference, differences, different, differing, differs
memory	6	33	0.84	memory
interactive	11	29	0.74	interact, interaction, interactional, interactive
processing	10	29	0.74	process, processes, processing
classroom	9	28	0.71	classroom, classrooms
use	3	28	0.71	use, used, usefully, uses, using
noticing	8	27	0.69	notice, noticed, noticed', notices, noticing
words	5	27	0.69	word, words
correct	7	26	0.66	correct, corrected, correction, corrections, corrective, correctness
gass	4	26	0.66	gass, gass'
task	4	26	0.66	task, tasks
mackey	6	25	0.64	mackey
attention	9	24	0.61	attention, attentional
following	9	24	0.61	follow, followed, following, follows
provides	8	22	0.56	provide, provided, provider, providers, provides, providing
see	3	22	0.56	see
example	7	22	0.56	example, examples
two	3	21	0.53	two
comprehension	13	20	0.51	comprehensibility, comprehensible, comprehension
form	4	20	0.51	form, forming, forms
study	5	20	0.51	studies, study, studying
role	4	19	0.48	role, roles
capacity	8	18	0.46	capacities, capacity
information	11	17	0.43	information
recasts	7	17	0.43	recast, recasts
test	4	16	0.41	test, tested, testing, tests

FIGURE 4.6 Word frequency results

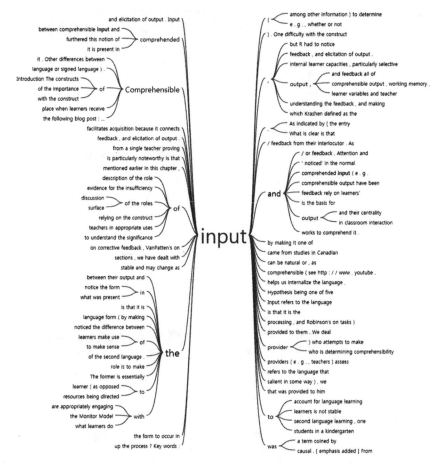

FIGURE 4.7 Word tree—input

4.7 CONCLUSION

Data coding is one of the most time-consuming and painstaking aspects involved in carrying out a second language research project. There are many decisions to be made, and it is important to remember that many of the processes involved in data coding can be thought through ahead of time and pilot tested. These include the preparation of raw data for coding, transcription, the modification or creation of appropriate coding systems, and the plan for determining reliability. Careful coding is a key component of good research. In the next chapter, we focus on research variables, validity, and reliability.

POINTS TO REMEMBER

- Determine coding conventions appropriate for data and research questions.

- Three major types of data: nominal, ordinal, interval.

- Coding depends on the type of data being coded.

- Coding categories adopted depend on research question.

- At times, tailor-made coding systems are necessary.

- For qualitative data, coding must be grounded in the data.

- Reliability ensures that the data are being coded consistently.

- Coding software exists and should be matched with the needs of the researcher.

MORE TO DO AND MORE TO THINK ABOUT ...

1. Classify the following as nominal, ordinal, or interval data:

   a. The number of T-units in a 100-utterance transcript.
   b. The presence or absence of a verb form in an obligatory context.
   c. 10 students ranked from 1 to 10 based on their recall of prepositions from a reading passage.
   d. The number of final words in 10 sentences that were recalled correctly in a test of working memory.
   e. The 10 different L1s of a group of 15 ESL children.
   f. The number of errors in a single student essay.

2. What are the advantages and disadvantages of using or modifying an existing coding scheme as opposed to devising a scheme of one's own to fit the data?

3. Name three methods for inter-rater reliability checks.

4. When is the optimal time to make decisions about coding? What factors should you consider, and what can help you in making your decisions?

5. Suggest coding categories for the following data set, which was collected to address the question of the relationship between frequency of input and the development of third-person singular "s."

Teacher:	She goes to the park in this video
Learner 1:	She go to the park
Teacher:	Goes, she goes there every day
Learner 2:	She went yesterday?
Teacher:	She went yesterday, and today she goes again
Learner 3:	Again today she go to the park. She like the park fine.
Teacher:	She goes to the park most days. She likes it. She will go tomorrow, she went yesterday, and she goes there today as well.
Learner 3:	Always she go to the park. Not too boring for her?

NOTES

1. Ratio scales have a true zero point where zero represents the absence of the category.
2. As discussed, with examples, in Chapter 8, a comprehensive set of coding systems has also been developed for classroom observations.

CHAPTER FIVE

Research Variables, Validity, and Reliability

This chapter focuses on concepts necessary for understanding how to design a second language research study. We begin with an outline of variables and scales followed by descriptions of specific types of validity and reliability. We also discuss sampling, representativeness and generalizability, and the collection of biographical data.

5.1 INTRODUCTION

In Chapter 1, we introduced the concepts of research questions and research hypotheses. Research questions can take a range of forms. One example of a specific and answerable research question might be, "What is the effect of form-focused instruction on the acquisition of English relative clauses by French and Japanese-speaking learners of English?" Because of differences between Japanese and English and similarities between French and English, we might hypothesize as follows: "French-speaking learners of English will perform better following form-focused instruction than Japanese-speaking learners of English." Assuming that the research question is clearly phrased, answerable, and motivated by the literature, we can move on to the research hypotheses.

5.2 HYPOTHESES

A hypothesis is a type of prediction found in many experimental studies; it is a statement about what we expect to happen in a study. In research reports, there are generally two types of hypotheses: (1) research hypotheses; and (2) null hypotheses. The null hypothesis (often written as H_O) is a neutral statement used as a basis for testing. The null hypothesis states that there is no relationship between items under investigation. The statistical task is to reject the null hypothesis and to show that there is a relationship between x and y. Given our hypothesis above that French-speaking learners of English would perform better following form-focused instruction than Japanese-speaking learners of English, the null hypothesis would be:

There will be no difference between the performance of the French group and the Japanese group on a post-test.

We could then statistically test the differences in performance between these groups on a post-test following instruction to determine if any differences found were due to chance or due to treatment. We return to hypotheses and statistics in Chapter 10.

When, based on previous research reports in the literature, we expect a particular outcome, we can form research hypotheses. There are two ways that we can do this. The first is to predict that there will be a difference between two groups although we do not have sufficient information to predict the direction of the difference. For example, we might have a research hypothesis that states simply that the two groups will be different, as below:

There will be a difference between the performance of the French-speaking group and the Japanese-speaking group on a post-test.

This is known as a non-directional or two-way hypothesis.

On the other hand, we may have enough information to predict a difference in one direction or another. This is called a directional or one-way hypothesis. To take our example from above, we might believe (based on the closer linguistic relationship between English and French than between English and Japanese) that the French-speaking group will perform better than the Japanese-speaking group. We would then formulate our hypothesis as follows:

The French-speaking group will perform better on a post-test than the Japanese-speaking group.

TIME TO DO ...

Are the following directional or non-directional hypotheses?

a. German learners of Russian will outperform Spanish learners of Russian in the acquisition of case marking.

b. There will be more instances of relative clause production by Hindi learners of French than by Japanese learners of French.

c. There will be a difference between Hindi learners of French and Japanese learners of French in the amount of relative clause production.

d. Students in a lab setting will show more evidence of circumlocution than those in a classroom setting.

e. There will be a difference in learning between students who are presented with models of language as opposed to those who are given recasts.

f. Students who are induced to make an error through overgeneralization followed by immediate correction will outperform those who are presented with a correct form from the outset.

Based on topics that interest you, write one to two directional and one to two non-directional hypotheses.

As noted in Chapter 1, there are also research questions that are more appropriately addressed by degree rather than by absolutes. In such cases, hypotheses might be more of a comparative statement with an indication of degree of difference.

5.3 VARIABLE TYPES

In order to carry out any sort of measurement, we need to think about variables, that is, characteristics that vary from person to person, text to text, or object to object. Simply put, variables are features or qualities that change. For example, we might want to think about the effects of a particular pedagogical treatment on different groups of people (e.g., Spanish speakers learning English versus Japanese speakers learning English). Native language background, then, is a variable. What we are ultimately doing in experimental research is exploring whether there are relationships between variables and a constant.

Example: We want to examine the effects of different types of instruction on a group of foreign language learners. We take as our object of investigation students enrolled in first semester foreign language classes of Spanish. We use two equivalent classes of first semester Spanish (selecting classes is an issue that we discuss in Chapter 6). We have teachers provide one group with explicit grammar instruction. Another group receives no grammar instruction, but receives a significant amount of input on the specific linguistic structure in question.

The variable under investigation: Type of instruction

What is being held constant: Class level (1st semester Spanish, native language background of participants)

TIME TO DO ...

The following hypotheses were presented in Chapter 1, section 1.4.2.

Hypothesis 1. Null subjects in the four subjects' IL will decrease with time.

Hypothesis 2. There is a negative relation between the development of verb inflections and the use of null subjects; in other words, null subjects will decrease with the increase in verb inflections.

Hypothesis 3. The acquisition of obligatory verb inflections depends on the specific category of verb morphology.

Hypothesis 4. There is a positive relationship between the use of null subjects in is constructions and the development of is constructions.

Hypothesis 5. There are significant differences between the distribution of null subjects and lexically realized subjects in is constructions and non-is constructions. The frequency of occurrence of null subjects will be greater than the frequency of occurrence of lexically realized subjects in is contexts; the frequency of occurrence of null subjects in non-is contexts will be less than the frequency of occurrence of lexically realized subjects in non-is contexts.

Consider two of them and rewrite them as null hypotheses.

5.3.1 Independent and Dependent Variables

There are two main variable types: independent and dependent. The independent variable is the one that we believe may "cause" the results; the dependent variable is the one we measure to see the effects the independent variable has on it. Let us consider the examples in Table 5.1.

In each of the examples in Table 5.1, the independent variable is manipulated to determine its effect on the dependent variable. To elaborate on one of these, let us consider the third example: Does length of residence affect identification of word-final consonants? Let us assume that we have a well-motivated reason to believe that learners are able to recognize word-final consonants based on the amount of input that they have been exposed to. Assuming that one can operationalize (see section 5.4) amount of input (possibly as length of residence in a foreign country or amount of classroom exposure), we would then divide learners into groups depending on their exposure to the target language and see if there is a difference in the degree of correct identification of word-final consonants between or among the groups. The dependent variable would be expressed in terms of the number or percentage of word-final consonants correctly identified, and we would determine whether learners with longer or greater exposure (independent variable) had higher scores (dependent variable).

It is clear that the variables in Table 5.1 also differ in another way—some can be directly manipulated by the researcher (e.g., feedback types), while some exist independent of the research (e.g., amount of input). With those that exist, the researcher needs to find the right way of selecting the appropriate forum for investigating the effects. With those that can be manipulated, the task of the researcher is to determine how to manipulate the variable appropriately. For example, in the case of feedback types, one could select three different teachers

TABLE 5.1 Variable types

Research Question	Independent Variable	Dependent Variable
Does feedback type affect subsequent performance?	Feedback type	Performance measure
Can elements of child-directed speech aid in learning morphology?	Child-directed speech	Measure of morphological acquisition
Does length of residence affect identification of word-final consonants?	Length of residence	Measure of success in identifying word-final consonants
Is there a relationship between learners' noticing of recasts and L2 development?	Noticing of recasts	L2 development measure

who naturally employ different feedback types and use their classrooms for investigation. Alternatively, one could train teachers to use different feedback types.

5.3.2 Moderator Variables

Moderator variables are characteristics of individuals or of treatment variables that may result in an interaction between an independent variable and other variables. Let us assume again a study on the effect of length of residence on the recognition of word-final consonants. Let us further assume that we have a theoretical rationale for believing that length of residence might differentially affect recognition depending on gender. Gender might then be considered to be a moderator variable. In other words, a moderator variable is a type of independent variable that may not be the main focus of the study, but which may modify the relationship between the independent variable and the dependent variable. Of course, moderator variables can "sneak" into a study without the researcher realizing their importance.

5.3.3 Intervening Variables

One could imagine that in the hypothetical study mentioned above, it might not occur to the researcher that gender would be a factor. We have to be cognizant, therefore, of the fact that there may be variables that interfere with the actual results we are seeking. These are known as intervening variables. Intervening variables are similar to moderator variables, but they are not included in an original study either because the researcher has not considered the possibility of their effect or because they cannot be identified in a precise way. For instance, consider a study that measures the effect of pedagogical treatment (independent variable) on learners' overall language proficiency (dependent variable, as measured by TOEFL scores). A variable that cannot be measured or understood easily might be the individuals' test-taking abilities. In other words, the results may be due to test-taking abilities rather than to the treatment. As this variable was not controlled for, it is an intervening variable that could complicate the interpretation of the results.

TIME TO DO ...

You are completing a study on the effects of participation in a volunteer aiding program on later performance in ESL practice teaching. What is the dependent variable? What is the independent variable? You also believe that the type of class in which aiding was done (elementary school, adult school, university class) might have some relationship to success in student teaching. Identify this variable type.

5.3.4 Control Variables

When conducting research, one ideally wants to study simply the effects of the independent variable on a dependent variable. For example, consider the impact of feedback type on a performance measure. Variables that might interfere with the findings include the possibility that learners with different levels of proficiency respond differently to different types of feedback. Another possibility is that different students, depending on their prior language learning experiences, respond differently to different types of feedback. Whenever possible, researchers need to identify these possible factors and control for them in some way, although it should be recognized that identifying and controlling for all variables in L2 research may be difficult.

One way to determine if gender or possibly native language background might have an effect is to balance these variables by having an equal number of men versus women or an equal number of Korean versus Japanese versus Spanish speakers (or whatever languages one is dealing with). These then become moderator variables (see above). Another way to control for possibly interfering, or confounding, variables is to eliminate the variable completely (i.e., to keep it constant). In our hypothetical example, our study might include only men or only women, or only Korean or Japanese or Spanish speakers. Gender and native language then become control variables. This latter solution, of course, limits the degree of generalizability of one's study (see section 5.6.7 on external validity below).

TIME TO DO ...

The following is a description of a hypothetical study.

A teacher found that, in general, his students (English L1 speakers learning Italian) produced more accurate and more fluent second language speech (in terms of grammatical accuracy and lack of pauses) when describing pictures that had a predictable order than when describing a random assortment of pictures. Below are the characteristics of the participants in this study.

Name	M/F	Age	Accuracy score (1 is low; 6 is high)		Fluency score expressed in total pause length	
			Predictable Order	Random Order	Predictable Order	Random Order
Miranda	F	21	4.4	3.8	4.6	4.8
Octavia	F	22	5.2	4.6	3.2	3.5
David	M	26	4.5	4.7	3.9	3.4
Josh	M	28	4.1	4.6	3.8	3.2
Aaron	M	31	4.7	4.9	4.4	3.9
Seth	M	27	4.6	4.8	4.8	4.5
Ethan	M	25	4.5	4.4	5.2	4.6
Rebecca	F	18	3.8	3.2	1.0	1.0
Stefania	F	17	3.9	3.4	1.0	1.2
Kerry	F	24	4.4	3.9	4.1	4.6
Gabriel	M	24	4.4	3.9	1.9	2.0
William	M	32	1.9	2.0	4.1	4.6
Rachel	F	23	2.4	1.6	4.7	4.9
Jonah	M	19	1.0	1.2	2.4	1.6
Natasha	F	24	4.8	4.5	4.5	4.4
Samuel	M	23	1.0	1.0	4.4	3.9
Hannah	F	20	5.0	4.1	4.1	4.6
Michael	M	19	3.2	3.5	5.0	4.1
Robert	M	20	4.1	4.6	4.0	3.8
Sharona	F	22	3.9	3.2	4.5	4.7

What are the dependent, independent, and moderator variables? Do you think that the moderator variable is important in this study? Why or why not? To determine this, you might want to consider the averages for male versus female participants on the different conditions.

5.4 OPERATIONALIZATION

In many instances in second language research, it is difficult to measure variables directly so researchers provide working definitions of variables, known as operationalizations. An operational definition allows researchers to operate, or work with the variables. Operationalizations allow measurement. To return to the example above, we said that we need to operationalize *amount of input*, because this term, as stated, is vague. Although it might be difficult to come up with a uniform concept of amount of input, it is possible to think of examples in which groups vary along some parameter that seems close to the amount of input. For example, classroom learners could be classified based on how many years of exposure they have had to the target language. So "amount of input" could be operationalized as years of exposure in this case. In a natural setting, where exposure comes from everyday living, the operationalization of "amount of input" could be the number of years spent in the target language environment. Once a variable has been operationalized in a manner such as this, it is possible to use it in measurements.

TIME TO DO ...

What are some ways we can operationalize the following?

a. Amount of input
b. Attentiveness in class
c. Interest in class
d. Language proficiency
e. Prior language learning experience in L2
f. Prior language learning experience in other languages
g. Comprehensibility of non-native speaker speech

5.5 VALIDITY

After spending a great deal of time and effort designing a study, we want to make sure that the results of our study are valid. That is, we want them to reflect what we believe they reflect and that they are meaningful in the sense that they have significance not only to the population that was tested, but, at least for most experimental research, to a broader, relevant population. There are many types of validity, including content, face, construct, criterion-related, and predictive validity. We deal with each of these in turn before turning to internal and external validity, which are the most common areas of concern.

5.5.1 Content Validity

Content validity refers to the representativeness of our measurement regarding the phenomenon that we want information about. If we are interested in the acquisition of relative clauses in general and plan to present learners with an acceptability judgment task, we need to make sure that all relative clause types are included. For example, if our test consists only of sentences such as "The boy who is running is my friend," we do not have content validity because we have not included other relative clause types such as "The dog that the boy loves is beautiful." In the first sentence, the relative pronoun "*who*" is the subject of its clause, whereas in the second sentence the relative pronoun "*that*" is the object. Thus, our testing instrument is not sensitive to the full range of relative clause types, and we can say that it lacks content validity.

5.5.2 Face Validity

Face validity is closely related to the notion of content validity and refers to the familiarity of our instrument and how easy it is to convince others that there is content validity to it. If, for example, learners are presented with reasoning tasks to carry out in an experiment and are already familiar with these sorts of tasks because they have carried them out in their classrooms, we can say that the task has face validity for the learners. Face validity thus hinges on the participants' perceptions of the research treatments and tests. If the participants do not perceive a connection between the research activities and other educational or second language activities, they may be less likely to take the experiment seriously.

5.5.3 Construct Validity

This is perhaps the most complex of the validity types discussed so far. Construct validity is an essential topic in second language acquisition research precisely because many of the variables investigated are not easily or directly defined. In second language research, variables such as language proficiency, aptitude, exposure to input, and linguistic representations are of interest. However, these constructs are not directly measurable in the way that height, weight, or age are. In research, construct validity refers to the degree to which the research adequately captures the construct of interest. Construct validity can be enhanced when multiple estimates of a construct are used. For example, in the hypothetical study mentioned above in which exposure to input with accuracy was linked with the identification of final consonants, the construct validity of the measurement of *amount of input* might be enhanced if multiple factors, such as length of residence, language instruction, and the language used in the participants' formal education, were considered together.

5.5.4 Criterion-Related Validity

Criterion-related validity refers to the extent to which tests used in a research study are comparable to other well-established tests of the construct in question. For example, many language programs attempt to measure global proficiency either for placement into their own program or to determine the extent to which a student might meet a particular language requirement. For the sake of convenience, these programs often develop their own internal tests, but there may be little external evidence that these tests are measuring what the programs assume they are measuring. One could measure the performance of a group of students on the local test and a well-established test (for example, TOEFL in the case of English, or in the case of other languages, another recognized standard test). Should there be a good correlation (see Chapter 10 for a discussion of correlations in statistics), one can then say that the local test has been demonstrated to have criterion-related validity.

5.5.5 Predictive Validity

Predictive validity deals with the use that one might eventually want to make of a particular measure. Does it predict performance on some other measure? Considering the example above of a local language test, if the test predicts performance on some other dimension (class grades), the test can be said to have predictive validity.

We now turn to the two main types of validity that are important in conducting research: internal validity and external validity.

5.5.6 Internal Validity

Internal validity refers to the extent to which the results of a study are a function of the factor that the researcher intends. In other words, to what extent are the differences that have been found for the dependent variable directly related to the independent variable? A researcher must control for (i.e., rule out) all other possible factors that could potentially account for the results. For example, if we wanted to observe reaction times to a set of grammatical and ungrammatical sentences, we might devise a computer program that presents sentences on a computer screen one at a time, with learners responding to the acceptability/unacceptability of each sentence by pressing a button on the computer. To make the task easier for the participants in the study, we could tape the letter "A" for acceptable over the letter "t" on the keyboard and tape the letter "U" for unacceptable over the "y" key on the keyboard. After we have completed the study, someone might ask us if we checked for handedness of the participants. In other words, could it be the case that for those who are left-handed, the "A" key (acceptable) might be faster not because it is faster to respond to acceptable as opposed to unacceptable sentences (part of our hypothesis), but because left hands on left-handed people react faster? Our results would then have been compromised. We would have to conclude that there was little internal validity.

It is important to think through a design carefully to eliminate or at least minimize threats to internal validity. There are many ways that internal validity can be compromised, some of the most common and important of which include the following: (1) participant characteristics; (2) participant mortality (dropout rate); (3) participant inattention and attitude; (4) participant maturation; (5) data collection (location and collector); and (6) instrumentation and test effects.

5.5.6.1 Participant Characteristics

The example provided in the previous section concerning handedness is a participant characteristic. Clearly, not all elicitation techniques will require controlling for handedness. But what is important to keep in mind is that there may be elements of the research questions and/or elicitation technique that require a careful selection of one characteristic or another. Let us consider some relevant participant characteristics for second language research: language background, language learning experience, and proficiency level.

Language Background

In many studies, researchers want to compare one group of students with another group based on different treatments. For example, let us assume that a study on the role of attention in second language learning compared groups of students in a foreign language class who were exposed to a language structure with and without devices to ensure that they paid attention to that structure. It would be important that each group of students be relatively homogeneous. Were they not homogeneous, one could not be sure about the source of the results. For instance, let's further assume that one group of students had a large number of participants who were familiar with a language closely related to the target language (either through exposure at home or in the classroom). We then could not distinguish between the effects of the treatment and the effects of the background knowledge of the participants.

Language Learning Experience

Participants come to a language learning situation with a wide range of past experiences. In some instances, these experiences may have importance for research. For example, many students in an ESL setting have had prior English instruction in their home countries, and the type of prior instruction may differ from one country to another. If we wanted to conduct a study in which we compared implicit versus explicit methods of instruction, we might find that a group that received explicit instruction outperformed a group that received implicit instruction. If the two groups also differed in terms of prior learning experiences, we would be left with two variables: (a) learning experience; and (b) instruction type. We would not be able to distinguish between them. Are our results possibly due to the fact that explicit instruction yielded a better outcome because one group was more familiar with and thus more affected by that type of instruction? Or did one instruction type yield better results due to that type of instruction? It is the latter that we want our study to measure.

Proficiency Level

This is one of the most difficult areas to control for when conducting second language research. In foreign language environments, the issue is perhaps simpler than in second language environments because in the former, but not the latter, there is limited exposure outside the classroom although this is not always the case. In the area of foreign language research, there are some global proficiency measures such as the Oral Proficiency Interview (OPI) so that learners can be matched for proficiency. Another common measure is to use placement in class level (1st year versus 2nd year versus 3rd year, etc.). In a foreign language environment, this is relatively "safe" since exposure is more or less limited to what occurs in the classroom.[1] However, with second language learners, backgrounds and outside experiences are varied and there is typically unevenness in skill levels. For example, some potential participants in the same class level may have excellent oral skills but weak written skills and vice versa. It is therefore important to consider how this may bear on the specific research questions of the study.

We have discussed some of the ways in which participant characteristics differ. It is also important to ensure that participants are matched on the feature that is being examined. For example, if one is conducting a study that investigates the perception and production of phonological categories, it may not be sufficient to assume that advanced students are better than intermediate students since the intermediate students may have spent more time in the country where the language is spoken than the advanced students and, consequently, their perception and production of target language sounds may be more advanced even if their command of other aspects of the language is not. One must also be wary of using global proficiency tests when the testing instrument relies on one skill or another. For example, a global language test that provides information on grammar and vocabulary may obscure differences in participants' listening abilities. If listening is a major part of gathering data (e.g., as in elicited imitation tasks, discussed in Chapter 3), an additional measure of listening ability may be needed to make sure that difficulty with the instrument is not an issue causing problems with internal validity.

5.5.6.2 Participant Mortality

Some studies that are conducted in second language research are longitudinal in nature. That is, they seek to measure language development by sampling over time. As such, researchers may typically carry out immediate post-tests and also one or more delayed post-tests to determine the shorter- and longer-term effects of a treatment. In order to appropriately address research questions, it is best to ensure that all participants are present for all sessions. However, in many classroom research settings, it is inevitable that not all participants will be present at each testing period. A researcher must determine how to deal with this situation, and there are a number of factors that one might want to consider. For example, if a researcher has 50 participants and one participant has to be eliminated, the loss is probably not significant. If, on the other hand, participant numbers are balanced across groups, the loss of a participant in one group may necessitate the elimination of a matched participant in another group.

Some possible scenarios:

Scenario 1: Participant Missing from One Treatment Session

Purpose of study: Measuring the effect of quantities of input across groups

Number of participants: 25 per group

Method: Differing amounts of input per lesson; five lessons over a two-week period

Post-tests: One post-test

Situation: One student in one group misses one class period

Issue: Should the post-test data for that student be included in the final data pool?

Response: It might depend on how the groups vary in terms of input. Given that this study is measuring quantities of input and that one group may vary from others by only small differences in the amount of input, the inclusion of someone who missed one class session might make him or her more like someone in another group. Thus, data from this learner should probably be eliminated.

Scenario 2: Participant Missing from One Post-Test

Purpose of study: Determining the long-term effects of attention

Number of participants: Two groups of 10 each

Method: Computer-based input varying attention conditions

Post-tests: Five post-tests given at one-month intervals

Situation: One student in one group misses one post-test

Issue: Should the data for that student be included in the final data pool?

Response: Given that there are five post-tests, one could make a decision in advance that a student must participate in at least the first and the last of the post-tests and two of the remaining three. This would allow some flexibility in keeping as many participants in the data pool as possible while still providing the researcher with information from four data points following the treatment.

Scenario 3: Participant Missing from Part of Post-Test

Purpose of study: Determining the long-term effects of attention on syntax versus on vocabulary

Number of participants: Two groups of 10 each

Method: Computer-based input varying attention conditions

Post-tests: One post-test for syntax and one for vocabulary

Situation: One student in one group misses one post-test (either syntax or vocabulary)

Issue: Should the data for that student be included in the final data pool?

Response: Given that there are two separate post-tests and assuming that data are being aggregated rather than each student's performance on syntax being compared to his or her performance on vocabulary, one could maintain the data in the pool. This would mean that data for the statistical tests would include 10 syntax scores versus nine vocabulary scores (or vice versa).

If, on the other hand, one wanted to do a comparison of each person's data on the two tasks, then the individual who missed one would not be able to be kept in the final data pool.

We have presented three sample scenarios showing what some of the considerations might be in determining what to do about participant mortality. Each situation will, undoubtedly, be different and will require a different (and justifiable) solution. The point to remember is the importance of carefully thinking through the various possibilities given the design of the experiment or longitudinal sessions and making a principled decision as to how to solve the problem in the event of participant absences. These decisions should not be made *ad hoc*; when possible, they should be made in advance of data collection. They should also be fully reported in the research report.

TIME TO DO ...

Consider a study that deals with lexical learning based on repeated exposure. The researcher designs a study that lasts one week (three class meetings). She designs a study that is based on increasing exposure to words. She has selected 10 words and on day 1, each word is presented two times; on day 2, each word is presented three times; on day 3, each word is presented four times. At the end of each class period (day 1, day 2, day 3), she gives a vocabulary test to see at what point the words are learned. Fifteen students are in the class. On day 1, one student is absent; on day 2, two students are absent (one is the same as on day 1 and one is different); and on day 3, all students are present.

If this were your study, how would you handle the data from those students who were absent? Remember, one was absent one day (day 2) and one was absent on days 1 and 2.

Would you include data from these absent students? Why or why not?

5.5.6.3 Participant Inattention and Attitude

When we collect data from participants, we usually make the assumption that they are giving us their "best effort." In other words, we rely on the fact that the language data we are collecting are uncontaminated by the experiment itself.

This may not always be true. One factor that might affect participant behavior is what is known as the Hawthorne effect, which refers to the positive impact that may occur simply because participants know that they are part of an experiment and are, therefore, "different" from others. Participants may also try to please the researcher by giving the answers or responses they think are expected. This is known as the halo effect. Hawthorne and halo effects are also discussed in Chapters 6, 7, and 8 in relation to experimental designs and qualitative research.

Participating in a study also has potential negative effects. For example, researchers might want to consider factors such as fatigue and boredom when asking participants to perform tasks. This was mentioned in Chapter 3 when discussing the number of sentences to use in an acceptability judgment test. Whatever method is being used to gather data, one needs to think of the exhaustion and boredom factor. How much time can one reasonably ask a participant to perform without losing confidence in the results, especially if it is a repetitive and demanding task such as judging sentences? There is no magic answer; we must weigh the need to gather sufficient data against factors of boredom and/or fatigue. Presenting tasks or items in different orders to different individuals serves to balance these effects.

A second factor is general inattentiveness, whether from the outset of the experiment or as a result of the experiment. In a study by Gass (1994), which involved participants in the same task after a one-week interval, the author noted that some participants provided diametrically opposed responses at two time periods. In a stimulated recall after the second session, one of the participants stated that his results from the two sessions differed because his mind was wandering given that he had two academic tests that week. Clearly, one does not always know whether this is an issue, but one needs to be aware of this as a possible way of explaining what may appear to be aberrant or divergent results. In general, if time and resources permit, it is helpful to do a stimulated recall with participants (possibly using the test measure as a stimulus) or a post-experiment interview or exit questionnaire to ascertain if there might be extra-experimental factors that impacted learner responses or behaviors. Gathering such data from even a subset of participants can help in interpreting results.

5.5.6.4 Participant Maturation

Maturation is most relevant in longitudinal studies and particularly in those involving children. For example, a study that spans a year or longer will inevitably include participants who change in one way or another in addition to changes in language development. Adults may not change dramatically in a one-year period, but children certainly do. Moreover, people who were comparable at the outset of the study may change in different ways due to different experiences over time. Thus, one must find a way to balance regular maturational factors against the requirements of the study. When maturation is a consideration, a control group not subjected to the treatment or intervention is appropriate wherever possible. The inclusion of a control group provides one way to test whether any changes occurred because of the experimental treatment or because of maturation.

5.5.6.5 Data Collection: Location and Collector

Not all research studies will be affected by the location of data collection, but some might. Some obvious concerns relate to the physical environment; for example, the environment for two groups given the same test might influence the results if one group is in a noisy or uncomfortable setting and the other is not. A perhaps less obvious effect of setting might occur in a study in which a researcher is trying to gather information from immigrant parents (perhaps through an oral interview) about their attitudes concerning their desires for their children to learn the target language. Informal interviews in their home might yield results that differ from those obtained in a formal school setting, where teachers in proximity could influence what the parents think they should say.

Another factor in some types of research relates to the person doing the data collection. Given the scenario mentioned above concerning families being surveyed about their attitudes toward their children's learning of the target language, one could imagine different results depending on whether or not the interviewer is a member of the native culture or speaks the native language.

5.5.6.6 Instrumentation and Test Effect

The test instrument is quite clearly an important part of many research studies. In this section, we discuss three factors that may affect internal validity: equivalence between pre- and post-tests, giving the goal of the study away, and test instructions and questions.

Equivalence between Pre- and Post-Tests

One serious design issue relates to the comparability of tests. A difficult pre-test with an easier post-test will make it more likely for improvement to be apparent after a treatment. The opposite scenario will make it more likely for no improvement to be apparent following a treatment. There are a number of ways to address comparability of tests. For example, when testing grammatical improvement following a treatment, one can keep the grammatical structure the same and change the lexical items. Doing this, however, requires ensuring comparable vocabulary difficulty. For example, the sentence *The dog ate the chair* does not involve the same vocabulary difficulty level as *The deer consumed the rhododendron*. One way to address this issue might involve consulting a word frequency index (e.g., Brown Corpus, Academic English, Academic Word List; see Thorndike & Lorge, 1944 and Francis & Kucera, 1982) that lists words of the same frequency—that is, words that appear approximately the same number of times in a corpus of the same size and type.

Another way to ensure comparability is to establish a fixed group of sentences for all tests. If a set of 30 sentences were established, Participant A could have a random set of 15 of those on the pre-test and the remaining 15 on the post-test. Participant B could also have a random set of 15 on the pre-test and the remaining on the post-test, but the two participants would in all likelihood not have the same sets of 15. This is quite easy to do on a computer, but it could be done without a computer as well, counterbalancing the test by giving half of a group one set of sentences on the pre-test and the other set on the post-test and giving the sets of sentences to the other half of the group in the reverse order. This technique may also eliminate the possible practice effects or participant inattentiveness that might arise if learners were tested on the same set of sentences twice.

Another example of the importance of test comparability can be seen in conducting second language writing studies. Researchers need to be mindful of the need to choose appropriate topics to write about. A pre-test that is based on a compare and contrast essay might be quite different in structure and vocabulary than a post-test essay based on a topic of persuasion. It would not be meaningful to compare the two essays.

Giving the Goal of the Study Away

One of the problems in doing second language research is that one sometimes does not want participants to know the precise nature of the language area or behavior that is being tested. We might want to conceal the precise nature of the study because we want responses that reflect natural behavior rather than what participants think they should say or do (see Chapter 2 for a discussion of consent forms and how to strike a balance between not being deceptive and yet not revealing precisely what a study is about). This becomes particularly problematic when using a pre-test since the pre-test may in and of itself alert participants to what the study is about. One way of avoiding this problem is by conducting the pre-test a few weeks before the study, the idea being that participants will not associate the pre-test with the study itself. The disadvantage of this solution is that in the time interval between the pre-test and the actual treatment and post-test, participants' knowledge may change, making the results unreliable. A modification of this is to have a shorter time differential, but that, of course, weakens the original issue—that of not revealing the topic of the study.

A second solution, particularly in the case of assessment of discrete language knowledge, is to ensure that the grammatical/lexical point in question is embedded in a much larger test, thereby reducing the likelihood of participants figuring out the scope of the test. If the participants do not guess the topic from the pre-test, the study instruments are more likely to produce a valid characterization of their L2 knowledge.

TIME TO THINK ...

You want to conduct a study in which vocabulary gains are determined based on some treatment. You do not want to give a pre-test of these words because such a test will alert students to the words and might result in their being more sensitive to them or even looking them up in a dictionary. Your friend has suggested that you give the pre-test to a comparable group of students. What do you think about this idea? If you think it is something you want to pursue, how would you determine comparability? Are there other ways to document that the treatment group did not have prior knowledge of the words in question?

Instructions/Questions

In addition to guarding against the above threats to internal validity, one must make sure that the instructions are clear and appropriate to the developmental level of the participants in the study. We cannot rely on responses to questions when it is not clear whether the instructions have been adequately understood.

TIME TO THINK ...

While not a research questionnaire, consider the following statement that a large university added to the application form for all students, both domestic and international.

[We] seek to admit students who provide evidence of intellectual performance, good character, and potential which will permit them to profit from programs of the academic rigor of those offered by [this] University. The University recognizes that learning opportunities are enhanced by a secure environment. As part of the admissions process, we require applicants to respond to the following questions. Information provided in response to these questions needs to be reviewed, but rarely results in denial of admission.

1. Have you ever been expelled, suspended, disciplined, or placed on probation by any secondary school or college you have attended because of (a) academic dishonesty, (b) financial impropriety, or (c) an offense that harmed or had the potential to harm others?

2. Have you ever been convicted of a criminal offense (including in juvenile court) other than a minor traffic violation or are there criminal charges pending against you at this time?

If you answer yes to either of these questions, please submit a letter of explanation. If circumstances arise in the future (until the time you begin attending classes) that make your answers to the above questions inaccurate, misleading, or incomplete, you must provide the Office of Admissions with updated information.

Do you think that this language is appropriate for those whose English language abilities are not native-like? Why or why not? How could you change it to make it more appropriate?

Is the content appropriate (HINT: consider the phrase *juvenile court*)? Why or why not? How could you change it to make it more appropriate?

In second language research, the instructions and questions should be appropriate to the level of linguistic and cultural knowledge of those who are taking the test or filling out a questionnaire.

This section has dealt with threats to internal validity. In the next section, we turn to another type of validity, that known as external validity.

TIME TO THINK ...

Have you ever been a participant in a study? If so, were any of the topics discussed in this section on internal validity apparent to you in retrospect?

Summary of ways to minimize threats to internal validity

- Consider *participant characteristics* that may be relevant to the research questions and elicitation techniques, including but not limited to:
  - Language background
  - Past language learning experiences
  - Proficiency level
  - Specific features and/or skills being examined
- Consider the issue of *participant mortality*. Make decisions about it before carrying out your research, and justify your solution with respect to:
  - Research design
  - Research questions
  - How significant the loss of data would be
  (Then be sure to report on this in your research article.)
- Be aware of the possibility that the experimentation itself may affect the results through:
  - Hawthorne and halo effects
  - Fatigue and boredom of participants
  - Practice effects of the test material
- Get the participants' perspectives after the experiment to ascertain if extra-experimental factors may have impacted their behavior.
- Use a control group to balance *maturational factors* against any long-term requirements of the study.
- Consider how the participants' performance might be affected by:
  - Physical environment of the study
  - Characteristics of the researcher
- Ensure the comparability of pre- and post-tests.
- Don't give away the goals of the study.
- Make sure that the instructions are clear and appropriate to the developmental level of the participants.

5.5.7 External Validity

All research is conducted within a particular setting and using a specific set of characteristics (e.g., 2nd year L1 English learners of French at X university). However, most quantitative research is concerned with broader implications that go beyond the confines of the research setting and participants. The participants chosen for any study form a research population. With external validity, we are concerned with the generalizability of our findings, or in other words, the extent to which the findings of the study are relevant not only to the research population, but also to the wider population of language learners. It is important to remember that a prerequisite of external validity is internal validity. If a study is not conducted with careful attention to internal validity, it clearly does not make sense to try to generalize the findings to a larger population.

5.5.7.1 Sampling[2]

The basis of generalizability is the particular sample selected. We want this group of participants to be drawn randomly from the population to which we hope to generalize. Thus, in considering generalizability, we need to consider the representativeness of the sample. What this means is that each individual who could be selected for a study has the same chance of being selected as any other individual. To understand this, we introduce the concept of random sampling.

Random Sampling

Random sampling refers to the selection of participants from the general population that the sample will represent. In most second language studies, the population is the group of all language learners, perhaps in a particular context. Quite clearly, second language researchers do not have access to the entire population (e.g., all learners of Spanish at U.S. universities), so they have to select an accessible sample that is representative of the entire population.

There are two common types of random sampling: simple random (e.g., putting all names in a (figurative) hat and drawing from that pool) and stratified random sampling (e.g., random sampling based on categories). Simple random sampling is generally believed to be the best way to obtain a sample that is representative of the population, especially as the sample size gets larger. The key to simple random sampling is ensuring that each and every member of a population has an equal and independent chance of being selected for the research. However, simple random sampling is not used when researchers wish to ensure the representative presence of particular subgroups of the population under study (e.g., male versus female or particular language groups). In that case, stratified random sampling is used.

In stratified random sampling, the proportions of the subgroups in the population are first determined, and then participants are randomly selected from within each stratum according to the established proportions. Stratified random sampling provides precision in terms of the representativeness of the sample and allows preselected characteristics to be used as variables. In some types of second language research, it might be necessary to balance the number of learners from particular L1 backgrounds in experimental groups. For other sorts of second language questions, it might be important to include equal numbers of males and females in experimental groups, or to include learners who are roughly equivalent in terms of amount and type of prior instruction or length of residence in the country where the research is being carried out. As an example, assume that one is conducting a study on the acquisition of Arabic passives by speakers of English. Let's further assume that in Arabic language programs, there is a mixture of heritage speakers (those learners who have been exposed to Arabic prior to formal language study through family situations) and non-heritage speakers. Of the students who are available for the study, it turns out that 75 percent are heritage speakers, making it unlikely that the results will be generalizable to all learners of Arabic. To avoid this problem, the researcher could decide to obtain a sample containing 50 percent heritage learners and 50 percent non-heritage learners and randomly select accordingly. This would also make possible what might be an important comparison—that of heritage versus non-heritage learners.

There is yet another approach to sampling, and that is cluster random sampling. Cluster random sampling is the selection of groups (such as intact second language classes) rather than individuals as the objects of study. It is more effective if larger numbers of clusters are involved. In larger-scale second language research, for example, it might be important to ensure that roughly equal numbers of morning and evening classes receive the same treatments; however, as with any method, the research question should always drive the sampling choice.

How does one obtain a random sample? As mentioned above, the principle that should guide selection is that each member of the population has an equal and independent chance of being selected. The purest way of obtaining a true random sample is to take all members of the possible sample, assign each a number, and then use a random number table (available from most statistics books) or a computer-generated random number table (for example, using Microsoft Excel). The following is a small random number table:

068273	241371
255989	213535
652974	357036
801813	313669
188238	987762
858182	324564
539567	010407
874905	076754

705832	752953
394208	866085
532487	980193
717734	499039
965606	256844
442732	809259
128056	843715
398907	972289
999451	782983
016511	525925
980529	329844
657643	501602
123905	385449
941465	573504
311991	088504
594989	631367
163091	221076

If, for example, you have an available population of 99, but you only want to use 35 individuals for your study, you could assign each member a number from 1 to 99 and then use a random number generator to select the first 35. If the first number generated is 77, the person who has been assigned 77 will be part of the data pool. Let's assume that the second number generated is 55. The person who has been assigned 55 will also be a member of the data pool. This continues until 35 numbers have been generated. Alternatively, using the random number table above, you could decide to use the last two digits (or the first two or the middle two) and select the first 35 numbers that fall between 01 and 99 until you have the 35 individuals that you need for your study. Starting from the left column and using the last two digits, you would select 73, 89, 74, 13, 38, 82, 67, and so on until you had 35 participants.

TIME TO DO ...

Take the random number table given above and select 10 participants from a pool of 50, using whatever method you feel is appropriate.

Nonrandom Sampling

Nonrandom sampling methods are also common in second language research. Common nonrandom methods include systematic, convenience, and purposive sampling. Systematic sampling is the choice of every nth individual in a population list (where the list should not be ordered systematically). For example, in organizing a new class where learners have seated themselves randomly in small groups (although one must be sure that the seating was truly random rather than in groups of friends/acquaintances), teachers often ask learners to count themselves off as As, Bs, and Cs, putting all the As into one group and so on. In a second language study, researchers could do the same for group assignments, assuming random seating.

Convenience sampling is the selection of individuals who happen to be available for study. For instance, a researcher who wanted to compare the performance of two classes after using different review materials might select the two classes that require the review materials based on the curriculum. The obvious disadvantage to convenience sampling is that it is likely to be biased and should not be taken to be representative of the population. However, samples of convenience are quite common in second language research. For example, researchers may select a time and a place for a study, announce this to a pool of potential participants, and then use as participants those who show up. These learners will show up depending on their motivation to participate and the match between the timetable for the research and their own schedules and other commitments.

In a purposive sample, researchers knowingly select individuals based on their knowledge of the population and in order to elicit data they are interested in. The sample may or may not be intended to be representative. For example, teachers may choose to compare two each of their top, middle, and lower scoring students based on their results on a test, or based on how forthcoming these students are when asked questions about classroom processes. Likewise, a researcher may decide to pull out and present in-depth data on particular learners who did and did not develop as a result of some experimental treatment in order to illustrate the different pathways of learners in a study. Some consequences of nonrandom sampling will be discussed below.

5.5.7.2 Representativeness and Generalizability

If researchers want the results of a particular study to be generalizable, it is incumbent upon them to make an argument about the representativeness of the sample. Similarly, it is important to describe the setting. A study conducted in a university setting may not be generalizable to a private language school setting. It is often the case that to protect the anonymity of participants, one makes a statement such as the following about the location of the study: "Data were collected from 35 students enrolled in a 2nd year Japanese class at a large public U.S. university." It is important to minimally include this information so that one can determine generalizability. Private language school students may be different from students at large universities, who may in turn be different from students at other types of institutions.

When choosing a sample, the goal is usually that the sample be of sufficient size to allow for generalization of results, at least for most non-qualitative sorts of research. It is generally accepted that larger samples mean a higher likelihood of only incidental differences between the sample and the population. To reflect this, many statistical tests contain built-in safeguards that help prevent researchers from drawing unwarranted conclusions.

Novice researchers often wonder how many learners (the n size) are "enough" for each group or for their study overall.[3] In second language research, participant numbers vary enormously because of the wide range of different types of research carried out. These research types can range from an intensive experiment including several treatments, pre-tests, immediate post-tests, and multiple delayed post-tests, all entailing complex and finely grained linguistic analyses, to a large-scale second language testing study, in which simple numerical before and after scores may be utilized for hundreds of learners. In their text directed at educational research, Fraenkel and Wallen (2003) provide the following minimum sample numbers as a guideline: 100 for descriptive studies, 50 for correlational studies, and 15–30 per group in experimental studies (depending on how tightly controlled the study is). We must remember, however, that research in general education tends to have access to (and to utilize) larger pools than second language research. In second language studies, small groups are sometimes appropriate as long as the techniques for analysis take the numbers into account.

As we have said, a sample must be representative of the population in order for the results to be generalizable. If it is not representative, the findings have limited usefulness. If random sampling is not feasible, there are two possible solutions: First, thoroughly describe the sample studied so that others can judge to whom and in what circumstances the results may be meaningful. Second, as we also discussed in Chapter 1, conduct replication studies (and encourage the same of others) wherever possible, using different groups of participants and different situations so that the results, if confirmed, may later be generalized.

TIME TO THINK ...

Consider the context in which you are likely to conduct research. What is the most likely means you will have to collect data (e.g., intact classes)? What problems do you foresee and how might you overcome these challenges?

5.5.7.3 Collecting Biodata Information

When reporting research, it is important to include sufficient information to allow the reader to determine the extent to which the results of your study are indeed generalizable to a new context. For this reason, the collection of biodata information is an integral part of one's database. The major consideration is how much information to collect and report with respect to the participants themselves. In general, it is recommended that the researcher include enough information for the study to be replicable (American Psychological Association, 2010) and for our purposes in this chapter enough information for readers to determine generalizability. However, the field of second language research lacks clear standards and expectations for the reporting of data, and instances of underreporting are frequent.

In reporting information about participants, the researcher must balance two concerns. The first is the privacy and anonymity of the participants; the second is the need to report sufficient data about them to allow future researchers to both evaluate and replicate the study. There are no strict rules or even guidelines about what information should be obtained in the second language field; because of this, exactly what and how much detail is obtained will depend on the research questions and will vary for individual researchers.

It is generally recommended that major demographic characteristics such as gender, age, and race/ethnicity be reported (American Psychological Association, 2010), as well as information relevant to the study itself (e.g., the participants' first languages, previous academic experience, and level of L2 proficiency). Additional information that might be important for a study on second language learning could include the frequency and context of L2 use outside the classroom, amount of travel or experience in countries where the L2 is spoken, a learner's self-assessment of their knowledge of the target language, and the participants' familiarity with other languages. Additional information sometimes requested on biodata forms are facts that, while not appropriate for reporting, are necessary for carrying out the research, such as contact information and the association of the participant's name with a code number. The American Psychological Association publication manual also suggests that in reporting information about participants, selection and assignment to treatment groups also be reported. The manual further points out that "even when a characteristic is not an analytic variable, reporting it may give readers a more complete understanding of the sample and often proves useful in meta-analytic studies that incorporate the article's results" (American Psychological Association, 2010, p. 19).

A sample biodata form appears below (Figure 5.1). As can be seen from the form, depending on the data collection situation, some of the questions might require explanations. Not all learners would automatically understand *first language(s)*, for example. Does it mean chronologically first? Does it mean *best* language? They might be more easily able to answer a question about which language they speak at home, or a more specific question about the first language learned and still spoken, or they might understand the term mother tongue.

Name _____   Research Code _____

Sex: ___ Male ___ Female   Age ____   First language(s) _____

Email address _____   Phone number _____

For how many years have you studied English? _____

How old were you when you started to study English? _____

Where have you studied English? (tick as many as needed)	How long? (years)	Native English speaker? (yes/no)
_____ Kindergarten	_____	_____
_____ Elementary school	_____	_____
_____ Lower high school	_____	_____
_____ Upper high school	_____	_____
_____ Language schools	_____	_____
_____ Private tutoring	_____	_____

What English classes are you studying in now? (Class numbers and names)

_____

What English classes are you studying next semester? (Class numbers and names)

_____

Are you studying English anywhere else now? Where? What are you studying (TOEFL, grammar)?

_____

FIGURE 5.1 Sample biodata form

What was your score on the English test of the entrance exam?

_____

Have you ever taken the TOEFL test? Yes No

What was your score?_____

How many hours per week do you spend using English outside class to . . .

Do homework	0	1–2	3–4	5–6
Prepare for quizzes and exams	0	1–2	3–4	5–6
Listen to language tapes	0	1–2	3–4	5–6
Read for fun	0	1–2	3–4	5–6
Listen to music	0	1–2	3–4	5–6
Watch TV, videos & movies	0	1–2	3–4	5–6
Talk to friends	0	1–2	3–4	5–6
Talk to tourists	0	1–2	3–4	5–6
Talk to family members	0	1–2	3–4	5–6

Have you ever been to an English-speaking country (U.K., Canada, USA, Australia, etc.)?   Yes   No

If yes, how long were you there? _____

What did you do there?_____

Have ever been to a country where you spoke English to communicate? (Japan, Malaysia, Vietnam, etc.)   Yes   No

If yes, how long were you there? _____

Besides your first language and English, do you know any other languages?   Yes   No

If yes, which languages?

_____

How well do you know them?

_____

FIGURE 5.1 continued

In devising forms for the collection of biographical data, it is important for researchers to balance their need for answers to the questions that could impact their study with requests for extra information that take time to elicit and explain. However, biographical information can be very important when selecting participants; for example, the form above might elicit information about visits to English-speaking countries from even those learners who self-selected into a study on the basis of being beginners, but who then perform at a much higher level than the other learners in the study. This could be important in interpreting results.

There may, however, be instances when generalizability is not an issue. For example, if one is concerned about making curriculum changes or changes in the way assessment takes place in a particular language program, a research study may be conducted within the borders of that program. The results may turn out to be interesting enough to publish, but it should be understood that the results may or may not be applicable to other contexts and that it is only through empirical study in other contexts that one can determine the generalizability of the original findings.

In this section, we have pointed out that it is often difficult to ensure external validity and have shown ways to minimize threats to external validity.

Summary of ways of minimizing threats to external validity

- Random sampling
- Stratified random selection
- Systematic, convenience, and purposive sampling
- Sufficient descriptive information about participants
- Description of setting
- Replication of study in a variety of settings

5.6 RELIABILITY

Reliability in its simplest definition refers to consistency, often meaning instrument consistency. For example, one could ask whether an individual who takes a particular test would get a similar score on two administrations of the same test. If a person takes a written driving test and receives a high score, it would be expected that the individual would also receive a high score if the same written test were taken again. If so, we could say the test is reliable. This differs from validity, which measures the extent to which the test is an indication of what it purports to be (in this case, knowledge of the rules of the road). Thus, if someone leaves the licensing bureau having received a high score on the test and runs a red light not knowing that a red light indicates "stop," we would say that the test is probably not a valid measure of knowledge of the rules of the road. Or, to take another example, if we want to weigh ourselves on scales and with two successive weighings find that there is a 10-pound difference, we would say that the scales are not reliable (although many of us would undoubtedly take the lower weight as the true weight!).

In this section, we will discuss a number of ways that one can determine rater reliability as well as instrument reliability.

5.6.1 Rater Reliability

The main defining characteristic of rater reliability is that scores by two or more raters or between one rater at Time x and that same rater at Time y are consistent.

5.6.1.1 Inter-Rater and Intra-Rater Reliability

Because these concepts were dealt with in greater detail in Chapter 4 on data coding, this section on general reliability provides only a cursory discussion. In many instances, test scores are objective and there is little judgment involved. However, it is also common in second language research for researchers to make judgments about data. For example, a researcher might have a data set from which one wants to extract language-related episodes (LREs), defined as "any part of a dialogue in which students talk about the language they are producing, question their language use, or correct themselves or others" (Swain & Lapkin, 1998, p. 326). That researcher would want to make sure that the definition of LREs (or whatever construct we are dealing with) is sufficiently specific to allow any other researcher to identify them as such.

Inter-rater reliability begins with a well-defined construct, such as the one given above for LREs. It is a measure of whether two or more raters judge the same set of data in the same way. If there is strong reliability, one can then assume with reasonable confidence that raters are judging the same set of data as representing the same phenomenon. Inter-rater reliability, then, provides information about the extent to which independent raters evaluate a given construct and reach the same conclusion about that construct.

Intra-rater reliability is similar, but considers one researcher's evaluations of data, attempting to ensure that that researcher would judge the data the same way at different times—for example, at Time 1 and at Time 2, or even from the beginning of the data set to the end of the data set. To do this, one essentially uses a test-retest method (see section 4.7.2 below); two sets of ratings are produced by one individual at two times or for different parts of the data. Similar to inter-rater reliability, if the result is high, then we can be confident in our own consistency.

181

5.6.2 Instrument Reliability

Not only do we have to make sure that our raters are judging what they believe they are judging in a consistent manner; we also need to ensure that our instrument is reliable. In this section, we consider three types of reliability testing: (1) test-retest; (2) equivalence of forms of a test (e.g., pre-test and post-test); and (3) internal consistency.

5.6.2.1 Test-Retest

In a test-retest method of determining reliability, the same test is given to the same group of individuals at two points in time. One must carefully determine the appropriate time interval between test administrations. This is particularly important in second language research given the likelihood that performance on a test at one time can differ from performance on that same test two months later since participants are often in the process of learning (i.e., do not have static knowledge). There is also the possibility of practice effects, and the question of whether such effects impact all participants equally. In order to arrive at a score by which reliability can be established, one determines the correlation coefficient[4] between the two test administrations.

5.6.2.2 Equivalence of Forms

There are times when it is necessary to determine the equivalence of two tests, as, for example, in a pre-test and a post-test. Quite clearly, it would be inappropriate to have one version of a test be easier than the other because the results of gains based on treatment would be artificially high or artificially low, as discussed earlier. In this method of determining reliability, two versions of a test are administered to the same individuals and a correlation coefficient is calculated.

5.6.2.3 Internal Consistency

It is not always possible or feasible to administer tests twice to the same group of individuals (whether the same test or two different versions). Nonetheless, when that is the case, there are statistical methods to determine reliability: (1) split-half, (2) Kuder-Richardson 20, and (3) Cronbach's α are common ones. We provide a brief description of each.

Split-half procedure is determined by obtaining a correlation coefficient by comparing the performance on half of a test with performance on the other half. This is most frequently done by correlating even-numbered items with odd-numbered items. A statistical adjustment (Spearman-Brown prophecy formula) is generally made to determine the reliability of the test as a whole. If the correlation coefficient is high, it suggests that there is internal consistency to the test.

Kuder-Richardson 20 and 21 are two approaches that are also used. Although Kuder-Richardson 21 requires equal difficulty of the test items, Kuder-Richardson 20 does not. Both are calculated using information consisting of the number of items, the mean, and the standard deviation (see Chapter 10). These are best used with large numbers of items.

Cronbach's α is similar to the Kuder-Richardson 20, but is used when the number of possible answers is more than 2. Unlike Kuder-Richardson, Cronbach's α can be applied to ordinal data.

5.7 CONCLUSION

In this chapter, we have dealt with some of the general issues that must be considered in designing a research project, such as the importance of properly identifying, operationalizing, and controlling variables, ensuring the internal and external validity of the study, and determining reliability. In the next chapter, we deal in greater detail with design.

POINTS TO REMEMBER

- A hypothesis is a statement about what we expect to happen in a study.

- An independent variable is what we believe may be responsible for a result.

- A dependent variable is the variable that we measure to determine the effect of the independent variable.

- Other variables are moderator, intervening, and control. Operationalizational definitions are ones that allow researchers to work with a particular variable and which allow measurement.

- There are many types of validity all of which help to ensure that the results of a study reflect what we belief they reflect. Validity types are: content, face, construct, criterion-related, predictive, internal, and external.

- Reliability in a research study (a form of consistency) is central. Some types of reliability are: rater and instrument.

MORE TO DO AND MORE TO THINK ABOUT …

1. Read the following brief description of an experiment. Are the conclusions that this researcher came to valid? Why or why not?

> The researcher wanted to compare the effectiveness of: (a) instruction based on principles of cognitive linguistics coupled with an in-class teacher-led drill, with (b) instruction based on principles of task-based language teaching coupled with independent task work. Both focused on the acquisition of locative constructions by second language learners. The experiment was carried out during a seven-week term at the English Language School where the researcher was teaching. Six grammar teachers were assigned to six classes of 15 students each. Two classes were classified as beginning, two as intermediate, and two as advanced according to a placement test that consisted of listening comprehension, reading comprehension, and general grammar. The researcher randomly assigned one teacher at each level to each of the experimental instructional treatments. Students were given an essay to write based on some pictures that produced contexts for locative constructions at the beginning and end of the seven-week term. Each teacher scored his/her students' use of locative constructions based on the number of correct forms over the number of forms attempted. At the end of the seven weeks, the experimenter collected both sets of scores and compared them. She found that the teachers conducting in-class drill sessions had students with relatively fewer problems with locatives at the end of the session. She therefore concluded that classroom drill is superior to independent task work for the development of correct locative forms in second language learners.

2. Find three research articles published in different journals, or think of three research articles with which you are familiar.

    a.   What are the dependent and independent variables in the studies? Is there a moderator or an intervening variable?

    b.   What kinds of scales (nominal, ordinal, or interval) are used? Describe the scales and state why they are of the type you identified.

3. Find a study in which the researcher clearly operationalizes a variable. What needed to be operationalized? How was it operationalized? Are there alternative ways it could have been operationalized? What are they?

4. Consider the data below from two test administrations in which English students' knowledge of French relative clauses was being tested. The researcher was pilot-testing the instrument to see if it was reliable. Testing was done on two successive days so that it would be unlikely that any learning took place between test administrations. On each test, there was a maximum of 20 points (2 points for each of 10 sentences). Partially correct responses were awarded 1 point.

	Test 1	Test 2
Sally	18	12
Marie	15	12
Jean	10	14
Howard	15	16
Janice	14	14
Robert	19	18
Drew	8	15
Andrew	11	7
Marc	6	12
Grace	10	10

Given the scores above, are you confident that you have developed a reliable test? Why or why not?

5. Read the following abstract and answer the questions.

    Article title: Evidence in Favor of a Broad Framework for Pronunciation Instruction

    Article source: *Language Learning*, 1998, *48*, 393–410.

    Authors: Tracy Derwing, Murray Munro, and Grace Wiebe

Abstract:

We had native English-speaking (native speaker) listeners evaluate the effects of 3 types of instruction (segmental accuracy; general speaking habits and prosodic factors; and no specific pronunciation instruction) on the speech of 3 groups of English as a second language (ESL) learners. We recorded their sentences and extemporaneously produced narratives at the beginning and end of a 12-week course of instruction. In a blind rating task, 48 native English listeners judged randomized sentences for accentedness and comprehensibility. Six experienced ESL teachers evaluated narratives for accent, comprehensibility, and fluency. Although both groups instructed in pronunciation showed significant improvement in comprehensibility and accentedness on the sentences, only the global group showed improvement in comprehensibility and fluency in the narratives. We argue that the focus of instruction and the attentional demands on speakers and listeners account for these findings.

Segmental = phonetic features, i.e., vowel and consonant sounds, and no prosodic features

Prosodic features = generally stress, intonation, pitch, volume, i.e., suprasegmental features

Extemporaneously produced narrative = without any planning

Blind rating task = the evaluators did not know which set of sentences or narratives belonged to which treatment group.

Questions:

a. What is the independent variable in this study?
b. The dependent variable, pronunciation (=accentedness, comprehensibility, fluency), was measured in many different ways in this study. Do you think that those measures were categorical, ordinal, or interval? Explain.
c. How was the issue of validity in assessing the dependent variable dealt with in this study?
d. How would you check the reliability of the measures of pronunciation?
e. Was the blind rating done to ensure the internal or external validity of the study? Explain.

This problem was provided by Charlene Polio (adapted by Mackey & Gass).

6. Provide brief descriptions of second language studies in which you might want to use the following kinds of sampling and explain why: random, stratified random, cluster random, systematic, convenience, and purposive.

7. Why does (or why doesn't) replicating research make that research more generalizable?

8. Consider a study of the relationship between peer responses to L2 writing and linguistic accuracy, and explain why a researcher might want to obtain biographical data on the following:

- Age
- First language
- Length of residence
- Amount and type of prior L2 writing instruction

What else could a researcher find out about learners' profiles to inform this study?

NOTES

1. This is, of course, an oversimplification, since classroom learners will vary greatly in terms of the amount of time they spend out of class reading the foreign language or in the language laboratory.

2. As mentioned earlier, the sampling procedures discussed in this section relate primarily to quantitative studies. Qualitative research is discussed in Chapter 7.

3. At a large university, a chemist, a physicist, and a statistician were meeting with their Provost in a conference room to explain the real-life applications of their disciplines. During the meeting, a fire broke out in a wastebasket. The physicist whipped out a calculator and began crunching numbers, explaining, "I'm calculating the amount of energy that must be removed in order to stop the combustion." The chemist thoughtfully examined the fire and jotted down some notes, explaining, "I'm figuring out which reagent can be added to the fire to prevent oxidation." The Provost seemed impressed at the speed of their reactions and exclaimed, "I had no idea that there could be such immediate real-world applications of your disciplines to a situation like this." Meanwhile, the statistician pulled out a book of matches and began to set all the other wastebaskets on fire. The shocked Provost demanded, "What are you doing? Are you crazy?" "No, not at all," replied the statistician. "It's just that we won't understand anything until we have a larger N!"

4. A correlation coefficient is a decimal (between 0 and ±1) that indicates the strength of relationship between two variables. A high correlation coefficient indicates a strong relationship. Correlations are discussed in Chapter 10.

CHAPTER SIX

Designing a Quantitative Study

This chapter deals with design types in quantitative research. We begin by introducing the materials that are used along with ways of placing individuals into groups. We then move to the central part of the chapter where we focus attention on ways of designing a study, including pre-test/post-test designs, post-test only designs, time-series designs, and one-shot designs. This is followed by a discussion of meta-analysis. Throughout, we discuss the considerations researchers should make when designing a study for a given topic and population.

6.1 INTRODUCTION

In previous chapters, we discussed the need to specify clear and answerable research questions and we provided information on the development of questions and the selection of variables. In this and the following chapter, we deal with the design of a study. The focus of this chapter is quantitative research; in Chapter 7, we focus on qualitative research, and in Chapter 9 we discuss mixed methods, or those studies that use quantitative and qualitative approaches. We point out that not all questions that we want to answer can be researched experimentally. Some may require purely argumentation.

TIME TO DO ...

Which of the following questions are potentially researchable through an empirical study? Which are better "thought" questions?

a. Why should the government finance English as a Second Language classes for refugee families?
b. What are the characteristics of a good language learner?
c. Does articulatory explanation improve learners' ability to produce the /i/ vs. /I/ distinction in English?
d. Do high-anxiety students make fewer errors on compositions than low-anxiety students?
e. Do students remember more pairs of antonyms than pairs of synonyms when one member of the pair is presented in the first language and the other in the second language?
f. Should all nonnative speakers of a language be required to learn the target language in order to get a driver's license in that country?
g. Does the use of a bilingual dictionary help foreign language students learn more vocabulary than a monolingual dictionary in the L2?
h. Does a student's perception of similarities/differences between his or her first language and the second language influence transfer of syntactic forms from the first to the second language?
i. Is extended listening with delayed oral practice more effective than a total skills approach in initial language learning?

For the ones that you thought were researchable, is there further refinement that needs to be considered (e.g., operationalization)? If so, which ones and what needs to be operationalized?

Quantitative research can be conceptually divided into two types: associational and experimental. What is common in both types is that researchers are attempting to determine a relationship between or within variables. The goal of associational research is to determine whether a relationship exists between variables and, if so, the strength of that relationship. This is often tested statistically through correlations, which allow a researcher to determine how closely two variables (e.g., motivation and language ability) are related in a given population. Associational research is not concerned with causation, only with co-occurrence. In experimental studies, researchers deliberately manipulate one or more variables (independent variables) to determine the effect on another variable (dependent variable). This manipulation is usually described as a treatment and the researcher's goal is to determine whether there is a causal relationship. Many types of experimental research involve a comparison of pre-treatment and post-treatment performance.

TIME TO THINK ...

Think of an example in second language learning where a correlation might exist (e.g., motivation and learning success). Do you think that there might be a causal relationship between these variables? Why or why not?

In this chapter, we describe some of the issues that need to be considered in both associational and experimental research. It is important to note from the outset that all research designs involve decisions at each step of the way and typically, many of these decisions are fraught with compromises: if I do X, then I cannot do Y. Thus, in designing a research project, there is often a cost/benefit analysis to undertake.

Example:

You want to carry out research on the acquisition of past tense forms following recasts in an online chat session. One of your research questions involves the effects of recasts on participants of different language backgrounds (the languages vary in the degree to which their past tense system is similar to the target language past tense system). You need participants at a level of proficiency that is not too high so that there is some room for learning. Also, your participants' proficiency levels cannot be too low because otherwise they will not be able to carry out the task.

As you begin to look for participants of the right language background and the right proficiency level, you realize that this is more difficult than you had originally imagined. If you have students of an appropriate proficiency level, the right native languages are not available. Participants of the appropriate native languages are not available at the proficiency level that is right for your study.

Thus, you will be forced to make a compromise and possibly eliminate one of the variables of your study.

TIME TO THINK ...

If you were conducting this study, what variable would you eliminate and why?

TIME TO DO ...

A researcher wanted to investigate whether extensive reading was a more effective way of learning vocabulary than memorization of word lists. He also wanted to watch students (through the use of an eye-tracker) as they were reading to determine if the words in question were targeted during reading. He needed to find a long passage (short story) for participants to read. Also part of the research plan were the following:

- 60 Arabic learners of English
- Same proficiency level (a level with sufficient knowledge of English to read a short story)
- Background questionnaire
- Post-test of vocabulary

He soon realized that the amount of time needed was approximately 90 minutes. He also realized that the number of participants (Arabic speakers at the same proficiency level) was not available.

What decisions/compromises need to be made? Which ones could jeopardize his study and which ones are less important?

6.2 RESEARCH MATERIALS

One of the key components of designs involves the actual materials used. In Chapter 3, we presented various data elicitation techniques and discussed ways to avoid some of the pitfalls that occur in data elicitation, the most important of which is to ensure that the data obtained can truly address the research questions. Likewise, all materials need to be pilot tested, as discussed in Chapter 3, in order to ensure that what you want to elicit is in fact what you are eliciting. In the box below, we list some of the ways that materials can be the source of a problem.

- Insufficient tokens

Example 1 (Spanish copular *ser* and *estar*): You want to determine whether learners of Spanish understand the difference between the two copular forms (there are subtle semantic and pragmatic differences between the two) and only one example of each is elicited by a 10-item sentence completion task. It would be difficult to draw reliable conclusions from these data because there are not enough examples.

Example 2 (English past tense): You try to elicit examples of the past tense in English as a Second Language by using a narrative task. You give instructions to participants to recount a past event, but they *describe* rather than *narrate*, again providing you with data with very few examples of past tense. For example, when asked to describe his favorite birthday party, one learner begins by narrating "my brother gave me a party" and then continues by describing "my brother is a very good brother. He always do many things for me. He always call me, he always visit with me. He give me very good party." Such descriptions do not constitute past tense contexts.[1]

- Task appropriateness for the elicitation of target structure

Example (Italian noun-adjective agreement): You want to elicit noun-adjective agreement in Italian as a foreign language, but in your task there are very few opportunities to describe items, or learners can easily avoid the structure, as in the following exchange:

NNS:	Quella cosa (f) è blu (f. & m.)
	"That thing is blue"
NS:	Quale cosa?
	"What thing?"
NNS:	Libro (m)
	"Book"

If the target structure can be easily avoided in the task, it is inappropriate for use in the study.

- Imprecise instructions

Example (English relative clause formation): The following data elicitation exercise was designed to produce relative clauses.

Version 1:

Combine the two sentences below making one sentence. Start with the first sentence.
The boy loves chocolate. I saw the boy.

Expected response:
The boy that I saw loves chocolate.

Actual response:
The boy loves chocolate and I saw the boy.

Version 2:

Combine the two sentences below making one sentence. Do not use the words and, or, or but. Start with the first sentence.

The boy was running. I saw the boy.

Expected response:
The boy that I saw was running.

Actual response:
The boy was running even though I saw him.

Version 3:

Combine the two sentences below making one sentence. Do not use the words and, or, but, although, even though, or however. Start with the first sentence.

Result: These instructions worked well except that the participants did not always begin with the first sentence. Thus, the targeted structure was not elicited. (Fortunately, this "violation" of the instructions [see Gass, 1980] turned out to have interesting implications for relative clause acquisition.)

- Insufficient examples for learners to understand what to do

Example (English questions): A spot the difference task was used to study English as a Second Language question use among learner dyads.

Instructions: You and your partner each have a picture. Your pictures are very similar, but there are 10 differences. Don't show your partner your picture; ask questions to find the differences.

NNS1: what the man is doing on the floor?
NNS2: the man is sleeping
NNS1: Is not floor but is next beach, is it, next to beach.
NNS2: I don't have in my picture
NNS1: Is the same picture.
NNS2: No is not similar
(Adams, 2004)

In this situation, NNS2 did not understand that she and her partner had different pictures. Rather than looking for the differences, she became upset when her partner did not confirm her description of her picture. While tasks and directions may seem obvious to researchers, they may be new and confusing for each participant. Sufficient examples should always be provided.

The above examples illustrate some problems that can occur. As mentioned above, the best and perhaps the only way to ensure that your materials will allow you to answer the research questions that you have posed is to pilot them. In your research report, you can then justify your choice of research materials by discussing the pilot data. An example of this can be seen in the selection of vocabulary items in a study of attention (Gass, Svetics, & Lemelin, 2003). The authors selected vocabulary items and piloted them on a separate group of learners to make sure that the words would be unfamiliar to a group of learners similar to those in the experiment. They stated in their article: "Five words were selected for focus in this study that pilot-testing showed were unlikely to be known by the participants" (p. 512). It would not have been possible to ask participants in the actual study if they knew the words or to test their knowledge of the words in this particular experiment because the fact of asking or testing could have served as a forum for learning.

TIME TO THINK ...

What way can you think of that might be used to make sure that the participants did not know the words of the experiment?

6.3 INTACT CLASSES

In Chapter 5, we discussed the ways in which randomization can enhance the experimental validity of a study. However, there are situations when randomization of individuals may not be feasible. For example, in second language research we often need to use intact classes for our studies, and in these cases the participants cannot be randomly assigned to one of the experimental or control groups. Intact classes are often by necessity used in research for the sake of convenience or by necessity. Consider the following design (Gass et al., 1999), which used intact classes to examine the effects of task repetition on learners' subsequent production.

Research questions:

Does task repetition yield more sophisticated language use?

Will more accurate and/or sophisticated language use carry over to a new context?

Method:

Show film clips a different number of times to different Spanish classes (at the same proficiency level) followed by the showing of a new film clip of the same genre.

Groups:

Experimental Group 1: This class saw one episode three times followed by a fourth viewing of a different episode.

Experimental Group 2: This class also had four viewings of a film, but each video was different (the first was the same as Group 1's first and the fourth was the same as Group 1's fourth).

Control group: This class saw only two episodes: the first and the fourth.

In this case, the alternative to using intact classes would have been to randomly assign individuals to one of the three groups (two experimental and one control). Given that this study took place on a university campus where students have varied academic (and sometimes work) schedules, it would have been unlikely that all the individuals assigned to Group 1 would have been able to meet at one time to view the video. The alternative would have been multiple video showings. This would have represented a significant time burden for the researchers in addition to the problems of room and participant scheduling. To put this into a time frame, consider a classic experimental/control group study, with 20 learners in each group and treatments that last one hour each. If two intact classes participated (one designated control and the other experimental), data elicitation would require two hours. If participants from both classes were randomly assigned to control and experimental groups and the research had to conduct individual treatment sessions, data elicitation would require 40 hours. This obviously represents a greater strain on human resources. Thus, practicality is often part of the decision making of a study.

The use of intact classes, while not typical of experimental research, may have the advantage of enhancing the face validity of certain types of classroom research. For example, if the effects of a particular instructional method are investigated, an existing classroom may be the most ecologically sound setting for the research (for more in-depth discussion of classroom research, see Chapter 8).

If intact classes are used, the researcher should carefully consider how the classes are assigned to treatment groups. One way of dealing with non-randomization of individuals is to use a semi-randomization procedure by arbitrarily assigning classes to one treatment or another. However, there are other considerations as well. Suppose that you want to compare five sections of a German as a foreign language class. Unless students are randomly placed in sections, it might be the case that there is a different profile for students who opt to take an 8:00 a.m. class when compared with those who opt to take a 5:00 p.m. class. One group may include more learners with off-campus jobs, for example, while another group may include those who are exclusively studying full-time.

TIME TO THINK ...

Given the situation above (comparing multiple sections), what ways can you think of to resolve the problem and move forward with this study?

6.4 COUNTERBALANCING

Counterbalancing refers to an experimental design in which the test items or tasks are different for different participants. To look at this more closely, consider the two designs below in which the researcher wants to investigate the effect of writing topics (the independent variable) on the amount of coherence that is produced in the form of transition words (the dependent variable). For reasons of logistics, in this fictional study we cannot randomly assign individuals and we cannot do a pre-test to determine group equivalence.

Design 1: Non-random assignment of participants to groups

Research Question: Do different L2 writing topics yield different amounts of transitional words?

Design:

Group 1: Compare your two best teachers.

Group 2: Describe a traumatic event.

Group 3: Argue in favor of language programs in elementary schools.

Analysis: Compare number of instances of transitional words among three groups.

In this design, participants were not assigned randomly and because there was no pre-test, some might question the extent to which the groups are comparable (see further discussion on non-pre-test designs in section 6.5.3.2). One way to compensate for this lack of comparability is to counterbalance by having all groups do all tasks in a different order as in design 2 given below. Because each individual does all tasks, and the order is different for each group, the issue of the possible lack of comparability due to ordering effects can be minimized.

Design 2: Counterbalanced design

Research Question: Do different writing topics yield different amounts of transitional words?

Design:

Group 1: (1) Compare your two best teachers; (2) describe a traumatic event; (3) argue in favor of language programs in elementary schools.

Group 2: (1) Describe a traumatic event; (2) compare your two best teachers; (3) argue in favor of language programs in elementary schools.

Group 3: (1) Argue in favor of language programs in elementary schools; (2) compare your two best teachers; (3) describe a traumatic event.

Group 4: (1) Compare your two best teachers; (2) argue in favor of language programs in elementary schools; (3) describe a traumatic event.

Group 5: (1) Describe a traumatic event; (2) argue in favor of language programs in elementary schools; (3) compare your two best teachers.

Group 6: (1) Argue in favor of language programs in elementary schools; (2) describe a traumatic event; (3) compare your two best teachers.

Analysis: Compare number of instances of transitional words in each of the tasks.

In the analysis, the data are averaged across groups. In other words, all comparison and contrast results would be averaged across all six groups so that there is no ordering effect. The disadvantage is that one must rely on the "goodwill" and attentiveness of the participants to participate in three tasks, especially if all the data are being collected at one time. Another disadvantage is that because of the toll (e.g., in fatigue and boredom, see Chapter 5) that the experiment takes on participants (assuming each task takes approximately 10–15 minutes), one must limit the number of topics. In addition to counterbalancing treatments, researchers can also explicitly test for order effects, particularly when there are relatively few treatments, as in the example above.

TIME TO DO ...

You are conducting a study in which you want to know if a 30-minute spontaneous writing exercise produces a more coherent writing sample than a 45-minute writing exercise. Your study has 40 participants. Your plan is to develop two opinion topic-based questions and give participants one for 30 minutes and the other for 45 minutes. What are the problems? Are they resolvable? If so, how can you resolve them?

6.5 RESEARCH DESIGN TYPES

6.5.1 Correlational (Associational) Research

Correlation can be used in different ways, for example: (1) to test a relationship between or among variables; and (2) to make predictions. Predictions are dependent on the outcome of a strong relationship between or among variables. That is, if variables are strongly related, we can often predict the likelihood of the presence of one from the presence of the other(s). Correlation is often used in survey-based research (see Chapter 3), although it is by no means limited to that research area. Below, we provide examples of two types of survey-based correlational research (one relational and one predictive), both from a large survey-based study of motivation by Dörnyei and Clément (2001).

Example:

Research question: Are student motivational characteristics related to language choice?

Context: (1) Motivational characteristics (e.g. direct contact with L2 speakers, cultural interest, integrativeness, linguistic self-confidence) were collected through questionnaires from more than 4,700 Hungarian students.

(2) Information was gathered on their language of choice in school (e.g. American vs. British English, German, French, Italian, Russian).

Analysis: The study was set up so that the relationship between these variables could be examined.

Example:

Research question: Was integrativeness (represented by questions such as "How important do you think learning these languages is in order to learn more about the culture and art of its speakers?", "How much do you like these languages?", and "How much would you like to become similar to the people who speak these languages?") a predictor of language choice?

Analysis: The follow-up analysis showed that integrativeness was the best predictor of language choice.

The specific statistical analyses will be discussed in Chapter 10.

6.5.2 Experimental and Quasi-Experimental Research

In Chapter 4, we introduced the concept of random assignment of participants and the need to ensure that each participant in a particular population has an equal and independent opportunity for selection. Randomization is usually viewed as one of the hallmarks of experimental research. Design types can range from truly experimental (with random assignment) to what is known as quasi-experimental (without random assignment). Clearly, some design types are more prototypical of one end of the range than the other. In this section, we deal with both types beginning with those that include random assignment of individuals.

A typical experimental study usually uses comparison or control groups to investigate research questions. Many second language research studies involve a comparison between two or more groups. This is known as a between-groups design. This comparison can be made in one of two ways: (1) two or more groups with different treatments; or (2) two or more groups, one of which, the control group, receives no treatment.

6.5.2.1 Comparison Group Design

In a comparison group design, participants are randomly assigned to one of the groups, with treatment (the independent variable) differing between or among the groups.

Example:

A researcher wants to investigate whether aural input or input through conversational interaction yields better L2 learning.

Group 1: Hears a text with input containing the target structure.

Group 2: Interacts with someone who provides input on the target structure.

Assuming a pre-test/post-test design (see below), the results of the two groups would be compared, with inferences being made as to the more appropriate method of providing information to learners. In comparison research, more treatment groups can be added to the study if the research question is elaborated. The example below suggests a slightly different research question with a more elaborate design.

Example:

A researcher wants to investigate to what extent (1) aural input, (2) input through conversational interaction, or (3) a combination of aural and conversational input yields better L2 learning.

Group 1: Listens to a text containing the target structure.

Group 2: Interacts with someone who provides input on the target structure.

Group 3: Receives some input through listening and some through interaction.

TIME TO THINK ...

Can you think of a fourth question that could be asked? What would the fourth group do? Provide a brief description, as in the examples above.

6.5.2.2 *Control Group Design*

The second standard type of experimental design is a control group design. This is similar to the comparison group design, with the important difference that one group does not receive treatment. The control group would typically take the same pre-test and post-test as the experimental groups, but would not have any between tests. For control groups, some researchers may want to provide some language activity or input (of course, different from the treatment) in which the participants are doing something else with language. This is to ensure that it was the treatment, not the mere fact of doing something that led to any change.

One aspect that all researchers grapple with in second language research is how to control for outside exposure to the language. This is much easier to control in a foreign language environment than in a second language environment. In a foreign language setting, control for exposure can often be accomplished simply by ensuring that the particular language focus is not covered in the syllabus during the time of treatment. Another way to prevent external input influencing the results of the study is not to have long periods of time between testing sessions (although there are instances when long periods of time are desirable, as in delayed post-tests when testing longer-term effects of treatment), or, minimally to be able to argue that if there is additional exposure, the groups are equivalent in this regard. Each researcher must be cognizant of the problem and must determine how to deal with it in an appropriate manner.

In sum, a true experimental design will have some form of comparison between groups. The groups will differ in terms of some manipulation of the independent variable to examine the effect of manipulation on the dependent variable. Assignment will be random, or as random as possible, to avoid threats to internal validity caused by participant characteristics.

TIME TO DO ...

A researcher wants to know if working memory capacity (a continuous variable) helps comprehension of a short video with and without captions. How could an experiment be set up? What needs to be operationalized? What comparisons need to be made?

6.5.3 Measuring the Effect of Treatment

There are a number of ways of designing a study using the design characteristics discussed above. We will focus on two: (1) pre-test/post-test (with and without delayed post-tests); and (2) post-test only.

6.5.3.1 Pre-Test/Post-Test Design

In many second language studies, participants are given a pre-test to ensure comparability of the participant groups prior to their treatment, and a post-test to measure the effects of treatment. In Chapter 3, we discussed the need to ensure that our measures are assessing what we intend them to assess. Once we have determined that our measures are indeed appropriate for our research question, there is a further question to be addressed: Is the pre-test comparable in difficulty to the post-test? If the pre-test turned out to be more difficult than the post-test, participants might demonstrate artificially greater improvement; if the pre-test turned out to be easier, participants might demonstrate artificially less improvement. We discussed the importance of comparability of tests in Chapter 5 where we outlined one solution in the form of a study that randomly assigned some sentences to the pre-test and others to the post-test with the sentence assignment differing for each learner. In this way, the threat of test bias is reduced. Another way of accomplishing this is to test all sentences on a comparable group of individuals to ensure that no test items are more difficult than others and, if they are, to place a comparable number of difficult ones and a comparable number of easy ones in each test.

In a pre-test/post-test design, researchers can determine the immediate effect of treatment. But, clearly, the real question for studies of second language learning is to address to what extent a treatment truly resulted in learning. We must always keep in mind that learning is a process and in most cases is not something that occurs at a single moment. It is a process that may begin with a particular treatment, but it is not always clear that the effects of that learning are long-lasting. To measure the longer-term effects, researchers often want to include delayed post-tests in addition to the immediate post-tests, that is, those that occur shortly after a treatment. In fact, this is becoming increasingly common in second language research. With delayed post-tests, a test comparable to the post-test (and pre-test, if there is one) is administered one or more times at predetermined times after the treatment. Often this is one week following the first post-test and then two weeks later and even two or three months later. The advantage of delayed post-tests is that one gets a wider snapshot of treatment effects; the disadvantages are that there is a greater likelihood: (1) of losing participants; (2) that extra-experimental exposure will be greater; and 3) that there will be maturation. Because of the likely possibility of losing participants due to the burden on their time or, in the case of classroom research, due to absences on the day(s) of treatment or testing, it is important to make an *a priori* principled decision as to how many post-tests a participant must participate in before eliminating data.

TIME TO DO ...

Think of a study that you might want to conduct. Determine how many testing sessions you want and how many treatment sessions you will need. Let's assume that you have 40 participants who will participate. Make an *a priori* decision how many sessions (treatment and testing) a participant will have to be present at to include his or her data. Now assume that same study and make an *a priori* decision about how many sessions participants will have to be present at to include their data. Justify your decision.

6.5.3.2 Post-Test Only Design

In some instances, it is undesirable to give a pre-test because the pre-test itself might alert participants to what the treatment is about. In most cases, we do not want our participants to know or guess the purposes of the treatment (see Chapter 5 for a discussion of the problems of giving the goals of the study away and ways to address this). It is important to recognize that there are limitations to this type of design, the main one being that you cannot be sure if there is initial comparability of groups. This becomes an issue particularly when measuring improvement as a result of the manipulation of an independent variable. In post-test only designs, the focus of study is usually performance at a particular point in time and not development. Below are suggestions for ways to address the issue of lack of initial comparability measures, so that one can make assumptions about group comparability.

Ways to address group comparability

- When using intact classes (see section 6.3), if at all possible (it may be difficult if you are using more than two or three intact classes), select classes that meet at roughly the same time (8:00 a.m. classes versus 4:00 p.m. classes).
- Match learners on other measures, such as those that can be gained from a background biographical data questionnaire, for example:

  - gender
  - age
  - years of language study
  - type of language instruction

  - language(s) spoken in the home
  - class grades
  - teachers' ratings
  - placement test

- Match learners on a variable that you can argue is related to the dependent variable. For example, if you can argue that attitude and motivation are related and your study is about motivation, you could match participants on the variable of attitude.
- Match learners on performance on a first treatment.
- Base the investigation on language features that have not previously appeared in the syllabus or in the textbook (relevant for foreign language environments).
- Use low-frequency (or nonce [made-up]) words for vocabulary studies to minimize the possibility that participants will have prior knowledge of the items under consideration.

TIME TO THINK ...

What types of research questions do you think are best suited to a post-test only design?

6.5.4 Repeated Measures Design

As mentioned above in our discussion of randomization, a common way of dealing with the problem of non-randomization is through a repeated measures design, in which all tasks or all treatments are given to different individuals in different orders. The basic characteristic of a repeated measures design (also known as a within-group design) is that multiple measurements come from each participant. This is similar to the example of a counterbalanced design presented in section 6.4, where the goal was to elicit information on the effect of writing topic on the use of transitional words. In that study, all learners produced writings on each of the different topics. In the following example (Gass, 1994), data on the target structure are elicited from all learners at two different points in time.

Purpose:	To assess the reliability of using acceptability judgments in L2 research.
Research Question:	Do learners make similar judgments of acceptability at two different points in time?
Method:	L2 learners of English judged relative clauses on a 7-point scale (including a 0 point). Sentences were randomized for each participant. The judgment

Scoring:	exercise was repeated at a one-week interval with sentences of the same grammatical structure.
	Each person was given a score from –3 (definitely incorrect) to +3 (definitely correct) for each sentence at each time period. The responses at Time 1 and Time 2 were compared to determine the extent to which responses were similar/different at Time 1 and Time 2.

In this repeated measures study, each participant's score at Time 1 was compared with his or her score at Time 2. The research question itself dictated a repeated measures design.

6.5.5 Factorial Design

A factorial design involves more than one independent variable and can occur with or without randomization. A factorial design allows researchers to consider more than one independent variable, generally moderator variables (see Chapter 4 for a discussion of variables). The example below shows a possible factorial design.

Factorial design for the investigation of topic effect on word count/sentence

Research Questions:

Question 1:	Do different writing topics yield different word counts?
Question 2:	Does L1 background yield different word counts?
Question 3:	Do writing topics and L1 background interact to yield different word counts?

Make-up of group:

Native Language	Korean	Spanish	Arabic
	19	22	21

Analysis for Question 1:
Compare results across all topics for all learners (total number of learners is 62). This is a main effect.

Analysis for Question 2:
Compare results across L1 background groups for all writing topics. This is a main effect. The three groups would consist of: 19 (Korean), 22 (Spanish), 21 (Arabic).

Analysis for Question 3:
Compare the groups to see if the pattern is the same for all three language groups. This is an interaction effect.

A results table of the factorial design presented above might look like Table 6.1.

TABLE 6.1 Average number of words per sentence by topic and group

Topic	Native Language			
	Korean	Spanish	Arabic	Total
Compare two favorite teachers	6	12	5	23
Describe a traumatic experience	12	18	10	40
Argue in favor of language programs	10	15	8	33
Total	28	45	23	**96**

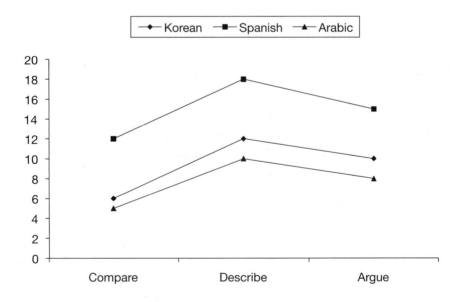

FIGURE 6.1 Words per sentence by topic and L1 background

These group means are different, as demonstrated by Figure 6.1. Without statistical testing, of course, it is not possible to determine whether these differences are significant. Figure 6.1 is a possible graph of the results of a factorial design.

The figure above provides a graphic representation of the data and suggests that the type of writing task influences the average words per sentence for each group. It also suggests that the effect of the type of writing task is similar for each group.

6.5.6 Time-Series Design

Time-series designs are frequently used with small groups of learners. A time-series design involves repeated observations (both pre- and post-treatment) over a set period of time. Before the treatments, a set of observations is made to establish a baseline. Following the treatment, further observations are made to ascertain the effects of the treatment. A typical pattern for a time-series design is the following, where O refers to observations:

$$O_1 \ O_2 \ O_3 \ O_4 \ O_5 \ \text{Treatment} \ O_6 \ O_7 \ O_8 \ O_9 \ O_{10}$$

If, for example, a researcher finds comparable results for all the observations prior to the treatment, there is evidence to determine the normal patterns that a particular group exhibits before the treatment. Similarly, one can obtain a sense of the patterns that occur following the treatment. An example cited by Mellow, Reeder, and Forster (1996) comes from data from Kennedy (1988). Kennedy was interested in dyadic grouping upon discourse. The participant pool consisted of four 4-year-old children and the study took place over a 10-week period. These deliberately paired dyadic interactions in which mathematics was discussed were compared with interactions in free play. Treatment was introduced at different points for each of the four dyads. Figure 6.2 (from Mellow et al., 1996) shows the results of one of the measures (number of NNS turns per episode) and provides information on the nature of the design. As can be seen, the pre-intervention time for each participant differed, ranging from three weeks (#1) to six weeks (#4). Similarly, the treatment time differed for each participant. Using a design such as this, one can look at each treatment session and determine the rank for whatever is being measured (the dependent variable). For example, if one looks at session 4, one can see that the highest score comes from the only participant who had already received the treatment (#1).

In summary, a time-series design can overcome some of the problems typical in second language research, where there can be both small numbers and non-comparability of individuals at the outset. It also reduces some of the problems inherent in research that does not utilize a control group. In a time-

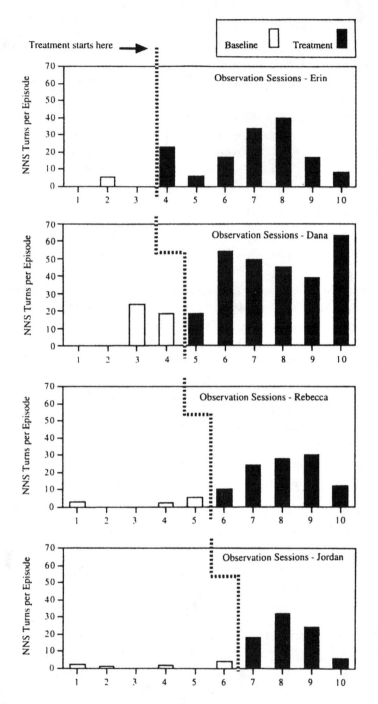

FIGURE 6.2 Number of NNS turns per episode

series design, as can be seen from the example above, multiple samples can be taken from an individual/groups before and after the treatment, allowing a researcher to generate certain baseline information about each participant/ groups, thereby allowing a comparison among individuals/groups at different points of the pre-test, treatment, post-test continuum. For example, we can see that at time 4, Erin (the only one with treatment at this time) has more turns per episode than the other three. In addition, the consistency in samples for each individual before treatment increases the confidence in the effects of the treatment and hence increases the internal validity.

Mellow et al. (1996) list various options for variations in time-series designs of which we mention only two:

- Treatment and withdrawal: One can gather baseline data on an individual in a classroom followed by treatment and then withdrawal of treatment. If the learner reverts to pre-treatment behavior following withdrawal, one would have confidence in the effects of the treatment.
- With multiple individuals, each individual can receive treatment at a different time.

Time-series designs have a great deal of flexibility. Mellow et al. (1996) isolate four reasons for utilizing this design type:

1. Practicality. Can be used even with small numbers of participants.
2. Can be used to reduce the Hawthorne effect (see Chapters 5, 7 and 8) because many instances of data collection are used.
3. Can be used as a means of exploration and hypothesis generation.
4. Given the longitudinal design and many instances of measurement, we have a richer picture of development.

In general, using a time-series design does not eliminate the possibility of maturational effects, but the use of multiple subjects, treated at different times, may make findings more convincing.

TIME TO THINK ...

Can you think of a research question for which a time-series design would be helpful?

6.5.7 One-Shot Designs

We have limited our discussion to the most common design types used in second language research, but there are others as well. One of these is what is generally known as a "one-shot" design. This is not usually considered part of a true experimental paradigm, because there is no treatment. Nevertheless, one-shot designs are often used in second language research within the UG or processing paradigms (see Chapter 3 for discussions of each of these) when the study does not have a pre-test/post-test design, but simply raises questions along the lines of: What do learners know at this particular point in time? How do learners interpret sentences in an L2? An example of this type of research comes from White (1985), who was following up on a well-motivated theoretical question from formal linguistics.[2]

Research Question: Is there a relationship among the following three types of sentences produced by Spanish-speaking learners of English?

That-trace

Spanish	English
Quien dijeste que vino?	**Who did you say that came?*
who you said that came	*Who did you say came?*
"Who did you say came?"	

Subject-verb inversion

Spanish	English
Vino Juan.	*John came.*
came Juan	**Came John.*
"Juan came."	

Null-subjects

Spanish	English
Anda muy ocupada.	**Is very busy.*
is very busy	*She is very busy.*
"She is very busy."	

Method: Present participants with sentences (both grammatical and ungrammatical) and ask for acceptability judgments.

Results: Spanish speakers continue to cluster these sentences in their L2, particularly at lower levels of proficiency.

Questions other than UG-based questions lend themselves to this design type as well. Consider this research question from Gass, Mackey, and Ross-Feldman (2003) where data were collected at one point in time.

Research Question: Is there a difference between the amount of interaction in classroom contexts versus lab contexts?

Operationalization of interaction: 1) Language-related episodes, 2) recasts, 3) negotiation

Method: Three tasks given to participants in their regular classrooms.

Identical three tasks given to a different and comparable group of participants in a laboratory context.

Results: No difference in the amount of interaction in the two contexts.

Thus, not all studies require a design that uses a control group and an experimental group or that necessitates a pre-test and a post-test.

6.5.8 Meta-Analyses

We discussed replication earlier in this book, as a way of verifying findings. There is another way of determining wider impact and that is through a meta-analysis. A meta-analysis is not truly a design type, but we discuss it here (also discussed in Chapter 10) because it is a way of setting up data for analysis. There are times when our research questions involve surveying a wide range of existing studies rather than collecting original data. In a sense, a meta-analysis is a way of stepping back and surveying and comparing what others have done on a particular topic. In other words, a meta-analysis is a way of synthesizing results across studies through a statistical procedure. It is an average of averages in which the data points are individual studies, not individual participants.

Often in meta-analyses, one has to exclude a study from consideration because the author(s) failed to include essential information. Thus, accurate reporting is particularly important when thinking about future researchers who might conduct a meta-analysis (see Plonsky and Oswald, 2012, for a discussion of how to conduct meta-analyses).

TIME TO THINK ...

What topics might be ripe for a meta-analysis? (Hint: the role of instruction.)

6.6 CONCLUSION

As has become clear in this chapter, there are many areas to consider when designing a research project. We have discussed the most commonly used design types in experimental and quasi-experimental research, identifying them along such dimensions as participant assignment to treatment group, testing, and variables included. Below is a checklist of some of the concepts discussed in this chapter that are useful to think about as you are designing and reporting a study. In the next chapter, we focus on issues of methodology in qualitative research.

POINTS TO REMEMBER

- Are your groups matched for proficiency?

- If you are using a particular type of task (e.g., listening), are your groups matched for (listening) abilities?

- Are your participants randomized?

- If intact classes are used, are their treatments randomly assigned?

- Are your variables clear and well described?

- Do you have a control group?

- Are control groups and experimental groups matched for everything but the specific treatment (including the time spent on the control and experimental tasks)?

- Have you described your control and experimental groups?

- Do you have a pre-test?

- If you are testing development, do you have a post-test or even multiple post-tests?

- If using a repeated measures design, are the treatments counterbalanced?

MORE TO DO AND MORE TO THINK ABOUT ...

1. You have asked each of your ESL students to go out in the "real world" and make five complaints during the next week. They will judge their success on a five-point "success" to "failure" scale. During the previous week, half of these students had watched a videotape of an American woman returning a watch to a store, complaining that it did not work properly. You want to know if the model helped with self-rated success. What is the dependent variable in this study? The independent variable? All your students are adult women from a variety of language backgrounds. Some of them work in factories, some in stores, and some in offices. How would you identify these variables? You decide that this might be a good pilot project on ESL learner success in speech events. Suggest another variable that might be important in such a study. How would you measure this variable?

2. Consider the following conclusions. Are they valid? Why or why not? If not, what would make them more convincing?

    a. Second language learners who identify with the target culture will master the language more quickly than those who do not. (**Evidence 1:** A case study of an unsuccessful language learner who did not identify with the target language. **Evidence 2:** Five case studies of unsuccessful language learners who did not identify with the target language and five case studies of successful language learners who did identify with the target language. **Evidence 3:** Same as #2, but the data are accompanied by verbal reports from learners showing that this is indeed an important connection.)

    b. Immigrants are more law abiding than native-born citizens. (**Evidence:** An analysis of court records.)

    c. Affective relationships between teacher and students influence proficiency gains. (**Evidence:** A longitudinal ethnographic study of an inner-city high school class.)

    d. Input followed by interaction promotes better learning than interaction followed by input. (**Evidence:** Two groups of 50 each where the group with input followed by interaction outperformed the group with interaction followed by input on (a) an immediate post-test; and (b) two subsequent post-tests.)

3. Read the following abstract and answer the questions.

    Article title: The Influence of Task Structure and Processing Conditions on Narrative Retellings

Article source: *Language Learning*, 1999, *49*, 93–120.

Authors: Peter Skehan and Pauline Foster

This article explores the effects of inherent task structure and processing load on performance on a narrative retelling task. Task performance is analyzed in terms of competition among fluency, complexity, and accuracy. In a study based on 47 young adult low-intermediate subjects the fluency of performance was found to be strongly affected by degree of inherent task structure; more structured tasks generated more fluent language. In contrast, complexity of language was influenced by processing load. Accuracy of performance seemed dependent on an interaction between the two factors of task structure and processing load. We discuss which aspects of performance receive attention by the language learner. The implications of such cross-sectional results for longer-term language development are considered.

Questions:

a. What is the research question addressed in this study?
b. Is this an experimental study? Why or why not?
c. What are the independent variables in this study?
d. For each independent variable, state what kind of variable it is— that is, what kind of scale is being used? Justify your response.
e. What are the dependent variables?
f. How might one operationalize each of the dependent variables?

This problem was provided by Charlene Polio (adapted by Mackey & Gass).

NOTES

1. A further difficulty with this situation is that we cannot be certain that these examples do not constitute actual attempts at the past. Given the possibility that the learner could produce the past tense, but contexts for the past to occur are not adequately targeted by the prompt (or that there is ambiguity), this prompt should probably be eliminated in favor of one where there is greater certainty of eliciting the target structure if the learner is at the correct level to produce it.
2. This study involved a comparison between Spanish and French native speakers where the French group served as a control, but the point is that a one-shot design can be used when one is interested in considering what a group of learners knows about the TL at one point in time.

CHAPTER SEVEN

Qualitative Research

The importance and utility of qualitative research has long been recognized in the field of second language studies. This chapter begins with a discussion of the nature of qualitative research and how it differs from other approaches. Next, commonly used methods for gathering qualitative data are outlined, including case studies, ethnographies, interviews, observational techniques, verbal protocols, and diaries/journals. We conclude with a discussion of practical considerations in conducting and analyzing qualitative research, including issues such as credibility, transferability, dependability, triangulation, and quantification. We continue the discussion of qualitative research in Chapter 9 where we focus on mixed methods.

7.1 DEFINING QUALITATIVE RESEARCH

The term "qualitative research" is associated with a range of different methods, perspectives, and approaches. As Mason (1996) points out, "qualitative research—whatever it might be—certainly does not represent a unified set of techniques or philosophies, and indeed has grown out of a wide range of intellectual and disciplinary traditions" (p. 3). Nonetheless, for the purposes of this chapter, we present a general definition of qualitative research in the second language field and outline several of its key characteristics. Briefly defined, the term qualitative research can be taken to refer to research that is based on descriptive data that does not make (regular) use of statistical procedures. Detailed definitions of qualitative research usually include the following characteristics:

- Rich description: The aims of qualitative researchers often involve the provision of careful and detailed descriptions as opposed to the quantification of data through measurements, frequencies, scores, and ratings.

- Natural and holistic representation: Qualitative researchers aim to study individuals and events in their natural settings (Tetnowski & Damico, 2001). That is, rather than attempting to control contextual factors (extraneous variables) through the use of laboratories or other artificial environments, qualitative researchers tend to be more interested in presenting a natural and holistic picture of the phenomena being studied. This picture includes both the broader sociocultural context (e.g., the ideological orientations of the speech community as a whole) as well as micro-level phenomena (e.g., interaction within the classroom).

- Fewer participants: Rather than using a large group of (generally randomly selected) participants with the goal of generalizing to a larger population like quantitative researchers, qualitative researchers tend to work more intensively with fewer participants, and are less concerned about issues of generalizability.

- Emic perspectives: Qualitative researchers aim to interpret phenomena in terms of the meanings people attach to them—that is, to adopt an emic perspective, or the use of categories that are meaningful to members of the speech community under study. For instance, it might be inappropriate in some cultures for students to laugh at, question, or make eye contact with their teachers. A qualitative researcher would aim to take this into account when investigating student affect in the classroom. Emic perspectives can be distinguished from the use of etic (or outsiders') categories and frameworks to interpret behavior. Etic perspectives are more common in quantitative studies.

- Cyclical and open-ended processes: Qualitative research is often process-oriented, or open-ended, with emergent categories. The research often follows an inductive path that begins with few preconceived notions, followed by a gradual fine-tuning and narrowing of focus. In contrast, quantitative research usually begins with a carefully defined research question that guides the process of data collection and analysis. So, while quantitative researchers set out to test specific hypotheses, qualitative researchers tend to approach the research context with the purpose of observing whatever may be present there, and letting further questions emerge from the context.

- Possible ideological orientations: Whereas most quantitative researchers consider impartiality to be a goal of their research, some qualitative researchers may consciously take ideological positions. This sort of research is sometimes described as "critical," meaning the research may have particular social or political goals. For example, Scollon (2001) has argued that critical discourse analysis, a form of qualitative research, is "a program of social analysis that critically analyzes discourse—that is to say language in use—as a means of addressing social change" (p. 139).

- Research-generated hypotheses: Research questions tend to be general and open ended and hypotheses may be generated as an outcome of qualitative research rather than in the initial stages of the study. According to Brown (2003), "One of the great strengths often cited for qualitative research is its potential for forming new hypotheses" (p. 485).

The following chart from Chaudron (2000) provides a useful overview of the distinctions between qualitative and quantitative approaches.

TIME TO DO ...

Based on the definition of qualitative research above, think about why a researcher would employ qualitative methods to investigate a problem rather than quantitative methods. Conduct a library search for both a quantitative and qualitative study and compare and contrast the research questions/issues under investigation.

Despite the fact that distinctions can be drawn between qualitative and quantitative research as shown in Chaudron's chart, these two research types are by no means as dichotomous as they sometimes appear to be. It is increasingly common for researchers to discuss both quantitative and qualitative data in the same report, or to use methods associated with both types of research in a process sometimes known as split methods or multiple methods, which we refer to as mixed methods and discuss in Chapter 9.

The growing practice in applied linguistics of utilizing qualitative and quantitative data illustrates the fact that these two research approaches should not be viewed as opposing poles in a dichotomy, but rather as complementary means of investigating the complex phenomena at work in second language acquisition.

7.2 GATHERING QUALITATIVE DATA

As noted earlier, a wide variety of different techniques are used in the collection of qualitative data. As with all methods, the advantages and disadvantages of each technique should be taken into consideration when deciding how to

	Qualitative Methods (Ethnography)	Quantitative Methods
Observation & Collection of Data	In data collection, ethnographic research (as the most typical and concrete example of qualitative research) doesn't usually use "instruments," rather "processes" that are supposedly free of bias and prior assumptions: free, prolonged observation, at times "participant observation," open-ended interviews, "triangulation" of information and interpretation, "informant checking," access to existing documents.	The observations in quantitative research (whether tests, attitudes scales of the subjects observed, behaviors categorized and counted according to instruments, etc.) usually are based on an observation scheme or descriptive categories that have been developed prior to the research. Moreover, these observations are made in a planned way, according to an order determined by the design of the research, and with categories that cannot be changed once the research is underway.
Nature of Data	Ethnographic research considers those data most relevant which arise from the natural events in the research context. The topics of greatest interest for qualitative researchers are human behaviors and sociocultural patterns and norms that underlie the behaviors. Data are viewed in a "holistic" fashion, without attempting to separate them into their components, and preferably following the interpretations of the people who are the object of the research ("emic" interpretations).	Data tend to be limited by the type of observation that is planned, and according to the method of observation; depending on the design and the effects of a "treatment," the data usually indicate stability or variability and development in events, attitudes, abilities, skills, knowledge, performance or production, etc., with respect to a language and its use. These are interpreted according to the theoretical model or hypotheses of the researcher, and not necessarily according to the views of the subjects involved ("etic" interpretation).
Use and Development of Theory	The qualitative researcher does not want to verify or prove theories; what he or she attempts is to observe without bias or narrow perspectives. However, the researcher always takes account of the relevant theories regarding the context or topic under study, and normally will remain aware of his or her own assumptions during observation and interpretation. Proper methodology will include the appropriate degree of "objectivity." In the end, the researcher will develop a "grounded" theory, which helps to relate the observations to one another and to larger contexts, or he or she will attempt to revise and perfect the conceptual framework that was adopted at an earlier stage. In the most radical form of qualitative research (from the tradition of phenomenology), causal explanations are not sought, but only a better "understanding" of the phenomenon.	The researcher constructs a design to prove some aspect of a theoretical framework (forming hypotheses about the goals of the research), and the results tend to either confirm or disconfirm the hypotheses. Although it is recognized that the researcher's subjectivity can influence interpretations, in order not to generalize beyond the research context, the design, which includes the means of sampling the subjects, should control the limits of conclusions to be drawn. Thus, a theoretical framework is slowly developed.

Source: Chaudron, C. (2000). Contrasting approaches to classroom research: Qualitative and quantitative analysis of language and learning. *Second Language Studies, 19*(1), 7. Copyright © 2000 by Craig Chaudron. Reprinted with the permission of Craig Chaudron and the *Working Papers in Second Language Studies*.

address a specific research question. Here, we present an overview of some of the most commonly used qualitative data collection methods, including:

- ethnographies
- case studies
- interviews
- observational techniques
- diaries/journals

As discussed above, since there is little general agreement in the field about what constitutes qualitative research, some of the data collection techniques we discuss in this chapter are associated with more descriptive than truly qualitative methods by some researchers. For example, Brown (2003) considers interviews and questionnaires to be a part of survey-based research, a distinct category from qualitative and quantitative research, or what he refers to as interpretive and statistical methods. Also, given that some of the data collection methods described here are associated with particular contexts or overlap with each other, some are also described in other chapters in this text. For example, diaries and journals are also discussed in Chapter 8 on second language classroom research contexts, with examples from teachers and learners. Each approach and method can be seen as contributing its own piece of the puzzle in qualitative researchers' attempts to obtain rich, detailed, participant-oriented pictures of the phenomena under study.

7.2.1 Ethnographies

Although there has been much debate concerning the nature of ethnography, it can be said from a second language research perspective that ethnographic research aims "to describe and interpret the cultural behavior, including communicative behavior, of a group" (Johnson, 1992, p. 134), as well as "to give an emically oriented description of the cultural practices of individuals" (Ramanathan & Atkinson, 1999, p. 49), or in other words, to carry out research from the participants' points of view, using categories relevant to a particular group and cultural system.

This focus on group behavior and the cultural patterns underlying that behavior is one of the key principles of ethnography identified by Watson-Gegeo in an interesting (1988) review article. Another important principle of ethnographic research is the holistic approach taken to describing and explaining a particular pattern in relation to a whole system of patterns. So, ethnography can be viewed as a qualitative research method that generally focuses on the group rather than on the individual, stresses the importance of situating the study within the larger sociocultural context, and strives to present an emic perspective of the phenomena under investigation, with the categories and codes for analysis being derived from the data themselves rather than being imposed from the outside.

Ethnographic approaches have been used in a very broad range of second language research contexts, ranging from ethnographies of schools and language programs, to personal accounts and narratives or life histories of learning and teaching (e.g., Duff, 2002; Pavlenko & Lantolf, 2000), home-school discontinuities among Native American children (e.g., Macias, 1987; Philips, 1972, 1983), bilingual language use outside educational settings (Goldstein, 1997), cultural and ideological processes in first and second language learning (King, 2000), and research on specific aspects of the L2 process, such as second language writing in different cultural contexts (e.g., Atkinson & Ramanathan, 1995; Carson & Nelson, 1996). However, as Johnson (1992) notes, one of the main uses of ethnographic research in the second language context "has been to inform us about the ways that students' cultural experiences in home and community compare with the culture of the schools, universities, and communities where they study, and the implications of these differences for second language and culture learning" (p. 135). A well-known piece of research of this nature, an ethnography of first language communication, was carried out by Brice Heath (1983), who spent a decade living in two working-class communities in the Carolinas, one black community, Trackton, and one white community, Roadville. Using data from these working class communities, as well as middle-class school-oriented black and white families in the town, Heath's research focused on how children learned to use language and how their use of language was related to their literacy. She showed how the different ways of learning language interacted with the children's integration into academic life and how their use of language in the home interacted with how they used print. The working-class communities had both different expectations and different usage patterns, as well as different attitudes towards the mainstream families and schools in terms of uses of language. Heath refers to these differing usage patterns as ritualized uses of language, such as the assignment of labels to objects, response to questions where answers were already known to the questioner (often known as display questions), and recitation of discrete points of factual material separated from context. In summary, the language and literacy practices of middle-class families mirrored expectations in the school. These differences in home language and literacy practices had implications for academic success.

The goal of such research is to be emic, detailed, holistic, and situated in context with a focus on exploring how complex factors interact. Ethnographies can profitably make use of methods specifically designed to tap into participants' perspectives, and as such, they often involve or overlap with the use of observations, interviews, diaries, and other means of data collection that will be discussed in more detail below. They also generally involve triangulation of data, which will also be discussed below.

TIME TO THINK ...

Brice Heath (1983) lived in the community she studied for over a decade. What is the role of the researcher in an ethnographic study?

7.2.1.1 Advantages

One advantage of using an ethnographic approach is that the research questions employed in these studies can be dynamic, subject to constant revision, and refined as the research continues to uncover new knowledge. For example, an ethnographer studying second language writing classrooms may enter the research process with the aim of describing the patterns of interaction between teachers and students and illustrating how those patterns are related to the writing process. However, over the course of many classroom observations, analyses of student essays, and interviews with both students and teachers, the researcher may alter the focus of the study and begin concentrating on the types of feedback that are provided by both teachers and students. Ethnographies are usefully employed when not enough is known about the context or situation to establish narrowly defined questions or develop formal hypotheses. For example, why do a particular group of heritage language learners do poorly when learning in formally instructed foreign language classroom settings? An ethnographic approach to this question could examine the context, the attitude of the teacher and the students, the influence of home and social groups, and so on in an attempt to uncover information relevant to addressing the question. If the researcher shares the heritage language background, participant observation could be used, that is, the researcher might be able to participate in the language classes or share social occasions where the language is used in some way. Since ethnographies typically employ multiple methods for gathering data, such as participant observations and open-ended interviews, as well as written products, the researcher may be able to provide an holistic, culturally grounded, and emic perspective of the phenomena under investigation.

As Schilling (2013) has pointed out, in addition to providing an emic perspective, ethnography is often associated with research participants feeling more comfortable than in other sorts of data-gathering situations. The extended nature of ethnographic research allows the relationship between researcher and participants to develop organically over time. This may encourage participants to be more candid and may ultimately lead to richer data (Schilling, 2013, p. 125).

7.2.1.2 Caveats

In embarking upon an ethnographic study, researchers need to be aware of some potential challenges and sensitive issues. First of all, ethnographies involve intensive research over an extended period of time. They require a commitment to long-term data collection, detailed and continuous record keeping, and repeated and careful analysis of data obtained from multiple sources. It is also important for the researcher to realize that ethnographic approaches to research may create potential conflicts between the researcher's roles as an observer and a participant. If the researcher participates in an event he or she is observing, this may leave little time for the carefully detailed field notes that ethnographies may require. This can be rectified to a certain extent by audio and video tape recording. However, and more seriously, the researcher's participation may change the nature of the event (see also the discussion on observations in section 7.2.4). Researchers thus need to be aware of how they can supplement and triangulate ethnographic data obtained through participant observation, and they must carefully consider how their dual roles might influence the data collected.

In addition to these practical concerns, there are theoretical issues that the researcher should take into consideration. First of all, it has been argued that an ethnographer's focus on describing a culture is problematic, as "there is no such thing as a social group that is not constantly destabilized by both outside influences and personal idiosyncrasy and agency" (Ramanathan & Atkinson, 1999, p. 45). In its strong form, this criticism implies that any attempt to describe a culture is to some extent misguided on the part of the ethnographer. A second theoretical concern about ethnographies has to do with the act of writing up the research. Since research reports adhere to certain (culturally influenced) standards of writing, the otherwise accurate picture an ethnographer has recorded may come out skewed. In other words, the very act of transcribing the events that were observed may inevitably entail a misrepresentation of them. Finally, it is often difficult to generalize the findings of ethnographic research to other problems or settings because of the highly specific nature of such work.

7.2.2 Case Studies

Like ethnographies, case studies generally aim to provide a holistic description of language learning or use within a specific population and setting. However, while ethnographies focus on cultural patterns within groups, case studies tend to provide detailed descriptions of specific learners (or sometimes classes) within their learning setting. As Duff (2008) highlights, case studies explore the behaviors and attitudes of individuals, groups (e.g., a whole class), organizations (e.g., a language program), or events (e.g., a tutorial or seminar), while ethnography explores the cultural basis for those group behaviors and values. Case studies are also usually associated with a longitudinal approach, where observations of the phenomena under investigation are made at periodic intervals for an extended period of time.

Case studies have been used in a wide variety of second language research studies. One well-known longitudinal case study investigating the development of L2 communicative competence is Schmidt's (1983) study of Wes, an ESL learner. Wes was a 33-year-old native speaker of Japanese who had little formal instruction in English. Schmidt studied Wes' language development over a three-year period when he was residing in Japan but visited Hawaii, the research site, regularly on business. The study focused on a small number of grammatical features, including plural "s," third-person singular "s," and regular past tense. Schmidt transcribed conversations between Wes and friends and also transcribed monologues that he asked Wes to produce and record while at home in Japan. Although Wes attained relatively high levels of pragmatic ability and acculturation (for example, in the use of formulae such as "So, what's new?" and "Whaddya know?"), he had very limited improvement in terms of linguistic accuracy for the grammatical forms over the three years of the study, thus providing evidence for the separability of linguistic and pragmatic competence.

TIME TO THINK ...

Take a closer look at Schmidt's (1983) study of Wes. What was the main research question in this study? Why do you think Schmidt decided to employ a case study approach to his research rather than a quantitative approach?

Another well-known case study is Ellis' (1984) investigation of two child learners in an L2 context. J was a 10-year-old Portuguese boy, and R was an 11-year-old boy from Pakistan. Both children were learning ESL in London in a program that catered to new arrivals with the aim of preparing them for transfer to high schools. Ellis investigated the learning patterns of the two children in an instructed context, as opposed to the naturalistic context in which Schmidt had studied Wes' language development. In order to examine the learners' use of requests, Ellis visited the classrooms regularly, writing down the samples of requests the two children produced. Ellis' analysis documented different stages in the children's use of requests over time, also noting their tendency to use formulae. In another second language case study where the focus was the role of collaborative interaction in second language development, Ohta (1995) examined the language of two intermediate learners of Japanese as a foreign language, finding that their patterns of interaction facilitated a form of scaffolding, or assisted help, which benefited both learners. Cases are not limited to individuals, but can also be classes or schools. For example, Willett (1995) observed an entire classroom of first-grade ESL students for a year in her exploration of the development of ESL students' identities and communicative competence. Her case study focuses on four students who were audio-recorded in addition to the observations. She found that the three girls in her study were able to appear more competent and successful in the academic setting through their collaboration. However, the single boy in the study was viewed as a problematic learner in the classroom context due to his more independent work and because his social displays of communicative competence were disruptive (e.g., shouting "This is easy" when he completed a task).

7.2.2.1 Advantages

One main advantage of case studies is that they allow the researcher to focus on the individual in a way that is rarely possible in group research. As Johnson (1993) notes, "too often, because of the nature of correlational, survey, and experimental research, and their privileged status in L2 research, very little is learned about individual language learners, teachers, or classes. Case studies stand in sharp contrast to these approaches by providing insights into the complexities of particular cases in their particular contexts" (p. 7). In addition, case studies can be conducted with two individual learners or two existing groups of learners for the purpose of comparing and contrasting their behaviors within their particular context. Case studies have the potential for rich contextualization that can shed light on the complexities of the second language learning process.

7.2.2.2 Caveats

An essential point to bear in mind with case studies, however, is that the researcher must be careful about the generalizations drawn from the study. Although this is true for all forms of research, it is particularly pertinent to case studies, which often employ only a few participants who are not randomly chosen. For this reason, any generalizations from the individual or small group (or classroom) to the larger population of second language learners must be made tentatively and with extreme caution. From a single case study, it may be difficult to recognize idiosyncrasies as such, with the potential that they are misinterpreted as typical language learning behavior. To address this concern, the findings from multiple longitudinal case studies can be combined to help researchers draw firmer conclusions from their research. For example, Wray (2001) summarizes 14 case studies that focused on the role of formulaic sequences in child second language acquisition. The cases involved 21 children

(12 girls and nine boys), aged approximately 2 to 10. Based on these multiple case studies, Wray argues that children express themselves holistically in a second language by employing formulaic sequences. In short, interesting case studies may provide valuable insights into certain aspects of second language learning, but single case studies are not easily generalizable.

7.2.3 Interviews

A number of different interview types can be employed to gather data for qualitative research. As noted in the introduction to this chapter, interviews are often associated with survey-based research, as well as being a technique used by many qualitative researchers. In structured (also known as "standardized") interviews, researchers usually ask an identical set of questions of all respondents. Structured interviews resemble verbal questionnaires and allow researchers to compare answers from different participants. Less rigid are semi-structured interviews, in which the researcher uses a written list of questions as a guide, while still having the freedom to digress and probe for more information. In unstructured interviews, on the other hand, no list of questions is used. Instead, interviewers develop and adapt their own questions, helping respondents to open up and express themselves in their own terms, and at their own speed. Unstructured interviews are more similar to natural conversations, and the outcomes are not limited by the researcher's preconceived ideas about the area of interest. Some interviews can also be based around a stimulus, for example a completed questionnaire, or a videotape of a lesson. Focus-group sessions are related to such interviews, and usually involve several participants in a group discussion, often with a facilitator whose goal it is to keep the group discussion targeted on specific topics, again often using a stimulus for discussion, such as a videotape or previously elicited data.

7.2.3.1 Advantages

Interviews can allow researchers to investigate phenomena that are not directly observable, such as learners' self-reported perceptions or attitudes. Also, since interviews are interactive, researchers can elicit additional data if initial answers are vague, incomplete, off-topic, or not specific enough. Another advantage of interviews is that they can be used to elicit data from learners who are not comfortable in other modes. For example, some learners are more at ease speaking than writing and are more likely to provide extended answers in a conversational format. Depending on the research question and the resources available, interviews can also be conducted in the learner's L1, thus removing concerns about the proficiency of the learner impacting the quality and quantity of the data provided.

7.2.3.2 Caveats

Researchers must also take note of the potential drawbacks of interviews. For example, Hall and Rist (1999) make the point that interviews may involve "selective recall, self-delusion, perceptual distortions, memory loss from the respondent, and subjectivity in the researcher's recording and interpreting of the data" (pp. 297–298). Multiple interviews—that is, interviewing the same subject more than once, or interviewing many different subjects—is one potential means of addressing such issues. Another concern is that good interviewing is a skill. It may not be easy for novice researchers to conduct unstructured interviews without practice and/or training in drawing participants out, encouraging them to express themselves, and gathering valuable data on the area of interest. Given that participants' attitudes toward other people can impact what they say, there is also the danger of the so-called halo effect, discussed earlier in Chapter 5. This halo effect happens when the interviewees pick up cues from the researcher related to what they think the researcher wants them to say, thus potentially influencing their responses. In addition to these concerns, the possibility of cross-cultural pragmatic failure exists. Some questions may be considered inappropriate in particular cultures, and because of the different connotations words carry in different linguistic and cultural contexts, miscommunications may arise.

To address some of these concerns, the following suggestions may be useful in interviewing:

- Be sensitive to (and/or match the interviewer's characteristics with) the age, gender, and cultural background of the interviewee.
- Encourage open-ended discussion, for example by keeping silent, or by saying "Anything else?" rather than accepting a first answer as the interviewee's final and complete response to a question.
- Develop skills in anticipating and addressing communication problems.
- Try to make the interviewee as comfortable as possible. This can be done by conducting the interview in a familiar place, beginning with smalltalk to relax the interviewee, and/or using the L1 if a communication problem arises or if the interviewee so prefers.
- Place the key questions in the middle of the interview, as the interviewee may be nervous in the beginning and tired by the end.
- Mirror the interviewee's responses by repeating them neutrally to provide an opportunity for reflection and further input.

TIME TO DO ...

Consider a situation where you are a language teacher and you want to investigate your own students' perceptions and attitudes towards oral activities in class. What type of interview will you use, structured, semi-structured, or unstructured? How will you take the halo effect into consideration while conducting your interviews? Generate a sample list of questions you would ask of your students.

7.2.4 Observations

As Mason (1996) notes, observation usually refers to "methods of generating data which involve the researcher immersing [him or herself] in a research setting, and systematically observing dimensions of that setting, interactions, relationships, actions, events, and so on, within it" (p. 60).

When collecting data using observational techniques, researchers aim to provide careful descriptions of learners' activities without unduly influencing the events in which the learners are engaged. The data are often collected through some combination of field notes (which can involve detailed descriptions of the researcher's intuitions, impressions, and even questions as they emerge) and audio or visual recordings (which allow the researcher to analyze language use in greater depth later and to involve outside researchers in the consideration of the data). In the field of second language research, observations have been used in a wide variety of studies, ranging from naturalistic studies to the rather more common classroom observations that are discussed at length in Chapter 8.

Different types of observations can be identified, depending upon their degree of structure. In highly structured observations, the researcher often utilizes a detailed checklist or rating scale. In a complex L2 environment such as the language school, workplace, or community, a structured observation can facilitate the recording of details such as *when, where*, and *how often* certain types of phenomena occur, allowing the researcher to compare behaviors across research contexts in a principled manner. In less structured observations, the researcher may rely on field notes for detailed descriptions of the phenomena being observed, or transcripts of recordings of those events.

7.2.4.1 Advantages

Observations are useful in that they provide the researcher with the opportunity to collect large amounts of rich data on the participants' behavior and actions within a particular context. Over time and repeated observations, the researcher can gain a deeper and more multilayered understanding of the participants and their context.

7.2.4.2 Caveats

Observations typically do not allow the researcher access to the participants' motivation for their behaviors and actions. For this reason, observations are best combined with one or more of the other methods discussed in this book (see section 7.3.2 on triangulation below). However, perhaps the most serious concern is the "observer's paradox" (Labov, 1972). This refers to the fact that although the goal of most observational research is to collect data as unobtrusively as possible, the presence of an observer can influence the linguistic behavior of those being observed. There is also some possibility of the Hawthorne effect (discussed in Chapters 5 and 8), which may occur when learners perform better due to positive feelings at being included in a study. Simply put, if learners realize that they are under observation, their performances might improve because of the fact of that observation. To minimize these threats, researchers should consider the ways in which they may influence an L2 setting and take steps to mitigate the effect of their presence. For example, if the goal of a study involves observing the use of a second language among immigrants in their workplace, researchers may try to blend into the background of the workplace to make the participants more accustomed to their presence. Another less obtrusive option is participant observation, where researchers are members of the group they are observing. They play a dual role of observing while fully participating in activities with other group members. While participant observation can limit the effects of the observer's paradox, it can also be difficult to both observe and participate, as discussed above. Participant observation is generally most feasible in adult learning contexts where the researcher can easily blend in—for example, in conversation or language exchange clubs. Ethical issues related to participant observations also need to be considered. It is important to keep issues related to partial and full disclosure of the goals of a study in mind, as discussed in Chapter 2.

7.2.5 Diaries/Journals

Since learners' reports about their internal processes and thoughts can be elicited by carefully tailoring the questions researchers choose to ask, verbal protocols and other introspective methods are often used to gather data for qualitative studies (see Chapter 3 for additional discussion of verbal protocols). Second language diaries, also referred to as L2 journals or learner autobiographies, can also be used to allow learners and language professionals (and teachers, as discussed in Chapter 8 on classroom research) to write about their language learning experiences without the constraints imposed by specific questions.

One well-known diary study in the second language research field is Schmidt and Frota's (1986) research on the language-learning diary of one of their own experiences learning Portuguese in Brazil. Schmidt used a diary to record his language learning experiences in classes of Portuguese as a second language as well as in his daily interactions while living in Brazil. His diary included the specific second language forms that he was taught in class, as well as those he observed during conversations and those that he found himself using. Additionally, he met with his co-researcher, a native speaker of Portuguese, for periodic communicative second language testing. Through an examination of the diary entries and results of the testing, he was able to detect an interesting pattern: Schmidt consistently consciously noticed forms in the input shortly before acquiring them. Another often-cited study in the second language research field is the work of Schumann and Schumann (1977), who reported on diaries they kept as they attempted to learn Arabic in North Africa at the introductory level, and as they learnt Persian (Farsi) in a U.S. University setting as well as in Iran as intermediate-level learners. Schumann and Schumann remark that the diary itself is "a possible vehicle for facilitating the language learning process" (p. 241). They also point out that the detailed records of emotional issues, such as transition anxiety, found in their diaries suggest that individual variables can promote or inhibit second language learning. On the topic of transition anxiety and second language learning, one of their diary entries reveals, "I found one reasonably effective way to control this stress during travel to the foreign country. En route to Tunisia and during the first week or so after arrival, I devoted every free minute to working through an elementary Arabic reader . . . Learning more of the language gave me a sense of satisfaction and accomplishment that went a long way toward counter-acting the anxiety" (p. 246). Other diary studies in second language research involve researchers analyzing the diaries of language learners, often in instructed settings.

TIME TO THINK ...

Why do you think both Schmidt and Frota (1986) and Schumann and Schumann (1977) involve a researcher participating in their own diary study?

7.2.5.1 Advantages

In many diary studies, learners are able to record their impressions or perceptions about learning, unconstrained by predetermined areas of interest. This form of data collection can yield insights into the language learning process that may be inaccessible from the researcher's perspective alone. Even in studies where researchers provide a structure for the diarists to follow (such as certain topics to address and guidelines for the content), the researchers are still able to access the phenomena under investigation from a viewpoint other than their own. In addition, since diary entries can be completed according to the participants' own schedules, this approach to data collection allows for greater flexibility than, for example, observations and interviews, which must be scheduled to fit the time constraints of multiple individuals. Bailey's (1983, 1990) work provides a classic introduction to the use of diaries in second language research.

7.2.5.2 Caveats

One of the concerns with diary research is that keeping a diary requires a commitment on the part of the participants to frequently and regularly provide detailed accounts of their thoughts about language learning. As this is often a significant burden to place on study participants, many researchers participate in their own diary studies. However, it is important to note that while the diaries of second language researchers have yielded interesting insights, this is a highly specialized population, and the insights from these studies cannot often be extended to other contexts. Another potential complication is that due to the lack of structure of diary entries, data analysis can become a complex affair, making it more difficult for researchers to find and validate patterns in the data.

7.3 ANALYZING QUALITATIVE DATA

In this section, we discuss approaches that are often used to guide the analysis of qualitative data. We also address three important issues in qualitative data analysis (credibility, transferability, and dependability), as well as methods for ensuring that a qualitative study possesses these characteristics.

In analyzing qualitative data, researchers often make use of cyclical data analysis. This refers to the process of data collection followed by data analysis and a hypothesis-formation stage utilizing the first round of data collection, followed by a second and more focused round of data collection where hypotheses are tested and further refined. The process continues until a rich and full picture of the data is obtained. Thus with qualitative research, data analysis is not a discrete stage, but is integrated throughout the process (Friedman, 2012). Watson-Gegeo (1988, 1997) divides cyclical data analysis into three distinct stages:

- comprehensive—where all possible aspects of a chosen context are researched;

- topic-oriented—where the topic is clarified through preliminary analysis and focused data collection; and
- hypothesis-oriented—where hypotheses are generated based on data.

The hypotheses are then tested through further focused and structured interviews, observations, and systematic analysis. In short, cyclical research is the process by which researchers bring increasing focus to their topic of interest.

A similar approach that guides qualitative data analysis is known as grounded theory. This also involves developing theory based on, or grounded in, data that have been systematically gathered and analyzed. Grounded theory attempts to avoid placing preconceived notions on the data, with researchers preferring to let the data guide the analysis. Using grounded theory, researchers often aim to examine data from multiple vantage points to help them arrive at a more complete picture of the phenomena under investigation.

In inductive data analysis, the goal is generally for research findings to emerge from the frequent, dominant, or significant themes within the raw data, without imposing restraints as is the case with predetermined coding (see Baralt, 2012) or analysis schemes. Inductive data analysis is determined by multiple examinations and interpretations of the data in the light of the research objectives, with the categories induced from the data. The framework for analysis is often shaped by the assumptions and experiences of the individual researcher.

7.3.1 Credibility, Transferability, Confirmability, and Dependability

In analyzing qualitative data, researchers must pay attention to three concerns that arise as part of the research: credibility, transferability, and dependability.[1]

In terms of credibility, because qualitative research can be based on the assumption of multiple, constructed realities, it may be more important for qualitative researchers to demonstrate that their findings are credible to their research population. Fraenkel and Wallen (2003) suggest several techniques to enhance credibility, including continuing the data collection over a long enough period of time to ensure that the participants have become used to the researcher and are behaving naturally. They also suggest collecting data in as many contexts and situations as possible to make certain that the picture provided in the research is as full and complete as it can be.

For transferability in qualitative research, the research context is seen as integral. While qualitative research findings are rarely *directly* transferable from one context to another, the extent to which findings may be transferred depends on the similarity of the context. Important for determining similarity of context is the method of reporting known as "thick description," which refers to the process of using multiple perspectives to explain the insights gleaned from a study, and taking into account the actors' interpretations of their actions and the speakers' interpretations of their speech. Davis (1995) distinguishes three essential components of thick description:

1. particular description (representative examples from the data);
2. general description (information about the patterns in the data); and
3. interpretive commentary (explanation of the phenomena researched and interpretation of the meaning of the findings with respect to previous research).

The idea behind thick description is that if researchers report their findings including sufficient detail for readers to understand the characteristics of the research context and participants, the audience will be able to compare the research situation with their own and thus determine which findings may be appropriately transferred to their setting. Other steps can be taken to augment the transferability of research.

For confirmability, researchers are required to make available full details of the data on which they are basing their claims or interpretations. This is similar to the concept of replicability in quantitative research, with the point being that another researcher should be able to examine the data and confirm, modify, or reject the first researcher's interpretations.

For dependability, researchers aim to fully characterize the research context and the relationships among the participants. To enhance dependability, researchers may ask the participants themselves to review the patterns in the data. Electronically recorded data can help to recreate the data collection context and allow the researcher to make use of all interpretive cues necessary to draw inferences and evaluate the dependability of the inferences that have been drawn. Recordings can also help research participants and other researchers working in similar contexts to assess whether dependable inferences have been drawn from the data.

TIME TO DO ...

Conduct a library search for a qualitative study in your area of interest. Evaluate the credibility and transferability of the results of the study. How does the author(s) deal with these issues in the discussion of the findings? What reporting technique is used? Could it be characterized as rich or thick?

7.3.2 Triangulation

Triangulation involves using multiple research techniques and multiple sources of data in order to explore the issues from all feasible perspectives. Using the technique of triangulation can aid in credibility, transferability, and dependability of qualitative research. Different types of triangulation have been identified, including theoretical triangulation (using multiple perspectives to analyze the same set of data), investigator triangulation (using multiple observers or interviewers), and methodological triangulation (using different measures or research methods to investigate a particular phenomenon). The most common definition of triangulation, however, is that it entails the use of multiple, independent methods of obtaining data in a single investigation in order to arrive at the same research findings.

As Johnson (1992) notes, "the value of triangulation is that it reduces observer or interviewer bias and enhances the validity and reliability (accuracy) of the information" (p. 146). By collecting data through a variety of means, the researcher helps address many of the concerns with the various qualitative data collection methods that were pointed out earlier in this chapter. One method alone cannot provide adequate support. It may take two or more independent sources to support the study and its conclusions.

For example, in their study of the effects of training on peer revision processes in second language writing, McGroarty and Zhu (1997) assessed the effects of training in terms of: (1) students' ability to critique peer writing; (2) quality of student writing; and (3) students' attitudes toward peer revision and writing in general. Their experiment included four instructors and 169 students, with each instructor teaching one class in the experimental condition, which included training for peer revision via instructor conferences, and one class in the control condition, which employed peer revision without such training. Their research used a range of different measures, data sources, and methods. The authors pointed out that "the combination of measures, data sources, and methods not only allowed triangulation of the finding that training for peer revision improves students' ability to critique peer writing and their attitudes toward peer revision, but also illuminated other aspects of peer revision processes" (p. 2). We return to this discussion in Chapter 9.

TIME TO DO ...

Imagine that you are a researcher interested in investigating how two children enrolled in a bilingual immersion class at the elementary level respond to corrective feedback provided by their ESL teacher. What method(s) would you employ to gather information about this topic? How would you go about triangulating your findings?

7.3.3 The Role of Quantification in Qualitative Research

As we saw above, some qualitative researchers make use of cyclical data analysis, examining patterns of occurrence in their data and then using them to draw inferences and recursively generate and test hypotheses. Although some qualitative researchers eschew the practice of quantification, others are interested in patterns of occurrence and do not exclude the use of the sorts of numbers and statistics that are usually found in quantitative research. Quantification can play a role both in the generation of hypotheses and in the verification of patterns that have been noticed; it can also be used later for the purpose of data reporting.

For example, in Qi and Lapkin's (2001) case study exploring the relationship between quality of noticing, written feedback processing, and revision, they coded two learners' verbal protocols in terms of "language-related episodes" and used quantification to conclude tentatively that higher-proficiency learners may be better able to make use of feedback than lower-proficiency learners. They also suggested that quality of noticing was directly related to L2 writing improvement and that reformulation may be a better technique than error correction in helping learners to notice the gap and produce more accurate language.

While quantification can assuredly be helpful in the generation of hypotheses and detection of patterns, its practicality is especially evident when the time comes for communicating the findings through publication. As a simple, concise way of reporting general research findings, quantification of some kind is used by many qualitative researchers, who commonly gather enough data to fill a book, to pare down their data and findings to a length that conforms to publication requirements. Quantification is also valuable in that numerical descriptions can make it readily apparent both why researchers have drawn particular inferences and how well their theories reflect the data. Another benefit of quantification is its usefulness to other researchers who may be interested in ascertaining quickly whether the research findings are relevant to other contexts.

7.4 CONCLUSION

In this chapter, we have contrasted qualitative research with other approaches and discussed common methods used for qualitative data collection. We have also addressed key issues in carrying out qualitative research, including credibility, transferability, dependability, triangulation, and quantification. As we have seen, qualitative research can yield valuable and unique insights into the second language learning process. When appropriate qualitative research methods are chosen to address a particular problem, and when the proper standards of empirical rigor are met through triangulation of research perspectives, consideration of emic perspectives, and cyclical data collection and analysis, qualitative research can reliably help us to gain a deeper understanding of the nature of second language learning.

POINTS TO REMEMBER

- Qualitative research refers to research that is based on descriptive data that does not make (regular) use of statistical procedures.

- Split or multiple-methods research employs both quantitative and qualitative data in the same report.

- Ethnographic research aims to carry out research from the participants' point of view, using categories relevant to a particular group and cultural system.

- Case studies provide detailed descriptions of specific learners (or sometimes classes) within their learning setting typically utilizing a longitudinal approach.

- Interviews can be employed to gather data for qualitative research and can take the form of structured, semi-structured, or unstructured interviews.

- With observational techniques, researchers aim to provide careful descriptions of learners' activities without unduly influencing the events in which the learners are engaged. Data are collected through some combination of field notes and audio or visual recordings.

- Second language diaries, also referred to as L2 journals or learner autobiographies, are used in qualitative research to allow learners and language professionals to write about their language learning experiences without the constraints imposed by specific questions.

- Cyclical research is the process by which researchers bring increasing focus to their topic of interest through rounds of data collection, analyses, and hypothesis formation.

- Grounded theory involves developing theory based on, or grounded in, data that have been systematically gathered and analyzed where the data guide the analysis.

- In analyzing qualitative data, issues of credibility, transferability, confirmability, and dependability must be taken into account just as internal and external validity are in quantitative research.

- Triangulation involves using multiple research techniques and multiple sources of data in order to explore the issues from all feasible perspectives.

MORE TO DO AND MORE TO THINK ABOUT ...

1. Jick (1984) argued that qualitative and quantitative approaches to research should be viewed "as complementary rather than as rival camps" (p. 135). Based on the information you have read in this chapter and your own ideas, why would this comment be valuable to keep in mind in designing a second language case study of two adult learners acquiring English as a Second Language in their place of employment, an inner-city restaurant kitchen?

2. What is a *split (or combination) methods* study and what are some of the advantages of taking this approach?

3. Take a look at the following chart. Based on the information in the chapter and your own ideas, what are the benefits and limitations of each method? Also, in the far right-hand column, provide suggestions for how some of the limitations could be addressed or mitigated.

Method	Benefits	Limitations	Addressing Limitations
Ethnographics			
Case studies			
Interviews			
Observations			
Diaries/Journals			

4. Choose three of the methods above. For each, find a research report that makes use of this method. To what extent do you think the method was appropriate to the research question?

5. Provide thumbnail definitions for *credibility, transferability*, and *dependability*. Why are these important for qualitative studies?

6. What are *cyclical data analysis* and *grounded theory*? How do these approaches to qualitative data collection and analysis differ from those taken in quantitative studies?

7. Why might qualitative researchers choose to employ quantification?

8. In both qualitative and quantitative studies, it is important to discuss the role of the researcher in the data collection process. However, why would this be especially important in a qualitative study?

9. Think about your own research interests for a moment. If you were considering taking a qualitative approach to investigating your topic, how would you begin your study? In particular, think about: (a) your research question and how it might change over the course of gathering data; (b) what methods you would use to collect data; and (c) what conclusions you could draw from those data.

NOTE

1. In Chapter 5, we discussed the importance of internal and external validity to quantitative research. In qualitative research, the notion of internal validity can be related to credibility, and the notion of external validity to transferability. Although they are related, credibility and transferability differ from validity.

CHAPTER EIGHT

Classroom Research

This chapter addresses common practices in classroom-based research. We begin with a description of classroom observation techniques and a range of observation schemes. We then present three commonly used introspective measures followed by a discussion of some of the practical and logistical considerations involved in carrying out research in L2 classrooms. Finally, we move on to a description and discussion of methodology in three areas of classroom research, the role of instruction in second language development, action research, and aptitude-treatment interaction research.

While classrooms constitute a distinct *context* for research, many of the methodological practices and data collection techniques associated with classroom research are not unique to classroom settings and some are also discussed elsewhere in this book. For example, we discuss diary studies both in Chapter 7 as part of qualitative research methods, and in the current chapter where we focus exclusively on diary use by learners and teachers in second and foreign language classroom contexts. We begin the chapter with a general discussion of the nature of classroom research.

8.1 CLASSROOM RESEARCH CONTEXTS

Traditionally, second language researchers have distinguished between classroom-based research and research conducted in controlled laboratory contexts. Typical laboratory-based research has the advantage of allowing the researcher to tightly control the experimental variables, randomly assign subjects to treatment groups, and employ control groups—all of which are difficult, and sometimes impossible, to implement in classroom-based research contexts.

Such concerns regarding classroom research have led some second language researchers to claim that although laboratory settings are more abstract, the benefits connected with being better able to control and manipulate intervening variables may be worth the potential costs of abstraction (Hulstijn, 1997).

Whether research carried out in the laboratory can (or cannot) be generalized to the L2 classroom is an empirical question. In any case, in light of the complementary strengths and limitations of laboratory and classroom studies, second language researchers are increasingly recognizing that studies must be carried out in different contexts and that a range of different approaches must be used to gain a deeper understanding of the complexity of second language learning. Thus, while classroom research can enhance our understanding of how to effectively improve learners' second language skills, laboratory studies can provide more tightly controlled environments in which to test specific theories about second language development.

Combined approaches to classroom research—that is, those involving a range of different approaches, including both experimental and observational techniques—are also increasingly popular. As long ago as 1991, Allwright and Bailey pointed out that "increasingly it appears, second language classroom researchers are calling for judicious selection and combined approaches rather than rigid adherence to one approach over another" (p. 68). We also believe that research in a wide range of contexts and using multiple methods and techniques is necessary for developments in the ongoing investigation of how second languages are learned and consequently, how languages may best be taught. This is particularly true given today's increasing methodological sophistication. We now turn to a discussion of some of the common data collection techniques used in research set in second language classrooms.

TIME TO THINK ...

Some researchers (e.g., Foster, 1998) have claimed that research findings from laboratory contexts cannot be applied to classroom settings. Do you agree or disagree with this position? Why?

8.2 COMMON TECHNIQUES FOR DATA COLLECTION IN CLASSROOM RESEARCH

8.2.1 Observations

As we discussed in Chapter 7, observational data are common in second language research and observations are a useful means for gathering in-depth information about such phenomena as the types of language, activities, interactions, instruction, and events that occur in second and foreign language classrooms. Additionally, observations can allow the study of a behavior at close range with many important contextual variables present. Here, we will focus on the particular concerns that can arise when carrying out observations in intact classrooms, as well as providing information about the different types of observation schemes that have been developed by second language classroom researchers.

8.2.1.1 Conducting Classroom Observations

Obtrusive Observers

Observation etiquette may initially seem secondary to the more practical nuts and bolts of carrying out a thorough observation, but conforming to good observation etiquette is essential. Any observer in the classroom runs the risk of being an obtrusive observer, which can be problematic for research. An obtrusive observer's presence may be felt in the classroom to the extent that the events observed cannot be said to be fully representative of the class in its typical behavior, and therefore the observation data may have limited validity (we also discuss this in Chapter 7 as the observer's paradox).

An obtrusive observer may also be problematic for the instructor and students in terms of compromising the quality of the lesson, preventing instructors from delivering the lesson to the best of their ability, and, consequently, preventing the students from learning to the best of theirs. For example, younger learners in particular can become very easily distracted by observers. They may be interested in playing with the recording equipment and may pay more attention to a new person in their classroom with equipment like a lavaliere microphone than to their instructor.

The Hawthorne Effect

Another potential problem for observational research is the so-called Hawthorne effect, also discussed in Chapters 5 and 7. This effect was first described by observers at the Hawthorne, Chicago branch of the Western Electric Company (Brown, 1954; Mayo, 1933). When the observers were present, the productivity of workers increased regardless of whether or not there were positive changes in working conditions. The workers were apparently happy to receive attention from researchers who expressed an interest in them by observing them, and this impacted their behavior. Accordingly, while in observational research it may be difficult to be sure that the observed classes are the same as they would be without the observation, in controlled research it may be difficult to separate

Hawthorne effects from experimental variables. Although Hawthorne effects in management have been queried by some (e.g., Adair, 1984), including those who have pointed to the small number of participants in the original study, educationalists usually make efforts to take such effects into account when conducting observations. For example, as mentioned in Chapter 6, Mellow et al. (1996) argue that time-series designs are particularly useful for investigating and evaluating different approaches to second language teaching, pointing out that one of their benefits is that they may reduce the Hawthorne effect as students and teachers begin to feel more comfortable and natural about being observed.

Objectivity and Subjectivity

Classroom observations are not only conducted by researchers external to the school or educational environment. Instructors often observe each other's classes for professional development as well as for research purposes, and they may also carry out observations of their own classes, usually using audio or videotapes to assist with this process. This brings us to another consideration that needs to be taken into account when conducting observations: namely, the level of objectivity or subjectivity of the observer. The level and impact of this on the study is often debated and needs to be clearly recognized and reported in research. While objectivity is typically valued in second language research, particularly in experimental work, both objectivity and subjectivity have their respective roles in research on second language learning. Therefore, in classroom studies, it is necessary for researchers both to strive for objectivity and also to be aware of the subjective elements in that effort—for example, in how they gather data, analyze data, and report the results of analyses.

TIME TO DO ...

Imagine teaching Spanish to L1 English-speaking elementary school students. You are interested in conducting a study on the impact of instruction on your own students' acquisition of vocabulary. How would you strive to maintain objectivity and subjectivity? How will you limit the Hawthorne effect? Brainstorm a method for gathering data with these ideas in mind.

Obtaining Permission to Observe and Enlisting the Help of the Instructor

In addition to keeping issues of objectivity and subjectivity in mind, there are several further precautions for observers to take into account. First of all, it is

241

important to obtain the permission of the instructor to observe the class well in advance of the scheduled observation(s). This is, of course, not only a professional courtesy, but may also help the instructor to lessen any impact of the observation on their lesson planning and implementation. When working with schools and language programs, the researcher should not assume that the permission of administrators indicates that individual classroom instructors have been informed and that their instructional schedules have been considered. It is important to contact the instructor in advance in order to obtain consent and to negotiate the schedule and observation process. It is also important to seek the instructor's input about matters such as when to arrive. For example, arriving a little before the learners, or at the same time, or during an activity when their attention will be focused elsewhere, can all be options for lessening the impact of the observer. The instructor may also have the best idea about where the observer can sit in the classroom so as to be minimally intrusive. Some instructors prefer observers to sit in the back or off to the side of the class, and some may recommend that researchers begin coming to class several days before they conduct the research in order to habituate the students to their presence. Instructors may feel that by minimizing the presence of the observer, their students will not become distracted by note taking or the direction of the observer's gaze or equipment, and will concentrate on the lesson.

For some classes, students may be used to the occasional presence of a supervisor or instructor-trainer, and little explanation will need to be provided. However, other classes, especially those early in the semester or program, may never have experienced an observer before. For these classes, depending on the research problem being studied, it might be possible to introduce the researcher into the classroom so that they participate in the instructional activities and are seen as an instructor's aid. Another reason to be sure to have made personal contact with the instructor beforehand is that having more than one observer in the classroom at any time could be disruptive for the instruction, and the instructor is usually in the best position to know the schedule for who plans to observe and when. If the observation is to be ongoing, it may also be wise to ask the instructor for feedback after the class in case they would prefer something to be done differently the next time around. Murphy (1992) recommends that observers who are there for research purposes keep in mind that their role is not to judge, evaluate, criticize, or offer constructive advice, and also that if asked by the learners what they are doing in the classroom, observers keep their responses as short as possible.

Debriefing the Instructor

It is also important as part of the negotiation surrounding the observation process to debrief the instructor about the research findings or the content of the observation notes or scheme. Timing is also an important consideration here.

For example, researchers might provide instructors with a copy of their notes after each lesson or arrange a time to meet in order to discuss the research. By keeping the observation process as transparent and interactive as possible, researchers can often establish a more trusting and cooperative relationship with instructors. Of course, in some cases, the instructors may be the focus of the research, or it may unduly influence the research if they are kept continually debriefed. In these cases, it may be preferable to make such contact after the project has been completed.

Finally, of course, it is always important to thank the instructor for allowing the observation, together with any other parties who have been helpful to the research, including both administrators and students. It can be easy to overlook such simple things, but in fostering good relationships between instructors and future researchers, the importance of expressing courtesy and appreciation cannot be overstated. As such, when research is published with acknowledgments made to schools, principals, instructors, and students, it is helpful to send copies of the publication to the schools and instructors since they may not have access to the same journals and publications as the researcher.

Helpful checklist to consider in setting up observations

- Contact the classroom instructor (in person if possible).
- Determine the schedule for observation.
- Negotiate the observer's role in the classroom, including regular pre-visits, arrival time, introductions, and seating arrangements.
- Debrief the instructor (either during or after the observational period) on the findings of the study.
- Clearly express appreciation to the instructor, students, and administration.

8.2.1.2 Observation Procedures and Coding Schemes

When considering observation procedures and coding schemes, the first critical step is to carefully consider the goals of the research and the observation. If an existing observation procedure or coding scheme can be used or adapted, this can prevent duplication of effort in developing new schemes. Readily available observation schemes address a wide range of classroom phenomena, and a number of observation schemes have been developed for researchers working in L2 classrooms (schemes have been developed by Allen, Fröhlich, & Spada, 1984; Fanselow, 1977; Mitchell, Parkinson, & Johnstone, 1981; Moskowitz, 1967, 1970; Nunan, 1989; Sinclair & Coulthard, 1975; Ullman & Geva, 1983).

Existing coding schemes can vary considerably in their organization and complexity, ranging from simple checklists and tallies of behaviors to highly complex schemes for judging the meaning or function of particular behaviors, as well as combination schemes. In their classic book focusing on the second language classroom, Allwright and Bailey (1991) provide examples of seven different published coding schemes (pp. 202–223). Other useful discussions and examples are provided by Chaudron (1988), Lynch (1996), and McDonough and McDonough (1997).

TIME TO THINK ...

Why might it be important to utilize an observation scheme in classroom-based research? What issues can arise if no observation scheme is employed?

Description of Observation Schemes

In most observation schemes, the observer marks the frequency of an observed behavior or event at a regular time interval; for example, observations may be made of every instructor question or of the students' reactions to the writing on the board every five minutes. In Nunan's (1989) classroom observation tally sheet, for instance, there are categories for such classroom events as the instructor's praise, instructions, and explanations of grammar points, as well as learners' questions, answers, and peer interactions. Categories such as Nunan's are considered low-inference, that is, "clearly enough stated in terms of behavioral characteristics . . . that observers in a real-time coding situation would reach high levels of agreement or reliability" (Chaudron, 1988, pp. 19–20). Nunan's scheme appears in Table 8.1 below.

Other observation schemes incorporate both low-inference and high-inference categories. High-inference categories are those that require judgments, such as the function or meaning of an observed event. For example, the Target Language Observation Scheme (TALOS) (Ullman & Geva, 1985) consists of two parts. The first is a real-time, low-inference checklist for describing live classroom activities (e.g., drills, dialogues, translation, free communication), linguistic content (e.g., sounds, words, phrases, discourse), and skill focus (e.g., reading, writing, listening, speaking), as well as teaching behaviors (e.g., drills, narrations, explanations, comparisons, answers, discipline) and student actions (e.g., types of questions asked). The second part of the observation scheme is a high-inference rating scale to be completed after the observation. Here, the observer

TABLE 8.1 Classroom observation tally sheet from Nunan (1989)

	Tallies	Total
1. Teacher asks a display question (i.e. a question to which she knows the answer)	///	3
2. Teacher asks a referential question (i.e. a question to which she does not know the answer)	////	4
3. Teacher explains a grammatical point		0
4. Teacher explains meaning of a vocabulary item		0
5. Teacher explains functional point		0
6. Teacher explains point relating to the content (theme/topic) of the lesson	/	1
7. Teacher gives instructions/directions	//// /	6
8. Teacher praises	/	1
9. Teacher criticizes		0
10. Learner asks a question	///	3
11. Learner answers question	////	4
12. Learner talks to another learner		0
13. Period of silence or confusion		0

Source: Nunan, D. (1989). *Understanding language classrooms: A guide for instructor initiated action* (p. 78). New York: Prentice Hall. Copyright © 1989 by Prentice Hall. Reprinted with the permission of Prentice Hall. All rights reserved.

provides ratings on a five-point scale (extremely low to extremely high) for categories such as enthusiasm, humor, and negative and positive reinforcement. The TALOS scheme appears in Table 8.2.

The Communicative Orientation of Language Teaching, or COLT, is a similar sort of structured observation scheme (Allen et al., 1984). Developed in the 1980s to describe differences in communicative language teaching, the COLT scheme focuses on pedagogic and verbal behavior in two sections—one section for real-time coding (Part A) and the other section (Part B) for post-observation analysis of recordings. In Part A, more than 40 categories are provided for participant organization and activities, as well as topic type, content, and control. In Part B, the observer is provided with a chart that allows for post-hoc analyses of student-instructor and student-student interaction within various activity types. This observation scheme has been used in original or modified forms in a wide range of classroom studies (e.g., Lightbown & Spada, 1990, 1994; Lyster & Ranta, 1997; Spada & Lightbown, 1993; White et al. 1991). Table 8.3 shows the COLT scheme.

TIME TO DO ...

Consider the following examples and decide if they represent high or low-inference observations:

- Use of humor extremely high
- Peer-to-peer interaction
- Explicit instruction of a grammar point
- Effective use of positive reinforcement
- Use of L1 by students

In Lyster and Ranta's (1997) study of corrective feedback and learner uptake, they examined four immersion classrooms, with their transcripts totaling 18.3 hours of classroom interaction. They note that:

> although the teachers knew we were interested in recording classroom interaction, they were unaware of our research focus related to classroom feedback. The teachers continued with their regular program while recordings were being made, and one or more observers coded classroom activities using Part A of the Communicative Orientation to Language Teaching coding scheme (Spada & Fröhlich, 1995), which we had adapted for use in immersion classrooms. Because we were interested in analyzing teacher behaviour in this first phase of a larger program of research, we focused exclusively in our analyses on teacher-student interaction . . .
>
> (p. 43)

This illustrates Lyster and Ranta's (1997) research process. First, they identified a helpful starting point for their observation scheme, the COLT. Then they adapted it to their particular immersion classroom context. Finally, they narrowed their focus to teacher-student interactions only.

Although classroom observation coding schemes vary considerably, some common elements may be identified. For example, many schemes include a category relating to the identity of the participants and their groupings (e.g., small or large groups). Most schemes also have categories for the content or topic of the lesson, as well as the types of activities and materials used. There may also be categories dealing with the language employed during an activity or event (e.g., L1 or L2) and the targeted skill. Depending on the researcher's particular goals and questions, the scheme may additionally include categories for marking the frequency or duration of targeted activities or behaviors. Observation schemes may be used to code broad categories related to classroom instruction, or they may be focused on specific characteristics of a single classroom phenomenon.

TABLE 8.2 The TALOS observation scheme

Expanding Evaluation Perspective The High-Inference TALOS	Extremely low	Low	Fair	High	Extremely high
Teacher					
Use of L_1	0	1	2	3	4
Use of L_2	0	1	2	3	4
teacher talk time	0	1	2	3	4
explicit lesson structure	0	1	2	3	4
task orientation	0	1	2	3	4
clarity	0	1	2	3	4
initiate problem solving	0	1	2	3	4
personalized questions and comments	0	1	2	3	4
positive reinforcement	0	1	2	3	4
negative reinforcement	0	1	2	3	4
corrections	0	1	2	3	4
pacing	0	1	2	3	4
use of audio-visual aids	0	1	2	3	4
gestures	0	1	2	3	4
humour	0	1	2	3	4
enthusiasm	0	1	2	3	4
Students					
Use of L_1 on task	0	1	2	3	4
Use of L_2 on task	0	1	2	3	4
student talk time on task	0	1	2	3	4
initiate problem solving	0	1	2	3	4
comprehension	0	1	2	3	4
attention	0	1	2	3	4
participation	0	1	2	3	4
personalized questions & comments	0	1	2	3	4
positive effect	0	1	2	3	4
negative effect	0	1	2	3	4
S to S interaction on task	0	1	2	3	4
Program					
linguistic appropriateness	0	1	2	3	4
content appropriateness	0	1	2	3	4
depth	0	1	2	3	4
variety	0	1	2	3	4
listening skill focus	0	1	2	3	4
speaking skill focus	0	1	2	3	4
reading skill focus	0	1	2	3	4
writing skill focus	0	1	2	3	4
formal properties	0	1	2	3	4
functional properties	0	1	2	3	4
integration with general curriculum	0	1	2	3	4

Source: Ullmann, R., & Geva, E. (1985). Expanding our evaluation perspective: What can classroom observation tell us about Core French Programs? *The Canadian Modern Language Review, 42*(2), 319–322. Reprinted with permission from University of Toronto Press (www.utpjournals.com).

TABLE 8.3 The COLT scheme

COLT PART A
Communicative Orientation of Language Teaching Observation Scheme

School   Grade   Observer

Teacher   Lesson (min.)   Visit No.

Subject   Date   Page

Time	Activities and Episodes	Participant Organisation							Content									Content Control			Student Modality					Materials							
		Class			Group		Indiv.		Manag.		Language				Other topics		Teacher/Text	Teacher/Text/Stud.	Student	Listening	Speaking	Reading	Writing	Other	Type Text		Audio	Visual	Source			
		T □ S/C	S □ S/C	Choral	Same task	Different tasks	Same task	Different tasks	Procedure	Discipline	Form	Function	Discourse	Sociling	Narrow	Broad									Minimal	Extended			L2-NNS	L2-NS	L2-NSA	Student-made
	2	3	4	5	6	7	8	9	10	11	12	13	14	15	16	17	18	19	20	21	22	23	24	25	26	27	28	29	30	31	32	33
1																																

TABLE 8.3 The COLT scheme

COLT PART B: COMMUNICATIVE FEATURES
Communicative Orientation of Language Teaching Observation Scheme

School
Teacher

Subject

Date of visit
Coder

Teacher Interaction

Category	Subcategory	Feature	No.
Off task			1
Target language gap		L1	2
		L2	3
Informaton gap	Giving info.	Predict.	4
		Unpred.	5
	Request info.	Pseudo requ.	6
		Genuine requ.	7
Sustained speech		Minimal	8
		Sustained	9
Reaction to form/ message	Incorporation of student utterences	Form	10
		Message	11
		Correction	12
		Repetition	13
		Paraphrase	14
		Comment	15
		Expansion	16
		Clarif. request	17
		Elab. request	18
Discourse initiation			19

Student Verbal Interaction

Category	Subcategory	Feature	No.
Target language		L1	20
		L2	21
Informaton gap	Giving info.	Predict.	22
		Unpred.	23
	Request info.	Pseudo requ.	24
		Genuine requ.	25
Sustained speech		Minimal	26
		Sustained	27
		Form	28
Form restriction		Message	29
		Correction	30
		Repetition	31
Reaction to form/ message	Incorporation of student utterences	Paraphrase	32
		Comment	33
		Expansion	34
		Clarif. request	35
		Elab. request	36
Sustained speech	Incorporation of student utterences	Minimal	37
		Sustained	38
		Form	39
		Message	40

As illustrated in Table 8.4 below, there are many possible categories that could be included in even the most focused observation scheme, and it is unlikely that any one scheme could capture all the potentially relevant aspects of information about classroom events. Table 8.4 shows a sample observation scheme that could be used in a study of feedback in second language classrooms. There is increased interest, mostly in ESL classes, in the presence and benefits of feedback in classroom settings (e.g., Doughty & Varela, 1998; R. Ellis, 2000; Mackey, 2000; Oliver, 2000; Samuda, 2001; Williams, 1999). One way to code data in this context is to use a scheme, such as the following, to determine the frequency of the provision and use of feedback by instructors and students in Japanese EFL classes. The highly structured nature of the scheme would also allow the researcher to compare the frequency of feedback types, feedback focus, and uptake in classes at different institutions or among learners with different ages or different language abilities.

By making tallies and notes on the sample observation sheet given in Table 8.4, a researcher could record the sources and types of feedback, the linguistic objects of the feedback (i.e., the errors), and what sort of uptake has occurred, if any. There is space for examples of any of these categories, together with space to note how many times they occur in units of 10 minutes.

The text in the box below briefly notes some of the advantages of using or modifying existing observation schemes, followed by a more in-depth discussion of some important caveats in the next section.

Advantages of using or modifying existing observation schemes

- Relative ease of use when compared with non-systematic classroom descriptions with no preexisting guidelines or descriptions of data based on the schemes.
- Comparability with other studies, with a potentially concomitant increase in the generalizability of the research.
- Simplified analysis of complicated and rich, but possibly overwhelming, classroom data.
- Possibility of measuring change or status over different time periods.
- More reliable focus of the researcher's attention on facets of the instruction related to the research problem.
- Imposition of regularity on classroom observations, allowing researchers to systematically compare instruction in different classroom contexts.

TABLE 8.4 Possible categories to include in a feedback-focused observation tally scheme

	Instances per ten-minute intervals (present/absent)				Notes:
Source of feedback: • Instructor • Student • Other (note at right)					Other feedback sources
Type of feedback: • Recast • Metalinguistic explanation • Confirmation check • Clarification request • Repetition • Nonverbal cue • Other (note at right)					Notes: Other examples of feedback types
Target of feedback: • Lexical item • Pronunciation • Morphology • Syntax • Pragmatics • Other (note at right)					Notes: Other examples of student errors
Feedback uptake: • Feedback incorporated into next utterance • Feedback incorporated later utterance • No opportunity for feedback incorporation • Ignored feedback					Notes: Other examples of uptake

Caveats to Using or Modifying Existing Observation Schemes

In general, when evaluating, selecting, adapting, or devising an observational coding scheme, there are several questions regarding potential limitations that the researcher should keep in mind. Most importantly, as with any elicitation technique, it is necessary to determine whether the scheme is appropriate for the research goals. To determine this, the researcher should consider whether the scheme has a clear focus that is relevant to the research questions. For example, a scheme focused on instructor-learner dialogues may not allow a researcher to adequately characterize the nature of language use in the classroom if the research question is focused primarily on small-group dynamics in the L2 classroom. In this case, the observation scheme would have to be adapted. Observation schemes can promote valid findings only when they are appropriate and applicable to the research question. Additionally, researchers should consider the type of findings that are likely to emerge from an observation scheme. If the research question goes beyond descriptions of behaviors, for instance, an observation scheme based on low-inference categories is not likely to highlight the items of interest in the data.

Another consideration is the use of time as a unit in an observation scheme. If the overall occurrence of a phenomenon is of interest (e.g., how many times an instructor recasts learner utterances), then a category system such as the COLT is most appropriate. In a category system, the observer checks a behavior each time it occurs in order to record its frequency. Alternatively, if the distribution of a phenomenon throughout the class is of interest, the observer can employ a sign system, in which an observation is made at regular intervals of time. Also, it is important to note that unless more than one observer is present in the classroom, or the data are videotaped and later replayed for a second person, with most coding schemes only one rater observes (and at the same time codes) the data. Issues of coding and inter-rater reliability were discussed in Chapter 4.

TIME TO THINK ...

Suppose you are investigating how often and in what contexts students use their L1 in a second language classroom.

What type of coding scheme would you implement in this case? Why?

By helping to ensure not only that relevant aspects of the classroom lesson are noted and remembered, but also that significant patterns of interaction are identified, observation schemes have allowed researchers to gain a deeper understanding of the inner workings of second language classrooms. However, some researchers have argued that the use of observation schemes with their predetermined categories "seriously limits and restricts the observer's perceptions—that it creates a kind of tunnel vision because the observer sees only those behaviors that coincide with the categories in the observation scheme" and may fail to observe other important features (Spada, 1994, p. 687). As we discussed in Chapter 4, the coding scheme may result in data reduction, where potentially important patterns are missed. As one simple example, making an observation every five minutes ignores the potentially rich events that occur in between. In addition, even the most thorough observation schemes cannot allow the researcher to reach conclusions about what the participants themselves are experiencing. Another criticism leveled at observation schemes is that there is insufficient evidence showing that the categories are valid predictors of learning processes and outcomes. One way to address such criticisms may be to record the classroom data and then to develop custom-made coding schemes based on the observations, with the coding developing out of the observations. Custom-made schemes are further discussed in Chapter 4 and coding where categories emerge from the data are further discussed in Chapter 7. Whether customized or preexisting schemes are used, additional data-gathering methods may be useful in order to triangulate classroom data and provide multiple perspectives by accessing the learners' insights into the events that have been observed.

8.3 INTROSPECTIVE METHODS IN CLASSROOM RESEARCH

Introspective methods, or data elicitation techniques that encourage learners to communicate their internal processing and perspectives about language learning experiences, can afford researchers access to information unavailable from observational approaches. In second language research, a range of intro-spective methods have been employed. These methods vary with respect to the practicality of their application to classroom research. Uptake sheets, for example, described in the next section, allow researchers to investigate learners' perceptions about what they are learning. Stimulated recalls (see also Chapter 3) may yield insights into a learner's thought processes during learning experiences, while diaries (discussed in Chapter 7) can present a more comprehensive view of the learning context from a participant's viewpoint. The following discussion provides an overview of the use of some introspective methods that are particularly relevant in second language classrooms and discusses the advantages and applicability of each.

8.3.1 Uptake Sheets

One way to elicit learners' perspectives on second language classroom events is through the use of uptake sheets. Uptake sheets were initially developed as a method of data collection following Allwright's (1984a, 1984b, 1987) interest in learners' perceptions about what they learned in their language classes. He collected learners' reports about their learning, which he termed "uptake" or "whatever it is that learners get from all the language learning opportunities language lessons make available to them" (Allwright, 1987, p. 97). In classroom research, uptake sheets are often distributed at the beginning of the lesson, and learners are asked to mark or note things that the researcher or teacher is focusing on. Whether used to uncover information about learning, noticing, attitudes, or a range of other interesting phenomena, uptake sheets can allow researchers to compare their own observations and other triangulated data with information obtained from the learners, creating a more detailed picture of classroom events in the process.

An example of an uptake chart can be found in Table 8.5. This sheet is designed for classroom learners to fill out during a lesson or activity by a teacher or researcher who wanted to elicit information about what learners were noticing about second language form.

In their study of the effects of different uptake sheet formats on learner reports about their learning, Mackey et al. (2001) asked learners to mark uptake sheets in order to address research questions focusing on the relationship between the format of the uptake sheet and the quantity and quality of learner reporting. Learners were asked on all three formats to indicate "(a) which language forms or concepts they noticed, for example, pronunciation, grammar, vocabulary, or business; (b) who produced the reported items, for example, the learner, the instructor, or their classmates; and (c) whether the reported items were new to the learner" (p. 292). The learners in this study were given sheets at the beginning of class for each of six consecutive classes and asked to fill them out as they noticed language forms or concepts during the instruction.

8.3.2 Stimulated Recall

Another way to obtain the perspective of classroom learners is through stimulated recall. In this method, as described in Chapter 3, the observer tapes or video records a lesson for the stimulus, and then plays the tape to a participant, periodically stopping the tape to ask what he or she was thinking at that particular point in time. Stimulated recall can be used to provide the researcher with access to the learners' interpretations of the events that were observed and can be a valuable source of information for researchers interested in viewing a finely

TABLE 8.5 Sample uptake chart

Language focus format

What are you noticing about …	Who said it? (check as many as you want)				Was this **new** to you? (check as many as you want)		
	Teacher	Classmate	Me	Book	Yes, new	No, heard of it	No, knew it
Pronunciation • • • • • •							
Vocabulary • • • • • • •							
Grammar • • • • • •							

detailed picture of the classroom. A detailed account of stimulated recall methodology, as well as considerations in applying it in classroom and laboratory studies, can be found in Gass and Mackey (2000, in press).

Stimulated recall has been used to investigate various aspects of second language classrooms, with one of the early studies being Roberts (1995). Roberts used stimulated recall in a study of learners' recognition of feedback in a university Japanese as a Foreign Language class. He recorded a 50-minute class period, which was viewed several days later by three volunteers from the class. The participants were asked to write down their perceptions about episodes from the tape involving instructor feedback and to note the error being corrected. This study exemplifies one of the contributions that stimulated recall can make to classroom research by allowing researchers to view instruction from the learners' perspectives.

TIME TO DO ...

Compare and contrast stimulated recall and uptake sheets as methods of introspective data elicitation in a second language classroom. What are the advantages and disadvantages of each? Could you use both?

8.3.3 Diary Research in Classroom Contexts

Bailey (1990) defines a diary study as "a first person account of a language learning or teaching experience, documented through regular candid entries in a personal journal and then analyzed for recurrent patterns and salient events" (p. 215). Diaries of classroom contexts can produce useful data on a range of aspects of the second language learning process. These include individual learners' and instructors' insights into their own learning and teaching processes, their self- and other-comparisons, decision-making processes, the process of language development (or not) over time, attitudes towards classroom learning and teaching, the use of language learning strategies, and the recognition and use of feedback. Diary studies have the additional advantage of time sensitivity. Since most diary research is longitudinal, it can illuminate how perceptions develop over time. However, as discussed in Chapter 7 on qualitative research, there are also some drawbacks to the use of diaries, including the highly subjective nature of the data.

In classroom research, some structure can be provided for the diary entries. It is increasingly the case that instructors ask learners to keep diaries as a part of coursework (and even course assessment), where the goal is enhancement of pedagogy. The diaries might be required to address specific points, including how well the learners have followed specific lessons, what is enjoyable, easy, or difficult about the instruction, and their reactions to the instructor and other learners, as well as to specific classroom activities and group and pair work.

Instructor diaries are also common in educational research, and explorations of language instructor diaries are popular in the second language research field. For example, Bailey et al. (1996) used instructor diaries to investigate the role of language-learning and -teaching beliefs in decision-making by student instructors. An examination and comparison of the instructors' diaries indicated that conscious examination of long-held beliefs about language learning helped to shape pedagogical decisions, and that student teaching was experienced differently according to the student instructor's gender, educational background, and language learning experiences. In general, instructors' diaries have tended to focus on classroom experiences, perceptions about student reactions and learning, and instructional decision-making (and decision-changing) where the method matched the goals of the research.

Diary research represents a significant expenditure of time, both for those who write the diaries as well as for the researchers who analyze them. When embarking on diary research, it is important for diary writers to schedule regular times for writing. The quality of the diaries can also be enhanced if the researcher includes guidelines for the range and amount of writing expected per entry or provides sample questions that the writer may want to consider for each entry. Diary writers should be encouraged to keep a notebook, mini audio recorder, or personal digital assistant with them to jot down insights as they occur and transfer them later to the diary (or leave them on tape/disk in the case of oral diaries). They should also be reminded to include examples to illustrate their insights in the diary entries and can be asked to include their own questions about teaching and learning that occur as the research progresses.

Bailey's (1983) survey of journal studies and discussion of her own journal describing her learning of French illustrates such phenomena as the role of self-esteem in second language learning, operationalized as competitiveness and anxiety, as in the following quotations:

> I feel very anxious about this class. I know I am (or can be) a good language learner, but I hate being lost in class. I feel like I'm behind the others and slowing down the pace . . .
>
> (pp. 75–76)

> Today I was panicked in the oral exercise where we had to fill in the blanks with either the past definite or the imperfect. Now I know what ESL students go through with the present perfect and the simple past. How frustrating it is to be looking for adverbial clues in the sentence when I

257

don't even know what the words and phrases mean. I realized that the teacher was going around the room taking the sentences in order so I tried to stay one jump ahead of her by working ahead and using her feedback to the class to obtain confirmation or denial of my hypotheses. Today I felt a little scared. I'm so rusty!

(p. 74)

The analysis of diary data involves a careful and thorough search for patterns in the writing or tapes in order to find recurrent themes of interest. When reviewing the data, it is important to be conscious of one's own beliefs, experiences, and orientations to the question of interest and how these may influence interpretations both of individual diary entries and of the emergent patterns. When diaries from several participants are included in the research, it is important to note not only how many times a phenomenon is noted, but also by whom it is noted. This will help researchers to avoid seeing the experiences of only a few participants as reflective of the experiences of the whole. Similarly, the salience of the phenomena in the diary entries should be considered in order to prevent decontextualized over- or under-emphasis of the above-mentioned points.

8.4 PRACTICAL CONSIDERATIONS IN CLASSROOM RESEARCH

Studies carried out in second language classrooms take a wide variety of forms, ranging from ethnographic work on "naturalistic" classroom discourse or interaction to quasi-experimental studies of the effects of specific instructional practices such as form-focused instruction, extensive reading, and processing instruction. Classroom research has enhanced our understanding of second language learning in a variety of contexts, including second and foreign language contexts, as well as in classes with differing orientations to language teaching. It contributes in important ways to our understanding of both second language learning and second language teaching. However, the process of carrying out classroom research is both complex and time-consuming. The purpose of this section is to detail some of the considerations, logistical and conceptual, that researchers should weigh when designing classroom studies.

8.4.1 Logistical Issues to Consider When Carrying out Classroom Research

Together with decisions about particular data collection methods to use in obtaining data on second language classroom contexts, researchers also need to consider matters of logistics. As mentioned above, conducting observations in classrooms raises a unique set of concerns and issues, and indeed logistical matters in classrooms are quite different from those in laboratories (see Schachter & Gass, 1996, for further discussion).

When observing a classroom, it is common not only to use field or observation notes and/or a coding scheme, but also to triangulate or supplement this method with a mechanical means of recording the lesson, such as audio or video recording. In a laboratory research setting, recording can be a relatively straightforward matter, although the quality required of the recording will differ, of course, depending on the emphasis of the research. However, in classrooms, recording can present a unique set of problems.

First of all, in selecting the most appropriate way to record, the particular nature of the data collection should be considered. For example, the use of microphones is a choice. Many recorders currently available, including apps for smartphones, will provide quality sufficient for transcription and analysis. However, if a very careful phonetic transcription is needed, for example for examining the effects of corrective feedback on Chinese tone acquisition, high quality recordings are needed, and microphones are typically the best way to achieve this. If children are involved, though, not using a microphone may be less distracting and more foolproof, as fewer pieces of equipment (and therefore less possibility for fiddling and equipment malfunction) are involved. However, if the goal is to capture small-group or pair work, or a number of individuals in a classroom, and if participants share a gender and an L1, distinguishing individual voices can be hard, and again, external microphones are often needed. One type of external microphone, the lapel microphone, can make it easier to distinguish the wearer's voice from other voices on a recording. Boom microphones, on the other hand, can capture the speech of several participants. The specific selection of a microphone again will also depend on the nature of the research. If the data collection calls for recording a large class activity, the most sensitive microphone possible should be used. However, if the research involves recording separate, simultaneous group activities, using a very sensitive microphone might pick up talk from both the target group and adjacent groups, making it more difficult to transcribe and analyze the group discussion. In general, if the research question allows grouping or pairing of learners into male/female sets with different L1s, this can make transcription easier.

The research questions may also suggest the appropriateness of video recording (e.g., a study on nonverbal communication). Even if only audio is required, it can be very useful to have a supplementary video—to check non-verbal signals, for example, or as a backup for the audio, to aid in transcription, and so on. When video recording, the focus of the study needs to be carefully considered. More than one recording device might be necessary to capture student interactions in small-group and pair work as well as instructor input. However, more than one device can require more than one operator, and this can double the intrusion into the classroom. Sometimes classrooms are equipped with concealed cameras that allow remote operation. This is the exception rather than the rule, however, and it is important to note that fully informed consent must always be sought. If only one camera is available, it can help to try to place it in a corner of the room so that not only the instructor, but also as many of the students as possible, are captured on tape. In this way, more information can be gathered on the interactions between the instructor and the students and between the students themselves.

When using audio recorders, researchers should keep in mind that as a general rule, it is important to use more than one as a backup in classroom research. This is both to pick up more data and to account for equipment failure or human intervention such as learners turning equipment on and off and so on. It might also be possible to position the recorder near the instructor and place microphones (if available) at various locations in the classroom to pick up the students' voices. Movable chairs and tables are useful in this regard; if there are only a limited number of recorders or microphones, the researcher can arrange the students around whatever equipment is available.

When recording younger children, as noted above, researchers must also keep in mind that any equipment will be novel, interesting, and thus a target for fiddling. One way to help ensure that the equipment will remain intact is to ask colleagues or adult volunteers to come to the class and keep an eye on it. However, again, this may be disruptive for the class and alter its nature. Alternatively, a researcher could start bringing the equipment to the class a few weeks before the observation. In that way, the children could become accustomed to the presence of both the researcher and seeing whatever is being used to record switched on.

In any class, there will also most likely be learners who have not consented (or whose parents have not consented for them) to be recorded. In such cases, it is necessary to make arrangements for these learners to sit behind the recorder so that images of them are not recorded, and away from any microphones that may be placed in the class. They also need to be assured that any recording inadvertently picked up will be deleted wherever possible, and never shared. IRBs, as discussed in Chapter 2, will have their own specific guidelines as to how to best deal with these situations.

TIME TO DO ...

Think of a classroom that you are familiar with. Now, imagine you want to conduct a study with audio and video recording for that classroom. Sketch out where you would position your equipment in the room and explain your decisions.

Other logistical concerns relate to the physical environment of the classroom. In some data-gathering situations, it will be important to ascertain whether or not the chairs and tables are movable, the quality of the acoustics in the classroom, and the availability of writing implements and boards. Issues such as the temperature, light, and the scheduling of breaks can also impact data collection.

Helpful checklist for classroom research logistics

- Select a recording format that will facilitate the ultimate uses of the data (e.g., transcription, analysis, presentation).
- Consider whose voices and actions need to be recorded, as well as how sensitively and distinguishably this needs to be done and in which situations.
- Determine what kinds of microphones and other equipment should be used for these purposes and where they should be placed to collect as much relevant data as possible.
- Supplement your primary recording method with a backup, but try to gauge what is necessary and sufficient for the job in order to avoid equipment malfunction or undue complexity. Pilot testing can help.
- Consider the amount of intrusion in the classroom caused by equipment and equipment operators.
- Take anonymity concerns seriously and act accordingly.
- Plan the physical arrangement beforehand, taking into account the suitability and adaptability of the environment.
- Consider human factors such as the age of the participants and how the equipment may affect them; acclimate participants if necessary.

8.4.2 Problematics

In addition to the logistical concerns arising out of classroom observations, there are other issues that need to be addressed when conducting classroom-based research. In this next section, we will discuss several of the most serious, including dealing with relevant non-participating parties (i.e., parents and administrators), debriefing participants, accessing test scores if necessary, and segmenting the data for presentation.

8.4.2.1 Informed Consent

As detailed in Chapter 2 in the section on informed consent, it is necessary to obtain the consent of all interested parties when conducting research. In the case of classroom-based research, this usually means that consent must be obtained from learners (and their parents if the learners are children), the instructor, and the school administrators. As in all research, all parties must be informed as to the purpose of the research and what participation entails. In classroom research, it is particularly important that potential participants do not feel pressured by their instructors and are assured that non-participation in the research will incur no penalties. As just mentioned, they must also be assured that every effort will be made to accommodate those individuals who do not wish to participate by not using any data inadvertently collected, such as their voices on tape.

8.4.2.2 Debriefing Participants and Facilitators

It is also important that participants—especially parents, instructors, and administrators—be debriefed after the conclusion of the study. Researchers may, for example, wish to send a letter to the parents detailing the results of the study. For administrators, a researcher may also consider setting up a meeting to discuss the results of the research. In this way, they can be assured that the research was beneficial and a worthwhile use of their limited time and resources. While research may not have direct applications that benefit a particular school or language program, any well-designed and well-motivated research project should enhance our understanding of the nature of second language learning, and it may therefore have eventual benefits for second language teaching. Many instructors and administrators appreciate knowing how individual research projects conducted in their context fit into the theory and practice of second language research.

8.4.2.3 Ensuring Confidentiality and Minimizing Disruption

In addition to participant issues, the classroom researcher will also face concerns related to the gathering of data. To triangulate the findings from classroom observations, for instance, the researcher may also wish to obtain test scores or report cards. It is important to remember that student grades are a highly sensitive matter. Permission to view grades or any graded material should be included in the informed consent and discussed with both instructors and administrators, and participants should be assured of confidentiality. If researchers prefer to administer their own tests, arrangements will need to be made so that the testing does not take away more class time than absolutely necessary. Indeed, it is always important to consider the most judicious use of class time when conducting classroom research. Researchers need to be sensitive to the perspectives of both instructors and learners in the classroom, and they should be careful not to disrupt learning during the research wherever possible.

8.4.2.4 Data Segmentation and Coding

As we discussed in Chapter 4 on coding, once the data have been gathered, the researcher must also decide how to segment the data for presentation. No data can speak for themselves; it is the responsibility of the researcher to analyze and present the data in a manner that will be accessible to interested parties. When determining units of analysis for classroom data, it is important to consider both the aims of the research and the classroom context. With regard to research questions, data should be analyzed and presented in ways that can shed light on the specific questions asked. For example, if the researcher is interested in the quantity of talk by learners in groups or pairs, one appropriate unit of analysis might be the word. If, on the other hand, the researcher wants to investigate the organization of talk in groups or pairs, the turn might be an appropriate unit for analysis. As with all studies, classroom researchers should be careful not to reduce the data too far. For example, in a study of the quantity of student talk in the classroom, segmenting the data at the word level would not distinguish between learners who have a few extended turns and learners who have many short turns. Data can always be collapsed for analysis, but in data collection and coding it is best to keep the categories as narrow as possible.

8.4.2.5 Considering the Instructional Setting

Finally, there are contextual factors that must be kept in mind when conducting classroom-based research—including whether the research takes place in a foreign or a second language setting, and the particular type of foreign or second language classroom of interest. In the foreign language setting, for example, instruction and expectations for learning might be very different between an EFL course at the university level and an English immersion primary school. It is thus important for researchers to consider the particular characteristics of the context in which they conduct research. To clarify further, if you are teaching or researching English instruction in a foreign language environment with students who do not encounter the language outside of the classroom, you may find that your views on teaching and research differ from those of your colleagues and administrators, or you may have difficulty gaining access to sources of information, such as test scores, interviews, and even learners, and your research plans may not fit in with the instructors' schedules. There is also the issue of subject mortality, or the dropout rate. In some instructional settings, it may be acceptable to offer compensation or some kind of reward, whereas this may be inappropriate in other contexts or situations. Compensation for participation in research is further discussed in Chapter 2.

However, such impediments to conducting research are neither limited nor applicable in blanket fashion to particular language learning situations; even if you are carrying out research in your home country and examining second language learners rather than foreign language learners, you may still find that your research goals and plans are incompatible with those of the instructors with whom you need to work. In addition, in a second language context, it can be more difficult to control all of the variables in quasi-experimental research. For example, the students will be exposed to the target language outside their schools or language programs, thus making firm conclusions about the effect of any treatment more questionable, and perhaps requiring more wide-ranging collection of data by classroom ethnographers. In any case, it is clear that foreign and second language learning research situations must be considered with regard to their own particular characteristics.

8.4.2.6 Summary of Problematics

In pointing out the concerns listed above, we do not wish to discourage novice or experienced researchers from investigating areas of interest in second language classrooms, but rather to emphasize that classroom research is a particularly complex and multifaceted endeavor that must be planned carefully. We must also stress the importance of flexibility. Even the most carefully designed studies rarely go exactly according to plan in second language classrooms; unforeseen events and problems arise from many sources, and matters which might otherwise be trivial can require the use of quick thinking and adaptation— from there being an odd number of students in the classroom when an experiment calls for pair work to some students having to leave early and not being able to complete the tasks. However, if researchers are aware of this likelihood in advance and can be patient, flexible, and ready to utilize contingency plans, classroom research is ultimately extremely valuable for the field of second language research.

TIME TO DO ...

Scan the methodology and any limitations sections of classroom-based research papers you know. What logistical problems can you identify from reading these studies? What logistical problems that are not mentioned can you foresee in the studies?

8.5 PURPOSES AND TYPES OF RESEARCH CONDUCTED IN CLASSROOM SETTINGS

Despite the concerns that need to be addressed when carrying out classroom-based research as discussed above, many successful studies have been carried out in a wide range of second language and foreign language classroom contexts. Some of the different types of research have included large-scale investigations of the effects of instruction, smaller-scale analyses of activities or lessons in classroom settings, detailed ethnographies of specific classes over time, research on learners' aptitude and learning strategies, and qualitatively oriented descriptions of classroom discourse. A range of topics has also been investigated through action research in classrooms, usually carried out by individual instructors on what works in their own instructional contexts. Helpful summaries of the many different classroom research studies can be found in Ellis (1990, 1994) and Loewen (2015). Below, we briefly illustrate methodological practices in two quite different types of research carried out in classroom settings. Despite the wide range of existing classroom research, here we focus narrowly on two different types for illustrative purposes. First, we illustrate traditional classroom-based research by focusing on work carried out on the role of instruction in second language learning. Next, we move on to describe a different type of research set in classrooms, known as action research.

8.5.1 The Relationship between Instruction and Learning in Second Language Classrooms

The role of instruction in the acquisition of a second language has been studied using a number of different methods in second language classrooms. The majority of researchers have examined the role of instruction in the context of a particular second language learning theory, with a second concern being to inform pedagogical practices.

For example, VanPatten and Cadierno (1993) examined the relationship between explicit instruction and input processing (i.e., perceiving the relationship between grammatical form and meaning). In a study using intact classes, VanPatten and Cadierno compared three groups of learners of Spanish as a second language. One class received traditional instruction in object pronoun placement, the second received "processing" instruction on the same topic, and the third received no instruction on this grammar point. In the traditional instruction group, students received explanations on the form and position of direct object pronouns in Spanish and completed typical oral and written classroom exercises, including production exercises. Processing instruction, on the other hand, involved contrasting the forms, presenting the object pronouns, and explaining important points on pronoun position in Spanish. These learners participated in reading and listening exercises in which the focus was the comprehension of object pronouns. Comparing pre-test and post-test results for the three groups, the researchers found that the processing instruction group significantly outperformed the other two groups, leading VanPatten and Cadierno (1993) to conclude that "instruction is apparently more beneficial when it is directed toward how learners perceive and process input rather than when instruction is focused on having learners practice the language via output" (p. 54). This study is typical of many carried out in the instructed second language acquisition paradigm, particularly in the area of input processing, where intact classes, different instructional treatments, and a series of pre- and post-tests are often utilized.

TIME TO THINK ...

Consider the study described above (VanPatten & Cadierno, 1993). How do you think these researchers went about collecting the data? What logistical issues have the potential to arise in this context?

Other researchers have investigated the role of instruction in second language development by examining different approaches to instruction. For example, there is a great deal of work on the utility of the focus-on-form approach to instruction. Such research has tended to center on questions of how best to draw learners' attention to form, when to focus on form, and whether one type of focus on form is more effective than another (Long, 2015). Like the processing instruction study described above, research on focus on form has also often involved intact classes receiving different instructional methods. For example, Williams and Evans (1998) addressed the question of whether some linguistic forms were more amenable to focus-on-form instruction than others. They used three intact classes: a control group, a group that received an input flood of positive evidence, and a group that received explicit instruction and feedback. For the two experimental groups, the treatments were rotated for the different linguistic forms under investigation. That is, each class received different treatments for participial adjectives and passives. However, the researchers ensured that the instructional materials were not only appropriate for and similar to but also integrated with the normal activities and focus of the course. Each treatment lasted for approximately two weeks. The analysis, which combined quantitative and qualitative data, suggested that not all forms were equal in terms of the effectiveness of focus-on-form activities and that individual learners could vary greatly in terms of readiness and ability to learn.

Other research on focus on form involving a different methodological approach has been carried out by Ellis, Basturkmen, and Loewen (2001). They recorded and examined a large database of naturalistic classrooms in a descriptive study of what practicing teachers do, finding both teacher-generated and learner-generated incidental focus on form in meaning-based ESL lessons, and reporting that preemptive focus-on-form techniques occurred as frequently as reactive techniques (38 percent student-initiated, 10 percent teacher-initiated). In a similar series of descriptive studies, Lyster (1998a, 1998b; Lyster & Ranta, 1997) also examined the different techniques that teachers used when reacting to student errors, suggesting that some types of feedback facilitate student responses more than others.

Research has also been conducted on the effectiveness of instruction for younger learners. For example, in a well-known series of studies involving many years of collaboration with classroom teachers, Lightbown, Spada, and their colleagues have described the ESL development of young Francophone learners in Canada, using both description and experimentation to investigate the roles of instruction and error correction. Spada and Lightbown (1993) examined the impact of instruction on question formation in ESL. Following a two-week period of explicit instruction and corrective feedback, they found that learners improved and maintained their gains on a delayed post-test five weeks later. Illustrating the many complexities involved in second language classroom research, Spada and Lightbown reported that control group comparisons were not possible because their control group teacher had used similar instruction and correction techniques to the experimental group teachers, despite the researchers' assumptions (based on several data points) that her focus was to be meaning only in a communicative approach.

There are methodological concerns in research on instructed second language learning. As discussed, research on the effects of instruction on second language learning has involved a number of different types of methodologies, ranging from observational to experimental with combined methods and different levels of teacher involvement in the process. Findings have yielded mixed results, with some studies indicating that instruction promotes learning and others suggesting that instruction has little effect. There are many possible reasons for the disparity in findings. As shown above, it can be more difficult in classroom than in laboratory studies to isolate variables for study, opening possibilities for intervening variables to influence the research findings. Additionally, classrooms vary in significant ways, and instructional practices that seem to enhance learning in one setting may not do so in a different setting. And of course, the different types of methodologies employed, the different units of analysis, and measures of learning all contribute to the difficulty in comparing results.

In an attempt to determine whether there is an overall pattern of positive effects of instruction, Norris and Ortega (2000) performed a meta-analysis of studies of classroom instruction. Meta-analyses were discussed in Chapter 6 and will be dealt with again in Chapter 10 on analysis. While this was one of the first major meta-analyses of the field, it has been followed by more syntheses and meta-analyses (see, for example, Plonsky, 2013, 2014). Simply put, meta-analyses examine the findings of a range of different studies and try to synthesize them. Norris and Ortega's overview suggested that instruction does promote second language learning. While lending support to more explicit instructional approaches, their analysis also illuminates the necessity of considering the nature of the classroom setting, the instructional style, and the many intervening variables when carrying out and interpreting research set in second language classrooms. Their 2006 book on meta-analysis continues this line of argument. In their words:

> A more complex agenda has begun to unfold within L2 type-of-instruction research that investigates not only the relative effectiveness of particular instructional techniques but also the potential impact of a range of moderator variables (e.g., learner factors such as aptitude, age, and learning style; linguistic factors, such as the relative structural complexity of L2 forms; cognitive factors, such as the learner developmental readiness, degree of noticing; and pedagogical factors, such as timing, duration and intensity of instruction, and integration of interventions within the language curriculum) . . . [R]esearchers will need to turn to more rigorous practices for experimental and quasi-experimental designs.
>
> (p. 502)

8.5.2 Action Research

8.5.2.1 Definitions

Although there is little general agreement as to an all-encompassing definition of action research, it is important to realize that action research can be defined and is being implemented in many different ways in the field. For example, Wallace (1998) believes that action research is "basically a way of reflecting on your teaching . . . by systematically collecting data on your everyday practice and analyzing it in order to come to some decisions about what your future practice should be" (p. 4). In this view, action research is a mode of inquiry undertaken by teachers and more oriented to instructor and learner development than it is to theory building, although it can be used for the latter. Although according to Chaudron (2000), action research does not "imply any particular theory or consistent methodology of research" (p. 4), several steps in the action research process have been usefully identified by action researchers (see Nunan, 1993, for a helpful overview of the process involved in conducting action research). In all empirical research on second language classrooms, whether effect-of-instruction, descriptive, or action research, the investigators share similar goals. These include wanting a better understanding of how second languages are learned and taught, together with a commitment to improving the conditions, efficiency, and ease of learning.

8.5.2.2 Theory and Background to Action Research

Teachers can bring a wealth of background knowledge and experience to the research process, offering a unique perspective on the dynamics of second language learning and teaching. Also, teachers may believe that others' research findings are not sufficiently related or applicable to their own unique teaching situations (Crookes, 1993). As Johnson (1992) notes, when discussing research initiated and carried out by teachers, "if what is missing from the research on classroom language learning is the voices of teachers themselves, then the movement provides ways for teachers' voices to be heard and valued" (p. 216). Action research is one form of teacher-initiated research. Crookes (1993) provides a useful discussion of the origin of the term, suggesting that "in action research it is accepted that research questions should emerge from a teacher's own immediate concerns and problems" (p. 130). In contrast to most second language classroom research that is carried out by parties outside the classroom for the purposes of theory construction and testing, action research is typically carried out by practitioners in order to address an immediate classroom problem or need (Allwright & Bailey, 1991). Like most research, action research usually stems from a question or problem, involves gathering data, and is followed by analysis and interpretation of those data and possibly a solution to the research problem. This can be followed by communication of the findings to others and sometimes by a change or modification to current practice.

8.5.2.3 Action Research in Practice

Before we outline some of the common steps involved in carrying out action research, it is important to note that not all action researchers agree on a process for doing action research, any more than they agree on the nature and content, or even the title of action research, which is sometimes referred to as "collaborative research" or "practitioner research" or "teacher research." For example, McDonough and McDonough (1997), with reference to "researcher-generated" and "teacher-initiated" research (p. 2), discuss the potential tension inherent in referring to teaching as "action" and research as "understanding," pointing out that both teachers and researchers can do both types and both be parties in research. Allwright and Bailey (1991) also refer to the dynamic nature of the action research framework, suggesting that all research centered on the classroom can be viewed under the unifying characteristic of attempting to understand what goes on in the classroom setting. With this in mind, we now turn to a discussion of the practice of action research.

First, practitioners identify problems or concerns within their own classrooms. For example, a practitioner may be concerned that the students seem to have particular problems with writing an essay. Next, the practitioner may conduct a preliminary investigation in order to gather information about what is happening in the classroom; for instance, the instructor may carefully observe the students during writing classes, examine their written products, and note where problems seem to arise. In this data-gathering phase, the practitioner may decide to create a database with information gathered from multiple sources. As discussed in Chapter 7 on qualitative research, triangulation, or the process of obtaining data from more than one source, is an important factor in many types of research, including action research. For our second language writing example, the practitioner may decide to supplement the information gathered from classroom observations and analyses of the students' written work with other sources of information, such as discussions with colleagues, questionnaires or diary entries tapping the students' perspectives, verbal protocols or think-alouds produced by the students while writing, and/or the administration of writing tests (such as timed essays) in order to gather more information on the students' strengths and weaknesses.

Based on the information obtained in the data, or sometimes before the data are collected, the practitioner may form assumptions or hypotheses. For example, if some of the students seem to have trouble finding and using low-frequency vocabulary words that are required to discuss the topic of the essay, the instructor may then devise and implement some form of intervention or treatment to address that problem. This could constitute a range of techniques, including a new method of teaching vocabulary, or a new technique for raising students' awareness of their own problems and providing them with resources to solve them. Finally, the instructor might evaluate the effects of this practice. This could be done, for example, through another round of data gathering, in which the instructor uses such techniques as observations, questionnaires, verbal protocols, or tests, or simply asks the students for their perspectives. These approaches might help the instructor to determine whether or not the students have benefited from the treatment and also to ascertain the learners' own views about the change in instructional practice, including if and how they feel they have benefited. If the outcome on essay writing is positive, the practitioner may disseminate the results of the process at this point, or return to the stage of reflection. In disseminating results, it is important to remember that much action research is not intended to be generalized. It is situated, or context-dependent. In cases where instructors' treatments, changes in practice, or actions have not been effective, they can consider what other measures could be taken to improve the students' writing. If the changes have been effective, they can consider what else could be done to further support their writing efforts. As can be seen, action research of this form is a cyclic process, and one that many teachers engage in as part of their everyday practice.

TIME TO DO ...

If you are a teacher, think of a problem in your classroom that you would like to further investigate. If you are not a teacher, think of a problem you experienced in your own language learning in a classroom. Design an action research project to investigate this problem further, and explain how you would execute it.

Action research is often motivated by teachers' curiosity and their wish to understand their classrooms. An example of this is the following study of the effectiveness of introducing second language adults to reading in English, carried out by Tse (1996). Tse implemented a reading instructional program in her class of adult ESL learners. During the reading program, the learners, none of whom had ever previously read a book in English, read six novels. The class also participated in activities and discussions based on the ideas the stories introduced and kept regular reports of their experiences with the reading. Tse found that the learners' orientation to reading and reading behaviors changed throughout the study. The learners' attitudes towards reading in English became increasingly positive. Additionally, learners reported that they relied less on dictionaries and were better able to focus on the comprehension of the text as a whole as the semester progressed.

This study demonstrates a typical use of teacher-research: the teacher identified a question she wanted to investigate in her classroom; she then gathered and analyzed data from her class to determine how well the instruction worked.

As with research on instructed second language acquisition, concerns have also been expressed about various kinds of action research. For example, many types of action research do not typically utilize control groups, and it is often easy to lose sight of concerns with validity or reliability. A further question arises about how to resolve potential conflicts that arise where the intuitions of teachers run counter to empirical findings about second language learning. It is hard to know exactly how to deal with these criticisms especially in the light of some discussions (for example, in Johnson, 1992) that action research might best be considered as an independent genre with its own features and standards, and a legitimate rejection of quantitative paradigms. Essentially, it may not always be appropriate to hold action research, or other evolving research paradigms, to the same standards as established research. However, if action research is intended to be read by a wider research community, it will need to meet the basic standards for publication and presentation. Conducted in the complex, dynamic context of the classroom, action research can be "difficult, messy, problematic, and, in some cases, inconclusive" (Nunan, 1993, p. 46). Nevertheless, action research can provide valuable insights both to individual teachers and to the field of second language learning.

8.5.3 Aptitude-Treatment Interaction

It is also important to note that there is a growing trend towards carrying out aptitude-treatment interaction (ATI) research. Studies of this sort look at how variation in learners' individual differences (aptitude, motivation, styles, strategies, working memory, cognitive creativity) is related to the effectiveness of different kinds of instruction. In ATI studies, aptitude-learning relationships are compared across a variety of instructional settings and conditions. Work by Goo (2012), Li (2014), Mackey and Sachs (2012), and Sheen (2007) utilizes ATI to provide insights on language learning processes so that L2 instruction can be optimized to fit the individual needs of the learner. We also see calls for more of this kind of research in position papers (e.g., DeKeyser, 2009). These studies usually combine methodologies using laboratory and classroom methods, and analyses often use correlations and comparisons of means. An example of an ATI study is by Révész (2011). She explored the relationship between the complexity of a task and learners' ability to focus on form-meaning connections as they interact in a classroom. The study investigated how individual difference factors such as linguistic self-confidence, anxiety, and self-perceived communicative competence mediate that relationship. Utilizing 43 ESL learners in naturalistic classroom settings, Révész asked participants to perform two versions of the same argumentative task, a simple and complex version, and then had learners fill out a questionnaire that measured individual differences. She found relationships between task complexity and syntactic complexity, but no effects for individual differences. ATI research has important implications for language pedagogy. As the study from Révész (2011) shows, careful manipulations of tasks and task design can induce different interaction and learner behaviors in the classroom.

8.6 CONCLUSION

As noted earlier in this chapter, second language learning theory is unlikely to be fully developed without some understanding of how second languages are learned in the classroom and, consequently, how they may be more effectively taught. Second language classroom research, regardless of the specific approach taken, allows researchers and teachers to better understand the multitude of factors involved in instruction and learning in different contexts, enhancing our insights into how languages are learned and should be taught. It is worthwhile to note that in recent years, together with the general trend towards the use of multiple methods in classroom research methodology, collaborative approaches to research are becoming increasingly common and valued, with language teachers and researchers working together as a team to investigate various aspects of second language learning.

POINTS TO REMEMBER

- When conducting classroom observations, it is important to conform to good observation etiquette such as avoiding being an obtrusive observer and the Hawthorne effect, maintaining objectivity and subjectivity, and staying in communication with the instructor.

- In classroom observation schemes, the observer marks the frequency of an observed behavior or event at a regular time interval. Two commonly used observation schemes are the Target Language Observation Scheme (TALOS) and the Communicative Orientation of Language Teaching (COLT).

- Uptake sheets are a method of introspective data collection that elicit learners' perspectives on second language classroom events.

- Stimulated recall is used to provide the researcher with access to the learners' interpretations of classroom events by using a stimulus to ask the student what they were thinking at a particular point in time.

- Diary studies obtain a first-person account of a language learning or teaching experience through regular entries in a personal journal that are then analyzed for recurrent patterns and salient events.

- When conducting classroom research, it is important to consider logistics such as selecting the appropriate microphones and audio/visual equipment necessary, positioning of audio/video recording devices in the classroom, acclimating students to the recording devices and researcher, and being aware of issues of informed consent.

- Action research is a mode of inquiry undertaken by teachers and is typically carried out in order to address an immediate classroom problem or need. It is more oriented to instructor and learner development than it is to theory building, although it can be used for the latter.

MORE TO DO AND MORE TO THINK ABOUT ...

1. Examine the COLT observation scheme, found in this chapter. Devise a research question and a short description of a possible research context for a study using the COLT.

2. Consider the context you wrote about for question 1. How could you triangulate the data in this study? How might introspective methods (e.g., uptake sheets, stimulated recall, or diaries) be used to better understand the research phenomenon?

3. Take the following generalized research question: "How are idioms acquired by college-aged ESL learners?" How would you go about setting up a classroom research study? What considerations would you need to make (e.g., recordings, consent, etc.)? Now consider a similar study conducted in an elementary school EFL classroom in Japan. How would you change the study? What different issues might arise in this context?

4. Teachers may choose to carry out action research in their own classrooms to find ways to improve their own teaching. If you are currently a classroom teacher, write a list of questions about your own classes that you would be interested in researching. Try to write at least five questions, noting why they might be important for your teaching. If you are not a current teacher, consider a language learning class you previously taught or participated in, and come up with five questions you would be interested in investigating.

CHAPTER NINE

Mixed Methods

Thus far in this book, we have dealt with quantitative and qualitative methods as separate entities. However, as we have alluded to in many places throughout this text, there are times when both approaches are appropriate within a single study. In Chapter 7, we introduced the notion of triangulation, a term originally used in surveying and navigation by using triangles as a base for determining distances. We return to this concept in this chapter as it is the most common way of referring to mixed methods (along with multiple data sources or even quantitative and qualitative) in second language and applied linguistics research (see Hashemi & Babaii, 2013, p. 835). In recent years, in social science research, in general, and applied linguistics and second language research, in particular, combining quantitative and qualitative data has become frequent; this chapter addresses the why and how of mixed-methods research.

9.1 INTRODUCTION

Mixed-methods discussions have been in place since the 1980s, but their acceptance in social science research has become apparent if not prominent in recent years with publications of books devoted to this area (e.g., Creswell, 2015; Tashakkori & Teddlie, 2010), articles relevant to SLA and applied linguistics (Hashemi & Babii, 2013; Jang, Wagner, & Park, 2014), and a journal dedicated to this research area, *Journal of Mixed Methods Research* (http://mmr.sagepub. com, retrieved April 19, 2015), begun in 2007. The scope of this journal "includes delineating where mixed-methods research may be used most effectively, illuminating design and procedure issues and determining the logistics of conducting mixed-methods research" (http://mmr.sagepub.com, retrieved April 19, 2015).

There is not a single name that has been standard when referring to this area of research. For example, one will find the following referring to what we refer to as mixed methods:

- Multi-method
- Triangulation
- Integrated
- Combined
- Quantitative and qualitative methods
- Multi-methodology
- Mixed methodology
- Mixed-method
- Mixed research

In the first edition of this book, we referred to these as split methods and multiple methods. In the current edition, we will stick to the term more commonly used in social science research, namely mixed methods.

Often in applied linguistics research, the quantitative-qualitative distinction has been seen as a dichotomy with some researchers "aligned" with one type of research being at odds with those of the other persuasion. It is our view that multiple approaches are often needed to understand a particular second language issue. This same position is echoed by Trochim (2006), who said:

To say that one or the other approach is "better" is, in my view, simply a trivializing of what is a far more complex topic than a dichotomous choice can settle. Both quantitative and qualitative research rest on rich and varied traditions that come from multiple disciplines and both have been employed to address almost any research topic you can think of. In fact in almost every applied social research project I believe there is value in consciously combining both qualitative and quantitative methods in what is referred to as a "mixed methods" approach.

He goes on to say:

the line between qualitative and quantitative is less distinct than we sometimes imagine. All qualitative data can be quantitatively coded in an almost infinite varieties of ways. This doesn't detract from the qualitative information. We can still do any kinds of judgmental syntheses or analyses we want. But recognizing the similarities between qualitative and quantitative information opens up new possibilities for interpretation that might otherwise go unutilized.

The fields of applied linguistics and SLA are fortunately turning the corner on this debate. In fact, the coming together of minds was demonstrated in a recent issue of the journal *Studies in Second Language Acquisition* (35[3], 2014), in which nine prominent scholars debated ways in which the gap between cognitive (primarily quantitative) and social (primarily qualitative) approaches to second language learning and teaching could be bridged.

This chapter is intended to demonstrate ways that the two data types can complement and supplement one another, yielding a more complete understanding of the phenomenon under investigation.

9.2 WHAT ARE MIXED METHODS?

A very simple definition is the following: a mixed-methods study is one in which both quantitative and qualitative data are combined in a single study (Bergman, 2008, p. 1). As Hashemi and Babaii (2013) point out, this definition is limited; true mixed-methods research must include both quantitative and qualitative data at all stages of a research project, including data collection, data analysis, and interpretation. Tashakkori and Creswell (2007, p. 4) provide the following definition: "research in which the investigator collects and analyzes data, integrates the findings, and draws inferences using both qualitative and quantitative approaches in a single study or program of inquiry." It is this definition that we find most useful.

The National Institute of Health, cognizant of the growing use of mixed methods and the need to establish best practices, in 2010 commissioned a white paper titled *Best Practices for Mixed Methods Research in the Health Sciences* (Creswell et al., 2010). The guidelines specified in the document are applicable to all social science research. Their definition (p. 4) includes the following elements:

- focusing on research questions that call for real-life contextual understandings, multi-level perspectives, and cultural influences;
- employing rigorous quantitative research assessing magnitude and frequency of constructs and rigorous qualitative research exploring the meaning and understanding of constructs;
- utilizing multiple methods (e.g., intervention trials and in-depth interviews)
- intentionally integrating or combining these methods to draw on the strengths of each; and
- framing the investigation within philosophical and theoretical positions.

When conducting research, one often wants to investigate a particular research question from a variety of perspectives and using both quantitative and qualitative data tools allows us to do just that. As we have discussed elsewhere in this book, quantitative data can provide researchers with a large numerical database, but qualitative data often provide the richer contextualized data important for a fuller understanding. Using both approaches competently and responsibly gives the best of all possible worlds when attempting to draw conclusions from data. As pointed out by Duff (2010, p. 59) (citing Hornberger, 2006), mixed-method research provides "a greater triangulation of findings and help[s] identify and interpret 'rich points' in research."

TIME TO THINK ...

Think about the benefits of using captions or subtitles in second language classrooms in a listening activity. One could use eye-tracking to determine whether second language learners actually look at the captions/subtitles more than the video images. This might lead to an interesting set of quantitative data. What types of data could also be gathered to supplement the quantitative results that would require a qualitative approach?

9.3 WHY USE MIXED METHODS?

In a 2006 article, Bryman surveyed the reasons generally provided in articles for their use of mixed methods although interestingly practice was not always in a 1:1 relationship with the rationale provided. Although not everyone provided justification, the following represent the various stated rationale from the survey (pp. 105–107):

a. Greater validity (triangulation). Findings can be corroborated.
b. Offset. This refers to the idea that both quantitative and qualitative methods have their specific strengths and weaknesses. Combining them results in researchers building on strengths and minimizing weaknesses.
c. Completeness. A picture of the phenomenon under investigation is more complete when multiple approaches are used.
d. Process. Qualitative data can provide a better picture of process, something that quantitative data are less likely to do.
e. Different research questions. This refers to the idea that different research questions can be addressed using mixed methods.
f. Explanation. Better explanations can be provided for the other approach (quantitative can explain qualitative results; qualitative can explain quantitative results).

g. Unexpected results. Similar to explanation, this category refers to the ability to use both method types to help explain surprising findings.

h. Instrument development. Qualitative data can be used to develop instruments (e.g., questionnaires where one might want data to generate choices).

i. Sampling. One approach can assist with the sampling of respondents.

j. Credibility. Integrity of responses is enhanced. In other words, if findings are similar from two different approaches, they are more likely to gain traction in the research community.

k. Context. Often one needs context to understand quantitative data; qualitative data can provide that context for interpretation. Quantitative data provide information for generalizability.

l. Illustration. Qualitative data can "illustrate" quantitative data.

m. Utility. Combining data types is more useful to actual practitioners.

n. Confirm and discover. Qualitative data is the data source for generating hypotheses. Quantitative data tests those hypotheses.

o. Diversity of views. This justification is one that essentially argues for a need to include researchers' and participants' viewpoints.

p. Enhancement. This refers to using one form of data as the "base" data and building upon that with the other data source.

The important point is that one needs to have a well-reasoned rationale for any research approach; mixed methods are no exception.

TIME TO DO ...

Look at the methodology section of some of the following research studies. Is there a justification for using a mixed-method design? If so, what is it? If not, why do you think they used the particular design adopted?

1. Davis, J. M. (2007). Resistance to L2 pragmatics in the Australian ESL context. *Language Learning, 57,* 611–649.

2. Brandl, K. K. (2000). Foreign language TA's perceptions of training components: Do we know how they like to be trained? *The Modern Language Journal, 84,* 355–371.

3. Graham, S., & Macaro, E. (2008). Strategy instruction in listening for lower-intermediate learners of French. *Language Learning, 58,* 747–783.

4. Sasaki, M. (2004). A multiple-data analysis of the 3.5 year development of EFL student writers. *Language Learning, 54,* 525–582.

5. Mackey, A. (2006). Feedback, noticing and instructed second language learning. *Applied Linguistics, 27,* 405–430.

6. Copland, F., Garton, S., & Burns, A. (2014). Challenges in teaching English to young learners: Global perspectives and local realities. *TESOL Quarterly, 48,* 738–762.

9.4 TYPES OF MIXED-METHODS STUDIES

There are numerous ways to design quantitative and qualitative studies. Similarly, there are multiple ways of combining these two research traditions. Creswell, Plano Clark, and Garrett (2008), based on Creswell and Plano Clark (2007), present five typical research designs which differ, *inter alia*, on whether data collection takes place concurrently or sequentially; the first two exemplify concurrent designs and the latter three, sequential deigns.

Triangulation in this model (see Figure 9.1) is a concurrent design that involves collecting two sets of data simultaneously and considering them in parallel as a way of understanding the research question more thoroughly. In other words, the data types complement one another. A second design type is what they refer to as concurrent embedded design (see Figure 9.2). In this design type, rather than both contributing equally to the interpretation, there is an effort to determine the impact of an intervention. Qualitative data are collected along with the intervention, for example, when one wants information on the experience of the intervention itself. Thus, the two data types are used for different purposes, quantitative data to determine the impact of the intervention and qualitative data to understand the ways in which participants relate to the intervention. Both, then, contribute to the overall understanding of the impact of the intervention.

Creswell et al. (2008) illustrate three sequential designs: explanatory, exploratory, and sequential embedded (see Figures 9.3–9.5). These three all involve data collection at different parts of the data-collection process. In the first (explanatory), qualitative data are collected after the collection of quantitative

FIGURE 9.1 Triangulation design

Source: Reproduced by permission of SAGE Publications, London, Los Angeles, New Delhi and Singapore, from Creswell, J. W., Plano Clark, V. L., & Garrett, A. L. (2008). Methodological issues in conducting mixed methods research designs. In M. Bergman (Ed.), *Advances in mixed methods research* (pp. 66–84). London: Sage (© Sage, 2008).

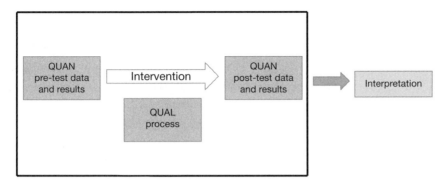

FIGURE 9.2 Concurrent embedded design

Source: Reproduced by permission of SAGE Publications, London, Los Angeles, New Delhi and Singapore, from Creswell, J. W., Plano Clark, V. L., & Garrett, A. L. (2008). Methodological issues in conducting mixed methods research designs. In M. Bergman (Ed.), *Advances in mixed methods research* (pp. 66–84). London: Sage (© Sage, 2008).

FIGURE 9.3 Explanatory design

Source: Reproduced by permission of SAGE Publications, London, Los Angeles, New Delhi and Singapore, from Creswell, J. W., Plano Clark, V. L., & Garrett, A. L. (2008). Methodological issues in conducting mixed methods research designs. In M. Bergman (Ed.), *Advances in mixed methods research* (pp. 66–84). London: Sage (© Sage, 2008).

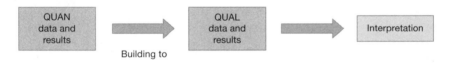

FIGURE 9.4 Exploratory design

Source: Reproduced by permission of SAGE Publications, London, Los Angeles, New Delhi and Singapore, from Creswell, J. W., Plano Clark, V. L., & Garrett, A. L. (2008). Methodological issues in conducting mixed methods research designs. In M. Bergman (Ed.), *Advances in mixed methods research* (pp. 66–84). London: Sage (© Sage, 2008).

FIGURE 9.5 Sequential embedded design

Source: Reproduced by permission of SAGE Publications, London, Los Angeles, New Delhi and Singapore, from Creswell, J. W., Plano Clark, V. L., & Garrett, A. L. (2008). Methodological issues in conducting mixed methods research designs. In M. Bergman (Ed.), *Advances in mixed methods research* (pp. 66–84). London: Sage (© Sage, 2008).

data and are used to help explain the quantitative results. In exploratory designs, qualitative data are the original data source with quantitative data being collected at a later time with the purpose of verifying and/or generalizing the conclusions from the qualitative data. Finally, with an embedded approach, qualitative data are collected before or after quantitative data collection. Qualitative data collected prior to quantitative data may serve the purpose of instrument verification or even participant selection; qualitative data collected after data collection are often used as a way of explaining outcomes.

As with all data collection measures (see Gass & Mackey, 2007), no data collection is foolproof and problem-free. Creswell et al. (2008) detail some of the issues, including concerns with contradictory findings, data integration, sampling, introduction of bias, implementing actual data collection, and the skills needed to successfully elicit data stemming from different traditions.

There has been an increase in the number of mixed-methods studies in second language research. Magnan (2006) reported on a 10-year period (1995–2005) of articles published in *The Modern Language Journal*. At that time, the total percentage of mixed-methods studies was only 6.8 percent (p. 4). In a study by Hashemi and Babaii (2013), in which the authors surveyed 205 applied linguistics/second language articles from 1995–2008 in which mixed methods were used, 36 percent of the articles fell into the period 2005–2008. This suggests that the use of mixed methods has greatly increased since the time of Magnan's study (the database for Hashemi & Babaii was larger). Despite the increased emphasis on mixed methods, the range of types is quite narrow. Hashemi and Babaii found that the vast majority of the mixed-methods studies in applied linguistics use concurrent triangulation (66 percent), with the next highest category being sequential explanatory (16 percent).

TIME TO THINK ...

Winke, Gass, and Sydorenko (2013) conducted a study on the use of captions by English-speaking learners of Spanish, Arabic, and Russian. They stated in their abstract that quantitative "[r]esults are triangulated with qualitative findings from interviews" (p. 254).

Following is a synopsis of their study.

The participants then followed a standard eye-tracking calibration procedure . . . This was followed by a short calibration validation procedure. Each participant then watched one of the videos two times, the first time with captions, the second time without. This was followed by a comprehension test . . . After the experiment, the learners were interviewed. The interview questions were: 1) What did you think of the videos?, 2) Was one video easier than another, or were they the same?, 3) What did you think of the captions that were presented when you saw the videos for the first time?, 4) Were you able to learn new vocabulary from the videos? Why or why not?, 5) Did the captions help you to learn new vocabulary? Why or why not?, 6) Did you like the captioning?, 7) When seeing a video twice, which do you prefer, seeing the video with captions first or seeing it with captions second?

What do you think was the purpose of the interview questions? Which of the design types do you think this was? Was it sequential or consecutive? Once you have decided that, which subtype was it?

TIME TO THINK ...

Pritchard and Nasr (2004) conducted a needs analysis with the goal of improving an L2 reading program. The study had three parts. The first phase was the needs analysis itself (these were qualitative data). A subsequent phase involved a quantitative study in which actual materials were tested to determine reliability and validity. The third phase involved the collection of quantitative and qualitative data from users (students and teachers) as part of the evaluation of the materials.

Does this fit into one of the design categories described above? If not, how would you describe this organization?

9.5 CONDUCTING A MIXED-METHODS STUDY

In the previous sections, we presented some of the types of mixed-methods studies. We also pointed out that the most common form of mixed-methods research in applied linguistics/second language acquisition is what has been referred to as triangulation. This latter term is perhaps the most common one and refers to using multiple data sources to shed light on the same research problem. In conducting mixed-methods research, one must guard against the method becoming prominent and the actual problem being investigated taking a secondary role. It is always important to match the purpose of the study with the methods (quantitative, qualitative, or mixed). Table 9.1 suggests a way for researchers to determine design type. Note that some names are in all caps and others in lower case. This is the standard way of indicating which of the data types is dominant.

TABLE 9.1 Design types

Data Type	Order	Rationale
QUAL + QUAN	Concurrent	Fuller understanding of research question
QUAN + qual + QUAN	Concurrent	To understand two perspectives of an intervention
QUAN + Qual	Sequential	Qualitative data to enrich quantitative data
QUAL + Quan	Sequential	Verification and generalization
(QUAL) + QUAN + (QUAL)	Sequential	

TIME TO DO ...

The last box in Table 9.1 has been left blank. Fill in what you think the rationale would be for a sequential embedded design.

9.5.1 Deciding Whether or Not to Conduct a Mixed-Methods Study

Most researchers lean toward doing either quantitative or qualitative research. It is the rare researcher who has a truly balanced background in both research types. In mixed-methods research, it is often the case that teams of researchers are needed so that the appropriate expertise can be brought to bear at each stage of the project. But, most important is the initial consideration: Is there a strong rationale for mixing methods and if so, will there be a greater likelihood of a richer result than there would be with only quantitative or qualitative data? In other words, what are the benefits of conducting a study of this sort? In the end, pragmatism must reign.

9.5.2 Planning Phase

Some early decisions need to be made: (1) How will the quantitative and qualitative data relate to one another? Does one dominate or do quantitative and qualitative data have equal importance? (2) What is the sequential order? Are they gathered at more or less the same time or are they to be gathered consecutively, perhaps after data from one or the other have been analyzed?

After you have determined that a mixed-methods study is feasible and after the rationale for such a study has been thoroughly explored and understood, and after you have assembled a team of researchers with sufficient expertise to conduct the study, subsequent actions/questions are as follows:

1. What are your specific research questions?
2. What is the design and what types of data will you be collecting?
3. How will you collect quantitative and qualitative data (see design types above)?
4. How will you analyze both sets of data (see design types above)?
5. How will you determine how to present the data in a written report (are the data types part of one large study or are they to be presented as two separate studies)?

Mixed-method studies can be highly complex. Ivankova, Creswell, and Stick (2006, p. 15) suggest that a graphical representation of the design is the easiest way to comprehend the various stages of the project. They list 10 rules for developing visual models:

1. Give a title to the visual model.
2. Choose either horizontal or vertical layout for the model.
3. Draw boxes for quantitative and qualitative stages of data collection, data analysis, and interpretation of the study results.
4. Use capitalized (QUAN) or small letters (quan) to designate priority of quantitative and qualitative data collection and analysis.
5. Use single-headed arrows to show the flow of procedures in the design.
6. Specify procedures for each quantitative and qualitative data collection and analysis stage.
7. Specify expected products or outcomes of each quantitative and qualitative data collection and analysis procedure.
8. Use concise language.
9. Make your visual diagram simple.
10. Size your visual diagram to one page.

They present a visual model for a sequential explanatory design (p. 16) presented in Table 9.2.

This design is particularly complex, but the point, nonetheless, is that it is important to explicitly present the various steps along the way, particularly if there are multiple research participants.

TABLE 9.2 A visual model of a mixed-methods design

Phase	Procedure	Product
Quantitative Data Collection	• Cross-sectional Web-based survey (n = 278)	• Numeric data
Quantitative Data Analysis	• Data screening (univariate, multivariate)	• Descriptive statistics, missing data, linearity, homoscedasticity, normality, multivariate outliers
	• Factor analysis	• Factor loadings
	• Frequencies	• Descriptive statistics
	• Discriminant function analysis	• Canonical discriminant functions, standardized and structure coefficients, functions at group centroids
	• SPSS quan. Software v. 11	
Connecting Quantitative and Qualitative Phases	• Purposively selecting one participant from each group (n = 4) based on typical response and maximal variation principle	• Cases (n = 4)
	• Developing interview questions	• Interview protocol
QUALITATIVE Data Collection	• Individual in-depth telephone interviews with four participants	• Text data (interview transcripts, documents, artifact description)
	• Email follow-up interviews	• Image data (photographs)
	• Elicitation materials	
	• Documents	
	• Lotus Notes courses	
QUALITATIVE Data Analysis	• Coding and thematic analysis	• Visual model of multiple case analysis
	• Within-case and across-case theme development	• Codes and themes
	• Cross-thematic analysis	• Cross-thematic matrix
	• QSR N6 qualitative software	• Image data (photographs)
Integration of the Quantitative and Qualitative Results	• Interpretation and explanation of the quantitative and qualitative results	• Discussion
	• Implications	
	• Future research	

Source: From Ivankova, N. V., Creswell, J. W., & Stick, S. (2006). Using mixed methods sequential explanatory design: From theory to practice. *Field Methods*, *18*(1), 3–20. (c) 2006 by Sage Publishers. Reprinted by permission of Sage Publications.

9.6 ANALYZING DATA FROM A MIXED-METHODS STUDY

Analysis of data from a mixed-methods study in some sense is not unlike the analysis of data from quantitative or qualitative studies (see previous chapters for details). In another sense, presenting a coherent report of a mixed studies report is more complex because results must be integrated in some fashion. With different data types for the qualitative part of the study (e.g., survey, interview, recall data) and for the quantitative data (essentially numeric, statistical), certain challenges present themselves.

Jang et al. (2008) investigated school success in a Canadian context (including special education and ESL students). As they describe their study, it was a concurrent mixed-methods research design in which they used qualitative data, namely interviews and focus groups with constituents (principals, teachers, students, parents) and quantitative data, a survey of principals and teachers. The survey data (quantitative data) were to be "enriched, elaborated, and clarified with contextually specific accounts of school success from interviews involving multiple perspectives" (p. 226). The main analysis had multiple stages. First, data from the different sources were analyzed in parallel, using standard data analytic methods. A second stage involved "member checking" with the school principals. The purpose was to ensure that the analyses from stage one corresponded to the perspectives that the principals had of the school context. This was done relatively early in the process to avoid issues of validity at later stages. The third phase involved the creation of data that could be compared. This is known as data transformation. This was necessary because, although the data from the quantitative and qualitative analyses overlapped, there were also areas of difference. This was done by taking the categories from the quantitative analyses and building support narratives. Additionally, a matrix was created with three columns: theme, interviews and focus groups, and survey for ease of comparison wth data from the different sources. An example of one such theme (Distributed Leadership) includes the following comment from an interview or focus group: "Many school participants, rather than just the principal, are involved in leadership activities." The following is from the survey: "School leaders provide a supportive climate for the development of teacher capacity" (p. 234). The fourth phase involved data consolidation in which data were recoded to make a more concise relationship between themes from qualitative data and survey questions. This led to a set of reorganized variables that were submitted to descriptive statistics and correlations, allowing cross-school comparisons. Not all designs are as complex as the one presented in Jang et al. (2008), but their study illustrates the way in which quantitative and qualitative data are viewed separately and combined and allow richer descriptions as the data types build upon, support one another, and, in general, provide insight into a particular learning context.

9.7 SOFTWARE FOR ANALYSIS

There are many computer programs that can be used for the analysis of data that are discussed elsewhere in this book. One tool that is common in applied linguistics research is NVivo (see Chapter 4), which allows for analysis of quantitative and qualitative data. Other tools for qualitative analysis are described (along with step-by-step guides for their use) in *Using Software in Qualitative Research* (Silver & Lewins, 2014; a companion website is also available). Particularly noteworthy is their discussion of Dedoose given that is a program that is specifically designed for mixed-methods research and allows for the integration of text, audio, and video files.

9.8 CONCLUSION

We have seen an increase in mixed-methods studies in the recent SLA literature. In fact, as seen in numerous venues, there is an understanding and appreciation of the value and richness of multiple approaches. Notable is the call by Lazarton (2005, p. 219), "I would also hope that we would see more studies that combine qualitative and quantitative research methods, since each highlights 'reality' in a different, yet complementary way." Duff (2010, p. 59) points the way to the future: "as new perspectives, genres, and media for reporting and disseminating research are transformed, new areas for AL [applied linguistics] research and new challenges, too, will surface for the evaluation of innovative, nontraditional forms of research." Mixed-methods research is clearly one of the innovative, nontraditional forms of research that will undoubtedly become more prevalent in future research.

POINTS TO REMEMBER

- Mixed-methods research is referred to in many different ways.

- Mixed-methods research uses quantitative and qualitative data at all phases of a research project.

- A major advantage of mixed-methods research is to gain a richer and more fulsome picture of the phenomenon under investigation.

- In a mixed-methods study, there are multiple ways of incorporating both sets of data (concurrent or sequential data collection).

- In mixed-methods research, data types can contribute equally to the conclusions drawn; they can be used for different purposes; one data type can be used to explain the other.

- Quantitative data can be used for generalizing the findings of qualitative data.

- With the complexity of mixed-methods research, it is important to lay out a visual diagram of the design.

- Decisions need to be made about the ways the analysis of quantitative and qualitative data will utilize both and at what stages.

MORE TO DO AND MORE TO THINK ABOUT ...

1. Consider the figure below (Figure 9.6), which illustrates the design of a study whose purpose was to investigate whether learners of English as a Second Language (ESL) acquired the use of English articles (*a/an* and *the*) better based on receiving oral or written corrective feedback (CF).

    Identify the parts that were probably analyzed quantitatively and those that were probably analyzed qualitatively. Justify your decision.

2. Using Figure 9.6, analyze the design in terms of:

    - association/experimental
    - groups
    - materials
    - treatment
    - dependent/independent variables

3. How might you modify the scheme to investigate:

    - The different effects of recasts and explicit feedback?
    - The effects of learning with music?
    - The effects of anxiety on oral productions?

4. Assume that you are interested in determining goals for foreign language study among high school students.

    a. What sort of data might you collect? Quantitative? Qualitative? Both?
    b. Will data be collected concurrently or sequentially? Why?

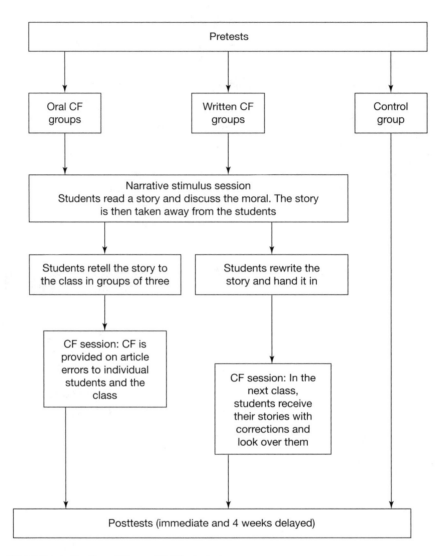

FIGURE 9.6 Design of Sheen (2010) study

Source: Sheen, Y. (2010). Differential effects of oral and written corrective feedback in the ESL classroom. *Studies in Second Language Acquisition*, *32*, 214. Copyright © 2010 by Cambridge University Press.

    c.   How would you collect the data (observations, surveys, interviews)?

    d.   Now assume that you are collecting both quantitative and qualitative data. How would you integrate the two?

    e.   Present your design visually. Don't forget to use the 10 rules suggested by Ivankova et al. (2006) presented in this chapter.

5.   You have read the following in an abstract of a study that investigated high school in a college preparatory program (Knaggs, Sondergeld, & Schardt, 2015):

> Through the use of an explanatory sequential mixed methods design, our study found that significantly more students [enrolled in program x] . . . showed greater college attendance and persistence outcomes over those who did not participate.

    a.   What sorts of quantitative data do you think were collected?

    b.   What sorts of qualitative data do you think were collected?

    c.   How could the data be integrated?

    d.   Draw a visual of a, b, and c above.

CHAPTER TEN

Analyzing Quantitative Data

This chapter presents introductory information about statistics to enable the reader to begin to understand basic concepts. We focus on issues and methods of analysis that are common in second language research. The chapter deals with descriptive as well as analytic measures and also addresses concepts such as normal distribution, standard scores, probability, and effect sizes, all of which are necessary to an understanding of basic statistical procedures. This chapter serves only to briefly familiarize the reader with central topics; for more extensive information, it is recommended that statistics books be consulted.

10.1 INTRODUCTION

In Chapter 4, we considered issues of data coding and basic data description. These were important prerequisites to the topic of analyzing data. This chapter focuses on issues of analysis and, in particular, provides background information on statistical procedures commonly used in second language research.[1] We recommend that before conducting statistical analyses of data, researchers gain greater knowledge of statistics through academic coursework, statistical texts, and/or consultations with statistical experts.

10.2 DESCRIPTIVE STATISTICS

The first issue we deal with has to do with description and data display. Descriptive statistics can help to provide a simple summary or overview of the data, thus allowing researchers to gain a better overall understanding of the data set.

Because raw data are not in and of themselves revealing, they must be organized and described in order to be informative. In this section, we present an overview of three different types of descriptive statistics: (1) measures of frequency; (2) measures of central tendency; and (3) measures of variability or dispersion. We will also discuss ways of displaying these data visually to facilitate the exposition of summaries of findings. Data displays are generally prescribed by the particular style manual one is using. Many journals with a second language research focus require APA, but one needs to consult each journal for the required style sheet.

TIME TO DO ...

Look up two to three journals you are familiar with and find out the style formatting required.

10.2.1 Measures of Frequency

Measures of frequency are used to indicate how often a particular behavior or phenomenon occurs. For example, in second language studies, researchers might be interested in tallying how often learners make errors in forming the past tense, or how often they engage in a particular classroom behavior. One of the most common ways to present frequencies is in table format. For example, in Table 10.1 below, we present a sample frequency table from Storch and Tapper (1996), who provide the frequencies of different types of annotations that second language writers made on their own texts, indicating the areas where they felt they were having difficulty.

In addition to tables, frequencies may also be represented graphically in forms such as histograms, bar graphs, or frequency polygons. In these graphic representations, the categories are typically plotted along the horizontal axis (x-axis), while the frequencies are plotted along the vertical axis (y-axis). For example, if we were to convert Storch and Tapper's (1996) frequency table (Table 10.1) into a graphic representation, one possible way would be through the bar graph seen in Figure 10.1a, with the same data displayed using a line graph (Figure 10.1b).

Frequencies, as well as measures of central tendency (which are described below), are often presented in second language studies even when they do not relate directly to the research questions. This is because frequency measures provide a succinct summary of the basic characteristics of the data, allowing readers to understand the nature of the data with minimum space expenditure.

TABLE 10.1 Sample frequency table

Content of student annotations

Content of annotation	Number	Total
(i) Syntactic		
Preposition or verb + preposition	21	
Verb tense	17	
Word order/sentence structure	17	
Articles	10	
Singular/plural agreement	8	
Word form	6	
Other	37	116
(ii) Lexical	70	70
(iii) Blanket requests		
Tenses	13	
Grammar	7	
Sentence structure	6	
Punctuation	4	
Other	29	59
(iv) Discourse organization	5	5
(v) Ideas	5	5
TOTAL		255

Source: Storch, N., & Tapper, J. (1996). Patterns of NNS student annotations in identifying areas of concern in their writing. *System*, *24*(3), 323–336 (excerpt from p. 329). Copyright ©1996 by Elsevier Science Ltd. Reprinted with the permission of Elsevier Science Ltd.

TIME TO THINK ...

Consider Table 10.1 and Figures 10.1a and 10.1b, which represent three ways of displaying data. Which of these ways is most useful to you as you try to interpret the results of the study from which these data came? Why? Is a line graph a reasonable way of displaying these data? Why or why not? Consider whether there really is a relationship between the category types.

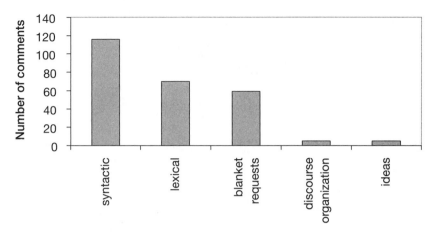

FIGURE 10.1a Sample frequency bar graph

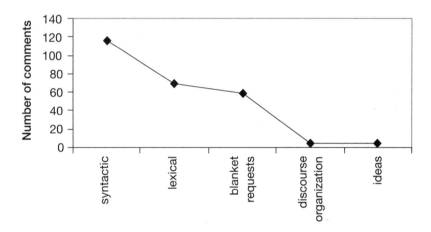

FIGURE 10.1b Sample line graph

Also, frequencies and measures of central tendency can help researchers determine which sorts of statistical analyses are appropriate for the data.

In order to visualize trends in the data, it is almost always useful to plot the data even before carrying out statistical analyses. In this section, we show various ways of visually representing data (e.g., see Figure 10.2 and bar graphs); these and other visual means of representation are useful in order to gain an overall impression of the patterns in the data. For example, creating a scatterplot (Figure 10.3) to assist with visualization of a data set (see correlation figures in section 10.12.1) can provide an early picture of any outliers in one's data (see, for example, the person who arrived at age 2, but had the lowest proficiency test

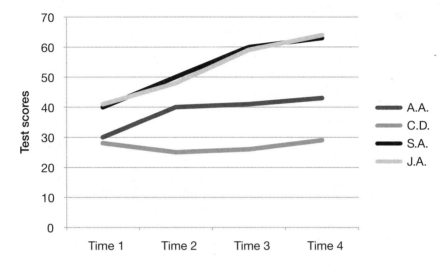

FIGURE 10.2 Sample line graph

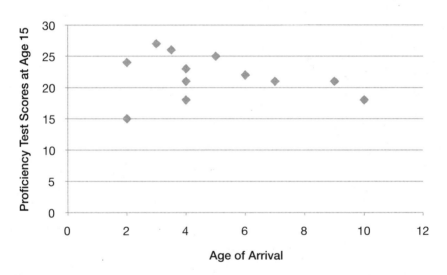

FIGURE 10.3 Scatterplot showing relationship between age of arrival and a proficiency test score (maximum score of 30)

TIME TO DO ...

Consider Figure 10.2. How would you verbally interpret this line graph? Which student(s) showed the greatest improvement over time? Which the least?

score [15]). Providing visual representations of results in graphical form can also contribute to a clearer understanding of any patterns confirmed through statistical testing.

10.2.2 Measures of Central Tendency

While simple frequencies are useful ways of providing an initial picture of the data, they are not as precise as other measures, particularly when the data are obtained from different groups. Second language researchers often use one or more measures of central tendency to provide precise quantitative information about the typical behavior of learners with respect to a particular phenomenon. There are three commonly used measures of central tendency, each of which will be discussed below.

10.2.2.1 Mode

Arguably the easiest measure of central tendency to identify is the mode. Simply put, the mode is the most frequent score obtained by a particular group of learners. For example, if the ESL proficiency test scores recorded for a group of students were 78, 92, 92, 74, 89, and 80, the mode would be 92 because two students in this sample obtained that score. Although this measure is convenient in that it requires no calculations, it is easily affected by chance scores, especially if the study has a small number of participants. For this reason, the mode does not always give an accurate picture of the typical behavior of the group and is not commonly employed in second language research.

10.2.2.2 Median

Another measure of central tendency that is easy to determine is the median. The median is the score at the center of the distribution—that is, the score that splits the group in half. For example, in our series of ESL proficiency test scores (78, 92, 92, 74, 89, and 80), we would find the median by first ordering the scores (74, 78, 80, 89, 92, 92) and then finding the score at the center. Since we have an even number of scores in this case (namely, six), we would take the midpoint between the two middle scores (80 and 89), or 84.5. This measure of central tendency is commonly used with a small number of scores or when the data contain extreme scores, known as outliers (see section 10.2.2.4 for an explanation of outliers).

10.2.2.3 Mean

The most common measure of central tendency is the mean, or the arithmetic average.[2] Furthermore, since the mean is the basis for many advanced measures (and statistics) based on group behavior, it is commonly reported in second language studies. For our scores (78, 92, 92, 74, 89, and 80), the mean would be the sum of all scores divided by the number of observations, or (Σx /n =) 84.2. It should be kept in mind that even though the mean is commonly used, it is sensitive to extreme scores especially if the number of participants is small.

The mean may be represented visually through the use of graphics, including a *bar graph*. For example, Toth (2000) created the graph in Figure 10.4 for his study of the role of instruction, L2 input, and Universal Grammar in the acquisition of the Spanish morpheme *se* by English-speaking adult learners. In this graph, he provides a visual representation of the means of three different groups on three acceptability judgment tests (pre-test, post-test, and delayed post-test). This visual presentation using a bar graph succinctly summarizes the information.

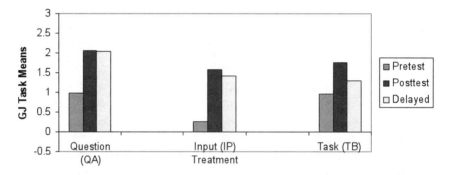

FIGURE 10.4 Visual presentation of group means: bar graph

Source: Toth, P. D. (2000). The interaction of instruction and learner-internal factors in the acquisition of L2 morphosyntax. *Studies in Second Language Acquisition*, *22*(2), 189. Copyright © 2000 by Cambridge University Press. Reproduced with the permission of Cambridge University Press.

TIME TO DO ...

Interpret this figure. How would you interpret the post-test results? Which group did better? For which group did learning persevere? Which group gained the most? At which point in time?

Alternatively, means may be shown through the use of a frequency polygon, also known as a line graph. For example, Zsiga (2003) compared patterns of consonant-to-consonant timing at word boundaries in Russian and English to investigate the roles of transfer and the emergence of linguistic universals in second language articulation. Zsiga provided the following graph to illustrate a significant interaction between L1 and language spoken, showing that the articulatory timing patterns of native Russian and English were different (Figure 10.5). The graph shows the mean duration ratios for English speakers and Russian speakers speaking their L1s and L2s, respectively.

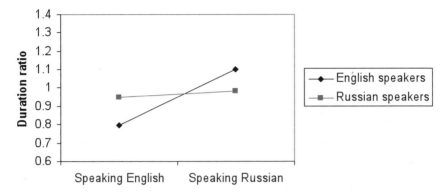

FIGURE 10.5 Visual presentation of means: line graph

Source: Zsiga, L. (2003). Articulatory timing in a second language. *Studies in Second Language Acquisition, 25*(3), 413. Copyright © 2003 by Cambridge University Press. Reproduced with the permission of Cambridge University Press.

In terms of measures and displays of central tendency and summaries of the data, it is always important to be flexible to the needs of your particular research questions and data set. In the words of Woods, Fletcher, and Hughes (1986):

> Although it will usually be possible to display data using one of the basic procedures . . . you should always remain alive to the possibility that rather special situations may arise where you may need to modify or extend one of those methods. You may feel that unusual data require a rather special form of presentation. Remember always that the major purpose of the table or graph is to communicate the data more easily without distorting its general import.
>
> (pp. 20–21)

10.2.2.4 Outliers

Earlier in this section, we raised the concept of outliers. This refers to data that seem to be atypical of, or lying outside, the rest of the data set. The presence of outliers strongly suggests that the researcher needs to take a careful look at the data and determine whether the data collected from specific individuals are representative of the data elicited from the group as a whole. There are times when researchers may decide not to include outlier data in the final analysis, but if this is the case there needs to be a principled reason for not including them beyond the fact that they "don't fit right." Should researchers decide that there are principled reasons for eliminating outlying data, a detailed explanation in the research report needs to be provided. Below, we provide two hypothetical examples where a researcher might, after careful consideration, decide to eliminate some data.

Example 1:

Data elicitation: Sentence matching (see Chapter 3 for further discussion of this elicitation technique). Participants are instructed to press the Yes button (the J key on the keyboard) if the sentences match or the No button (the F key on the keyboard) if the sentences do not match.

Problem: One participant has: (a) pressed only the Yes button throughout the experiment for all the sentences; and (b) consistently pressed it very quickly (i.e., the reaction times are much faster than the average).

Possible reason: Participant was not attentive to the task and repeatedly pressed only one button, suggesting that there was little processing going on.

Decision: Delete this individual's data.

Justification: These data did not represent the processing that one has to assume for sentence matching.

Example 2:

Data elicitation: Child-child interactions in which the researcher is measuring feedback provided by children to their peers.

Problem: One child's behavior appears to be unlike the others in that no feedback is ever provided.

Further exploration: In talking to the teacher, it was found that the child had a severe learning disability. It was also typical for this child not to stay on task in other classroom activities.

Decision: Delete this individual's data.

Justification: This child was most likely not on task. This child did not represent the population from which data were being collected.

Both of the examples are based on data that appeared to be unlike the rest of the data set. The data were not immediately deleted, but because they were outliers, the researchers took a closer look at what might have been going on. It was only after careful consideration and a determination that these data did not reflect a valid characterization of the construct of interest that the researchers decided that it was not appropriate to include the data in the final data pool. As mentioned earlier, information and justification of decisions like this should be included in a final research report.

Examples 1 and 2 illustrate occasions where it may be necessary to eliminate all of an individual's data when the extent to which he or she was on task is questionable. There are also cases when it may be appropriate to remove a subset of the data. For example, Duffield and White (1999) excluded from analysis responses on a sentence-matching task from any participant who had an overall error-rate of greater than 15 percent (e.g., said sentences were different when they were actually the same, and vice versa). Or, in some reaction time experiments, such as the one described in Example 1, a researcher might eliminate responses greater than a certain length of time, known as a cutoff point (e.g., 5000 msec [Lotto & de Groot, 1998]). A researcher might also move responses longer than the cutoff time to that cutoff point. For example, Duffield and White (1999) calculated the mean response time on a sentence-matching task for each individual. All responses that "fell outside a cut-off of ±2 standard deviations (see below) of a particular subject's personal mean were corrected to the corresponding cut-off value" (p. 145). In other words, there was a maximum response time value that was used in their analysis.

TIME TO THINK ...

Think of a situation where you might want to eliminate data. What would your rationale be for eliminating those data? And think of a situation where you would not want to eliminate data. Why not?

10.2.3 Measures of Dispersion

Measures of central tendency are useful in that they give both the researcher and the reader an idea of the typical behavior of the group. However, the use of measures of central tendency alone may also obscure some important information. For instance, consider the hypothetical case of two groups of learners who take a final exam. One group of students obtains scores of 45,

99, 57, 17, 63, and 100, while the other group obtains scores of 66, 62, 65, 64, 63, and 60. Both groups have approximately the same mean (63.5 and 63.3, respectively). However, if you report only the mean, you will not be able to show that the groups have a fairly different dispersion of scores: one group's scores are all close to the mean; the other group's scores are more widely dispersed. How can we present this additional information on the dispersion, or variability, of scores?

One informal way to do so is by presenting the range of scores. The range is the number of points between the highest and lowest scores on the measure. For example, the range for the first group of test scores would be 83 (17–100), while the range for the second would be 6 (60–66). The range, though easy to calculate, is not commonly reported in second language studies because it is sensitive to extreme scores and thus is not always a reliable index of variability.

A more common way of measuring variability is through the calculation of the standard deviation. Simply put, the standard deviation is a number that shows how scores are spread around the mean; specifically, it is the square root of the average squared distance of the scores from the mean. In other words, one takes the differences between each score and the mean and squares that difference. The next step is to add up these squared values, and divide by the sample size. The resulting number is called the variance. The standard deviation is the square root of the variance. As an example, consider the scores given above, 45, 99, 57, 17, 63, and 100. To calculate the standard deviation, the following steps are taken:

1. Calculate the mean. $\Sigma x / n = 63.5$
2. Subtract the mean from each score and square the difference $(63.5-x)^2$.

Score (x)	Mean	Difference	Difference squared
49	63.5	−14.5	210.25
99	63.5	35.5	1260.25
57	63.5	−6.5	42.25
17	63.5	−46.5	2162.25
63	63.5	−0.5	0.25
100	63.5	36.5	1332.25

3. Sum the differences squared and divide by the number of scores (6) to arrive at variance.

Score (x)	Mean	Difference	Difference squared
49	63.5	−14.5	210.25
99	63.5	35.5	1260.25
57	63.5	−6.5	42.25
17	63.5	−46.5	2162.25
63	63.5	−0.5	0.25
100	63.5	36.5	1332.25

Σ = 5007.5
variance = 834.58

4. Take the square root of the variance.

    SD = 28.89

The second set of scores given above (66, 62, 65, 64, 63, and 60) are closer to one another. If we do the same calculation as above, we see that the variance is 3.89 and the standard deviation is 1.97. Thus, while the means are similar, the amount of dispersion from the mean is quite different.

The larger the standard deviation, the more variability there is in a particular group of scores. Conversely, a smaller standard deviation indicates that the group is more homogeneous in terms of a particular behavior. We return to standard deviations below in our discussion of normal distributions.

Because the mean does not provide information about how scores are dispersed around the mean, the standard deviation (SD) should always be reported in second language research, often in a table along with the mean (M) and the number of participants (n). An example of a table (Table 10.2) with this information comes from Rodríguez and Abreu (2003), who investigated the construct of *anxiety* in pre-service teachers (native speakers of Spanish) majoring in English and French. The teachers were at different proficiency levels and came from two universities. Below, we present only the results from one of the universities in their example. This shows a table that portrays descriptive information.

One can examine the SDs and means in relation to one another. All groups (Table 10.2) (with the exception of level 5 for French Anxiety) are more or less equally dispersed from the means. If SDs are consistently large compared to the mean, you have groups with little homogeneity. In general, researchers should closely examine data with SDs that are consistently larger than the mean. Measures of dispersion (particularly standard deviations) can serve as a quality control for measures of central tendency; the smaller the standard deviation, the better the mean captures the behavior of the sample.

TABLE 10.2 Sample mean and standard deviation table

Level	English Anxiety			French Anxiety		
	M	SD	n	M	SD	n
1	74.42	14.87	12	76.75	17.32	12
3	90.42	14.98	12	89.08	13.99	13
5	94.38	14.00	8	93.50	120.52	8
Overall	84.39	17.45	33	85.15	15.80	33

Note: Maximum Score = 165.

Source: Rodríguez, M., & Abreu, O. (2003). The stability of general foreign language classroom anxiety across English and French. *The Modern Language Journal*, *87*, 371. Copyright © 2003 by Blackwell. Reproduced with the permission of Blackwell.

As was the case with frequencies, this information can also be represented visually. For example, Morgan-Short et al. (2012) provided the graph shown in Figure 10.6 in their study of the effect of different instruction conditions on the ability of adult Japanese ESL learners to acquire a rule about verbs. In this graph, the mean scores are represented by the height of the bars, while the black line extending from the top of each bar represents the size of the standard deviation.

As we noted earlier, it is important to include measures of variability in descriptions of data. Each offers different information, but when taken together they provide a richer understanding of the data than when viewed alone. As will be seen later in this chapter, means and standard deviations figure prominently in many statistical analyses.

10.3 NORMAL DISTRIBUTION

A normal distribution (also known as a bell curve) describes the clusterings of scores/behaviors. In a normal distribution, the numbers (for example, scores on a particular test) cluster around the midpoint. There is an even and decreasing distribution of scores in both directions. Figure 10.7 shows a normal distribution. As can be seen, the three measures of central tendency (mean, mode, median) coincide at the midpoint. Thus, 50 percent of the scores fall above the mean and 50 percent fall below the mean. Another characteristic of a normal distribution relates to the standard deviation. In a normal distribution, approximately 34 percent of the data lie within one standard deviation of the mean (above and

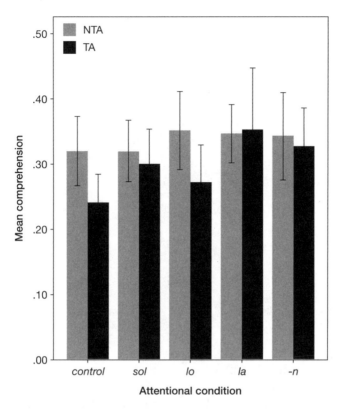

FIGURE 10.6 Sample visual representation of mean and standard deviation (comprehension scores per TA group per attentional condition)

Source: Morgan-Short, Heil, Botero-Moriarti, & Ebert (2012). Allocation of attention to second language form and meaning: Issues of think-alouds and depth of processing. *Studies in Second Language Acquisition*, *34*, 675. Copyright © 2012 by Cambridge University Press. Reproduced with the permission of Cambridge University Press.

below) and thus comprise 68 percent of the data. If we look at two standard deviations above and below the mean, we capture an additional 27 percent for a total of 95 percent. Thus, only 5 percent of the data in a normal distribution lies beyond two standard deviations from the mean. Finally, approximately 2.13 percent of the data fall between two and three standard deviations, leaving only approximately 0.3 percent of the data beyond three standard deviations above and below the mean. If we know that a group of scores is normally distributed and if we know the mean and the standard deviation, we can then determine where individuals fall within a group of scores. Many statistics assume normal distribution of scores. We return to this concept below. Figure 10.7 represents a normal distribution with the mean, mode, and median corresponding at the midpoint.

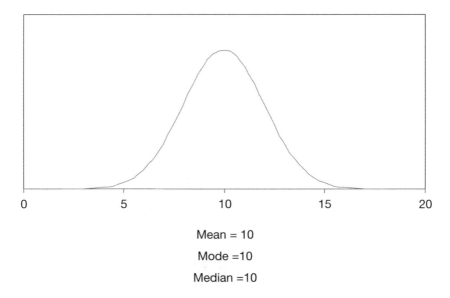

Mean = 10
Mode =10
Median =10

FIGURE 10.7 Normal distribution

10.4 STANDARD SCORES

There are times when we want to compare an individual's performance on different tests. For example, we might want to compare a score on a vocabulary test with a score on a test of grammar. Given the nature of the two tests, it is also likely that the maximum score on each is different. It would, of course, not be prudent to compare a score of 22 on one test with a score of 22 on another when one was based on a total possible score of 75 and the other based on a total possible score of 25. One way to make a more meaningful comparison is to convert these raw scores into standard scores.

The two most common standard scores are z scores and T scores. Z scores use standard deviations to reflect the distance of a score from a mean. If a score is one standard deviation above the mean, it has a z score of +1, a score that is two standard deviations above the mean has a z score of +2, and a score that is one standard deviation below the mean has a z score of −1. The calculation of a z score is straightforward: we subtract the mean from the raw score and divide the result by the standard deviation. The formula is given in Appendix G.

A second common standard score is the T score. In essence, it is a converted z score. Z scores are often expressed in negative terms (when they are below the mean) and in fractions. For certain manipulations of scores, negative scores are inappropriate. If non-negative standard scores are needed, T scores are commonly used. T scores are calculated by multiplying the z score

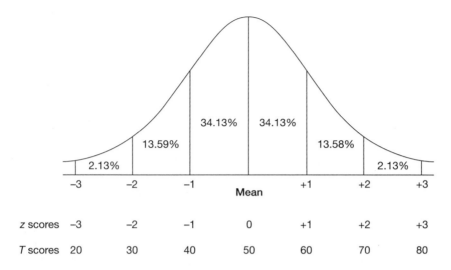

FIGURE 10.8 Means, standard deviations, z scores, T scores

by 10 and adding 50 ((z × 10) + 50). Consider a test with a mean of 60 and a standard deviation of 14. A learner who receives a score of 39 on this test has scored one and one-half standard deviations below the mean, and would have a z score of −1.5 and a T score of 35. The relationship between means and standard deviations and the two standard scores discussed here can be seen in Figure 10.8.

TIME TO THINK …

Think of a circumstance when you might want to convert scores to a standard score.

10.5 PROBABILITY

The purpose of conducting statistical tests is to provide information about the likelihood of an event occurring by chance. The probability value (referred to in research reports as the p-value) that is reported is designed to provide confidence in the claims that are being made about the analysis of the data. We are all familiar with the concept of probability from everyday life. Insurance companies rely on the concept of probability to determine rates using various factors such as age, and health (for life insurance) or age and driving record (for automobile insurance). The general way of expressing probability is through a percentage (.20 = something occurring 20 percent of the time). Probability is an expression of the likelihood of something happening again and again. For example, if the probability is .05, there is a 5 percent possibility that the results were obtained by chance alone. If the probability is .50, there is a 50-50 possibility that the results were obtained by chance. The generally accepted p-value for research in second language studies (and in other social sciences) is .05. A p-value of .05 indicates that there is only a 5 percent probability that the research findings are due to chance, rather than to an actual relationship between or among variables. In second language research reports, probability levels are sometimes expressed as actual levels and sometimes as simply greater or less than .05 or some other probability level. Table 10.3 (modified from Ortega, 1999) shows actual p-values from a study on planning and focus on form with L1 English speakers learning Spanish. The column labeled F-value reflects the specific statistical procedure that Ortega used, analysis of variance (ANOVA), and will be discussed later in this chapter, a less preferred method of reporting given that best statistical programs present actual p values.

Table 10.4, from a study on word meaning by L1 English speakers learning Spanish (modified from Barcroft, 2003), shows p-values being expressed in relation to .05 and .01.

In Chapter 5, we introduced the concept of null hypotheses. Null hypotheses predict that there is no relationship between two variables; thus the statistical goal is to test the hypothesis and reject the null relationship by showing that there is a relationship. Let us take the following hypothesis: "Resumptive pronouns [*The man that I saw him is very smart*] will decrease with time." This hypothesis predicts change in a particular direction, that is, the occurrence will decrease over time. We could express this hypothesis as a null hypothesis as

TABLE 10.3 Example of expression of probability levels

Summary of findings from ANOVAs on IL measures

Measure	F-Value	P-Value
Words per utterance	8.444	.0002
Noun-modified TLU	5.8472	.0217
Pruned speech rate	16.0625	.0004
Type-token ratio	1.5524	.2221
Article TLU	4.3599	.0451

Source: Ortega, L. (1999). Planning and focus on form in L2 oral performance. *Studies in Second Language Acquisition*, *21*, 126. Copyright © 1999 by Cambridge University Press. Reprinted with the permission of Cambridge University Press.

TABLE 10.4 Example of expression of probability levels

Repeated measures ANOVA for effect of condition and time on cued recall

Source	F
Time	4.84*
Condition	9.06**

$*p < .05. **p < .01$

Source: Barcroft, J. (2003). Effects of questions about word meaning during L2 Spanish lexical learning. *The Modern Language Journal*, *87*, 557. Copyright © 2003 by Blackwell. Reproduced with the permission of Blackwell.

follows: "There is no relationship between the use of resumptive pronouns and the passage of time." We can then test whether the null hypothesis can be rejected. Consider the hypothetical scenarios below representing the number of instances of null subject use over time.

Time 1	Time 2	Time 3	Time 4
Scenario 1			
4	2	2	1
Scenario 2			
30	20	8	1

We can see that the difference in the number of instances in Scenario 1 is slight, suggesting that this may be a random finding and that were we to repeat this study many times, the results would be different. If we were to do a statistical test, we would probably come up with a high *p*-value and we would have little confidence that our results would be the same were the test to be repeated. On the other hand, the difference in the numbers in Scenario 2 is such that we would have more confidence in our results not being due to chance alone. A low level of probability would indicate this.

As noted above, probability is an estimation of the likelihood of something occurring due to chance. Two potential problems with such estimates, commonly referred to as Type I and Type II errors, are noteworthy. Type I errors occur when a null hypothesis is rejected when it should not have been rejected; Type II errors occur when a null hypothesis is accepted when it should not have been accepted. Examples are provided below.

Error Type	Definition	Example
Type I	Reject null hypothesis when it should not be rejected.	A statistical test shows a significant difference between an experimental and a control group ($p < .05$) and the researcher confirms that a treatment has been successful when in actuality it was unlikely that the two groups were different.
Type II	Accept null hypothesis when it should not be accepted.	A statistical test shows no significant difference between an experimental and a control group and the researcher confirms the treatment has not been successful when there really was a difference.

The approach discussed above is also known as null hypothesis significance testing (NHST) and relies on establishing a hypothesis that is then supported or rejected at some level of confidence (p-value). This discussion will be expanded when we return to the construct of effect sizes (section 10.11.2). Before moving to a discussion of statistics, we utter a word of caution about the difference between significance and meaningfulness. When we have a large sample size, it is often not difficult to get statistical significance. Assume, for example, that you are testing the effect of recasts versus models for the learning of irregular past tense verbs in English. Assume also that you have a sample size of 500 learners in the recast group and 500 in the model group (a highly unlikely event in second language research). Following the treatment, you give a post-test, and the model group has a mean score of 8.8 and the recast group has a score of 9.1. With such a large sample size, it is possible that this difference is significant, but given the small difference (.3), we might not want to make strong claims based on these results. However, in second language research we generally deal with much smaller sample sizes, making it difficult to get statistical significance.

As mentioned earlier, the commonly accepted level for significance in second language research is .05. This is known as the alpha (α) level; alpha levels should be established by the researcher at the onset of the research. For certain research, for example where high-stakes decisions will not be based on the analysis, the researcher may decide to set a less conservative alpha level. In fields such as medicine where the stakes are high, the alpha levels are much more conservative, thereby reducing the likelihood of chance occurrences. In sum, the p-value is the exact probability level matching the calculated statistic. The actual p-value must be lower than the predetermined alpha level for the results of the analysis to be considered significant. In second language research, even when the alpha level of .05 is used, researchers occasionally describe their findings in terms such as "approaching significance" or "demonstrating trends" when the p-value is between .05 and .075 or even .10.

In considering the difference between meaningfulness and significance (in the statistical sense), we need to recognize that second language learning is a slow and complex process often involving a period of production of correct forms only to be followed by a later period of production of incorrect forms. Therefore, we often need longer periods of observation, but the exigencies of research do not often allow long periods of time. Thus, it may be that meaningful trends are worthy of discussion, independently of statistical significance. As Gass et al. (1999, pp. 575–576) noted:

> The need to have all results adhere to a .05 standard may be questionable. Shavelson (1988) noted that the convention of using .05 or .01 "grew out of experimental settings in which the error of rejecting a true H_0 was very serious. For example, in medical research, the null hypothesis might be that a particular drug produces undesirable effects. Deciding that the medicine is safe (i.e., rejecting H_0) can have serious consequences. Hence, conservatism is desired" . . .
>
> (p. 248)

Given the essential arbitrariness in setting significance levels and given the constraints in conducting (second language research, particularly) classroom research, we feel that trends are important and at least point to the notion that experiments should be replicated, particularly when it is impractical or impossible for experiments to cover a long period. We also believe that trends may at times be as meaningful as statistical significance.

We are not suggesting that different levels or standards for significance should apply to second language research than those that apply to education, social, or cognitive sciences in general; what we are suggesting is that given the nature of second language research, it is not always necessary to completely discount trends in all data that do not fit within the narrow confines of the standard alpha level of .05. In fact, some researchers have argued that alpha levels are essentially unnecessary in the field of second language research, and instead we should focus on large sample sizes, and on other means of determining relationships.

10.6 INFERENTIAL STATISTICS

The goal of some types of second language research is to go beyond uncovering information about how a particular group of students, for example those enrolled in first-year Spanish, learn a particular part of the language. Rather, the goal is to generalize beyond the results. In other words, such researchers want to make inferences from the particular sample to the population at large. Given that it is impossible to gather data from all members of the population, inferential statistics can allow researchers to generalize findings to other similar language learners, that is, to make inferences. In the following sections, we deal with some of the most common inferential statistics that are used in applied linguistics and second language research.

10.6.1 Prerequisites

Before moving to present information about specific statistical analyses, we briefly discuss some basic concepts that relate to statistical procedures. While the first two, standard error of the mean and standard error of the difference between sample means, are not concepts that are presented in research reports, they are important for conceptualizing the statistics presented later in the chapter.

10.6.1.1 Standard Error of the Mean

Standard error of the mean (SEM) is the standard deviation of sample means. The SEM gives us an idea of how close our sample mean is to other samples from the same population. If we know that the mean for the total population is 50 and if we know that the SEM is 5, we also know that if our sample mean is 52, it is within one SEM of the population mean and is within 34 percent of all sample means taken from the population. Because we do not know the mean for the total population, this is not a precise measure, but is important in determining the standard error of the difference between sample means, discussed in the next section.

10.6.1.2 Standard Error of the Difference between Sample Means

Standard error of the difference between sample means (SED) is based on the assumption that the distribution of differences between sample means is normal. This distribution, because it is normal, will have its own mean and standard deviation. This standard deviation is known as the SED. In order to calculate the SED, one needs to know the SEM of the two samples in question (see Appendix G).

10.6.1.3 Degrees of Freedom

The concept of degrees of freedom is necessary as we consider the determination of significance of statistical tests. To put it simply, the degree of freedom is the number of scores that are not fixed. Suppose we know that our total value on a test adds up to 50 and we have five scores contributing to this value of 50. If we know what four of the scores are, the fifth one is fixed; it cannot vary. In other words, only one of the scores cannot vary. In this case, 4 represents the degree of freedom. This is important when we look up critical values on statistical tables. Statistics tables are organized by alpha-level (such as $p < .05$) and degrees of freedom and are expressed in terms of critical values. When a statistic is calculated, the numerical result of the calculation is compared against the statistical table, to determine whether it reaches the critical value. If the result of the calculation reaches or surpasses the appropriate value, the findings are considered statistically significant. In today's world of computer analyses, this information is provided in the output.

10.6.1.4 Critical Values

Researchers can look up critical values in a statistics table, although statistical packages that calculate statistics also provide the critical value. This is the value that we can use as a confidence measure to determine whether our hypothesis can be substantiated. The observed statistic (based on our statistical calculation) must exceed the critical value in order to reject the null hypothesis. This is further discussed below.

10.6.1.5 One-Tailed versus Two-Tailed Hypotheses

When we discussed hypotheses in Chapter 1, we presented some hypotheses that predicted differences in one direction or another and others that were neutral as to direction, that is, they predicted a difference but not in which direction the difference was expected. The former (those that predict a difference in one direction) are known as one-tailed hypotheses and require a different critical value than the "neutral" or two-tailed hypotheses. Examples of one-tailed and two-tailed hypotheses are provided below.

One-tailed hypothesis:

The group that received explicit grammar instruction before reading a passage with those grammatical elements will have higher comprehension scores than those who had vocabulary instruction before reading a passage with those vocabulary items.

This hypothesis clearly predicts which group will perform better.

Two-tailed hypothesis:

The group that received explicit grammar instruction before reading a passage with those grammatical elements will have a different level of comprehension than those who had vocabulary instruction before reading a passage with those vocabulary items.

This hypothesis predicts a difference in the performance of the two groups, but says nothing about which group will perform better. The critical value needed to reach significance depends on the concept of directionality.

TIME TO THINK ...

Think of an RQ and the corresponding hypothesis/prediction that would require a one-tailed test. And think of one that would require a two-tailed test.

10.6.2 Parametric versus Nonparametric Statistics

There are two broad categories of inferential statistics known as parametric and nonparametric tests. As the names suggest, they deal with the parameters of the population from which researchers have drawn samples.

With parametric statistics, there are sets of assumptions that must be met before the tests can be appropriately used. Some of the assumptions for parametric tests include the following:

Some assumptions of parametric tests

- The data are normally distributed and means and standard deviations are appropriate measures of central tendency.
- The data (dependent variable) are interval data (such as scores on a vocabulary test; see Chapter 4 for further information).
- Independence of observations – scores on one measure do not influence scores on another measure (e.g., a score on an oral test at Time 1 does not bias the score on an oral test at Time 2).

Again, we refer the reader to detailed descriptions in statistics books related to the specific sets of assumptions for each test.

The assumptions underlying nonparametric tests are minimal. Nonparametric tests are generally used with frequency data (such as the amount of other-correction in class discussion in different classrooms) or when the assumptions for parametric tests are not met.

Parametric tests have more power. This means that they are more likely to detect a genuine effect because they are more sensitive. Parametric tests are also more likely to detect an effect that does not really exist. One reason for the greater power of parametric tests is that there is more information that feeds into the statistic. If a statistical test lacks power, it may be difficult to detect the effect of the independent variable upon the dependent variable, resulting in a Type II error, or failure to reject the null hypothesis when it is incorrect. However, using a parametric statistic when it is not appropriate can lead to a Type I error, an incorrect rejection of the null hypothesis.

In the following sections, we briefly discuss some of the more frequently used parametric and nonparametric tests used in second language research.

10.6.3 Parametric Statistics

In this section, we deal with t-tests and analysis of variance.

10.6.3.1 T-Tests

The t-test can be used when one wants to determine if the means of two groups are significantly different from one another. There are two types of t-tests—one is used when the groups are independent and the other, known as a paired t-test, is used when the groups are not independent, as in a pre-test/post-test situation when the focus is within a group (a person's performance before treatment compared with his or her own performance after treatment). Below are examples of types of research in which a t-test and a paired t-test would be appropriate.

Example 1:

Description: You have completed a research study looking at the effectiveness of two kinds of feedback on learners' vocabulary test scores. Group 1 has 35 learners and Group 2 has 33. You have calculated the means and standard deviations of the end-of-semester exams of the two groups and you believe that all of the assumptions for a parametric test have been met.

Statistic: You compare the two groups using a t-test.

Example 2:

Description: You have conducted a study on the effectiveness of a particular way of teaching reading. You have given a pre-test and a

---

post-test. Each individual has two scores (pre-test and post-test). You want to know if the improvement following the treatment was significant.

Statistic: A paired t-test is appropriate; each person is paired with him or herself on the two tests.

Example 3:

Description: You have conducted a study on the acquisition of relative clauses by Korean and Spanish learners of English. There are two groups, matched for native language and gender. Group 1 consists of three male native speakers of Korean, four female native speakers of Korean, five male native speakers of Spanish, and four female speakers of Spanish. Group 2 has the same profile. (Groups could be matched on a variety of factors, such as age, pre-experiment tests, reading tests, listening tests, and so forth.) Group 1 receives instruction on subject relative clauses; Group 2 receives instruction on indirect object relative clauses. You have pre-test scores and post-test scores for each individual on a range of relative clause types and calculate a gain score for each. You want to see if there are differences in learning between Groups 1 and 2.

Statistic: Paired (matched) t-test is appropriate because you have matched pairs. That is, Korean male #1 in Group 1 can be compared with Korean male #1 in Group 2, and so forth.

A word of caution about the use of t-tests is necessary. As noted, they are appropriate when comparing two groups, but there is a tendency in second language research to run t-tests on different parts of a data set in a way that overuses the test. Using an alpha level of .05 means that there is a 5 percent possibility of getting significance by chance. In other words one time out of 20 we might have a significant result that in actuality should not be significant. If one carries out 10 t-tests, for example, the odds are increased that a Type I error will be produced. For example, if you have conducted an experiment in which there were four groups, carrying out multiple two-way comparisons or carrying out multiple t-tests on sub-parts of the data (e.g., native speakers of one language versus native speakers of another language or males versus females) could be considered overusing the test. If there are multiple groups, rather than doing multiple two-way comparisons using t-tests, another statistic, such as an analysis of variance, may be more appropriate because analysis of variance calculations mathematically account for the increased chance of error that occurs as multiple comparisons are made.

TIME TO THINK ...

Come up with a small research project in which you might want to use a t-test (paired or not). What would you be comparing? And, why would a t-test be appropriate?

10.6.3.2 Analysis of Variance (ANOVA)

In the previous section, we discussed t-tests, which enable researchers to compare performance on two groups. Many research designs require comparisons with more than two groups, and ANOVA may be appropriate in this context. ANOVA results provide an F value, which is a ratio of the amount of variation between the groups to the amount of variation within the groups.

Example

You have conducted a study in which you are comparing the effectiveness of three different types of instruction. You are confident that the assumptions of a parametric test have been met. You want to compare the results and use an ANOVA to see if group differences are due to chance or are sufficient to reject the null hypothesis.

A sample result from an analysis of variance is presented in Table 10.5. This table includes the information that is relevant to understand an analysis of variance result (see Appendix G for formula).

TABLE 10.5 Example of an ANOVA results table

Source of variance	SS	df	MS	F
Between groups	521.43	2	260.71	53.98*
Within groups	202.66	42	4.83	
Total	724.09	44		

* $p < .01$

317

An ANOVA provides information on whether or not the three (or more) groups differ, but it provides no information as to the location or the source of the difference. That is, is Group 1 significantly different from 2 or 3, or is Group 2 significantly different from Group 3? To determine the location of the difference when the F value is significant, a post-hoc analysis is used. Common post-hoc analyses include the Tukey test, the Scheffé test, and Duncan's multiple range test. A typical display showing the source of a difference for the possible study described in the above example is presented in Table 10.6.

In this hypothetical example, differences were found between the groups who had Instruction 1 and Instruction 2, and between the groups who had Instruction 1 and Instruction 3. No other differences were found; the differences between Instruction 2 and Instruction 3, for example, were not significantly different.

10.6.3.3 Two-Way ANOVA

In second language research, there is often a need to consider two independent variables, for example instruction type and proficiency level. Where there is more than one independent variable, the results will show main effects (an effect of each independent variable without considering the effect of the other) and an interaction effect, which is the effect of one independent variable that is dependent on the other independent variable. In Figure 10.9, we can see that there is not a straightforward relationship between test scores and instruction type. Rather, there is an interaction between instruction type and proficiency level such that high proficiency students do better with instruction type 1, whereas low-proficiency students perform better with instruction type 3.

10.6.3.4 Analysis of Covariance (ANCOVA)

There are times when there might be a preexisting difference among groups and the variable where that difference is manifested is related to the dependent

TABLE 10.6 Example of a post-hoc table

	Group		
Group	Instruction 1	Instruction 2	Instruction 3
Instruction 1		•	•
Instruction 2	•		
Instruction 3	•		

• Pairs where there was a significant difference at the .05 level

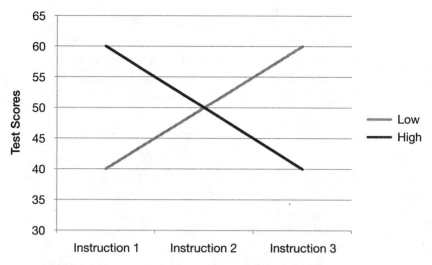

FIGURE 10.9 Instruction type as a function of proficiency level

variable. In other words, differences in means on variable X will show up on a pre-test. The preexisting difference will need to be controlled for and is referred to as the covariate. Because of differences among groups, the post-test results will need to be adjusted. The amount of adjustment will depend on two factors: (1) how large the difference is between the pre-test means; and (2) the change between the pre-test and the post-test (the dependent variable).

Example

You are testing three types of pedagogical treatments for learning the orthographic writing system of Arabic (explanation, visual repetition, practice). To do this, you use three separate first-semester university-level Arabic classes. You have a pre-test, treatment, post-test design. You find that your groups are not matched at the outset on language proficiency. Thus, your pre-test score, the covariate, will have to be adjusted to compensate for the fact that one group starts at a higher level than the other. If no adjustment is made, we would not know whether the group with the initial higher score learned more or appeared to learn more because of the higher initial score. An ANCOVA is appropriate.

10.6.3.5 Multivariate Analysis of Variance (MANOVA)

The MANOVA is part of the family of analyses of variance. It differs from an ANOVA in that it has more than one dependent variable. In order to appropriately use a multivariate analysis of variance, there has to be justification for believing that the dependent variables are related to one another.

Example

You have conducted a study of the effectiveness of different interlocutor types on learner performance (as measured by oral abilities and grammar). You devise a spoken proficiency test as well as an acceptability judgment task to measure learning. Because you are interested in the relationship between oral abilities and grammatical knowledge for the different interlocutor types, a multivariate analysis of variance is appropriate.

10.6.3.6 Repeated Measures ANOVA

There are times when we might want to compare participants' performance on more than one task.

Example

You have conducted a study of different writing prompts on learner performance as measured by writing accuracy. You have developed a measure of accuracy that includes length of essay, error-free T-units, and sophistication of vocabulary. You have carefully devised a counterbalanced design where each participant writes an essay under four conditions:

1. timed with a prompt;
2. untimed with a prompt;
3. timed with no prompt; and
4. untimed with no prompt.

Because each individual does all the tasks, we have a repeated measures design. And, because we have three different sets of results to be compared, a repeated measures ANOVA is appropriate.

10.6.4 Nonparametric Tests

As discussed above, nonparametric tests are generally used with frequency data or when the assumptions for parametric tests have not been met. In this section, we discuss some of the most frequently used nonparametric tests in second language and applied linguistics research.

10.6.4.1 Chi Square (χ^2)

Chi square tests are often used with categorical (i.e., nominal) data. Examples of categorical data include age groups (e.g., 8–10 years old, 11–13, 14–16), gender, native language, types of relative clauses, and so forth. The chi square statistic relies on observed frequencies and expected frequencies.

Example

You want to determine whether ESL learners from different L1 backgrounds and of different genders are more likely to use stranded prepositions (*That's the man I talked to you about*). You elicit this structure from 40 learners with the same gender distribution (20 L1 Japanese and 20 L1 Spanish—10 males and 10 females each). You construct a table that looks like the following:

Participants who use stranded prepositions

	Japanese	Spanish
Male	8	4
Female	6	10

If native language and gender did not matter in the use of stranded prepositions, we would expect the values in each square in the table to be equal. You can determine whether the actual values are different from the expected values by using a chi square analysis. If the actual values differ from the expected values, it can be assumed that at least one of the variables (native language or gender) influences the use of stranded prepositions. The expected frequency is determined by taking the sum total of the observations (in this case, 28) and dividing it by the number of cells (in this case, 4). So the expected frequency for each cell is 7. These are the values that feed into a chi square formula. Degrees of freedom are then determined by subtracting one from the number of columns. In this example, there is one degree of freedom. Degrees of freedom and corrections are generally built into computer programs that automatically calculate chi squares. When there is one degree of freedom, Yates' correction factor is often used.

Just as with many parametric statistics, chi square analyses rely on assumptions as to the type of data needed. Primary among these assumptions are the following:

- Each observation is independent, that is, it only falls in one cell. In the example above, an individual is either male or female and is either Japanese or Spanish.
- The data are raw frequencies (not relative frequencies or percentages).
- Each cell has an expected frequency of at least 5.

The Fisher's exact test, a variant of the chi square test, may be more appropriate than a chi square in some situations, including those in which there are several cells with expected frequencies that are less than 5, or where there are cells with a value of 0.

When chi square tests are calculated to determine the relationship among several variables, the results will indicate significant relationships. However, as with ANOVA tests, the location of the significance is not identified. There are procedures (e.g., Haberman's residuals) that can be used to locate the significant relationships.

10.6.4.2 Mann-Whitney U/Wilcoxon Rank Sums

Other nonparametric tests are used with ordinal or interval data rather than categorical data. Mann-Whitney U and Wilcoxon Rank Sums are two such tests; we discuss these together as they are essentially the same test. These are comparable to the t-test in that they compare two groups but are used when the results are rank scores (i.e., with ordinal scale dependent measures). Both sets of scores are pooled and the scores are compared in relation to the median.

Example

You want to determine the effects of interaction on the ability of the interlocutor to comprehend descriptions. You design a study with two groups, each made up of 10 dyads: in one group interaction is allowed, and in the other interaction is not allowed. You subsequently observe

---

where objects were placed on a board (dependent variable, measure of comprehension). The object placement scores are quantified and converted into rank scores.

A Mann-Whitney U is appropriate because the interval data assumption of a parametric test was not met. Had that assumption been met, a t-test could have been used.

10.6.4.3 Kruskal-Wallis/Friedman

A Kruskal-Wallis is a nonparametric test comparable to an ANOVA, but used when parametric test assumptions are not met. It is used when a researcher wants to compare three or more independent groups. In other words, a between-groups comparison is being made. A Friedman test is the nonparametric counterpart to a repeated measures ANOVA. That is, when you have non-independent samples and need to compare within groups, a Friedman may be appropriate.

In the preceding sections, we dealt with some commonly used parametric and nonparametric statistics in second language research. Below, we summarize some of the different types of second language data together with possible statistical techniques in Table 10.7.

10.7 STATISTICAL TABLES

In closing this discussion on parametric and non parametric tests, we present two statistical tables to illustrate how they can be read and used. Most statistical textbooks include full versions of tables that can be consulted to determine if your test results are significant. If statistics are carried out using a computer-based statistical package (see below), the results will be provided for you and

TABLE 10.7 Summary of statistics

Type of comparison/type of test	Parametric	Nonparametric
Two independent samples	T-test	Mann-Whitney
Two related samples	Paired t-test	Wilcoxon
More than two independent samples	ANOVA	Kruskal-Wallis
More than two related samples	Repeated measures ANOVA	Friedman

there will be little need to consult a statistical table such as the ones given in this section. Table 10.8 provides a partial display of the distribution of t.

This table and other statistical tables display the minimum value (i.e., critical value—see section 10.6.1.4) based on the desired probability level and degrees of freedom that one must have to claim significance. There are two points to note about this table. First, to determine significance, one looks at the left-hand column at the relevant degrees of freedom. Second, one has to determine whether one has a one-tailed or a two-tailed hypothesis. The figures given across the top (p-levels) are for a two-tailed hypothesis. For a one-tailed hypothesis, one halves the probability level. For example, column 2 (headed by .1) is .05 for a one-tailed hypothesis. Thus, if one has 14 degrees of freedom on a two-tailed test, and a value of 2.98, one can claim that the significance is < .01.

The second table (Table 10.9) is from a nonparametric test χ^2.

The method for reading this table is the same as that for reading the t-test table. If one has 15 degrees of freedom and a χ^2 value of 33.021, one has a significance level of < .01.

TABLE 10.8 Distribution of t

p	.1	.05	.02	.01	.001
df					
11	1.796	2.201	2.718	3.106	4.437
12	1.772	2.179	2.681	3.055	4.318
13	1.771	2.160	2.650	3.012	4.221
14	1.761	2.145	2.624	2.977	4.140
15	1.753	2.131	2.602	2.947	4.073

Note: p refers to the probability level; df refers to the degrees of freedom

TABLE 10.9 Distribution of χ^2

p	.1	.05	.02	.01	.001
df					
11	17.275	19.675	22.618	24.725	31.264
12	18.549	21.026	24.054	26.217	32.909
13	19.812	22.362	25.472	27.688	34.528
14	21.064	23.685	26.873	29.141	36.123
15	22.307	24.996	28.259	30.578	37.697

Note: p refers to the probability level; df refers to the degrees of freedom

As mentioned above, many second language researchers will not often have to read a statistical table since most computer programs provide exact probability levels, for example in the form $p = .023$, rather than in the form of $p < .05$. Many journals require reporting of exact probability levels and the use of notations such as $<.05$ or $<.01$ is no longer accepted.

10.8 STRENGTH OF ASSOCIATION

There are times when we might want to determine how much of the variation is actually due to the independent variable in question (e.g., the treatment, the learner's language background, the learning context, etc.). That is, if we find a difference, for instance, in performance between native speakers of Japanese learning English and native speakers of Arabic learning English on some measure, we don't know how much of the difference is due to the fact that their native languages are different or to something else (which we probably cannot specify). The following sections discuss some statistical procedures that can help us address these questions.

10.9 ETA² AND OMEGA²

The most common measurement that can be used after a t-test is eta^2 (expressed as $\eta 2$), which goes beyond the fact that there is a significant difference and gives us an indication of how much of the variability is due to our independent variable. Consider Example 1 of a t-test in the study of two different types of vocabulary instruction. Suppose that the t-test indicates that the learners from Group 1 score significantly better on their end-of-semester exam than the learners from Group 2. You know that there is a difference between these groups, but you don't know how much of that difference can be explained by the independent variable (instruction type). You calculate η^2 and determine that $\eta^2 = .46$. That means that 46 percent of the variability in their scores can be accounted for by the instruction type.

The same reasoning applies for ANOVAs. Omega² (ω^2) is the statistic used when all groups have an equal n size. Otherwise, eta^2 is appropriate. The formulae for these tests are given in Appendix G.

10.10 CORRELATION

One differentiating factor between correlational research and what we have discussed in previous sections is that in correlational research, no variables are manipulated. Correlational research attempts to determine the relationship between or among variables; it does not determine causation. Consider the fictitious example below.

The relationship between infant-directed speech and growth spurts

Introduction

A research team believes that talking to young children (infants) is related to their growth; the more talk addressed to young children, the more they grow. To test this, they consider two mother/child pairs. They gather speech and growth data from children aged 6 months to 18 months (twice a month, 30 minutes each time). To measure the amount of talk, they count all words in that two-hour period. The table below shows the data for both mother/child pairs.

| | Pair #1 | | | Pair #2 | |
Month of data collection (week)	# of words	Height in inches	Month (week)	# of words	Height in inches
1(1)	72	24	1(1)	65	28
1(3)	75	24	1(3)	70	28
2(1)	75	25	2(1)	66	28
3(3)	70	25.5	3(3)	72	29
3(1)	90	25.5	3(1)	59	29.5
2(3)	92	25.5	2(3)	64	29.75
4(1)	89	26	4(1)	64	30
4(3)	90	27	4(3)	80	30
5(1)	91	27	5(1)	82	30
5(3)	102	27.5	5(3)	100	30
6(1)	93	28	6(1)	125	30.25
6(3)	94	28	6(3)	152	30.5
7(1)	91	28	7(1)	145	30.5
7(3)	121	28.5	7(3)	150	30.5
8(1)	132	29	8(1)	145	31
8(3)	120	29.5	8(3)	180	31
9(1)	145	30	9(1)	92	31.25
9(3)	145	30	9(3)	165	32
10(1)	120	30	10(1)	172	33
10(3)	105	31.5	10(3)	170	33.5
11(1)	75	31.5	11(1)	200	34
11(3)	105	32	11(3)	180	35
12(1)	190	32	12(1)	178	36
12(2)	190	32	12(2)	180	36

Problematic Interpretation

Using the data presented above, a correlation coefficient of .70 for Pair 1 ($p < .001$) and .82 (Pair 2) was obtained ($p < .001$). The team conclude that because there is a relatively high correlation, this proves that the number of words used was the source of the growth.

What is wrong with this picture? There are a number of issues that could be raised, but the important one for this section is the interpretation. The first is that nothing has been "proven." All that has been shown is that there is a relationship between the number of words used when addressing a child and a child's height. The relationship is not necessarily one of cause and effect. While it is true that there is a relationship, the source of each variable is different. Increased amount of talk to an infant is possibly due to a relatively high interactive capability of the infant; increased height is a natural part of increased age in most children.

The above example focused on the interpretation of correlational data. We now turn to how to determine the strength of a correlation. Correlations are calculated between two sets of scores (in the previous example, one score is the amount of talk and the second is height). We can plot this information on a graph. The amount of talk can be plotted along the x-axis and the height on the y-axis. The result would be a graph with many individual points. If there were a relationship between the two scores, the dots would cluster around an imaginary line. When we calculate a correlation, we come up with a correlation coefficient (r) that characterizes the direction of the line and how well the line represents the patterns in the data. Depending on the direction of the line, correlation coefficients can be expressed as positive and negative values. A positive value means that there is a positive relationship; for example, the more talk, the taller the child. Conversely, a negative value means a negative relationship—the more talk, the shorter the child. A value of zero means that there is no relationship between the variables. These three possibilities are illustrated in Figures 10.10–10.12. The first figure (Figure 10.10) comes from the data showing a positive relationship between amount of talk and height of child for Pair 2. Figure 10.11 represents a graph that would depict a negative relationship and Figure 10.12 is a graph showing no relationship between two variables.

10.10.1 Pearson Product-Moment Correlation

We now turn to the Pearson product-moment correlation, a common means for determining the strength of relations (see formula in Appendix G). There are four assumptions that underlie this particular statistic; these are provided below.

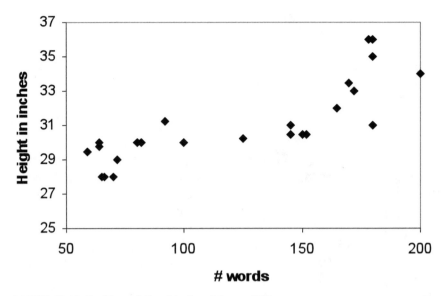

FIGURE 10.10 Positive relationship ($r = .82$, $p < .001$)

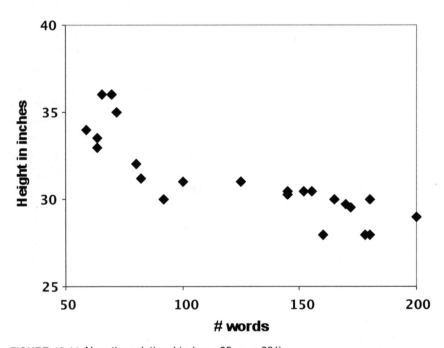

FIGURE 10.11 Negative relationship ($r = -.85$, $p < .001$)

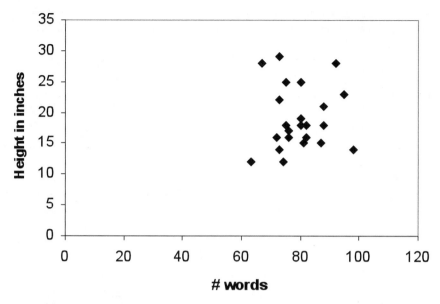

FIGURE 10.12 No relationship ($r = -.051$; $p = .808$)

Assumptions underlying the Pearson product-moment correlation

1. Normal distribution
2. Independence of samples
3. Continuous measurement scale (generally interval or sometimes ordinal if continuous)
4. Linear relationship between scores for each variable

The correlation coefficient gives information about the extent to which there is a linear relationship between the variables.

Frequently, correlations are calculated between multiple sets of scores in research studies. One concise way of presenting this data is in a correlation table, in which correlation coefficients for different sets of scores are listed. An example of a Pearson's correlation table (Table 10.10) comes from a study by de Graaff (1997) on the role of explicit instruction versus implicit instruction in an artificial language by native speakers of Dutch as it relates to language aptitude. This table is to be interpreted in such a way that if we look at T2 in task type 3 in the explicit condition, there is a .56 correlation between the mean aptitude score and the immediate post-test score on the gap-filling task. The probability level is based on the value of the correlation coefficient and the sample size.

TABLE 10.10 Pearson's product correlation table

Correlations (Pearson's r) between the language aptitude mean scores and the mean scores per task type and test session, under explicit and implicit conditions

Task Type	Test Session	Explicit (n = 27)	Implicit (n = 27)
1	T1	.38	.15
	T2	.47*	.42*
	T3	.50*	.55*
2	T1	.21	.02
	T2	.34	.34
	T3	.39	.34
3	T1	.52*	.32
	T2	.56*	.50*
	T3	.54*	.39
4	T1	.19	.36
	T2	.45*	.51*
	T3	.40	.50*

Note: Task type 1 = judgment task with time pressure; task type 2 = judgment task without time pressure; task type 3 = gap-filling task; task type 4 = correction task. T1 = mid-test; T2 = immediate post-test; T3 = delayed post-test

$^*p < .01$

Source: de Graaff, R. (1997). The eXperanto experiment: Effects of explicit instruction on second language acquisition. *Studies in Second Language Acquisition*, *19*, 263. Copyright © 1997 by Cambridge University Press. Reprinted with the permission of Cambridge University Press.

10.10.1.1 Linear Regression

We now turn to another use of correlations, that of prediction. Again considering our fictitious study of the relationship between infant-directed speech and growth, we repeat Figure 10.13 below.

As can be seen from the figure and the correlation coefficient (.71), there is a positive relationship, but if we had reason to believe that the relationship was meaningful, we might want to make predictions. For example, if the amount of words addressed to one specific child was 145, what might we expect her height to be? A straight line, called a regression line, might help us to address this question. A prediction equation can be used once we know the slope of the line and the intercept. While the details of these calculations go beyond the scope of this chapter, it is useful to know that if we want to predict one variable from another, and we know details of the regression line, we can calculate, for any

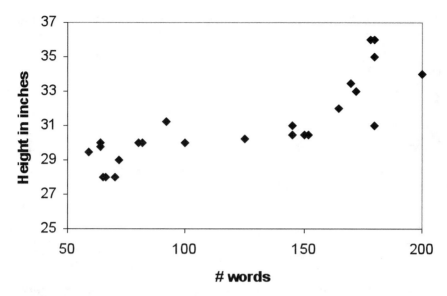

FIGURE 10.13 Relation between #words and height

given words addressed, the predicted height. Note that the validity of regression for prediction is dependent on the variables selected. A theoretically sound explanation for suspecting a relationship between the variables should be presented when regression is used to predict values.

10.10.1.2 Multiple Regression

This type of analysis is increasingly being used in the second language research field, probably because as studies get more methodologically sophisticated, our methods of analysis are also becoming more finely tuned. There may be instances when we want two or more variables to be used to predict a third variable. We can use multiple regression to do that. For example, we might want to predict how ESL learners will do in college based on two factors: (1) their results on a standardized test (e.g., TOEFL—Test of English as a Foreign Language); and (2) their performance in an Intensive English Program (IEP) on their own campus. A multiple regression prediction formula enables us to do this.

To test the validity of the predictor variables for predicting the third variable, data on the third variable should be collected from a subset of the population of study. For example, if we want to know how well TOEFL scores and IEP grades predict college grades, we could obtain actual college grades from a group of students and correlate our predicted grades based on a multiple regression formula with the actual grades. The resulting coefficient is called a coefficient of multiple correlation (R). The same idea applies as to r: R refers to the strength of the relationship among the variables in question (including the variable that is being predicted). Thus, as with other correlations, R can vary from +1 to −1, with +1 being a perfect positive correlation and −1 a perfect inverse relationship. The higher the absolute R value, the more confident we can be in our predictions.

TIME TO THINK ...

Which of the following research questions would lend themselves to a correlational analysis? Justify your answer.

a. Attitudes toward target culture and success in language learning.
b. Feedback type and language learning.
c. Attention paid to form and success in vocabulary acquisition.
d. Number of times male and female learners respond to feedback.

10.10.2 Spearman Rho/Kendall Tau

Both Spearman rho (ρ) and Kendall Tau are used for correlational analyses when there are ordinal data (or with interval data when converted to ranks). Spearman rho is more common, but the Kendall Tau is more suitable when there are many ties in the rankings.

10.10.3 Factor Analysis

Factor analysis is a complex procedure for determining common factors that underlie measures that test different (possibly related) variables. Researchers search for groups of variables that are correlated with one another; each group can be referred to as a factor. In doing a factor analysis, researchers take into account the variance that is common to all individual variables, the variance that is specific to each variable and sampling error. Factor analysis can be used to determine overall patterns found in correlation coefficients, and is particularly useful when analyzing results from surveys.

10.11 NEW APPROACHES[3]

We call this section "new approaches" (cf. Cumming, 2012, who refers to this suite of approaches as *new statistics*) recognizing that in fact we are not dealing with new statistics in the sense that they have just been invented, but rather in the sense that they represent a set of statistics that have recently entered into the common suite of approaches used in second language research. This is a reflection of the emphasis on study quality and methodological rigor that has become prevalent as part of accepted practice in SLA. Many of these issues were detailed in Plonsky and Gass (2011) and Plonsky (2013), and include such issues as reporting practices, design practices, and statistical power and significance. In what follows, we deal briefly with some of these constructs. Nick Ellis, then editor of the prominent journal *Language Learning*, raised the collective consciousness of the field in 2000 when he required that all articles submitted to the journal *Language Learning* include effect sizes which form the basis of power analyses and meta-analyses. According to Plonsky (2013), *TESOL Quarterly*, *The Modern Language Journal*, and *Language Learning and Technology*[4] also require the reporting of effect sizes along with "other reporting practices that include stating the hypotheses to be tested, describing whether or not assumptions for statistical tests were met, and using graphs and tables to complement in-text presentations and explanations of quantitative data" (p. 662). While other journals are not currently requiring reports of effect sizes, the sixth edition of the *Publication Manual of the American Psychological Association* (2010) strongly encourages the reporting of these statistics, emphasizing that "[f]or the reader to appreciate the magnitude or importance of a study's findings, it is almost always necessary to include some measure of effect size in the Results section" (p. 34).

The approaches discussed in this section take as a basis the inadequacy of null hypothesis significance testing (NHST). One of the main arguments in favor of alternative approaches to data analysis is that NHST is highly dependent on the sample size, as we saw in preceding sections. In general, NHST does not give an indication of the magnitude of a relationship. Rather, it relies on a yes/no (significant/not significant) decision. Further, the typical cutoff point in applied linguistics and second language research is .05, but when one considers this more carefully, one has to question whether there really is a difference between a result that is .054 (significant) and .055 (not significant).

TIME TO THINK ...

Think of a study you recently read. What were the research questions? Were they phrased dichotomously (Do . . .? Is there a difference?)

If so, what kind of an answer can come from such an RQ?

How might the findings and implications differ with an emphasis on magnitude rather than the presence/absence of a relationship or effect?

10.11.1 Power Analyses

Power analyses are associated with inferential statistics and are frequently used when we want to know how many participants are appropriate for a particular study. For this, we can conduct a power analysis, which is "a procedure designed to determine a priori the sample size necessary to reliably detect whether or not an effect will be found using inferential statistics" (Plonsky, 2012, p. 201). Plonsky (2013, p. 674) reported that only 1 percent of the studies he examined (6/606) actually conducted power analyses. Power analyses can be conducted relatively easily (e.g., http://danielsoper.com/statcalc3/calc.aspx?id=47, retrieved April 19, 2015).

10.11.2 Effect Size

An effect size is a measure that gives an indication of the strength of one's findings. It is not dependent on sample size and therefore can allow comparisons (meta-analyses) across a range of different studies with different sample sizes. A standard measure of effect size is Cohen's d (see Appendix G for formula), which can be used to test differences in means between two groups or differences in gain scores between two groups. A value of .2 is generally considered a small effect size, .5 a medium effect size, and .8 or more a large effect size. Effect size can be calculated based on a number of statistics (correlations, parametric, and nonparametric). Two useful references are: http://web.uccs.edu/lbecker/Psy590/es.htm (retrieved April 19, 2015) and Wilkinson et al. (1999). However, these interpretations have recently been challenged by Plonsky and Oswald (2014), who argue for a more nuanced and field-specific scale for interpreting effect sizes.

Consider the data in Table 10.11 below. Note how in the three hypothetical studies, the p-value changes based on variation in the sample size, whereas the effect size (d) is resistant to such variation. In other words, it is relatively easy to obtain significant results by increasing sample size.

TABLE 10.11 Effects of sample size and effect size

Study	N_1	N_2	M_1 (SD_1)	M_2 (SD_2)	p	d
1	5	5	15 (3)	18 (4)	.2265	.085
2	15	15	15 (3)	18 (4)	.0276	.085
3	45	45	15 (3)	18(4)	.0001	.085

TIME TO THINK ...

What are the implications of the results of Table 10.11 for consistency/lack of consistency in studies in second language? Does it make it more difficult to determine the real effects of a treatment? Why or why not?

Thus, effect sizes can be a useful tool for researchers who want to compare results with other research that addresses similar questions (see section on meta-analysis below) and who want to better understand the magnitude of a relationship.

TIME TO THINK ...

Compare the following:

1. Are there differences in the mean ratings that experienced ESL teacher raters and novice raters assign on measures of comprehensibility, accentedness, and fluency? (Isaacs & Thomson, 2013)
2. To what degree do (a) raters' background characteristics . . . (b) . . . affect students' ratings of ITAs' oral performances? (Kang, 2012)

Do you think that the analysis is based on NHST? Why? Which is more likely to have used effect sizes? Why? And which is more informative?

10.11.3 Confidence Intervals

A confidence interval (CI) is an estimate of the larger group from which a particular sample is taken. Assume that you know that the students in a fourth-semester Spanish class in the U.S. all have a particular proficiency level (on a scale from 1 to 10). What you really want to know is the proficiency level of all fourth-semester Spanish students within the state of California but for reasons of logistics and expense, you are unable to obtain that information. A CI is a way of determining the extent to which the proficiency level mean will actually contain the mean of the entire population of interest (students within the state of California) and thereby represents the boundaries within which we believe the actual population value falls. A 95 percent CI means that if one were to take multiple samples and compute confidence intervals, 95 percent would include the actual mean of the proficiency levels within the state of California. In other

TABLE 10.12 A way of expressing CIs in tabular form

Regression Output (Fixed Effects) for Finished Reading with Regression

Predictors	Odds	OR	95% confidence interval	p
Intercept	3.70	2.53	5.41	< .001
L1-L2 status	0.95	0.62	1.44	.801
Time	0.51	0.44	0.59	< .001
Grammaticality	0.95	0.83	1.10	.476
Sentence length (centered)	0.95	0.92	0.99	.013
Sentence-final length (centered)	1.00	0.93	1.07	.951
L1-L2 status × Time	0.35	0.25	0.51	< .001
L1-L2 status × Grammaticality	1.20	0.82	1.77	.351
Time × Grammaticality	1.98	1.32	2.98	.001
L1-L2 status × Time × Grammaticality	0.68	0.39	1.20	.187

Note: The intercept represents the odds for a NS reading a grammatical, untimed sentence of average total length (7.81 words) and average length of sentence-final region (0.61 words). OR = odds ratio

Source: A. Godfroid, S. Loewen, S. Jung, J-H. Park, S. Gass, & R. Ellis. (2015). Timed and untimed grammaticality judgments measure distinct types of knowledge: Evidence from eye-movement patterns. *SSLA*, *37*. Copyright © 2015 by Camgridge University Press. Reprinted with permission of Cambridge University Press.

words, it is a way of expressing our level of confidence that our interval includes the wider population mean. Many journals require or at least strongly recommend the inclusion of confidence intervals as part of the statistics presented. Table 10.12 shows a table display of confidence intervals.

10.12 META-ANALYSES

There are times when our research questions involve surveying a wide range of existing studies rather than collecting original data. In most instances, it will be difficult to directly compare studies given the unevenness of available data, size of experimental and control groups, and so forth. To make a meaningful comparison and to synthesize results, effect sizes become the main comparative tool. Norris and Ortega (2000) exemplify this in a study on the effectiveness of second language instruction. They outline the following five uses of effect sizes in their study.

- Average effect sizes across studies were calculated for specific predetermined categories.
- Average pre-test to post-test effect sizes were calculated.
- Average effect sizes across studies were calculated based on duration of treatment.
- Average effect sizes were calculated for delayed post-tests.
- Average effect sizes were calculated by type of dependent variable.

In essence, meta-analysis is an average of results from numerous studies. This is done by averaging effect sizes which are taken from original studies that focus on a particular research domain (e.g., interaction-based studies, strategy instruction, instructional effects). Effect sizes become the primary unit for analysis because they are not dependent on sample size. Meta-analyses provide an objective measure for determining the strength of an effect (for information on how to conduct a meta-analysis, see Plonsky & Oswald, 2012). One can see from this brief description why effect sizes are an integral part of what is reported in studies (see Plonsky, 2013; Plonsky & Gass, 2011, for a discussion of reporting practices).

In the preceding sections, we have dealt with statistical approaches. In the next sections, we deal with statistical packages that can assist in analyzing data and preparing those data for presentation.

10.13 STATISTICAL PACKAGES

There are commercially available statistical packages that can be used with a number of different operating systems, including Macs and PCs. In addition to the ones we deal with in this section, some basic statistics and graphing can be done using Excel. Others have been discussed elsewhere in this book. Two of the most common packages are SPSS and VARBRUL.[5] Learning to use either of these requires some initial effort and practice, but there are many courses or workshops in the use of these programs. Specific detail on statistical packages is beyond the scope of this book. Below, we give an indication of the use that can be made of each.

10.13.1 SPSS

SPSS is a basic analytic program. There are add-on packages for more sophisticated statistical use, but the standard statistical tests such as frequency statistics (chi square), t-tests, ANOVAs (with post-hoc tests), regression, correlations, and other more complex statistics are included. One can also convert raw data and output from SPSS to charts and graphs. Further details on SPSS are available through www.spss.com (see Larson-Hall, 2009, 2015) for detailed information on using SP55 in second language research).

10.13.2 VARBRUL

VARBRUL (Pintzuk, 1988; Rand & Sankoff, 1990) is a statistical package that is designed for analyzing variation data. For example, Young (1991) investigated –s plural marking in English by Chinese speakers. He wanted to know what the possible influence might be that would predict when the English plural form was used. He hypothesized 10 possible influences, including who the interlocutor was (Chinese or English), whether the noun was animate or inanimate, whether the noun was definite or not, and phonological surroundings. Each category could be divided into at least two levels. Because of the large number of factors and because many of the cells have a value of zero, an ANOVA is not appropriate for this comparison. VARBRUL, on the other hand, is designed to handle data of this sort. Young and Bayley (1996) provide detailed instructions on how to conduct a VARBRUL analysis and how to use data from this program.

10.14 CONCLUSION

This chapter has provided an overview of some of the statistical techniques commonly used in second language research. In the final chapter, we provide guidelines on what to do as you complete your research and prepare your findings for presentations and/or publication.

POINTS TO REMEMBER

- Numerous ways to report data exist (e.g., frequency, measures of central tendency, measures of dispersion).

- It is important to report standard deviations when reporting means.

- Determine carefully what you will do with outliers (if anything).

- At times, it is important to use standard scores when, for example, one wants to compare results on different tests.

- Probability is crucial in dealing with inferential significance and exact levels of probability should be reported.

- Inferential statistics allows generalizations beyond the specific group of participants being tested.

- Assumptions for parametric statistics should always be checked.

- Nonparametric tests are used with frequency data or when the assumptions for a parametric statistic have not been met.

- Correlations are used to determine relationships; no variables have been manipulated. Check assumptions.

- Power analyses are a way of determining the appropriate number of participants needed for a study.

- Effect size allows one to understand the strength of findings and is not dependent on sample size.

- Confidence intervals are a way of determining the range of values (with a certain level of certainty) within which the population value falls.

- Meta-analysis is a way of comparing studies and coming up with an average across many studies.

MORE TO DO AND MORE TO THINK ABOUT ...

1. You are in charge of student services in an intensive ESL program and notice that the students who are doing well in their reading class are not doing well in their writing class. This is surprising, but you want to make sure that there is a relationship before bringing it to the attention of the Director. Below are the two sets of scores from the 14 students enrolled in the class. You determine that the Pearson product-moment correlation is the most appropriate and can be used because you have interval data. Calculate the correlation coefficient (it has been started for you) and determine if the results are worth bringing to the attention of the Director. All scores have a maximum of 100.

	Reading Class	Writing Class
Maria	92	72
Juan	85	85
Toshi	78	93
Yoon-soon	61	51
Bob	25	32
Sachiko	87	62
Young-Ahn	67	78
Gunter	59	57
Angelika	84	72
Noriko	85	82
Jean-Marc	77	55
Antonio	62	77
Giovanna	88	87
Susana	87	88

$\Sigma X = 1037$ $\Sigma Y = 991$
$\Sigma X^2 = 81025$ $\Sigma Y^2 = 74035$
  $\Sigma XY = 76336$

Using the formula given in Appendix G, calculate the correlation between the two class scores (you will either need a calculator or you can use a program such as Excel). Given your results, would you notify the Director? Why or why not?

2. The statistical table below was discussed in this chapter. You have just conducted a study and have compared two means. You had 13 degrees of freedom. What must your critical value be to claim that your results are significant at the .05 level? At the .01 level? If you had 15 degrees of freedom, what would the critical value have to be to claim significance at the .01 level? At the .05 level?

Distribution of t

p	.1	.05	.02	.01	.001
df					
11	1.796	2.201	2.718	3.106	4.437
12	1.772	2.179	2.681	3.055	4.318
13	1.771	2.160	2.650	3.012	4.221
14	1.761	2.145	2.624	2.977	4.140
15	1.753	2.131	2.602	2.947	4.073

3. Consider the data below from a study comparing two groups of second language learners: one who received feedback and one who received no feedback. Compare the means of these two groups using the formula given below for a t-test (maximum score was 50). (Note that there are somewhat different formulae that are to be used with different group sizes. Consult a statistics book for the precise formula.)

	Feedback group (n=9)	No feedback (n=8)
Mean	42	29
Standard deviation (SD)	1.23	1.59
Standard error of the mean (SEM)		
Standard error of the difference (SED)		

The t value is _____. With _____df, the results are (not) significant.

4. Assume that you have gathered data on use by English speakers of correct noun-adjective gender agreement in Spanish. You have four groups of learners ranging from first-semester to fourth-semester Spanish classes. You want to determine whether learners from different classes are more likely to have acquired gender agreement. You define acquisition as 90 percent suppliance in obligatory contexts. Based on this standard, you determine which learners have and have not acquired gender agreement. The data can be seen in the table below.

Number of correct instances	Acquired Gender Agreement	Not Acquired Gender Agreement	TOTAL
Semester of study			
First semester	5	25	30
Second semester	10	22	32
Third semester	25	4	29
Fourth semester	26	6	32
TOTAL	66	57	123

Calculate the value using the formula given in Appendix G where f_E is the expected frequency and f_O is the observed frequency. Using the table below, determine if the results are significant and then write a summary statement about how to interpret the results.

Distribution of t

p	.1	.05	.02	.01	.001
df					
1	2.71	3.48	5.41	6.64	10.83
2	4.60	5.99	7.82	9.21	13.82
3	6.25	7.82	9.84	11.34	16.27
4	7.78	9.49	11.67	13.28	18.46
5	9.24	11.07	13.39	15.09	20.52

5. Describe a study in which measures of central tendency would be the only necessary analysis.

6. A researcher is interested in whether there is a connection between native language and ESL reading. He administered a reading comprehension test to high intermediate-level learners in a community education program. Means and standard deviations were calculated for each L1 group and are displayed in the table below. How can these data be represented in a figure? Sketch two possible figures. Sketch one that also represents the standard deviation.

Hypothetical reading comprehension study

L1 Group	Mean (x/100)	SD
Spanish	75	8.5
French	78	2.6
Russian	67	5.4
Mandarin Chinese	60	7.3
Korean	61	11.7

7. Locate three articles that use statistical analyses (select articles that differ in the statistics used). For each:

   a. What statistical analyses were used?
   b. Why were these statistical tests used?
   c. Were data presented in tables, graphs, or both?
   d. If tables were used, describe the information presented in the tables.
   e. If graphs were used, interpret the graph(s).

NOTES

1. This chapter deals with statistics rather than parameters. When researchers provide basic information about all members of a population (e.g., all first-year Spanish students at U.S. universities), they have information about the parameters of that population. It should be obvious that these data would be quite difficult to obtain; thus researchers draw information from a representative subset of that population, known as a sample. The information that we have about that population is referred to as statistics.

2. Butler (1985) suggests, "The 'mean' is what the layman means by an average although the statistician would regard all three measures of central tendency as types of average" (p. 27).

3. We acknowledge and are grateful to the contributions of Luke Plonsky to this section. He provided us with data and examples throughout.

4. *Studies in Second Language Acquisition* is now on this list.

5. SAS is another available statistical package (www.sas.com). It is more often used in business and in the hard sciences than in second language research, perhaps because it is perceived to be less user-friendly than SPSS, although it is used within the domain of language testing. SYSTAT (www.systat.com) is another program for statistical analysis and display. An example of its use in second language research is to investigate bilingual education. R, a free statistical package, has also gained traction in second language research (see Larson-Hall, 2015).

CHAPTER ELEVEN

Concluding and Reporting Research

In this chapter, we provide information about the final stages of research projects, including tips for drafting sections or chapters where results are discussed, together with limitations and conclusions sections. We also consider issues such as the audience for the research to be reported. We conclude the chapter with a checklist for researchers to think about when research is being prepared for submission for publication or presentation. While much of this chapter focuses on the more prescriptive requirements of concluding and reporting quantitatively oriented research, we also include information about preparing qualitative reports.

11.1 THE IMPORTANCE OF REPORTING RESEARCH

As we discussed at the beginning of this book, the purpose of research is to discover answers to pertinent questions. In order for answers to be meaningful, they must be reported to an audience. If research findings are not reported and heard or read, even the most carefully executed and elucidating studies are essentially meaningless. Therefore, we consider reporting findings to an audience to be one of the most crucial elements in the process of second language research. Reports about research generally involve a clear description of the problem and the methodology used to address the problem, together with the results, the researchers' interpretations of the data based on their theoretical framework, and a conclusion. The nature of research reports often differs for quantitative and qualitative studies, as well as for mixed-method designs. In this chapter on the final stages of research, we build upon many of the terms and concepts discussed in earlier chapters. First, we discuss the final stages in research reporting, namely the discussion and conclusion sections. Then, we move on to a consideration of the whole research report, and the steps to be taken before publication.

11.2 THE FINAL STAGES IN REPORTING QUANTITATIVE RESEARCH

In quantitative research, the results and discussion of findings may be combined into one section or presented in separate sections. The sections can be combined if the research design is relatively simple and the implications of the analyses are straightforward. However, with a more complicated research design and/or results that are complex, separating the results and discussion may add clarity to the reporting. The results section should include a clear description of the data collected and the outcomes of any statistical procedures. The analyses are often organized in terms of the relevant research questions or hypotheses so that it is clear whether the hypotheses are confirmed or rejected. In discussion sections, the authors present their interpretation of the results. In addition, they should address the implications the results might have for theory and/or practice, together with the limitations of the study and any suggestions they may have for further research.

TIME TO DO ...

Find two articles in which results and discussion sections are combined. In your opinion, is this combination justified?

Although the structure and organization of the final sections of research reports can vary from author to author and from one type of study to another, these final sections do share several common elements in second (and first) language research. As can be seen in Table 11.1, the closing segments of articles in different areas of second language research typically include discussion sections, together with additional sections concerned with the limitations, conclusions, and sometimes the pedagogical implications of the research. We outline the common elements of each of these sections in more detail below and provide examples from eight studies representing a range of interests in second language research.

TABLE 11.1 Organization of final sections in language research journal articles

Berg (1999)	Ellis and He (1999)	Leow (2000)	Willett (1995)	Philp (2003)	Williams (1999)	Melzi and King (2003)	Hafner (2013)
Journal of Second Language Writing	*Studies in Second Language Acquisition*	*Studies in Second Language Acquisition*	*TESOL Quarterly*	*Studies in Second Language Acquisition*	*Language Learning*	*Journal of Child Language*	*TESOL Quarterly*
Experimental (quantitative) study of the effect of trained peer response on L2 writing	Experimental (quantitative) study of modified output and L2 learning	Experimental (quantitative and qualitative) study of the effects of awareness on intake	Qualitative ethnographic study of L2 socialization	Experimental (quantitative) study of recasts and L2 learning	Classroom-based (quantitative) focus on form study	Descriptive (quantitative) study on the use of Spanish diminutives in mother-child conversations	Classroom-based (qualitative) evaluation of an English course's use of technology in the classroom
Discussion	Discussion	Discussion		Discussion	Discussion	Discussion	Discussion
Future research		Limitations and future research		Limitations and future research	Pedagogical implications		
	Conclusion	Conclusion	Conclusion	Conclusion		Conclusion	Conclusion

11.2.1 The Discussion

To understand what information is typically included in a discussion section, it is helpful to review the organization of the final sections of some sample articles from the field of SLA, presented above in Table 11.1. Seven of the eight articles include discussion sections; Willett (1995) does not dedicate a section exclusively to discussion, but instead chooses to weave the discussion and results together. Additionally, Hafner's (2013) discussion includes limitations at the beginning of the discussion section, allowing the reader to view the discussion of results through the lens of possible limitations. The other seven discussion sections all include a summary of the results, an explanation of possible reasons for the results, a comparison of the results to those obtained in other studies, and a commentary on the significance or implications of the results.

Of these four elements, a summary of the results is the most common. This is often done by repeating or referring to the specific research questions posed at the beginning of the study and providing succinct answers to those questions. Alternatively, discussions can begin with a concise summary of the findings that were detailed in the results section and then move on to a more detailed discussion of each research question. Including such summarizing comments is useful because it clearly informs the reader, especially the reader who is skimming, about the purpose and outcomes of the study. Here are respective examples from the discussion sections of three of the studies outlined in Table 11.1:

Summary of the results in discussion sections:

- Ellis and He (1999): "The first research question asked about the relative effects of premodified input, interactionally modified input, and modified output on L2 learners' comprehension. The results of this study indicate that reasonable levels of comprehension can be achieved in all three conditions" (p. 297).
- Philp (2003): "In general, the results support the claim that learners notice a considerable amount of implicit feedback provided through interaction in a primed context" (p. 114).
- Hafner (2013): "The findings demonstrate that, in attempting the digital video task, students perceived rhetorical challenges related to both the audience and the multimodal orchestration of the documentary" (p. 679).

TIME TO THINK ...

Review the examples above from Ellis and He (1999), Philp (2003), and Hafner (2013). Based on the summaries, can you work out what the primary research questions were in these studies?

Another typical element in the discussion section is the provision of possible explanations for the results found in the study—that is, for researchers to go beyond merely reporting the results and speculate about why particular results were obtained. For example:

Possible explanations for results in discussion sections:

- Ellis and He (1999): "Why did the modified output group consistently outperform the two input groups in comprehension and vocabulary acquisition? . . . We believe that the modified output condition afforded the learners a qualitatively different discourse experience" (pp. 297–298). (They then go on to support this explanation with examples and further details.)
- Williams (1999): "It appears that learners, at least at lower levels of proficiency, do not frequently focus on formal aspects of language. One logical reason for this is that lower-level learners may have enough to do just to maintain communications and they are therefore unable to focus on form to the same degree as the more proficient learners" (p. 612).

Comparing the results of the present study with the results found in earlier studies is also a common element in discussion sections. Earlier findings are typically presented in the literature review as a way of contextualizing the study. Comparisons of results in the discussion section have the effect of helping the reader understand how the findings relate to previous work. The findings may provide evidence that supports and extends earlier findings, or they may indicate that existing frameworks need to be reconsidered and revised. For instance:

Relating findings to previous research in discussion sections:

- Leow (2000): "[While the findings] provide further empirical evidence for the association between awareness and subsequent processing of L2 data found in other classroom-based studies, [they do not support] a dissociation between awareness and learning as espoused by some researchers" (p. 568).
- Berg (1999): "Findings in this investigation lend support to the view often expressed in the literature that training is important for successful peer response" (p. 230).

Discussion sections also often provide comments about the significance of the results or their implications for either pedagogy or theory, which can make it easier for readers to incorporate the findings into a framework they already know. For an audience of fellow researchers, such comments may clarify fundamental concepts and facilitate further research, while an audience of teachers may be able to consider the results actively in relation to what they do in the classroom on a daily basis. The first three examples below point out pedagogical implications, while the third focuses on theory:

Providing comments about the significance of research for theory or pedagogy in discussion sections:

- Berg (1999): "Peer response can be an important learning tool in a writing course because it helps student writers do what they cannot yet do for themselves, and detect incongruities in their texts" (p. 232).
- Williams (1999): "It is possible to pinpoint activities that are more likely to foster such a focus [on form] than others . . . Teachers can use this knowledge as they plan lessons and actively encourage students to engage in activities that draw or attract attention to form-meaning connections" (p. 619).
- Hafner (2013): "One way to look at the digital video project is as a bridge to the subsequent academic task of writing a lab report . . . the project stages identity development, language, and literacy development in manageable chunks, moving from familiar to unfamiliar and ultimately increasing access to the more constrained genres of academic writing" (pp. 681–682).

> - Leow (2000): "From a theoretical perspective, no dissociation between awareness and learning was found in this study, the results of which are compatible with the claim that awareness plays a crucial role in subsequent processing of L2 data" (p. 573).

In summary, then, discussion sections are typically central components of the final stages involved in reporting research, providing the important functions of summary, explanation, comparison, and appraisal. They can inform readers about the purposes of the research, call attention to its context and implications, clarify theories and concepts, and promote further investigation and analysis.

TIME TO DO ...

Review a study you have recently read. What elements does the author include in the discussion section?

11.2.2 Limitations, Future Research, and Conclusion Sections

Once research projects have been concluded, providing full information about the limitations of a study is always necessary. This may be included in the discussion section; however, limitations often appear as a separate section, and sometimes as part of the conclusion. Regardless of the precise location, acknowledgment of the limitations of the research is essential, not only as a caution to the readers against overgeneralization of the findings, but also as a suggestion for how future studies could be improved and as an indication of possible avenues for further investigation. As explained in Chapter 1, and as can be seen in the examples below, such sections are often an important and rich source of research questions for other researchers:

> Outlining potential future research:
>
> - Willett (1995): "The question we must ask is not which interactional routines and strategies are correlated with successful language acquisition. Rather, we must first ask what meaning routines and strategies have in the local culture and how they enable learners to construct positive identities and relations and manage competing agendas" (p. 499).

- Berg (1999): "It is important to discover what takes place during trained versus untrained peer response negotiations . . . [and] it would be useful to study the different aspects of the training program to determine the most useful activities for reaching desired outcomes" (p. 233).
- Leow (2000) (suggesting that future studies should focus on methodology): "Robust research designs are clearly needed to address the issue of how representative participants' performance in experimental groups truly is, especially in the areas of attention and awareness in SLA" (p. 574).
- Melzi and King (2003): "It would also be of interest to collect and analyse similar data among younger children in order to investigate the developmental trajectory [of diminutive affix use]" (p. 302).

These sorts of comments help generate ideas for further research, point to areas that need to be addressed in order to advance the field, and serve as a useful roadmap for both novice and experienced researchers. In finalizing research for publication, the specification of directions for future research also demonstrates to the reader that the author has concluded one phase of the research and has carefully thought about the next phase.

Limitations sections usually also include a discussion of the generalizability of the results given the characteristics of the participants (e.g., L1, age, gender, proficiency level, socioeconomic status, instructional or experimental context for the research, country of origin, length of residence, etc.) or the linguistic focus of the study. For example, the first three studies below imply limited generalizability and a corresponding need for replication, while the last implies that linguistic and cross-linguistic study are necessary:

Comments relating to generalizability:

- Philp (2003): "The majority of learners were educated to at least postsecondary level, most were socio-economically advantaged, and, in general, they were motivated to study the L2" (p. 118).
- Willett (1995) (in relation to instructional context): "The kinds of interactional routines and strategies used in this particular classroom were local, not universal" (p. 499).
- Leow (2000): "The findings clearly cannot be extrapolated to other linguistic forms or structures" (p. 573).

- Melzi and King (2003): "[Our study] provides further support for the recent calls (e.g., Lieven, 1994) for increased study of non-English languages in the field" (p. 303).
- Hafner (2013): "Although the approach has worked well in the reported context, the study is limited to observations of one course in one institution at one point in time and must be interpreted with this limitation in mind" (p. 682).

Also to be found in limitations sections are contextual concerns (e.g., the need for a wider range of contexts to be addressed, including second vs. foreign language, or different discourse contexts), statements about the effect of the materials (e.g., tasks and tests) on the results obtained, the role of setting (e.g., different types of L2 classrooms such as communicative vs. forms-oriented classrooms), the need for longitudinal studies investigating the long-term effect of the treatment used, and also interaction effects such as the relationship between learner-internal factors, target language knowledge, and the effects of instruction and interaction.

Common elements in the final sections of second language research articles

- summarizing the results;
- explaining possible reasons for the results;
- comparing the results to those obtained in other studies;
- commenting on the significance or implications of the results;
- discussing limitations; and
- suggesting areas for further research.

It is important to remember that the exact sequence of these sections is not fixed, nor do all articles contain all elements. As Ruiyang and Allison (2003) note, "The structure of empirical RAs [research articles] in applied linguistics tends to be flexible towards the end, partly because rhetorical functions can overlap" (p. 381). It is important to bear in mind when examining checklists such as these that many research reports—whether articles, grant proposals, grant reports, book chapters, or books—can be written in sections and checked in sections, just as we propose here. However, consistency between sections is crucial as well, so researchers also need to check for obvious contradictions and repetition of information, in addition to making certain that the sections logically match each other.

11.3 THE FINAL STAGES IN REPORTING QUALITATIVE RESEARCH

In the opening sections of reports, qualitative and quantitative articles can be quite similar. For example, regardless of paradigm, authors usually clearly state their (initial) research questions and problems, and provide a theoretical background for their research. The context in which the research has been conducted should also be addressed, along with the many issues involved in the selection of participants. However, qualitative and quantitative research can be different in their final stages insofar as qualitative research reports can be more varied in terms of organization and in terms of the specific sections included (for instance, results and discussion might be grouped together). They also demand more persuasive writing in order to effectively summarize large amounts of data and to communicate the significance of the research to the reader. Qualitative research must also address many other elements that are inherent to non-quantitative research as discussed below.

Different paradigms of qualitative research potentially involve distinct standards for reporting and stylistic elements. As we have discussed in Chapters 3 and 7, qualitative research can involve a range of data collection methods, including, for instance, structured and unstructured classroom observations, structured and unstructured informal interviews, case studies, introspective analyses, and diary studies. Since acceptable reports vary based on the research paradigm and methods that the qualitative researcher adopts, qualitative researchers must decide how to organize their reports so that their ideas are best communicated to the intended audience.

Heath (1997) suggests that qualitative reports include introduction, research paradigm, and research method sections, and that they address preliminary biases, suppositions, and hypotheses. The introduction to qualitative reports might begin with a quotation or a vignette before describing the research question and situating it within a theoretical context. An example of a vignette comes from Pierce (1995), who begins her article on identity and investment in the following way:

> Everybody working with me is Canadian. When I started to work there, they couldn't understand that it might be difficult for me to understand everything and know about everything what it's normal for them. To explain it more clearly I can write an example, which happened few days ago. The girl [Gail] which is working with me pointed at the man and said:
>
> "Do you see him?
>
> "Yes, why?"
>
> "Don't you know him?"
>
> "No, I don't know him."
>
> "How come you don't know him. Don't you watch TV. That's Bart Simpson."
>
> It made me feel so bad and I didn't answer her nothing. Until now I don't know why this person was important.
>
> Eva, February 8, 1991

As a stylistic device, the reader is immediately brought into an interpersonal association.

The research design section should be used to represent the epistemological, conceptual foundations and assumptions of the qualitative research paradigm chosen and should contain citations of authors who have defined the paradigm, thus increasing the validity of the design. The research methods section should include sufficient detail in order to increase its verisimilitude (i.e., authenticity and credibility). As such, the instrumentation used to collect the data, as well as the specific procedures followed, should be described. Reports should clearly state how the researcher gained access to participants and what kind of relationship was established between the researcher and participants.

TIME TO THINK ...

Why is it particularly important to address the researchers' relationship to their participants, as well as how they gained access to those participants, in a qualitative research report?

The nature of the data and how they were collected should also be clearly stated. Particularly important for qualitative research is the inclusion of information about procedures such as how decision-making was carried out and how the researcher implemented data reduction and reconstruction. It is also important for researchers to give a clear sense of how much data were collected (for example, how many interviews, and of what length, how many hours of observation, and over what period of time) as this is important in assessing the strength of the research overall. Finally, as noted above, since researchers are usually primarily responsible for data collection and analysis, they need to report any preliminary biases, suppositions, and hypotheses prior to the study, as well as whether, and if so how, these changed over the period of the study. For instance, case study reports must be certain to specify the role of the researcher since this is often greater than that of a simple observer and may be relevant when interpreting the data. The boundaries of the case study must also be clearly described and motivated. For instance, why a particular case was selected, and how and in what contexts data were collected. In addition, while generalizations are seldom made based on case studies, the researcher should not only report findings but also draw conclusions that contribute to an overall understanding of a phenomenon within a theoretical framework. Like case studies of individuals, classroom observation research should make the role of the researcher in the classroom explicit. If an observation instrument is utilized, a full description of it needs to be reported. On the other hand, for unstructured classroom observations, the research report might need to focus on how data were tracked as well as the decision-making process that led to the study's focus. If a data collection instrument was adapted or designed and revised, this should be made clear, often with much more detail about the processes that led to the revisions than would be the case for quantitative research. If surveys or questionnaires are employed to supplement and triangulate qualitative data, the researcher should report issues such as what the response rates were, whether or not there was a non-response bias, how analyses were performed, and whether any generalizations can be drawn from the results. It is also common to include copies of survey or interview questions in the appendices. In summary, each qualitative research paradigm requires a unique consideration of its crucial elements when a report is written in part because there are different research paradigms and many means of collecting and analyzing data, so researchers need to take particular care to detail (and justify) how they collected and analyzed their data.

When reporting the results of a qualitative study, researchers should also take into account the importance of rich or thick description. If the purpose of the research is to describe and classify the observed data, rich description is often utilized. The evidence reported should be detailed, multi-layered, and comprehensive. Rather than reporting a limited number of anecdotes that support the conclusions, researchers should try to provide detail about a systematic selection of the data that represents both the central tendencies and variations. Researchers often also opt to present counter examples as well, that is "exceptions that prove the rule." The purpose of some qualitative research, such as ethnographies, is to go beyond mere description and attribute observations to underlying constructs and systems of meaning. This type of research will need to employ thick description, as discussed in Chapter 7. An important question in qualitative research write-ups is how much interpretation of the data the writer should provide. Many qualitative researchers suggest that while writers may offer their own interpretations, they should also provide an adequate basis for their audience to construct their own independent interpretations. This may be accomplished by separating presentation of data (e.g., vignettes, interview excepts, and so on) from discussion and analysis.

11.4 REPORTING MIXED-METHODS RESEARCH

As discussed in Chapter 10, it is frequently the case now that quantitative and qualitative research methods are not viewed as dichotomous. Survey-based research methods, such as the use of questionnaires, are often used to triangulate both more quantitative and more qualitatively oriented data. However methods are classified, second language researchers are increasingly taking into account the fact that data can be collected using a wide range and combination of methods. When included in a primarily quantitative report, qualitative data or analytic techniques may provide unique insights that would escape both the researcher and the reader if statistical counts and analyses were used in isolation. For example, we have argued elsewhere (Gass & Mackey, 2000) that stimulated recall protocols, when collected and coded, often provide a particularly rich source of information that can elucidate a trend, exemplify any variation in the data, or provide insights into results that turn out to be different from what was predicted. Similarly, qualitative reports may become clearer when some quantitative analysis is included. While a qualitative researcher may not be able to (or choose to) utilize parametric and comparative statistics, descriptive statistics can help make any tendencies or patterns in the data clear to readers. For example, graphs representing the data frequency distribution, measures of central tendencies (means, modes, or medians), and range and standard deviation characteristics of the data can help confirm the validity of any trends, patterns, or groupings that the researcher has identified through a qualitative analysis. Hence, it may be best if researchers, even if they identify their research as primarily qualitative or quantitative, do not rule out the inclusion of both types of data in their reports. In reporting their research, researchers need to consider all elements and requirements that will best explain the data to the audience.

TIME TO DO ...

Find a piece of research that employs both quantitative and qualitative methods but does not identify itself as a mixed-methods study. How does the author organize the report to include both methodologies? Compare and contrast this method to a study report that is exclusively quantitative or qualitative.

11.5 CHECKLIST FOR COMPLETING REPORTS OF RESEARCH

It can be helpful to carefully evaluate research before submitting it for publication or review. Most researchers recommend considering where they might want to submit research for publication before investing the time in drafting the final sections because research will be written up differently depending on the target journal or publisher. Even for dissertations or masters theses, it can be helpful if the researcher has a publication goal in mind after completing the empirical work. Next, we provide a list of questions to consider when finalizing quantitative research.

11.5.1 The Research Problem and Questions

When reporting research, the problem and questions need to be clearly stated and presented as part of a theoretical framework. Helpful questions to ask include the following:

- Are the research questions motivated by the literature review/your discussion of the literature?
- Are the research questions clearly formulated and unambiguously worded?
- Are the research questions appropriate for the theoretical framework?
- Why is the central research problem worth investigating? Is the argument for why the study is interesting clear? For example:
  - Does the study fill a gap in the literature by addressing a relatively under-researched area or an unresolved problem?
  - Does the study address a methodological concern observed in previous research?
  - Does the study replicate previous research? If it is a partial replication, is the new element clear and well motivated (e.g.,

357

a replication with a different population of learners, in a new context, or with different measures of learning)?

- In general, how does addressing these research questions make an original contribution to the field?
- How have practical constraints such as time, money, availability, and energy limits facing the researcher impacted the investigation?
- Has the investigation of the research question avoided placing the participants in any physical or psychological danger? That is, are there ethical issues that should be considered/discussed?

11.5.2 The Research Hypotheses

The research hypotheses or predictions, if any, need to be clearly stated and presented as part of a theoretical framework in the research report. It is important to note that not all quantitatively oriented papers specify hypotheses or predictions. If they are included, however, helpful questions to ask include the following:

- Are the hypotheses clearly stated?
- Do the hypotheses clearly specify the variables that might be related?
- Are the hypotheses appropriate for the theoretical framework?
- Are the hypotheses testable given the methods adopted for the research?
- Will the results lead to the generation of additional hypotheses to be tested in subsequent research?

TIME TO DO ...

Reconstruct the research questions that formed the following hypotheses from Philp (2003, p. 105):

- Accuracy of recall is correlated with the level of the learner such that the higher the level of the learner, the greater the accuracy of recall.
- Accuracy of recall will be higher for shorter recasts than longer recasts.
- Accuracy of recall will be higher the fewer the changes made in the recast utterance.

11.5.3 The Audience

It is important to take into consideration the needs, interests, and expectations of the audience when reporting research. In choosing where to publish or present, researchers need to consider their audience and the match between their work and what is usually either published by the journal or press or presented at the conference venue. A useful place to start is to look at the publication venues of comparable articles that influenced the development of the research. With this in mind, useful questions include the following:

- Who is the primary audience for this article, report, paper, presentation, or book?
- Is there a secondary audience?
- Has the write-up been targeted to the relevant interests?
    - To ensure that the research is compatible with audience expectations, as well as to be sure that it is a good fit for a given journal or press, it is useful to skim a number of articles (or books) in recent issues of the journal or press.
    - It is also helpful to read the brief reports or summaries of previously successful grantees. These are often available on the Internet or by writing to the grant-awarding body.
- Have the needs and expectations of the readers been carefully considered? For example:
    - If the paper is for a class, have the assignment guidelines been followed?
    - If the article is to be submitted to a journal or a press, have the guidelines on page length, formatting, and reporting been followed?
    - If the research is part of a grant application or report, have the guidelines set by the grant-awarding body been followed?

11.5.4 The Abstract

As noted in Chapter 1, the abstract provides a quick at-a-glance overview, which readers will usually use to determine whether the study is relevant to their current interests and research needs. In other words, the abstract is likely to be the most read component of any paper or chapter, and as such, needs to be well written. In addition to enticing a potential audience and convincing publishers, grant awarders, or conferences to accept the research, it is also important to write a good, representative abstract for retrieval purposes. A large number of online search databases typically include only abstracts, and these are catalogued and indexed so that interested parties can search for relevant topics. Thus, useful questions to ask when evaluating the abstract for research reports include the following:

- Does it provide a readable, concise yet representative overview of the topic and aim of the research?
- Are the sample and materials/methods briefly described?
- Are the results of the study summarized and is the relevance of the study clear?

11.5.5 The Literature Review

The literature review explains the context for the research, together with details about the findings, strengths, and weaknesses of previous studies in the area. Helpful questions to evaluate the literature review in the concluding phases of research include the following:

- Are all relevant studies surveyed?
- Does the review provide an accurate and objective summary of the current state of the art and the theoretical framework of the study?
- Does the review present readers with enough background to understand how the study fits in with other research?
- Now that the study is concluded, are any organizational changes or new inclusions to the literature review necessary to better contextualize the discussion of the results?
- Is the literature review relevant, that is, are studies that are peripheral to or irrelevant to the research question excluded?

11.5.6 The Design of the Study

In reporting studies, researchers must try to include enough detail about the design to allow other researchers to replicate the study and to be able to understand and evaluate the validity of the results, based on the methods used. Helpful questions include the following:

- Is it clear that the research design (e.g., experimental, quasi-experimental, correlational, qualitative, mixed method, and so on) was appropriate given the theoretical framework, purpose, and research questions of the study?
- Are all of the terms clearly defined and operationalized with examples wherever space permits?
- Are each of the variables clearly defined?
- Is the design explained in sufficient detail to permit replication wherever possible?

11.5.7 Logistics

In the final stages of research and before reporting, researchers should also carefully address practical issues with a series of checks. For example:

- Has the appropriate permission or consent from the participants and all other relevant bodies (e.g., school boards, guardians, teachers, parents) been appropriately checked and filed?
- Did any problems interfere with the basic timeline for the completion of the study, and if so, should they be reported in order to help others who collect data in the same context?
- Are the data from the study kept in a secure place?
- Have all identifying details been kept confidential in the report wherever possible?
- Was there a contingency plan for a problem or unforeseen event that arose? If so, is information about how this was solved conveyed in the research report to assist future researchers who might face the same problem?

11.5.8 Participants

- Are sufficient biographical details on the participants provided so as to permit replication?
- At the same time, have confidentiality/anonymity issues been taken into account when this information was reported?
- Is information on the selection or assignment of participants to particular groups provided?

361

11.5.9 Data Gathering

- Is it clear that the choice of sample (e.g., random, nonrandom, stratified random) was appropriate given the purpose of the study?
- Is it clear that the means for gathering data was appropriate for the research question?
- Was evidence of the validity and reliability of the instruments provided in the write-up?
- Is sufficient and detailed information provided about how, when, and where the data were gathered?
- Was the status of the researcher made explicit in the data-gathering process (i.e., Was the researcher an observer? A participant? What, if any, was the relationship of the researcher to the participants?)?

11.5.10 Data Analysis

Some questions to keep in mind when reporting on data analyses include:

11.5.10.1 Transcription

- Was transcription of the entire data set necessary for coding, or was partial transcription acceptable? Is this clearly reported?
- Were reliability checks performed on transcriptions (and results reported)?
- Is it useful for the target readers if detailed information is provided on how many transcriptions and/or hours of data were used?
- Is information about transcription conventions necessary for the audience (and if so, is it provided in an appendix or notes to any examples used)?

11.5.10.2 Coding Systems

- Was coding of the entire database necessary, or was partial coding acceptable? Is this clearly reported?
- Were reliable coding guidelines available?
- Are coding categories clearly defined and examples of each coding category provided?

11.5.10.3 Inter-Rater Reliability

- Was an inter-rater (or intra-rater) reliability check necessary for the research? If so, is the method of assessing such reliability clearly reported?
- Is the rationale for choosing that particular method explained?
- Was the inter-rater reliability statistic considered to be sufficiently high? If not, is information about the sources of disagreement provided? Is information about missed (rather than disagreed-upon) episodes provided?
- Is information about the coders provided?
- Are the rating/scoring guidelines necessary for the reader to understand the coding system? If so, are they provided?

11.5.10.4 Data Organization

- Do all important constructs in the research have clear theoretical definitions? Are all variables operationally defined?
- Is it clear that the constructs and variables were appropriate for the research?
- Is information provided clarifying the research variables and the scales that represent them?
- Is enough information provided for readers to determine what kinds of scales have been used for each variable?

11.5.10.5 Statistics

- Are the statistical tests and procedures used clearly identified?
- If the choice of a statistical test is not one of the standard ones used in the field, is its appropriateness clearly demonstrated (for example, by referencing statistics texts or published studies with similar data and tests)?
- If consultants were used, are they thanked in the author's note (see below)?

11.5.10.6 *Presentation*

- Are the data clearly summarized and presented in the report (e.g., charts, appendices, figures, etc.)?
- Are both descriptions and graphical representations of the data included where appropriate?
- Is the chosen method of presentation the clearest, most effective, and most elegant way of presenting the data?
- Is appropriate and consistent formatting followed throughout?

11.5.11 Conclusions

As discussed earlier in this chapter, there are several considerations to keep in mind when drafting the final sections of research reports:

- Are the results of the research succinctly summarized?
- Are the limitations of the research acknowledged?
- Are the implications of the results for either theory or pedagogy (or both) discussed?
- Are suggestions as to the direction of future research provided?

11.5.12 References

Most style guides require researchers to ensure that *all* citations in reports of research (whether books, articles, or chapters, and so on), and *only* those citations, are included in the correct format in the reference list. Also, all citations in the research report should be consistent with the same style guide. It is important to consider carefully how secondary sources will be cited (for example, when to include the complete and original reference in cases where you cite someone who cited someone). To illustrate the variation in referencing, we list below the different referencing styles used in seven journals specializing in second language research.

Language Learning

Studies in Second Language Acquisition

The Modern Language Journal

These three journals all use the same style:

Polio, C. (1997). Measures of linguistic accuracy in second language writing research. *Language Learning, 47*, 101–143.

Applied Linguistics

Duanmu, S. 1995. 'Metrical and tonal phonology of compounds in two Chinese dialects.' *Language* 71/2: 225–259.

Tomlin, R.S. and V. Villa. 1994. 'Attention in cognitive science and second language acquisition.' *Studies in Second Language Acquisition* 16: 183–204.

Second Language Research

Spada, N. and Lightbown, P.M. 1993: Instruction and the development of questions in L2 classrooms. *Studies in Second Language Acquisition* 15, 205–24.

System

R.C. Gardner, P.F. Tremblay and A. Masgoret, Towards a full model of second language learning: an empirical investigation. *The Modern Language Journal* **81** (1997), pp. 344–362.

The style guide also needs to be followed for details such as the ordering of references in the text. Some guides require multiple citations to be in alphabetical order; others allow ordering to be chronological or selected by the researcher, perhaps in order of relevance to the point being made. Guidelines as to how to cite multiple publications by the same author in the same year, for example Smith (1994a, 1994b), also need to be checked with the style guide used. Meticulous checking of references and reference formatting, especially in cases where multiple revisions have been made to a document, can be one of the most tedious and time-consuming factors involved in preparing reports of research. Software programs such as EndNote[1] (ISI ResearchSoft) have been designed to automate this task. In terms of the content, it is also the responsibility of the author to ensure the references are appropriate for the study described.

The selection of sources is usually seen as related to the issues involved in writing the literature review and statement of the problem.

11.5.13 Footnotes, Endnotes, Figures, and Tables

Like the reference list, footnotes, endnotes, figures, and tables must adhere to a standardized presentation that is consistent with a single style guide. Whereas for theses and dissertations they are customarily placed at appropriate points throughout the text (footnotes), journals and other publications often require that they appear at the end of the research article (endnotes).

11.5.13.1 Footnotes and Endnotes

Since many style guides suggest citing authors parenthetically within the text itself, footnotes and endnotes are generally not used for citing sources; rather, they are used to include information that, while relevant, does not fit into the flow of the text. They may include supplemental content supporting an idea expounded on in the text, concessions to a contrasting point of view, additional sources for further reading on the topic, or copyright information. It is generally advised that footnotes containing supplemental content should explain only one basic tangential idea. If they are longer or more involved than this, style guides suggest that authors consider incorporating the information into the body of the paper or including it as an appendix. Both footnotes and endnotes are usually indicated and referenced with superscript Arabic numerals, consecutively numbered. The choice of whether to use endnotes or footnotes is determined by the style sheet of the journal or publisher.

11.5.13.2 Figures

Figures are used to display information discussed in the text in a concise format that is easy to comprehend, and they generally consist of graphs, diagrams, charts, illustrations, or photographs. Second language researchers commonly use figures when an image would make an arrangement or relationship easier to visualize, or when a pattern of results would be clearer in visual format to augment or supplement a list of numbers in a table. A general rule of thumb is that a figure should not be used simply to duplicate textual information, or as extra material, but rather as a helpful complement to or amplification of what is expressed verbally in the text. Stylistically, each figure should be referred to in the body of the paper, where the author should also indicate what in the figure is relevant to the issue under discussion. Also, each figure must be identified by a number, ordered consecutively, and given a brief and descriptive caption. It is often the case with most theses or dissertations, in which figures appear in the text itself, that the figures are also listed in a separate table. Chapter 9 provides examples of a range of typical figures used in second language research.

11.5.13.3 Tables

Tables are often used to present quantitative data, statistics, and analyses in a format that makes them easy to understand and facilitates comparisons. In writing research reports, it is important for researchers to decide what in their data is relevant and worthy of notice rather than to present every aspect of a large data set. When discussing the data in a table, researchers should guide the audience toward the information they feel is significant. As with figures, tables must be identified numerically, numbered consecutively, and referred to in the text. They should be given brief, descriptive titles, and notes can be added to the bottom to explain specific aspects of their content. Even though they are discussed in the text, tables should also be relatively self-standing; as such, any abbreviations and units of measurement should be defined, and all of the rows and columns must be appropriately labeled. As mentioned above, tables are placed at the end of articles submitted for publication. In the text of a thesis or dissertation, however, it is important that they be placed as close as possible to where they are mentioned in the body of the paper while still fitting on a single page.

11.5.14 Author's Note/Acknowledgments

Many reports of research include a section where people who have helped with the research are thanked. These notes appear in different sections depending on the format of the report. For example, in journal articles and book chapters, the author's note may appear either as a footnote or as an endnote, whereas in a book it may be part of the preface or even the dedication. Researchers often wish to thank: (a) their participants, for example learners, native speakers, teachers, and so on; (b) any colleagues who may have read earlier drafts of the work and offered suggestions or feedback; (c) any assistants including students, colleagues, or co-workers who may have helped with data collection, materials development, transcribing, coding, or library work; and (d) any consultants who may have helped with statistics or ideas. Grant support is also often acknowledged in the author's note, usually with the number of the grant included. Anonymous reviewers are often thanked as well. Many authors finish their notes by stating that despite the help they have received with their articles, they are solely responsible for the content and for any errors.

11.5.15 Post-Research Concerns

Once the research has been completed, there are still tasks that the researcher must think about. For example:

- What feedback, if any, needs to be provided to the participants?
  - Do the participants need to receive brief, accessible reports about the research findings?
  - Do any other parties (e.g., teachers or administrators) need to receive such reports?
- If necessary, have any participants been given an oral debriefing on the purpose and outcome of the study? (Confidentiality must be considered when summarizing results for participants and involved parties.)
- Have the participants been thanked and/or remunerated? In the report or the author's note, have those who contributed to the research been appropriately acknowledged?

11.5.16 Final Touches and Formatting

When writing reports in a manner appropriate to the research paradigm, in addition to the content and organization of what is being reported, it is important to consider how the report is presented. For example, the front and back material (title page, abstract, author note, references, and appendices) and the formatting can be very important to publication. This material will depend on where the report is to be submitted for publication. If the research is to be submitted for conference presentation or poster display, clear guidelines are usually provided in the calls for papers. As discussed above, if the report is to be submitted to a journal in the field of second language research, many (although by no means all) journals follow the guidelines set forth in the *Publication Manual of the American Psychological Association.* Researchers must carefully consult the relevant style manual when preparing to submit their manuscript. These manuals contain clear guidelines as to how the manuscripts are to be formatted. For example, as mentioned earlier, tables and figures are often included as back matter and not included in the text. Style guides also often suggest that researchers practice gender-neutral writing wherever possible, for example by using the term "the learner."

As far as research proposals are concerned, when soliciting grants, researchers must pay close attention to the format requirements laid out by the relevant agency. While compelling content and arguments for the value of the research should be the most important component of a grant proposal, grant submitters must also adhere to the regulations for margins, font, spacing, page length, etc. Often a granting body will have an office that evaluates proposals in order to ascertain their compliance with formatting regulations before the proposal is sent out to be reviewed. Researchers should pay attention to the front and back material that needs to be included ahead of time, because scrambling to complete these at the last minute can lead to problems. For example, a grant-awarding institution may require the inclusion of such items as customized (and often abbreviated) curriculum vitæ or a biographical statement, a timeline for the research, and usually a budget proposal together with a prose justification for the budget. All of these can be used by reviewers when determining whether the researcher has an appropriate research background, realistic expectations, and a feasible financial plan and timeline for implementing the proposed research.

Equally important in reporting research are the guidelines outlined by particular universities for theses and dissertations. For example, some universities require that students follow a style manual approved by the mentor regarding formatting issues such as quotations, footnotes, and other stylistic details. Much of the front and back material, however, may also need to follow specific university guidelines. Among other elements, guidelines are often required in regard to the layout of the title page, the table of contents, the type of paper used, and the spacing and margins. Other common specifications include information about the formatting of the abstract; for example, for many schools, the abstract must contain a statement of the problem, the procedure or method followed, the results, and the conclusion, all within a word limit. Stories of excellent dissertations that were sent back for revision by universities because of formatting violations often make the rounds of graduate schools, together with stories about how reformatting then held up graduation. In short, the "packaging" of a research report is crucial, whether it is being submitted to a university committee, a grant-awarding agency, a journal for publication, or a publisher for a book.

In summary, the final stages of research consist of creating a complete product. Not only must ideas, theories, results, and conclusions of quantitative and qualitative research be clearly communicated, but the professionalism of the researcher should also be demonstrated through careful attention to the formatting and presentation of their work. The earlier a researcher gets used to conforming to the "packaging" of research, the easier a researcher's writing life will be.

11.6 CONCLUSION

We hope this chapter has provided a useful point from which both novice and more experienced researchers can evaluate their research at the point of its conclusion and, ultimately, finalize studies that will make a significant and lasting contribution to second language research.

POINTS TO REMEMBER

- Although the structure and organization of the final sections of research reports can vary, a typical report includes: results, discussion, limitations, directions for future research, and a conclusion.

- Typical elements of a discussion section are a summary of results, explanations for the results, a comparison of the results of the present study with the results found in earlier studies, and implications for either pedagogy or theory.

- Acknowledgment of the limitations of the research is essential, not only as a caution to the readers against overgeneralization of the findings, but also as a suggestion for how future studies could be improved and as an indication of possible avenues for further investigation.

- While the opening sections of qualitative and quantitative articles can be quite similar, they can be very different in their final stages insofar as qualitative research reports can be more varied in terms of organization and may include elements not inherent to quantitative research.

- Even if researchers identify their research as primarily qualitative or quantitative, it is recommended to not rule out the inclusion of both types of data in research reports as both quantitative and qualitative methods may provide unique insights that would not otherwise be possible.

- When reporting studies, researchers must try to include enough detail about the design to allow other researchers to replicate the study and to be able to understand and evaluate the validity of the results.

MORE TO DO AND MORE TO THINK ABOUT ...

1. Consider the four elements commonly discussed as part of limitations sections: a summary of the results, an explanation of possible reasons for the results, a comparison of the results to those obtained in other studies, and a commentary on the significance or implications of the

results. For the two articles you found for question one, discuss their limitations sections in the context of the four common elements.

2. Provide three guidelines for writing up and discussing the findings of *quantitative* research.

3. Provide three guidelines for writing up and discussing the findings of *qualitative* research.

4. You have carried out a study of the relationship between scores on an aptitude test, and the development of past time reference in English as a second language. However, rather than the 25 participants per group you had anticipated, you only have six per group, and your findings are not conclusive. What sorts of considerations should be borne in mind when deciding where to report the results of this research?

5. If research reports are to be submitted to a journal or a publisher for consideration for publication, how can the relevant style guidelines be obtained?

6. In the final phases of research, when and how should findings be communicated to the participants?

NOTE

1. EndNote (www.endnote.com) is a software program designed to organize bibliographic references and place them in an appropriate format for the journal for which one is preparing an article.

Sample Short Form Written Consent Document for Subjects Who Do Not Speak English

This document should be written in a language understandable to the subject.

Consent to Participate in Research

You are being asked to participate in a research study.

Before you agree, you must be informed about (i) the purposes, nature, and time range for the research; (ii) any procedures which are experimental; (iii) any reasonably foreseeable risks and benefits to the research; (iv) any potentially beneficial alternative procedures; and (v) how confidentiality will be maintained.

Where applicable, you must also be told about (i) any available compensation should injury occur; (ii) the possibility of unforeseeable risks; (iii) circumstances in which the investigator may decide to halt your participation; (iv) any costs to you; (v) what happens if you decide to stop participating; (vi) when you will be told about new findings which may affect your willingness to participate; and (vii) how many people will be in the study.

If you agree to participate, you must be given a signed copy of this document and a written summary of the research.

You may contact ____name____ at ____phone number____ any time you have questions about the research.

You may contact ____name____ at ____phone number____ if you have questions about your rights as a research subject or what to do if you are injured.

Your participation in this research is voluntary, and you will not be penalized or lose any benefits if you refuse to participate or decide to stop.

Signing this document means that the research study, including the above information, has been described to you orally, and that you voluntarily agree to participate.

_____   _____

signature of participant   date

_____   _____

signature of witness   date

Consent to Participate in Research

Project Name: L2 learners' performance on grammaticality judgment, oral production, and production, and listening tasks

Investigator _____ **Telephone** _____ **Email** _____

Sponsor None (*The University Institutional Review Board has given approval for this research project. For information on your rights as a research subject, contact* _____)

Introduction

You are invited to consider participating in this research study. We will be comparing the performance of EFL learners on three different tasks, a speaking activity, a written activity, and a listening activity. This form will describe the purpose and nature of the study and your rights as a participant in the study. The decision to participate or not is yours. If you decide to participate, please sign and date the last line of this form.

Explanation of the study

We will be looking at the kind of language you use when you do three different kinds of activities: a speaking activity, a writing activity, and a listening activity. About 40 students enrolled in ____ will participate in this study. As part of the study, you will meet with the researcher for an oral interview. At the same time, you will do the writing activity and then the listening activity. All three tasks will take about 30 minutes to complete. A tape-recorder will be used to record what you are saying during the speaking activities.

Confidentiality

All of the information collected will be confidential and will only be used for research purposes. This means that your identity will be anonymous; in other words, no one besides the researcher will know your name. Whenever data from this study are published, your name will not be used. The data will be stored in a computer, and only the researcher will have access to it.

Your participation

Participating in this study is strictly voluntary. Your decision to participate will in **no** way affect your grade. If at any point you change your mind and no longer want to participate, you can tell your teacher. You will not be paid for participating in this study. If you have any questions about the research, you can contact _____ by telephone at _____, by email _____, or in person at the office in _____.

Investigator's statement

I have fully explained this study to the student. I have discussed the activities and have answered all of the questions that the student asked.

Signature of investigator _____ Date _____

Learner's consent

I have read the information provided in this Informed Consent Form. All my questions were answered to my satisfaction. I voluntarily agree to participate in this study.

Your signature _____ Date _____

Sample Consent Form for a Study in a Foreign Language Context

Consent to Participate in Research

Project Name Conversation and second language development

Investigator _____ **Telephone** _____ **Email** _____

Sponsor

The University Institutional Review Board has given approval for this research project. For information on your rights as a research subject, contact _____

Introduction

You are invited to consider participating in this research study. We will be evaluating the effect of carrying out different activities on learning English as a foreign language (EFL). This form will describe the purpose and nature of the study and your rights as a participant in the study. The decision to participate or not is yours. If you decide to participate, please sign and date the last line of this form.

Explanation of the study

We will be looking at how different kinds of speaking activities help EFL learners in X country develop skills such as fluency and creative thinking. In particular, we are interested in the difference between activities that are carried out several times and activities that are done only once. We are also interested in comparing the language used during conversation activities with a native speaker with speaking activities done individually. About 105 students enrolled in xxx will participate in this study. You will carry out speaking activities with a native English speaker outside of class time on three different days. Each speaking activity will take approximately 15 minutes to complete. As part of the study, you will also complete some written practice activities, and do some individual speaking activities in the language lab during the regularly scheduled class times. Each quiz and individual speaking activity will take about 20 minutes to do. A tape-recorder will be used to record what you are saying during all speaking activities. All the activities will be completed over a nine-week period.

Confidentiality

All of the information collected will be confidential and will only be used for research and teacher training purposes. This means that your identity will be anonymous; in other words, no one besides the researcher will know your name. Whenever data from this study are published, your name will not be used. The data will be stored in a computer, and only the researcher will have access to it.

Your participation

Participating in this study is strictly voluntary. That means you do not have to be a part of the study. Your decision to participate will in **no** way affect your grade in any class. You will participate in the same activities, but nothing you say or do will be used as part of the data. If at any point you change your mind and no longer want to participate, you can tell your teacher. You will not be paid for participating in this study. If you have any questions about the research, you can contact _____ by telephone at _____, by email _____, or in person at _____ office.

Investigator's statement

I have fully explained this study to the student. I have discussed the activities and have answered all of the questions that the student asked. If necessary, I have translated key terms and concepts in this form and explained them orally.

Signature of investigator _____ Date _____

Student's consent

I have read the information provided in this Informed Consent Form. All my questions were answered to my satisfaction. I voluntarily agree to participate in this study.

Your signature _____ Date _____

Note: In many cases, a University IRB or ethics committee will also require approval and review by the overseas institution.

Sample Consent Form for a Classroom Study

Consent to Participate in Research

Project Title: Learner Uptake in the L2 Classroom

Researchers

Names

Email Addresses

Telephone Numbers

Office Addresses

The University Institutional Review Board has given approval for this research project. For information on your rights as a research subject, call the Institutional Review Board office at this number:

Introduction

We are currently undertaking a study to explore the effect of different variables in the language learning classroom. This form will describe the purpose and nature of the study. Please take whatever time you need to discuss the study with the researcher. The decision to participate or not is yours. If you do decide to participate, please sign and date the last line of this form.

Background and purpose of the study

We are particularly interested in the relationships among instructional materials designed for use in the language classroom, the ways that teachers use those materials, and the amount and nature of students' learning. We hope to use what we learn to improve the quality of language learning and teaching, and contribute to the growing body of knowledge in the area of language learning research.

Total number of participants

Approximately 12 people will take part in this study.

General plan

During the study, an audio recorder will be used to record your teacher's interactions with the students during 6 lessons. Instructional materials completed during class may also be used as part of the data. The lesson will follow the school curriculum and be no different from other lessons during the term.

Length of study

The study will last for 7 lessons.

Confidentiality

Every effort will be made to keep the data collected confidential. We will disclose personal information about you only if required to do so by the law. However, we cannot guarantee absolute confidentiality. Whenever data from this study are published, your name will not be used.

Data security

If information about your participation in the study is stored on a computer, the computer will not be part of a network and only the researchers will have access to the data.

New findings

If you would like us to, we will contact you to explain the results of our study after the study has been concluded.

Payment

You will not be paid for participating in this study.

Your rights as a participant

Your participation in this study is entirely voluntary. You have the right to leave the study at any time. Leaving the study will not result in any penalty or affect your relations with your teacher or school. Should you decide to leave the study, tell your teacher or a researcher. You will still participate in class activities, but nothing you say or do which happens to be on the tapes, and nothing you submit to your teacher, will be used as part of the data.

Problems and questions

Email _____ or call _____ if you have any questions or problems.

Call the IRB Office at this number:_____ with any questions about your rights as a research subject.

Withdrawal by researcher

The researchers may stop the study or take you out of the study at any time should they judge that you are no longer at the appropriate level for the study, or for any other reason.

Researcher's statement

I have fully explained this study to the participant. I have discussed the procedures and treatments and have answered all of the questions that the participant has asked.

Signature of researcher _____ Date _____

Participant's consent

I have read the information provided in this Informed Consent Form. All my questions were answered to my satisfaction. I voluntarily agree to participate in this study.

Your name _____

Your signature _____

Date _____

Sample Transcription Conventions: "Jeffersonian" Transcription Conventions

1. [[Simultaneous utterances:
   TOM: [[I used to smoke a lot when I was young
   BOB: [[I used to smoke Camels

2. [Overlapping utterances:
   TOM: I used to smoke a lot more than this
           [
   BOB: I see

3.]   End of overlapping or simultaneous utterance
   TOM: I used to smoke a lot more than this.
           [   ]
   BOB: Did you really?

4. =   Linked or continuing utterance (no overlap)
   a. for different speakers
       TOM: I used to smoke a lot=
       BOB: =He thinks he's real tough

   b. for even more than one
       TOM: I used to smoke a lot=
       BOB: =[[He thinks he's real tough
       ANN: =[[So did I

c. in either direction

TOM: I used to smoke a lot=

     [

BOB: I see=

ANN: =So did I

d. for the same speaker, simply to indicate that the turn continues

TOM: I used to smoke a lot more than this=

     [

BOB: You used to smoke-

TOM: =but I never inhaled.

5. Intervals

a.   (0.6) In tenths of a second

LIL: When I was (0.6) oh nine or ten

and between utterances

HAL: Step right up

(1.3)

HAL: I said step right up

b. - Untimed, brief pauses

LIL: When I was - oh nine or ten

or longer

LIL: When I was - - - oh nine or ten

and between utterances

HAL: Step right up

((pause))

HAL: I said step right up

6. Delivery

a. : Length

RON: What ha:ppened to you

and longer

RON: What ha::ppened to you

b. . Falling ("final") intonation (followed by a noticeable pause)

HAL: Step right up.

c. , Continuing ("list") intonation (slight rise/fall, followed by a short pause)

BOB: I saw Bill,

d.　?　Rising ("question") intonation (followed by a noticeable pause)
　　　　ANN: He left?

e.　underscore　　Emphasis
　　　　ANN: He left?

f.　(hhh)　breathe out
　　(.hhh)　breathe in
　　　　DON: (.hhh) Oh, thank you.
　　　　FRED: (hhh) That's a break.

g. (( ))　Noises, kinds of talk
　　　　TOM: I used to ((cough)) smoke a lot
　　　　((telephone rings))
　　　　BOB: ((whispered)) I'll get it

h.　!　Animated talk (wider intonational contours)
　　　　BETTY: Look out for that rock!

i.　(h)　"Breathiness" (often laughter during speech)
　　　　TOM: I woul(h)dn't do that.

j.　x-　Abrupt cutoff (glottal)
　　　　BETTY: Look ou-

7.　( )　Transcriber doubt
　　　　TED: I (suppose I'm not)
　　　　(BEN): We all (t-　　　　　　　)
　　　　ANN: (　　　　　　　)
　　　　　　(spoke to Mark)
　　　　LIL: I
　　　　　　(suppose I'm not)

8.　[ ]　Phonetic transcription
　　　　BILL: I saw the dog [dag]

Courtesy of Dennis Preston, adapted from J. Schenkein (1978). *Studies in the organization of conversational interaction.* New York: Academic Press, pp. ix–xvi.

Sample Transcription Conventions for the L2 Classroom

Transcription conventions for classroom discourse

General layout

1. Leave generous margins at least at first to permit legible annotations as transcription gets refined.
2. Double space everything for the same reason.
3. Number every fifth line in the left-hand margin, *but* do so only in pencil until transcription is complete, unless you are using wordprocessing with automatic line numbering.
4. Identify transcripts at the top of each page with some economical reference number.
5. Number all pages in the top right corner.
6. Identify participants, date, and location on a separate sheet (separate in case participants' identities need to be kept confidential).
7. Decide whether to supply pseudonyms for participants' names, or to substitute numbers.
8. Enter participants' pseudonyms, where used, with gender, classroom layout, etc., also on a separate sheet (especially if using a computer, since computer analysis must not include this page as data).
9. If using numbers, enter real name and associated numbers (with gender information) on a separate sheet.
10. On transcript pages, justify identifying material to the right, justify text to the left, as below.

Symbols to identify who is speaking

T	teacher
A	aide
M1	identified male learner, using numbers (M1, M2, etc.)
F1	identified female learner, using numbers (F1, F2, etc.)
Su	use such two-letter abbreviations for pseudonyms, where used (note: gender information may be lost by this method)
M	unidentified male learner
F	unidentified female learner
MV	male voice from, for example, an audio or videotape
FV	female voice, as above
LL	unidentified subgroup of class
LL	unidentified subgroup speaking in chorus
LLL	whole class
LLL	whole class speaking in chorus

Symbols for relationships between lines of transcript

M3	
F7	use curly brackets to indicate simultaneous speech
(M	
T	use to indicate same unidentified male speaker
(M	
(F	
T	use to indicate same unidentified female speaker
(F	
-T	use hyphen to indicate continuation of a turn without a pause, where overlapping speech intervenes

Symbols to use in text

[ ]	use for commentary of any kind (e.g. to indicate point in discourse where T writes on blackboard)
[=]	use to introduce a gloss, or translation, of speech
/ /	use for phonemic transcription instead of standard orthography, where pronunciation deviant; use with gloss if meaning also obscured
( )	use for uncertain transcription
(/ /)	use for uncertain phonemic transcription
([ ])	use for uncertain gloss
x	incomprehensible item, probably one word only
xx	incomprehensible item of phrase length
xxx	incomprehensible item beyond phrase length
x—x	use optionally at early stages to indicate extent of incomprehensible item, as guide to future attempts to improve transcription

... use dots to indicate pauses, giving length in seconds in extreme cases, if potentially relevant to aims

" " use to indicate anything read rather than spoken without direct text support

Further notes

1. Use indentation to indicate overlap of turns, otherwise start all turns systematically at extreme left of text space.
2. Use hyphen in text to indicate an incomplete word (for example, Come here, plea-).
3. Omit the full stop (period) at the end of a turn, to indicate incompletion (for example, As I was going to).
   Otherwise, punctuate as normally as possible, as if writing a playscript.
4. Use "uh" for hesitation fillers, or give phonemic transcription if meaning differences are potentially important.
5. Use underlining for emphasis, if using typewriter, or **bold** if wordprocessing (for example, Come **here!**).

General principle: the law of least effort

Avoid redundancy. Use only the conventions that are necessary for your particular purposes, to record the information you are sure you will need. If you are wordprocessing it will always be possible to update the transcript later (though admittedly this will be much more laborious if only typewriting facilities are available).

Allwright, D., & Bailey, K. M. (1991). *Focus on the language classroom: An introduction to classroom research for language researchers*. Cambridge: Cambridge University Press, pp. 222–223. Copyright © 1991 by Cambridge University Press. Reproduced with the permission of Cambridge University Press.

Commonly Used Formulae[1]

Statistic	Formula
Correlation	
Pearson product-moment	$$\dfrac{\sum xy - \left(\sum x\right)\left(\sum y\right)/N}{\sqrt{\left(\sum x^2 - \left(\sum x^2\right)/N\right)\left(\sum y^2 - \left(\sum y^2\right)/N\right)}}$$
Spearman rho	$$1 - \dfrac{6\sum d^2}{N\left(N^2 - 1\right)}$$
Standard error of the mean (SEM)	$$\dfrac{SD}{\sqrt{n-1}}$$
Standard error of the difference (SED)	$$\sqrt{\left(SEM_1\right)^2 + \left(SEM_2\right)^2}$$
T-test	$$\dfrac{\bar{x}_1 - \bar{x}_2}{SED}$$
Paired t-test	$$\sum \dfrac{\bar{x}_1 - \bar{x}_2}{s_{\bar{D}}}$$
ANOVA	MSB / MSW
MSB	$$\dfrac{SSB}{K-1}$$

MSW	$\dfrac{SSW}{N-K}$
SST	$\displaystyle\sum x^2 - \dfrac{\left(\sum x\right)^2}{N}$
Sum of squares between (SSB)	$\dfrac{\left(\sum x_1\right)^2}{n_1} + \dfrac{\left(\sum x_2\right)^2}{n_2} + \ldots + \dfrac{\left(\sum x_k\right)^2}{k_1} - \dfrac{\left(\sum x\right)^2}{N}$
Sum of squares within (SSW)	SST − SSB
χ^2	$\displaystyle\sum \dfrac{\left(f_O - f_E\right)}{f_E}$
z score	$\dfrac{x - \bar{x}}{sd}$
T score	$(10\,z) + 50$
η^2 (for t-test)	$t^2 / (t^2 + df)$
ω^2	$(SSB - (K \times -1)\,MSW) / (SST + MSW)$
Inter-rater reliability	$\dfrac{nr_{AB}\,{}^{**}}{1 + \left(n-1\right)r_{AB}}$
Cohen's d (effect size)	$(x^1 - x^2) / S_w$
Pooled standard deviation (S_w)	$((n_1 - 1)sd_1 + (n_2 - 1)sd_2) / ((n_1 - 1) + (n_2 - 1))$

* number of groups

** r_{AB} = correlation of two raters (if two) or average correlation if more than two

NOTE

1   This table uses some of the most commonly used statistics. In most cases, a computer package (e.g., SPSS) will be used so there is no need to "know" the formula. We present these formulae to acquaint the reader with the kind of information that goes into the calculation of these common statistics.

Glossary

Abstract A brief summary of research that includes the research questions, the methods used (including participants), and the results.

Acceptability judgment A judgment about the acceptability of a particular utterance (generally a sentence).

Action research Research carried out by practitioners in order to gain a better understanding of the dynamics of how second languages are learned and taught, together with some focus on improving the conditions and efficiency of learning and teaching.

Analysis of covariance (ANCOVA) A type of analysis of variance that adjusts the measurement of the dependent variable to take other variables, such as a pretest score or an aptitude score, into account.

Analysis of variance A parametric statistic that enables researchers to compare the performance between (generally) more than two groups.

Aptitude Treatment Interaction (ATI) research ATI research examines how variation in learners' individual differences (including constructs like aptitude, anxiety, motivation, styles, strategies, working memory, cognitive creativity) is related to the effectiveness of different kinds of instruction.

Associational research A research type that is concerned with co-occurrence and relationships between/among variables.

Average See *Mean*.

Bell curve See *Normal distribution*.

Biodata Basic information about a participant. The information gathered depends on the goal of a study. In general, age, amount and type of prior

L2 study, gender, first language of participant, and proficiency in L2s are collected and reported.

Case study   A detailed description of a single case, for example an individual learner or a class within a specific population and setting.

Chi square (χ^2)   A non parametric statistic used with frequency data to test the relationship between variables.

CHILDES   A database of transcribed language acquisition data.

Classroom observation   An observation carried out in a classroom setting, often using a structured scheme or tally sheet for recording data.

Classroom research   Research conducted in instructed second or foreign language settings, often involving variables related to teaching or teachers and second language learning.

Closed role play   Similar to discourse completion tasks, but in oral mode. Individuals are usually provided with a description of a situation and/or a character and asked to state what they would say in that particular situation. (See also *Open role play*.)

Coding   Organizing data into a manageable, easily understandable, and analyzable base of information, and searching for and marking patterns in the data.

Coding system   A means of organizing data prior to analysis. Coding systems usually involve coding sheets, charts, techniques, schemes, and so on. Researchers develop their coding scheme based on their specific research questions.

Comparison group design   Compares performance following a treatment with two or more groups.

Computer-mediated communication (CMC)   Communicative exchanges between participants using a computer. Exchanges are recorded and information on performance such as keystrokes, erasures, and times can be documented.

Confidence interval   An estimated range of values for a specific statistic that is likely (e.g., 95 percent) to include the actual value of that statistic. The actual value is the population value.

Confirmability   Similar to the concept of replicability in quantitative research, confirmability in qualitative research involves making available full details of the data on which claims or interpretations are based so that other researchers can examine the data and confirm, modify, or reject the first researcher's interpretations.

Consciousness-raising task   A task that is intended to facilitate learners' cognitive processes in terms of awareness of some language area or linguistic structure.

Consensus task   A task in which participants are presented with information to discuss, and if possible, come to agreement about something while utilizing that information.

Construct validity   The degree to which the research adequately captures the construct of interest.

Content validity   The extent to which a test or measurement device adequately measures the knowledge, skill, or ability that it was designed to measure.

Control group design   A type of design that includes one group which does not receive the experimental treatment but participates in the testing sessions.

Control variable   A variable that is held constant across groups in order to eliminate the effect of that variable on the outcome of the study.

Convenience sample   A sample of the most available and/or accessible subjects in the population.

Corpus/Corpora   A collection of authentic data, often with detailed information about the context of collection and/or use. Learner corpora are increasingly being used in second language research.

Correlation coefficient   A numerical value between +1 and −1 that indicates the strength of relationship between variables.

Correlational research   A type of research that involves data collection designed to determine the existence and strength of a relationship between two or more variables.

Counterbalancing   An experimental design in which the ordering of test items or tasks is different for different participants or groups of participants.

Covariate   A variable that is believed to influence the measurement of the dependent variable. Used in an analysis of covariance.

Credibility   A term used by qualitative researchers to ensure that the picture provided by the research is as full and complete as possible.

Criterion-related validity   The extent to which tests used in a study are comparable to other well-established tests of the construct in question.

Critical value   The value that is used as a confidence measure to determine whether a hypothesis can be substantiated or a null hypothesis can be rejected.

Cronbach's α   A means to determine internal consistency of a measure when only one administration of a measure exists. It is used when the number of possible answers is more than 2 and can be applied to ordinal data. (See also *Kuder-Richardson 20* and *Split-half procedure*.)

Cyclical data analysis   A process where data collection is followed by some type of data analysis and hypothesis-formation, leading to subsequent and more focused rounds of data collection where hypotheses are tested and further refined, with the process continuing until a rich and full picture of the data is obtained.

Data There are many forms of second language data. For example, data may be oral and recorded onto audio and/or videotapes; they may be written, in the form of essays, test scores, diaries, or check marks on observation schemes; they may appear in electronic format, such as responses to a computer-assisted accent modification program; or they may be visual, in the form of eye movements made while reading text at a computer or gestures made by a teacher in a classroom.

Data collection The general process of accumulating information pertaining to a particular research question, problem, or area.

Data elicitation A subset of data collection, data elicitation refers to the process of directly eliciting information from individuals, for example through an interview or a task.

Data sampling Selecting and segmenting data, sometimes using only a portion of it in a procedure known as data reduction. Also known as *Data segmentation*.

Data segmentation See *Data sampling*.

Debriefing Providing information after a study or data collection period. For example, participants may be informed about research findings, questions, or the content of observations.

Degrees of freedom The number of scores that can vary if others are given.

Delayed post-test In a pre-test/post-test design, delayed post-tests are tests given after the first (immediate) post-test (for example, one month or one year later) to measure the long-term retention of a skill or knowledge.

Dependability Qualitative researchers aim to ensure the dependability of inferences that have been drawn from data. For dependability, they aim to fully characterize the research context and the relationships among the participants.

Dependent variable The variable that is measured to determine the effects of the independent variable.

Diary research An individual's perspective on their own language learning or teaching experience, in the form of entries to a personal journal. Analyses usually focus on patterns and salient events. Can be oral or written.

Directional hypothesis A prediction that specifies the relationship between variables. This is generally stated in the form of X will be greater than Y. (See *One-way hypothesis*.)

Discourse completion test (DCT) DCTs are a means of gathering contextualized data. Generally, a situation is provided and then the respondent is asked what he or she would say in that particular situation. There is often a follow-up response (such as "I'm sorry that you can't come") so that the individual knows the type of response that is expected (for example, a refusal).

Distribution A way of showing the frequency with which scores occur in a data set.

Duncan's multiple range test A post-hoc test used to compare means following an analysis of variance.

Dyad Two participants working together.

Effect of instruction research A kind of classroom research that focuses on the role and learning outcomes of (different types of) second language instruction.

Effect size A measure that can be used to determine the magnitude of an observed relationship or effect.

Elicited imitation A procedure for collecting data where a participant is presented with a sentence, clause, or word, and is asked to repeat (imitate) it.

Elicited narrative Narratives that are gathered through specific prompts (e.g., "What did you do yesterday?" Or, "Tell me about a typical day for you.")

Emic An insider's understanding of his or her own culture.

Empirical research Research that is based on data.

Eta² A correlation coefficient that expresses the strength of association and can be used following a t-test. It is expressed as η^2.

Ethics review board See *Institutional review board*.

Ethnography Research that is carried out from the participants' point of view, using categories relevant to a particular group and cultural system. It aims to describe and interpret the cultural behavior, including communicative patterns, of a group.

Etic An outsider's understanding of a culture or group that is not his or her own.

Experimental research Research in which there is manipulation of (at least) one independent variable to determine the effect(s) on one (or more) dependent variables. Groups are determined on the basis of random assignment.

External validity Refers to the extent to which the results of a study are relevant to a wider population.

Face validity   Refers to the familiarity of an instrument and the ease with which the validity of the content is recognized.

Factor analysis   A means of determining common factors that underlie measures that test different (possibly related) variables. It allows the researcher to take a larger number of variables and reduce them to a smaller number of factors.

Factorial design   A design type that involves more than one independent variable. The goal is to determine the effects of each individually and in interaction on the dependent variable.

Fisher's exact test   A variant of the chi square test (χ^2) used for 2 × 2 contingency tables. Fisher's exact test can be used with low-frequency counts in cells.

Focus groups   Related to interviews, these involve several participants in a group discussion, often with a facilitator whose goal it is to keep the group discussion targeted on specific topics. A stimulus is generally used for discussion, such as a videotape or previously elicited data.

Friedman test   A nonparametric test used to compare three or more matched groups. This test is the nonparametric equivalent to repeated measures ANOVA.

Generalizability   The extent to which the results of a study can be extended to a greater population.

Grounded theory   Theory based on, or grounded in, data that have been systematically gathered and analyzed. Researchers often attempt to avoid placing preconceived notions on the data, and aim to examine data from multiple vantage points to help them arrive at a complete picture of the phenomena under investigation.

Halo effect   Participants provide information that they believe a researcher wants or expects.

Hawthorne effect   The presence of observers may result in changed behavior because those being observed feel positive about being included in a study.

Human subjects committee   See *Institutional review board*.

Hypothesis   A statement of what one believes the outcomes of a study will be. A research hypothesis predicts what the relationship will be between or among variables.

Independent variable   A variable that is believed to affect the dependent variable.

Inductive data analysis   The general goal is for research findings to emerge from the frequent, dominant, or significant themes within raw data. Involves multiple examinations and interpretations of the data in the light of the research objectives.

Inferential statistics   A type of statistic that determines the likely generalizability from a sample(s) to the general population.

Information-exchange tasks   A task in which two (or more) individuals must exchange information using the linguistic resources available to them in order to complete the activity. A spot the difference task, where each participant has a uniquely held picture and they must share information to complete the task, is a type of information-exchange task, also known as a jigsaw task.

Information-gap tasks   In an information-gap task, one individual usually has a gap in their information. For example, a picture drawing activity, where one person describes and another person draws, is a type of information-gap task.

Informed consent   Voluntary agreement to participate in a study about which the potential subject has enough information and understands enough to make an informed decision.

Institutional review board   A committee established to review research involving human subjects to ensure it is in compliance with ethical guidelines laid down by government and funding agencies. (This term is often used interchangeably with *Human subjects committee* and *Ethics review board*.)

Instrument reliability   Refers to the consistency of a particular instrument over time.

Intact class   A treatment group that is made up of all individuals in a given class.

Interaction effect   Associated with a factorial design. Combined effect of two independent variables. (See *Main effect*.)

Internal validity   The extent to which the results of a study are a function of the factor that is intended by the researcher.

Inter-rater reliability   Consistency between two or more raters.

Interval scale   A scale in which there is an ordering of variables and in which there is an equal interval between variables.

Intervening variable   A variable that is not controlled for but can have an effect on the relationship between the independent and dependent variables.

Interview   Comparable to a questionnaire, but in oral mode, interviews are often associated with survey-based research. Information is often gathered by means of open-ended questions and answers. Interviews can be based around a stimulus, for example a completed questionnaire, or a videotape of a lesson.

Intra-rater reliability   A single rater's consistency at two or more points in time.

Introspective methods   A set of data elicitation techniques that encourage learners to communicate about their internal processing and/or perspectives about language learning experiences.

Investigator triangulation   Using multiple observers or interviewers in the same investigation.

IRIS   IRIS (Instruments for Research into Second Languages) is a collection of instruments, materials, and stimuli used to elicit data for research into second and foreign languages. See www.iris-database.org.

Kendall Tau   A correlation analysis used for ordinal data or with interval data when converted to ranks. This analysis is used when there are many ties in the rankings. (See *Spearman rho*.)

Kruskal-Wallis   A nonparametric test used to compare two or more independent groups.

Kuder-Richardson 20   A means to determine the internal consistency of a measure. It is used when one administration of a measure exists. This is done when the instrument is not split into two parts. (See also *Split-half procedure* and *Cronbach's* α.)

Laboratory research   Generally taken to refer to experimental research, where variables can be manipulated and the setting is controlled.

Linear regression   A means of predicting the score on one variable from another score on another variable.

Magnitude estimation   A procedure whereby participants are asked to rank a stimulus by stating how much better or worse the stimulus is than the previous one.

Main effect   The effect of one independent variable. (See *Interaction effect*.)

Mann-Whitney U   A nonparametric test used with ordinal or interval data. It is used to compare two groups and is similar to the Wilcoxon Rank Sums test.

Mean   A measure of central tendency, the mean is a value obtained by summing all the scores in a score distribution and dividing the sum by the number of scores in the distribution.

Measures of central tendency   A way of providing quantitative information about the typical behavior of individuals with respect to a particular phenomenon, usually given through means, modes, and medians.

Measures of dispersion   A method for determining the amount of spread in a set of scores. It is a way of determining variability.

Measures of frequency Indicate how often a particular behavior or phenomenon occurs.

Median A measure of central tendency, the median is a value that represents the mid-point of all the scores. Half of the scores are above the median and half below it.

Meta-analysis A statistical tool used in research synthesis to convert the findings of individual studies to comparable values in order to estimate an overall observed finding about a given treatment or condition across studies.

Methodological triangulation Using different independent measures or methods to investigate a particular phenomenon.

Mixed-methods research Research where authors present and discuss both quantitative and qualitative data in the same report, or use methods associated with both types of research in collecting data or conducting studies.

Mode A measure of central tendency, the mode represents the most frequent score obtained in a score distribution.

Moderator variable A variable that may interact with other variables resulting in an effect on the relationship between the independent and dependent variables.

Moving window A technique, generally carried out on a computer, whereby words are presented visually or aurally one by one. This technique may be used to measure reaction times (i.e., how long it takes a participant to press a button to have the next word presented) and thus indirectly, ease of comprehension.

Multiple-methods research See *Mixed-methods research*.

Multiple regression A means of predicting a score from the scores of two or more variables.

Multivariate analysis of variance (MANOVA) A type of analysis of variance with more than one dependent variable.

Naturalistic data Data that come from naturally occurring situations and which are not experimentally manipulated.

Naturalistic setting A research context that involves no manipulation of variables. Data are collected through observations of settings in which data occur without specific intervention or control.

Nominal scale Used for attributes or categories. A nominal scale is used to place attributes into two or more categories (e.g., gender).

Non-directional hypothesis A prediction that a relationship between variables exists without specifying the precise nature of the direction. (See also *Two-way hypothesis*.)

Nonparametric statistics   A type of inferential statistics that are generally used with nominal or ordinal data or when the assumptions necessary for parametric statistics cannot be met.

Normal distribution   A theoretical distribution of scores. In a normal distribution, scores cluster around the mid-point.

Null hypothesis significance testing (NHST)   A statistical approach that establishes a null hypothesis and then uses the results of statistical tests (p value) to either reject or not reject the hypothesis.

Observations   Researchers systematically observe different aspects of a setting in which they are immersed, including, for example, the interactions, relationships, actions, and events in which learners engage. The aim is to provide careful descriptions of learners' activities without unduly influencing the events in which the learners are engaged.

The observers' paradox   The tension between the fact that the goal of observational research is to unobtrusively collect data that is as natural as possible, and the fact that the presence of an observer inherently influences the linguistic behavior of those observed.

Omega²   A measure used to determine the strength of association when all groups have an equal n size.

One-shot design   A design type that uses one treatment and one measurement afterwards; there is no measurement before the treatment (e.g., a pre-test) and there is no control group.

One-way hypothesis   A prediction that specifies the relationship between variables. This is generally stated in the form of X will be greater than Y. (See also *Directional hypothesis*.)

On-line task   See *Think-aloud*.

Open role play   Individuals are provided with a description of a situation and/or a character and each individual is asked to play out the part of one of the characters. In open role plays, limits are not provided as to the length of the exchange. (See also *Closed role play*.)

Operationalize   To provide a precise, concrete definition of a variable in such a way that it can be measured.

Ordinal scale   A scale in which there is an ordering of variables. There is no implication that there is an equal interval between variables.

Outlier   A score that is different from the other scores in a set. It may be considerably larger or smaller than all the other scores.

Paired t-test   A type of t-test used when the comparison is between matched samples (e.g., pre-test/post-test). It is also known as a matched t-test.

Parameters   A way of describing certain characteristics of a population numerically.

Parametric statistics   Inferential statistics that use sets of assumptions about the dependent variable. Generally used with interval data.

Participant   An individual whose behavior is being measured or investigated.

Participant mortality   The dropout rate for a study. It is also referred to as subject mortality. Participants drop out for many reasons, including scheduling conflicts (there is often a high rate of no-shows for delayed post-tests).

Pearson product-moment correlation   A measure of correlation used with interval data.

Pilot study   A small-scale trial of the proposed procedures, materials, and methods. It may also include a trial of the coding sheets and analytic categories.

Population   All instances of individuals (or situations) that share certain characteristics.

Post-hoc analysis   A follow-up statistical analysis performed after a comparison of more than two groups (e.g., analysis of variance) shows a significant difference. It is a way of pinpointing where, for example between which groups or tests, the significant difference lies.

Post-test   A test to determine knowledge after treatment.

Post-test only design   Uses one treatment and one measurement afterwards. Like a one-shot design, there is no measurement before the treatment (e.g., a pre-test); however, there is usually a control group.

Power (statistical)   Probability that a test will yield a statistically significant result when there actually is one; the null hypothesis will be rejected when it should be rejected, thereby avoiding a Type II error.

Practitioner research   See *Action research*.

Predictive validity   Refers to the use that one wants to make of a measure. If there is predictive validity, the measure can predict performance on some other measure.

Pre-test   A test to determine knowledge before treatment.

Pre-test/post-test design   Compares performance before treatment with performance following treatment.

Probability   An estimation of the likelihood of something occurring due to chance.

Purpose sample   A sample selected in order to elicit a particular type of data. The sample may or may not be representative of the population at large.

Qualitative research   Research in which the focus is on naturally occurring phenomena and data are primarily recorded in non-numerical form.

Quantification   The use of numbers and sometimes statistics to show patterns of occurrence.

Quantitative research   Research in which variables are manipulated to test hypotheses and in which there is usually quantification of data and numerical analyses.

Quasi-experimental research   A type of experimental research but without random assignment of individuals.

Questionnaire   A (usually written) survey often used in a large-scale study to gather information. Can utilize open-ended questions and/or questions followed by a selection from a set of predetermined answers.

R   Software environment for statistical computing.

Random sample   A sample that has been selected in such a way that each member of a population has an equal chance of being selected. (See also *Simple random sample* and *Stratified random sample*.)

Range   A measure of dispersion, range indicates the distance between the highest and lowest score. It measures the spread of a set of scores.

Ratio scale   An interval scale that displays information about frequencies in relation to each other.

Reaction time   The time between a stimulus and a learner's response. Reaction time experiments are usually computer-based and can also be used to investigate processing.

Regression line   A line that can be drawn through scores on a scatterplot. It is the line of best fit, that is, the one that allows for the clustering of scores on the line.

Reliability   The degree to which there is consistency in results.

Repeated measures design   Multiple measurements from each participant.

Replication   Conducting a research study again, in a way that is either identical to the original procedure or with small changes (e.g. different participants), to test the original findings. Many different types of replication exist, for example conceptual replication (the main concept or idea is the same) and partial replication (where one aspect of the original study might be changed).

Representativeness   The extent to which an individual who could be selected for a study has the same chance of being selected as any other individual in the population.

Research A systematic process of collecting and analyzing information that will investigate a research problem or question, or help researchers obtain a more complete understanding of a situation.

Research protocol A detailed set of guidelines for how research will proceed.

Research question A question that will be addressed/investigated in a study.

Research report A formal report in which the findings from research are presented.

Sampling The way participants or data for a study are selected.

SAS A statistical package for data analysis.

Scheffé A post-hoc test used to compare means following an analysis of variance.

Semi-structured interview An interview in which researchers use written lists of questions as a guide, but can digress and probe for more information.

Sentence matching A procedure (generally computer-based) whereby participants are asked if two sentences (usually appearing consecutively) are identical or not. This procedure is often used to determine grammaticality.

Simple random sample Refers to a sample that has been selected in such a way that each member of a population has an equal chance of being selected.

Small group Usually three or four members; however, depending on the context, five may also be considered a small group.

Spearman rho A correlation analysis used for ordinal data or with interval data when converted to ranks. (See also *Kendall Tau*.)

Split-half procedure A means of determining the internal consistency of a measure by obtaining a correlation coefficiency by comparing the performance on half of a test with performance on the other half. (See also *Kuder-Richardson 20* and *Cronbach's* α).

Split methods research See *Mixed-methods research*.

SPSS A statistical package for data analysis.

Standard deviation A measure of dispersion, it is a numerical value that indicates how scores are spread around the mean.

Standard error of the difference between sample means Difference between sample means.

Standard error of the mean Standard deviation of sample means.

Standard scores   A converted raw score that shows how far an actual score is from the mean.

Standardized interview   See *Structured interview*.

Statistic   A way of describing a sample numerically.

Stimulated recall   An introspective technique for gathering data that can yield insights into a learner's thought processes during language learning experiences. Learners are asked to introspect while viewing or hearing a stimulus to prompt their recollections.

Stratified random sample   Random sampling based on categories.

Strength of association   A way of determining how much variation in the data can be accounted for by the independent variable.

Structured interview   Researchers ask similar sets of questions of all respondents. Structured interviews resemble verbal questionnaires. (Also known as *Standardized interview*.)

Suppliance in obligatory conexts (SOC) measures   Whether or not a feature is produced when it is required. Usually, the number of times a particular feature (e.g., the past tense) is produced is divided by the number of times that it is required.

Survey   A means of gathering information about a particular topic, for example attitudes or opinions about a school program. A questionnaire is a type of survey.

SYSTAT   A statistical package for data analysis.

Systematic sample   A sample that has been determined by the selection of every nth individual or instance/occurrence for sampling data.

_T_ score   A standard score based on a z score (multiply z score by 10 and add 50).

Teacher-initiated research   See *Action research*.

Theoretical triangulation   Using multiple perspectives to analyze the same set of data.

Thick description   Using multiple perspectives to explain the insights gleaned from a study, and taking into account the participants' interpretations of their actions and speech. It also involves the presentation of representative examples and patterns in data, along with interpretive commentary.

Think-aloud   A type of verbal reporting in which individuals are asked what is going through their mind as they are solving a problem or performing a task. (Also known as *On-line task*.)

Time series design   A design type that involves repeated observations over a set period of time where the participants serve as their own control.

Transcription conventions   Notations used to facilitate the representation of oral data in a written format. While there are no generally agreed-upon conventions common to all studies, researchers may recognize certain symbols; for instance, the use of dots to convey pauses or silence is relatively common.

Transcription software   Designed to facilitate transcription of oral data, these applications often allow recordings to be stopped and the last few seconds replayed, to facilitate ease of listening and transcribing; rate of speech can also be adjusted, to make it easier to distinguish individual voices.

Transferability   How far qualitative research findings are transferable from one context to another. The extent to which findings may be transferred usually depends on the similarity of the context.

Triangulation   Triangulation involves using multiple research techniques and multiple sources of data in order to explore the issues from all feasible perspectives. Using the technique of triangulation can aid in credibility, transferability, and dependability in qualitative research.

Truth-value judgment   These judgments generally involve contextualized information and individuals are asked if a particular follow-up sentence is true or not based on prior contextualization.

T-test   A parametric statistic that is used to determine if the means of two groups are significantly different from one another. (See also *Paired t-test*.)

T-unit   Usually defined as one main clause and any attached dependent clauses.

Tukey   A post-hoc test used to compare means following an analysis of variance.

Two-way hypothesis   A prediction that a relationship between variables exists without specifying the precise nature of the direction. (See also *Non-directional hypothesis*.)

Type I error   A null hypothesis is rejected when it should not have been rejected.

Type II error   A null hypothesis is accepted when it should not have been accepted.

Type-token ratio   A measure of lexical diversity that involves dividing the number of types by the number of tokens. For example, types can refer to the different words that are used in one data set, and tokens can refer to the number of repetitions of those words.

Uptake sheets   Learners' reports about their learning, illustrating what they take up from the language learning opportunities they have through instruction.

Validity   The extent one can make correct generalizations based on the results from a particular measure.

VARBRUL   A statistical package for data analysis often used in sociolinguistic research.

Variable   A characteristic that differs from group to group or person to person (e.g., native language, handedness).

Verbal reporting   A type of introspection that consists of gathering information by asking individuals to say what is going through their minds as they are solving a problem or doing a task.

Wilcoxon Rank Sums   A nonparametric test used with ordinal or interval data. It is used to compare two groups and is similar to the Mann-Whitney U test.

Within-group design   See *Repeated measures design*.

Z scores   A standard score that provides information about the distance of a score from the mean in terms of standard deviations.

References

Adair, G. (1984). The Hawthorne effect: A reconsideration of the methodological artifact. *Journal of Applied Psychology*, *69*(2), 334–345.

Adams, R. (2003). L2 output, reformulation, and noticing: Implications for IL development. *Language Teaching Research*, *7*(3), 347–376.

Adams, R. (2004). Learner/learner interactions: Implications for second language acquisition (unpublished doctoral dissertation). Georgetown University, Washington, DC.

Akiyama, Y. (2002). Japanese adult learners' development of the locality condition on English reflexives. *Studies in Second Language Acquisition*, *24*(1), 27–54.

Allen, J. P. B., Fröhlich, M., & Spada, N. (1984). The communicative orientation of language teaching: An observation scheme. In J. Handscombe, R. A. Orem, & B. Taylor (Eds.), *On TESOL '83: The question of control* (pp. 231–252). Washington, DC: TESOL.

Allwright, D. (1984a). Why don't learners learn what teachers teach? The interaction hypothesis. In D. Singleton & D. Little (Eds.), *Language learning in formal and informal contexts* (pp. 3–18). Dublin: IRAAL.

Allwright, R. (1984b). The importance of interaction in classroom language learning. *Applied Linguistics*, *5*(2), 158–171.

Allwright, D. (1987). Classroom observation: Problems and possibilities. In B. K. Das (Ed.), *Patterns of classroom interaction in Southeast Asia* (pp. 88–102). Singapore: SEAMEO Regional Language Center.

Allwright, D., & Bailey, K. M. (1991). *Focus on the language classroom: An introduction to classroom research for language researchers*. Cambridge: Cambridge University Press.

Amazon Web Services (2015). *Amazon Mechanical Turk* [Crowdsourcing Internet Marketplace]. Retrieved April 19, 2015, from www.mturk.com.

American Psychological Association (2010). *Publication manual of the American Psychological Association* (6th ed.). Washington, DC: American Psychological Association.

Atkinson, D., & Ramanathan, V. (1995). Cultures of writing: An ethnographic comparison of L1 and L2 university writing programs. *TESOL Quarterly, 29*(3), 539–568.

Bailey, K. M. (1983). Competitiveness and anxiety in adult second language learning: Looking at and through the diary studies. In H. W. Seliger & M. H. Long (Eds.), *Classroom oriented research in second language acquisition* (pp. 67–103). Rowley, MA: Newbury House.

Bailey, K. M. (1990). The use of diary studies in teacher education programmes. In J. Richards and D. Nunan (Eds.), *Second language teacher education* (pp. 215–226). Cambridge: Cambridge University Press.

Bailey, K. M., Bergthold, B., Braunstein, B., Fleischman, N. J., Holbrook, M. P., & Zambo, L. J. (1996). The language learner's autobiography: Examining the "apprenticeship of observation." In D. Freeman & J. C. Richards (Eds.), *Teacher learning in language teaching* (pp. 11–29). Cambridge: Cambridge University Press.

Baralt, M. (2012). Coding qualitative data. In A. Mackey & S. Gass (Eds.), *Research methods in second language acquisition: A Practical Guide* (pp. 222–244). Malden, MA: Blackwell Publishing.

Barcroft, J. (2003). Effects of questions about word meaning during L2 Spanish lexical learning. *The Modern Language Journal, 87*(4), 546–561.

Bard, E., Robertson, D., & Sorace, A. (1996). Magnitude estimation of linguistic acceptability. *Language, 72*(1), 32–68.

Bardovi-Harlig, K. (1992). A second look at T-unit analysis: Reconsidering the sentence. *TESOL Quarterly, 26*(2), 390–395.

Bardovi-Harlig, K. (2000). *Tense and aspect in second language acquisition: Form, meaning, and use.* Oxford: Blackwell.

Bardovi-Harlig, K., & Dörnyei, Z. (1998). Do language learners recognize pragmatic violations? Pragmatic versus grammatical awareness in instructed L2 learning. *TESOL Quarterly, 32*(2), 233–262.

Bardovi-Harlig, K., & Hartford, B. S. (1996). Input in an institutional setting. *Studies in Second Language Acquisition, 18*(2), 171–188.

Bates, E., & MacWhinney, B. (1982). Functionalist approach to grammar. In E. Warmer & L. Gleitman (Eds.), *Language acquisition: The state of the art* (pp. 173–218). New York: Cambridge University Press.

Baumrind, D. (1990). Doing good well. In C. B. Fisher & W. W. Tryon (Eds.), *Ethical issues in applied developmental psychology* (pp. 17–28). Norwood, NJ: Ablex.

Beck, M. L. (1998). L2 acquisition and obligatory head movement: English-speaking learners of German and the Local Impairment Hypothesis. *Studies in Second Language Acquisition, 20*(3), 311–348.

Beebe, L., & Takahashi, T. (1989). Do you have a bag? Social status and patterned variation in second language acquisition. In S. Gass, C. Madden, D. Preston, & L. Selinker (Eds.), *Variation in second language acquisition: Discourse and pragmatics* (pp. 103–125). Clevedon, UK: Multilingual Matters.

Beebe, L., Takahashi, T., & Uliss-Weltz, R. (1990). Pragmatic transfer in ESL refusals. In R. C. Scarcella, E. S. Andersen, & S. D. Krashen (Eds.), *Developing communicative competence in a second language* (pp. 55–73). New York: Newbury House.

Belmont Report: Ethical Principles and Guidelines for the Protection of Human Subjects of Research (1979). From the National Commission for the Protection of Human Subjects of Biomedical and Behavioral Research. Retrieved January 23, 2015 from www.hhs.gov/ohrp/humansubjects/guidance/belmont.html and http://ohsr.od.nih.gov/mpa/belmont.php3.

Berg, E. C. (1999). The effects of trained peer response on ESL students' revision types and writing quality. *Journal of Second Language Writing*, 8(3), 215–241.

Bergman, M. (2008). *Advances in mixed methods research*. Thousand Oaks, CA: Sage.

Bernard, H. R. (1995). *Research methods in anthropology: Qualitative and quantitative approaches*. Walnut Creek, CA: AltaMira.

Birdsong, D. (1989). *Metalinguistic performance and interlinguistic competence*. Berlin & New York: Springer.

Bley-Vroman, R., Felix, S., & Ioup, G. (1988). The accessibility of Universal Grammar in adult language learning. *Second Language Research*, 4(1), 1–32.

Bley-Vroman, R., & Joo, H-R. (2001). The acquisition and interpretation of English locative constructions by native speakers of Korean. *Studies in Second Language Acquisition*, 23(2), 207–219.

Bley-Vroman, R., & Masterson, D. (1989). Reaction time as a supplement to grammaticality judgments in the investigation of second language learners' competence. *University of Hawai'i Working Papers in ESL*, 8(2), 207–245.

Bowles, M. (2010). *The think-aloud controversy in second language research*. New York: Routledge.

Brandl, K. K. (2000). Foreign language TAs' perceptions of training components: Do we know how they like to be trained? *The Modern Language Journal*, 84(3), 355–371.

Breen, M. P., Hird, B., Milton, M., Oliver, R., & Thwaite, A. (2001). Making sense of language teaching: Teachers' principles and classroom practices. *Applied Linguistics*, 22(4), 470–501.

British Association for Applied Linguistics (1994). *Recommendations on good practice in applied linguistics*. Retrieved January 23, 2015, from www.baal.org.uk/dox/goodpractice_full.pdf.

Brown, J. A. C. (1954). *The social psychology of industry*. Middlesex, UK: Penguin.

Brown, J. D. (2001). *Using surveys in language programs*. Cambridge: Cambridge University Press.

Brown, J. D. (2003). Research methods for applied linguistics. In A. Davies & C. Elder (Eds.), *The handbook of applied linguistics* (pp. 476–500). Oxford: Blackwell.

Brown, R. (1973). *A first language: The early stages*. Cambridge, MA: Harvard University Press.

Bryman, A. (2006). Integrating quantitative and qualitative research: How is it done? *Qualitative Research*, 6(6), 97–113.

Butler, C. (1985). *Statistics in linguistics*. Oxford: Basil Blackwell.

Center for Advanced Language Proficiency Education and Research (2012). *Assessing language development through learner corpora*. University Park, PA: The Pennsylvania State University. Retrieved January 23, 2015, from http://calper.la.psu.edu/corpus.php.

Carmines, E., & Zeller, R. (1979). *Reliability and validity assessment*. Beverly Hills, CA: Sage.

Carson, J., & Nelson, G. L. (1996). Chinese students' perception of ESL peer response group interaction. *Journal of Second Language Writing, 5*(1), 1–19.

Chalmers, D. (2003, July). *Ethical and policy issues in research involving human participants commissioned papers and staff analysis: Research ethics in Australia*. Retrieved January 23, 2015 from www.onlineethics.org/cms/8069.aspx and http://onlineethics.org/reseth/nbac/hchalmers.html-system.

Chaudron, C. (1988). *Second language classrooms: Research on teaching and learning*. Cambridge: Cambridge University Press.

Chaudron, C. (2000). Contrasting approaches to classroom research: Qualitative and quantitative analysis of language and learning. *Second Language Studies, 19*(1), 1–56. Retrieved April 19, 2015, from www.hawaii.edu/sls/uhwpesl/19_1/chaudron.pdf.

Chaudron, C., Crookes, G., & Long, M. H. (1988). *Reliability and validity in second language classroom research*. Hawaii: Center for Second Language Classroom Research, Social Science Research Institute, University of Hawaii. Retreived April 9, 2015, from http://sls.hawaii.edu/Gblog/wp-content/uploads/2011/08/Chaudron-Crookes-Long-1988-Tech-rep-8.pdf.

Chomsky, N. (1997). *The minimalist program*. Cambridge, MA: MIT Press.

Cohen, A. (1998). *Strategies in learning and using a second language*. London: Longman.

Cohen, J. (1960). A coefficient of agreement for nominal scales. *Educational and Psychological Measurement, 20*(1), 37–46.

Copland, F., Garton, S., & Burns, A. (2014). Challenges in teaching English to young learners: Global perspectives and local realities. *TESOL Quarterly, 48*(4), 738–762.

Creswell, J. W. (2015). *A concise introduction to mixed methods research*. Los Angeles, CA: Sage.

Creswell, J. W., & Plano Clark, V. L. (2007). *Designing and conducting mixed methods research*. Thousand Oaks, CA: Sage.

Creswell, J. W., Plano Clark, V. L., & Garrett, A. L. (2008). Methodological issues in conducting mixed methods research designs. In M. Bergman (Ed.), *Advances in mixed methods research* (pp. 66–84). London: Sage.

Creswell, J., Klassen, A., Clark, V., & Smith, K. (2010). *Best practices for mixed methods research in the health sciences*. National Institutes of Health. Retrieved January 23, 2015, from http://obssr.od.nih.gov/scientific_areas/methodology/mixed_methods_research/index.aspx.

Crookes, G. (1993). Action research for second language instructors: Going beyond instructor research. *Applied Linguistics, 14*(2), 130–144.

Cumming, G. (2012). *Understanding the new statistics: Effect sizes, confidence intervals, and meta-analysis.* New York: Routledge.

Dale, P., Harlaar, N., & Plomin, R. (2012). Nature and nurture in school-based second language achievement. *Language Learning, 62*(s2), 28–48.

Davis, K. A. (1995). Qualitative theory and methods in applied linguistics research. *TESOL Quarterly, 29*(3), 427–453.

Davis, J. M. (2007). Resistance to L2 pragmatics in the Australian ESL context. *Language Learning, 57*(4), 611–649.

de Graaff, R. (1997). The eXperanto experiment: Effects of explicit instruction on second language acquisition. *Studies in Second Language Acquisition, 19*(2), 249–276.

De Guerrero, M., & Villamil, O. (2000). Activiating the ZPD: Mutual scaffolding in L2 peer revision. *The Modern Language Journal, 84*(1), 56–68.

DeKeyser, R. M. (2009). Cognitive-psychological processes in second language learning. In M. H. Long & C. J. Doughty (Eds.), *The handbook of language teaching* (pp. 119–138). Malden, MA: Wiley-Blackwell.

Denzin, N., & Lincoln, Y. (Eds.) (1994). *Handbook of qualitative research.* Thousand Oaks, CA: Sage.

Department of Health and Human Services (DHHS) (2003). *Protection of human subjects 45, Code of Federal Regulations (CFR) 46, Subparts A and D.* Washington, DC: U.S. Government Printing Office.

Derwing, T., Munro, M., & Wiebe, G. (1998). Evidence in favor of a broad framework for pronunciation instruction. *Language Learning, 48*(3), 393–410.

Dörnyei, Z., & Clément, R. (2001). Motivational characteristics of learning different target languages: Results of a nationwide survey. In Z. Dörnyei & R. Schmidt (Eds.), *Motivation and second language acquisition* (pp. 399–426). Honolulu, HI: University of Hawaii Press.

Dörnyei, Z. (with Taguchi, T.) (2010). *Questionnaires in second language research: Construction, administration, and processing.* New York: Routledge.

Dörnyei, Z., & Csizér, K. (2012). How to design and analyze surveys in second language acquisition research. In A. Mackey & S. Gass (Eds.), *Research methods in second language acquisition: A practical guide* (pp. 74–94). Malden, MA: Blackwell Publishing.

Doughty, C., & Varela, E. (1998). Communicative focus on form. In C. Doughty & J. Williams (Eds.), *Focus on form in classroom second language acquisition* (pp. 114–138). New York: Cambridge University Press.

Duanmu, S. (1995). Metrical and tonal phonology of compounds in two Chinese dialects. *Language, 71*(2), 225–259.

Duff, P. (2002). The discursive co-construction of knowledge, identity and difference: An ethnography of communication in the high school mainstream. *Applied Linguistics, 23*(3), 289–322.

Duff, P. (2008). *Case study research in applied linguistics.* New York: Lawrence Erlbaum/Taylor & Francis.

Duff, P. (2010). Research approaches in applied linguistics. In R. Kaplan (Ed.), *The Oxford handbook of applied linguistics* (pp. 45–59). Oxford: Oxford University Press.

Duff, P., & Early, M. (1996). Problematics of classroom research across sociopolitical contexts. In J. Schachter & S. Gass (Eds.), *Second language classroom research: Issues and opportunities* (pp. 1–30). Mahwah, NJ: Lawrence Erlbaum Associates.

Duffield, N., Prévost, P., & White, L. (1997). A psycholinguistic investigation of clitic placement in second language acquisition. In E. Hughes, M. Hughes, & A. Greenhill (Eds.), *Proceedings of the 21st Boston University Conference on Language Development* (pp. 148–159). Somerville, MA: Cascadilla Press.

Duffield, N., & White, L. (1999). Assessing L2 knowledge of Spanish clitic placement: converging methodologies. *Second Language Research, 15*(1), 133–160.

Egi, T. (2003, October). *Learners' perceptions about recasts and L2 learning*. Paper presented at the Second Language Research Forum, Tucson, AZ.

Ellis, R. (1984). *Second language classroom development*. Oxford: Pergamon.

Ellis, R. (1990). *Instructed second language acquisition*. Cambridge, MA: Blackwell.

Ellis, R. (1994). *The study of second language acquisition*. Oxford: Oxford University Press.

Ellis, R. (2000). Task-based research and language pedagogy. *Language Teaching Research, 4*(3), 193–220.

Ellis, R. (2003). *Task-based language learning and teaching*. Oxford: Oxford University Press.

Ellis, R. (2005). *Planning and task performance in a second language*. Amsterdam: John Benjamins.

Ellis, R. (2009). The differential effects of three types of task planning on the fluency, complexity, and accuracy in L2 oral production. *Applied Linguistics, 19*, 474–509.

Ellis, R., Basturkmen, H., & Loewen, S. (2001). Learner uptake in communicative ESL lessons. *Language Learning, 51*(2), 281–318.

Ellis, R., & He, X. (1999). The roles of modified input and output in the incidental acquisition of word meanings. *Studies in Second Language Acquisition, 21*(2), 285–301.

Ellis, R., & Yuan, F. (2004). The effects of planning on fluency, complexity, and accuracy in second language narrative writing. *Studies in Second Language Acquisition, 26*(1), 59–84.

EndNote (Version 7.0) [Computer software]. Carlsbad, CA: Thomson ISI ResearchSoft. Retrieved April 19, 2015, from http://endnote.com.

Eubank, L. (1993). Sentence matching and processing in L2 development. *Second Language Research, 9*(2), 253–280.

Fanselow, J. F. (1977). Beyond "Rashomon"—conceptualizing and describing the teaching act. *TESOL Quarterly, 11*(1), 17–39.

Fiksdal, S. (1990). *The right time and place: A microanalysis of cross-cultural gatekeeping interviews*. Norwood, NJ: Ablex.

Foster, P. (1998). A classroom perspective on the negotiation of meaning. *Applied Linguistics, 19*(1), 1–23.

Fotos, S., & Ellis, R. (1991). Communicating about grammar: A task-based approach. *TESOL Quarterly, 4*(25), 605–628.

Fraenkel, J., & Wallen, N. (2003). *How to design and evaluate research in education* (5th ed.). New York: McGraw-Hill.

Francis, W., & Kucera, H. (1982). *Frequency analysis of English usage*. Boston, MA: Houghton Mifflin.

Friedman, D. (2012). How to collect and analyze qualitative data. In A. Mackey & S. Gass (Eds.), *Research methods in second language acquisition: A practical guide* (pp. 180–200). Boston, MA: Wiley-Blackwell.

Fukkink, R., Blok, H., & de Glopper, K. (2001). Deriving word meaning from written context: A multicomponential skill. *Language Learning, 51*(3), 477–496.

Gaies, S. J. (1980). T-unit analysis in second language research: Applications, problems and limitations. *TESOL Quarterly, 14*(1), 53–60.

Gardner, R. C., Tremblay, P. F., & Masgoret, A. (1997). Towards a full model of second language learning: an empirical investigation. *The Modern Language Journal, 81*(3), 344–362.

Gass, S. (1980). An investigation of syntactic transfer in adult L2 learners. In R. Scarcella & S. Krashen (Eds.), *Research in second language acquisition* (pp. 132–141). Rowley, MA: Newbury House.

Gass, S. (1994). The reliability of second-language grammaticality judgments. In E. Tarone, S. Gass, & A. Cohen (Eds.), *Research methodology in second-language acquisition* (pp. 303–322). Hillsdale, NJ: Lawrence Erlbaum Associates.

Gass, S. (1997). *Input, interaction, and the second language learner*. Mahwah, NJ: Lawrence Erlbaum Associates.

Gass, S. (2001). Sentence matching: A reexamination. *Second Language Research, 17*(4), 421–441.

Gass, S. (2015). Comprehensible input and output in classroom interaction. In N. Markee (Ed.), *Handbook of classroom discourse and interaction*. Boston, MA: Wiley-Blackwell.

Gass, S. with Behney, J. & Plonsky, L. (2013). *Second language acquisition: An introductory course*. New York: Routledge.

Gass, S., & Alvarez-Torres, M. (2005). Attention when? An investigation of the ordering effect of input and interaction. *Studies in Second Language Acquisition, 27*(1), 1–31.

Gass, S., & Houck, N. (1999). *Interlanguage refusals: A cross-cultural study of Japanese-English*. Berlin: Mouton de Gruyter.

Gass, S., & Mackey, A. (2000). *Stimulated recall methodology in second language research*. Mahwah, NJ: Lawrence Erlbaum Associates.

Gass, S., & Mackey, A. (2007). *Data elicitation for second and foreign language research*. Mahwah, NJ: Lawrence Erlbaum Associates.

Gass, S., Mackey, A., Alvarez-Torres, M., & Fernández-Garcia, M. (1999). The effects of task repetition on linguistic output. *Language Learning, 49*(4), 549–581.

Gass, S., Mackey, A., & Ross-Feldman, L. (2003, October). *The role of setting in classroom and laboratory interaction: From claims to data*. Paper presented at the Second Language Research Forum, Tucson, AZ.

Gass, S., Svetics, I., & Lemelin, S. (2003). Differential effects of attention. *Language Learning, 53*(3), 495–543.

Gass, S., & Varonis, E. (1994). Input, interaction and second language production. *Studies in Second Language Acquisition, 16*(3), 283–302.

Geertz, C. (1973). *The interpretation of cultures*. New York: Basic Books.

Glew, M. (1998). The acquisition of reflexive pronouns among adult learners of English (unpublished doctoral dissertation). Michigan State University, East Lansing.

Godfroid, A., Loewen, S., Jung, S., Park, J-H., Gass, S., & Ellis, R. (2015). Timed and untimed grammaticality judgments measure distinct types of knowledge: Evidence from eye-movement patterns. *Studies in Second Language Acquisition*, *37*, 269–297.

Goldschmidt, M. (1996). From the addressee's perspective: Imposition in favor-asking. In S. Gass & J. Neu (Eds.), *Speech acts across cultures* (pp. 241–256). Berlin: Mouton de Gruyter.

Goldstein, T. (1997). *Two languages at work: Bilingual life on the production floor*. Berlin/New York: Mouton de Gruyter.

Goo, J. (2012). Corrective feedback and working memory capacity in interaction-driven L2 learning. *Studies in Second Language Acquisition*, *34*(3), 445–474.

Graham, S., & Macaro, E. (2008). Strategy instruction in listening for lower-intermediate learners of French. *Language Learning*, *58*(4), 747–783.

Granger, S. (2002). A bird's-eye view of learner corpus research. In S. Granger, J. Hung, & S. Petch-Tyson (Eds.), *Computer learner corpora, second language acquisition and foreign language teaching* (pp. 3–33). Amsterdam: John Benjamins.

Granger, S. (2012). How to use foreign and second language corpora. In A. Mackey & S. Gass (Eds.), *Research methods in second language acquisition: A Practical Guide* (pp. 7–29). Malden, MA: Blackwell Publishing.

Grotjahn, R. (1987). On the methodological basis of introspective methods. In C. Færch & G. Kasper (Eds.), *Introspection in second language research* (pp. 54–81). Clevedon, UK: Multilingual Matters.

Gwet, K. (2001). *Handbook of inter-rater reliability*. Gaithersburg, MD: Stataxis.

Hafner, C. (2013). Embedding digital literacies in English language teaching: Students' digital video projects as multimodal ensembles. *TESOL Quarterly*, *48*(4), 655–685.

Hall, A., & Rist, R. (1999). Integrating multiple qualitative research methods (or avoiding the precariousness of a one-legged stool). *Psychology and Marketing*, *16*(4), 291–304.

Harrington, M. (1987). Processing transfer: Language-specific strategies as a source of interlanguage variation. *Applied Psycholinguistics*, *8*(4), 351–378.

Hashemi, M., & Babii, E. (2013). Mixed methods research: Toward new research designs in applied linguistics. *The Modern Language Journal*, *97*(4), 828–852.

Hawkins, R., & Chan, C. Y. (1997). The partial availability of Universal Grammar in second language acquisition: The "failed functional features hypothesis." *Second Language Research*, *13*(3), 187–226.

Heath, A. W. (1997, March). The proposal in qualitative research. *The Qualitative Report*, *3*(1). Retrieved Janaury 23, 2015, from www.nova.edu/ssss/QR/QR3-1/heath.html.

Heath, S. B. (1983). *Ways with words: Language, life and work in communities and classrooms*. Cambridge: Cambridge University Press.

Helms-Park, R. (2001). Evidence of lexical transfer in learner syntax: The acquisition of English causatives by speakers of Hindi-Urdu and Vietnamese. *Studies in Second Language Acquisition*, *23*(1), 71–102.

Hornberger, N. (2006). Negotiation methodological rich points in applied linguistics research: An ethnographer's view. In M. Chalhoub-Deville, C. Chapelle, & P. Duff (Eds.), *Inference and generalizability I: Applied linguistics* (pp. 221–240). Amsterdam: John Benjamins.

Hulstijn, J. H. (1997). Second language acquisition research in the laboratory: Possibilities and limitations. *Studies in Second Language Acquisition*, *19*(2), 131–143.

Hunt, K. W. (1965). *Grammatical structures written at three grade levels* (Research Report No. 3). Urbana, IL: National Council of Teachers of English.

Inagaki, S. (2001). Motion verbs with goal PPs in the L2 acquisition of English and Japanese. *Studies in Second Language Acquisition*, *23*(2), 153–170.

Ionin, T., & Wexler, K. (2002). Why is "is" easier than "s"? Acquisition of tense/agreement morphology by child second language learners of English. *Second Language Research*, *18*(2), 95–136.

Isaacs, T., & Thomson, R. I. (2013). Rater experience, rating scale length, and judgments of L2 pronunciation: Revisiting research conventions. *Language Assessment Quarterly*, *10*(2), 135–159.

Ivankova, N. V., Creswell, J. W., & Stick, S. (2006). Using mixed methods sequential explanatory design: From theory to practice. *Field Methods*, *18*(1), 3–20.

Iwashita, N. (2003). Negative feedback and positive evidence in task-based interaction: Differential effects on L2 development. *Studies in Second Language Acquisition*, *25*(1), 1–36.

Jang, E., McDougall, D., Pollon, D., Herbert, M., & Russell, P. (2008). Integrative mixed methods data analytic strategies in research on school success in challenging circumstances. *Journal of Mixed Methods Research*, *2*(3), 221–247.

Jang, E., Wagner, M., & Park, G. (2014). Mixed methods research in language testing and assessment. *Annual Review of Applied Linguistics*, *34*, 123–153.

Jiang, N. (2002). Form-meaning mapping in vocabulary acquisition in a second language. *Studies in Second Language Acquisition*, *24*(4), 617–637.

Jick, T. (1984). Mixing qualitative and quantitative methods: Triangulation in action. In J. Van Maanen (Ed.), *Qualitative methodology* (pp. 135–148). Beverly Hills, CA: Sage.

Johnson, D. M. (1992). *Approaches to research in second language learning*. New York: Longman.

Johnson, D. M. (1993). Classroom-oriented research in second-language learning. In A. O. Hadley (Ed.), *Research in language learning: Principles, processes, and prospects* (pp. 1–23). Lincolnwood, IL: National Textbook Company.

Johnson, J., & Newport, E. (1989). Critical period effects in second language learning: The influence of maturational state on the acquisition of ESL. *Cognitive Psychology*, *21*(1), 60–99.

Juffs, A. (2001). Discussion: Verb classes, event structure, and second language learners' knowledge of semantics-syntax correspondences. *Studies in Second Language Acquisition*, *23*(2), 305–313.

Juffs, A., & Harrington, M. (1995). Parsing effects in second language sentence processing: Subject and object asymmetries in wh- extraction. *Studies in Second Language Acquisition*, *17*(4), 483–516.

Just, M. A., Carpenter, P. A., & Wooley, J. D. (1982). Paradigms and processes in reading comprehension. *Journal of Experimental Psychology: General*, *3*(2), 228–238.

Kang, O. (2012). Impact of rater characteristics on ratings of international teaching assistants' oral performance. *Language Assessment Quarterly*, *9*(3), 249–269.

Kasper, G., & Rose, K. (2002). *Pragmatic development in a second language*. Malden, MA: Blackwell.

Kennedy, E. (1988). The oral interaction of native speakers and non-native speakers in a multicultural preschool: A comparison between freeplay and contrived NS/NNS dyads (unpublished master's thesis). University of British Columbia, Vancouver.

King, K. A. (2000). Language ideologies and heritage language education. *International Journal of Bilingual Education and Bilingualism*, *3*(2), 167–184.

Knaggs, C., Sondergeld, T., & Schardt, B. (2015). Overcoming barriers to college enrollment, persistence, and perceptions for urban high school students in a college preparatory program. *Journal of Mixed Methods Research*, *9*(1), 7–30.

Labov, W. (1972). *Sociolinguistic patterns*. Philadelphia, PA: University of Pennsylvania Press.

Lakshmanan, U. (1989). Accessibility to Universal Grammar in child second language acquisition (unpublished doctoral dissertation). University of Michigan, Ann Arbor.

Lakshmanan, U., & Teranishi, K. (1994). Preferences versus grammaticality judgments: Some methodological issues concerning the governing category parameter in second language acquisition. In E. Tarone, S. Gass, & A. Cohen (Eds.), *Research methodology in second language acquisition* (pp. 185–206). Hillsdale, NJ: Lawrence Erlbaum Associates.

Larson-Hall, J. (2009). *A guide to doing statistics in second language research using SPSS*. New York: Routledge.

Larson-Hall, J. (2015). *A guide to doing statistics in second language research using SPSS and R*. New York: Routledge.

Lazarton, A. (2005). Quantitative research methods. In E. Hinkel (Ed.), *Handbook of research in second language teaching and learning* (pp. 209–224). Mahwah, NJ: Lawrence Erlbaum Associates.

Leow, R. (1998). Toward operationalizing the process of attention in SLA: Evidence for Tomlin and Villa's (1994) fine-grained analysis of attention. *Applied Psycholinguistics*, *19*(1), 133–159.

Leow, R. (2000). A study of the role of awareness in foreign language behavior: Aware vs. unaware learners. *Studies in Second Language Acquisition*, *22*(4), 557–584.

Leow, R., & Morgan-Short, K. (2004). To think aloud or not to think aloud: The issue of reactivity in SLA research methodology. *Studies in Second Language Acquisition*, *26*(1), 35–57.

Li, S. (2014). The associations between language aptitude and second language grammar acquisition: a meta-analytic review of five decades of research.

Applied Linguistics, first published online October 7, 2014, doi:10.1093/applin/amu054.

Lieven, E. V. M. (1994). Crosslinguistic and crosscultural aspects of language addressed to children. In C. Gallaway & B. J. Richards (Eds.), *Input and interaction in language acquisition* (pp. 56–73). Cambridge: Cambridge University Press.

Lightbown, P. M., & Spada, N. (1990). Focus-on-form and corrective feedback in communicative language teaching: Effects on second language learning. *Studies in Second Language Acquisition*, *12*(4), 429–448.

Lightbown, P. M., & Spada, N. (1994). An innovative program for primary ESL students in Quebec. *TESOL Quarterly*, *28*(3), 563–579.

Loewen, S. (2015). *Introduction to instructed second language acquisition*. New York: Routledge.

Long, M. (1996). The role of the linguistic environment in second language acquisition. In W. C. Ritchie & T. K. Bhatia (Eds.), *Handbook of second language acquisition* (pp. 413–468). San Diego, CA: Academic Press.

Long, M. H. (2015). *Second language acquisition and task-based language teaching*. Oxford: Wiley-Blackwell.

Lotto, L., & de Groot, A. (1998). Effects of learning method and word type on acquiring vocabulary in an unfamiliar language. *Language Learning*, *48*(1), 31–69.

Lynch, B. K. (1996). *Language program evaluation: Theory and practice*. Cambridge: Cambridge University Press.

Lyster, R. (1998a). Form in immersion classroom discourse: In or out of focus? *Canadian Journal of Applied Linguistics*, *1*(1–2), 53–82.

Lyster, R. (1998b). Recasts, repetition, and ambiguity in L2 classroom discourse. *Studies in Second Language Acquisition*, *20*(1), 51–81.

Lyster, R., & Mori, H. (2006). Interactional feedback and instructional counterbalance. *Studies in Second Language Acquisition*, *28*(2), 269–300.

Lyster, R., & Ranta, L. (1997). Corrective feedback and learner uptake: Negotiation of form in communicative classrooms. *Studies in Second Language Acquisition*, *19*(1), 37–66.

Macaro, E. (2001). *Learning strategies in foreign and second language classrooms*. London: Continuum.

Macias, J. (1987). The hidden curriculum of Papago teachers: American Indian strategies for mitigating cultural discontinuity in early schooling. In G. Spindler & L. Spindler (Eds.), *Interpretive ethnography of education: At home and abroad* (pp. 363–380). Hillsdale, NJ: Lawrence Erlbaum.

Mackey, A. (1999). Input, interaction, and second language development: An empirical study of question formation in ESL. *Studies in Second Language Acquisition*, *21*(4), 557–587.

Mackey, A. (2000, August). *Feedback, noticing and second language development: An empirical study of L2 classroom interaction*. Paper presented at BAAL 2000, Cambridge, UK.

Mackey, A. (2006). Feedback, noticing and instructed second language learning. *Applied Linguistics*, *27*(3), 405–430.

Mackey, A., Gass, S., & McDonough, K. (2000). How do learners perceive implicit negative feedback? *Studies in Second Language Acquisition*, *22*(4), 471–497.

Mackey, A., McDonough, K., Fujii, A., & Tatsumi, T. (2001). Investigating learners' reports about the L2 classroom. *International Review of Applied Linguistics*, *39*(4), 285–307.

Mackey, A., & Oliver, R. (2002). Interactional feedback and children's L2 development. *System*, *30*(4), 459–477.

Mackey, A., & Philp, J. (1998). Conversational interaction and second language development: Recasts, responses, and red herrings? *The Modern Language Journal*, *82*(3), 338–356.

Mackey, A., & Sachs, R. (2012). Older learners in SLA research: A first look at working memory, feedback, and L2 development. *Language Learning*, *62*(3), 704–740.

MacWhinney, B. (1999). The CHILDES system. In W. C. Ritchie & T. Bhatia (Eds.), *Handbook of child language acquisition* (pp. 457–494). New York: Academic Press.

MacWhinney, B. (2000). *The CHILDES Project: Tools for analyzing talk* (3rd ed.). Mahwah, NJ: Lawrence Erlbaum Associates.

Magnan, S. (2006). The MLJ turns 90 in a digital age. *The Modern Language Journal*, *90*(1), 1–5.

Markee, N. (2000). *Conversation analysis*. Mahwah, NJ: Lawrence Erlbaum Associates.

Mason, J. (1996). *Qualitative researching*. London: Sage.

Mason, W., & Suri, S. (2012). Conducting behavioral research on Amazon's Mechanical Turk. *Behavior Research Methods*, *44*, 1–23.

Mayo, E. (1933). *The human problems of an industrial civilization*. New York: MacMillan.

McDonough, J., & McDonough, S. (1997). *Research methods for English language instructors*. London: Arnold.

McGroarty, M. E., & Zhu, W. (1997). Triangulation in classroom research: A study of peer revision. *Language Learning*, *47*(1), 1–43.

Mellow, J. D., Reeder, K., & Forster, F. (1996). Using time-series research designs to investigate the effects of instruction on SLA. *Studies in Second Language Acquisition*, *18*(3), 325–350.

Melzi, G., & King, K. (2003). Spanish diminutives in mother-child conversations. *Journal of Child Language*, *30*(2), 281–304.

Mitchell, R., Parkinson, B., & Johnstone, R. (1981). The foreign language classroom: An observational study. *Stirling Educational Monographs, No. 9*. Stirling, UK: Department of Education: University of Stirling.

Montrul, S. (2001). Agentive verbs of manner of motion in Spanish and English as second languages. *Studies in Second Language Acquisition*, *23*(2), 171–206.

Morgan-Short, K., Heil, J., Botero-Moriarty, A., & Ebert, S. (2012). Allocation of attention to second language form and meaning: Issues of think-alouds and depth of processing. *Studies in Second Language Acquisition*, *34*(4), 659–685.

Morrison, L. (1996). Talking about words: A study of French as a second language learners' lexical inferencing procedures. *The Canadian Modern Language Review*, *53*(1), 41–75.

Moskowitz, G. (1967). The Flint system: An observational tool for the foreign language class. In A. Simon & E. G. Boyer (Eds.), *Mirrors for behavior: An anthology of classroom observation instruments* (section 15, pp. 1–15). Philadelphia, PA: Center for the Study of Teaching, Temple University.

Moskowitz, G. (1970). *The foreign language instructor interacts*. Minneapolis, MN: Association for Productive Teaching.

Muchisky, D. (1983). Relationships between speech and reading among second language learners. *Language Learning, 33*(1), 77–102.

Murphy, J. M. (1992). An etiquette for the nonsupervisory observation of L2 classrooms. *Foreign Language Annals, 25*(3), 215–225.

Murphy, V. (1997). The effect of modality on a grammaticality judgment task. *Second Language Research, 13*(1), 34–65.

Nassaji, H. (2012). The relationship between SLA research and language pedagogy: Teachers' perspectives. *Language Teaching Research, 16*(3), 337–365.

National Institute for Health. (n.d.). *Human subject protections education for research teams*. Retrieved January 25, 2015, from http://cme.nci.nih.gov.

Neufeld, A., Harrison, M., Hughes, K., Spitzer, D., & Stewart, M. (2001). Participation of immigrant women family caregivers in qualitative research. *Western Journal of Nursing Research, 23*(6), 575–591.

Norris, J., & Ortega, L. (2000). Effectiveness of L2 instruction: A research synthesis and quantitative meta-analysis. *Language Learning, 50*(3), 417–528.

Norris, J. M., & Ortega, L. (2003). Defining and measuring L2 acquisition. In C. Doughty & M. H. Long (Eds.), *Handbook of second language acquisition* (pp. 717–761). New York: Blackwell.

Norris, J., & Ortega, L. (2009). Towards an organic approach to investigating CAF in instructed SLA: The case of complexity. *Applied Linguistics, 30*, 555–578.

Norris, J. M., & Ortega, L. (Eds.) (2006). *Synthesizing research on language learning and teaching*. Amsterdam: John Benjamins.

Nunan, D. (1989). *Understanding language classrooms: A guide for instructor initiated action*. New York: Prentice Hall.

Nunan, D. (1993). Action research in language education. In J. Edge & K. Richards (Eds.), *Instructors develop instructors research: Papers on classroom research and instructor development* (pp. 39–50). Oxford: Heinemann.

Nuremberg Code (1949). *From trials of war criminals before the Nuremberg Military Tribunals under Control Council Law No. 10*, Vol. 2, 181–182. Washington, DC: U.S. Government Printing Office. Retrieved January 25, 2015, from www.loc.gov/rr/frd/Military_Law/pdf/NT_war-criminals_Vol-II.pdf.

NVivo [Computer Software]. Retrieved April 19, 2015, from www.qsrinternational.com.

Office for Human Research Protections (OHRP) of the Department of Health and Human Services (DHHS) (n.d.). *IRB Guidebook*. Retrieved January 25, 2015, from www.hhs.gov/ohrp/archive/irb/irb_guidebook.htm.

Office for Human Research Protections (OHRP) of the Department of Health and Human Services (DHHS) (n.d.). *Training modules for assurances: Investigator responsibilities and informed consent*. Retrieved January 25, 2015, from http://ohrp-ed.od.nih.gov/CBTs/Assurance/login.asp.

Office for Human Research Protections (OHRP) (2013, March). Considerations and Recommendations Concerning Internet Research and Human Subjects Research Regulations, with Revisions (Secretary's Advisory Committee on Human Research Protections SACHRP). Retrieved January 25, 2015, from www.hhs.gov/ohrp/sachrp/mtgings/2013%20March%20Mtg/internet_research. pdf.

Ohta, A. S. (1995). Applying sociocultural theory to an analysis of learner discourse: Collaborative interaction in the zone of proximal development. *Issues in Applied Linguistics, 6*(2), 93–121.

Ohta, A. S. (2001). *Second language acquisition processes in the classroom: Learning Japanese.* Mahwah, NJ: Lawrence Erlbaum Associates.

Oliver, R. (1998). Negotiation of meaning in child interactions. *The Modern Language Journal, 82*(3), 372–386.

Oliver, R. (2000). Age differences in negotiation and feedback in classroom and pairwork. *Language Learning, 50*(1), 119–151.

Oliver, R. (2002). The patterns of negotiation for meaning in child interactions. *Modern Language Journal, 86*(1), 97–111.

Ortega, L. (1999). Planning and focus on form in L2 oral performance. *Studies in Second Language Acquisition, 21*(1), 109–148.

Orwin, R. G. (1994). Evaluating coding decisions. In H. Cooper & L. V. Hedges (Eds.), *The handbook of research synthesis* (pp. 139–162). New York: Russell Sage Foundation.

Pavlenko, A., & Lantolf, J. P. (2000). Second language learning as participation and the (re)construction of selves. In J. P. Lantolf (Ed.), *Sociocultural theory and second language learning* (pp. 155–178). New York: Oxford University Press.

Pedhazur, E., & Schmelkin, L. (1991). *Measurement, design, and analysis: An integrated approach.* Hillsdale, NJ: Lawrence Erlbaum Associates.

Philips, S. U. (1972). Participant structures and communicative competence: Warm Indian Springs children in community and classroom. In C. B. Cazden, V. P. John, & D. Hymes (Eds.), *Functions of language in the classroom* (pp. 370–394). New York: Teachers College Press.

Philips, S. (1983). *The invisible culture: Communication in classroom and community on the Warm Springs Indian Reservation.* New York: Longman.

Philp, J. (2003). Constraints on "noticing the gap": Nonnative speakers' noticing of recasts in NS-NNS interaction. *Studies in Second Language Acquisition, 25*(1), 99–126.

Pica, T. (1984). The selective impact of classroom instruction on second language acquisition. *Applied Linguistics, 6*(3), 214–222.

Pica, T. (1994). Research on negotiation: What does it reveal about second-language learning conditions, processes, and outcomes? *Language Learning, 44*(3), 493–527.

Pica, T., Kanagy, R., & Falodun, J. (1993). Choosing and using communication tasks for second language instruction. In G. Crookes & S. M. Gass (Eds.), *Tasks and language learning: Integrating theory and practice* (pp. 9–34). Clevedon, UK: Multilingual Matters.

Pienemann, M., & Johnston, M., (1986). An acquisition-based procedure for second-language assessment. *Australian Review of Applied Linguistics*, *9*(1), 92–122.

Pierce, B. (1995). Social identity, investment, and language learning. *TESOL Quarterly*, *29*(1), 9–31.

Pintzuk, S. (1988). *VARBRUL programs* [Computer program]. Philadelphia, PA: University of Pennsylvania, Department of Linguistics.

Plonsky, L. (2012). Effect sizes. In P. Robinson (Ed.), *The Routledge encyclopedia of second language acquisition* (pp. 200–202). New York: Routledge.

Plonsky, L. (2013). Study quality in SLA: An assessment of designs, analyses, and reporting practices in quantitative L2 research. *Studies in Second Language Acquisition*, *35*(4), 655–687.

Plonsky, L. (2014). Study quality in quantitative L2 research (1990–2010): A methodological synthesis and call for reform. *The Modern Language Journal*, *98*(1), 450–470.

Plonsky, L., & Gass, S. (2011). Study quality in interactionist research. *Language Learning*, *61*(2), 325–366.

Plonsky, L., & Oswald, F. (2012). How to do a meta-analysis. In A. Mackey & S. Gass (Eds.), *Research methods in second language acquisition: A practical introduction* (pp. 275–295). Malden, MA: Blackwell.

Plonsky, L., & Oswald, F. (2014). How big is "big"? Interpreting effect sizes in L2 research. *Language Learning*, *64*(4), 878–912.

Polio, C. (1997). Measures of linguistic accuracy in second language writing research. *Language Learning*, *47*(1), 101–143.

Polio, C., & Gass, S. (1997). Replication and reporting: A commentary. *Studies in Second Language Acquisition*, *19*(4), 499–508.

Porte, G. K. (2002). *Appraising research in second language learning: A practical approach to critical analysis of quantitative research*. Amsterdam: John Benjamins.

Porte, G. K. (Ed.) (2012). *Replication research in applied linguistics*. Cambridge: Cambridge University Press.

Portney, L. G., & Watkins, M. P. (1993). *Foundations of clinical research: Applications to practice*. Norwalk, CT: Appleton & Lange.

Pritchard, R. M. O., & Nasr, A. (2004). Improving reading performance among Egyptian engineering students: Principles and practice. *English for Specific Purposes*, *23*(4), 425–445.

Psychology Software Tools (2014). E-Prime (Version 2.0) [Software]. Retrieved April 19, 2015, from www.pstnet.com/eprime.cfm.

Qi, D. S., & Lapkin, S. (2001). Exploring the role of noticing in a three-stage second language writing task. *Journal of Second Language Writing*, *10*(4), 277–303.

Ramanathan, V., & Atkinson, D. (1999). Ethnographic approaches and methods in L2 writing research: A critical guide and review. *Applied Linguistics*, *20*(1), 44–70.

Rand, D., & Sankoff, D. (1990). *GoldVarb: A variable rule application for the Macintosh* (Version 2.0) [Computer program]. Montreal: Centre de recherches mathématiques, Université de Montréal. Retrieved April 19, 2015, from http://albuquerque.bioinformatics.uottawa.ca/goldvarb/goldmanual.dir/gvmanual.html.

Reichardt, C. S., & Cook, T. D. (1979). Beyond qualitative versus quantitative methods. In T. D. Cook & C. S. Reichardt (Eds.), *Qualitative and quantitative methods in evaluation research* (pp. 7–32). Beverly Hills, CA: Sage.

Reichle, E., Pollatsek, A., & Rayner, K. (2006). E-Z Reader: A cognitive-control, serial-attention model of eye-movement behavior during reading. *Cognitive Systems Research, 7*, 4–22.

Reichle, E. D., Pollatsek, A., & Rayner, K. (2012). Using E-Z Reader to simulate eye movements in nonreading tasks: A unified framework for understanding the eye-mind link. *Psychological Review, 119*, 155–185.

Révész, A. (2011). Task complexity, focus on L2 constructions, and individual differences: A classroom-based study. *The Modern Language Journal, 95*(s1), 162–181.

Révész, A., Sachs, R., & Hama, M. (2014). The effects of task complexity and input frequency on the acquisition of the past counterfactual construction through recasts. *Language Learning, 64*(3), 615–640.

Reynolds, D. (2001). Language in the balance: Lexical repetition as a function of topic, cultural background, and writing development. *Language Learning, 51*(3), 437–476.

Roberts, M. (1995). Awareness and the efficacy of error correction. In R. Schmidt (Ed.), *Attention and awareness in foreign language learning* (Tech. Rep. No. 3, pp. 163–182). Honolulu, HI: University of Hawaii, Second Language Teaching and Curriculum Center.

Rodríguez, M., & Abreu, O. (2003). The stability of general foreign language classroom anxiety across English and French. *The Modern Language Journal, 87*(3), 365–374.

Rounds, P. (1996). The classroom-based researcher as fieldworker: Strangers in a strange land. In J. Schachter & S. Gass (Eds.), *Second language classroom research: Issues and opportunities* (pp. 45–59). Mahwah, NJ: Lawrence Erlbaum Associates.

Ruiyang, Y., & Allison, D. (2003). Research articles in applied linguistics: Moving from results to conclusions. *English for Specific Purposes, 22*(4), 365–385.

Rust, R. T., & Cooil, B. (1994). Reliability measures for qualitative data: Theory and implications. *Journal of Marketing Research, 31*(1), 1–14.

Sachs, R., & Polio, C. (2007). Learners' uses of two types of written feedback on a L2 revision task. *Studies in Second Language Acquisition, 29*(1), 67–100.

Samuda, V. (2001). Guiding relationships between form and meaning during task performance: The role of the instructor. In M. Bygate, P. Skehan, & M. Swain (Eds.), *Researching pedagogic tasks: Second language learning, teaching and testing* (pp. 119–140). London: Longman.

Sasaki, Y. (1997). Material and presentation condition effects on sentence interpretation task performance: Methodological examinations of the competition experiment. *Second Language Research, 13*(1), 34–65.

Sasaki, M. (2004). A multiple-data analysis of the 3.5 year development of EFL student writers. *Language Learning, 54*(3), 525–582.

SAS Institute, Inc. (n.d.). SAS [Software]. Retrieved April 19, 2015, from www.sas.com.

Schachter, J., & Gass, S. (1996). *Second language classroom research: Issues and opportunities*. Mahwah, NJ: Lawrence Erlbaum Associates.

Schegloff, E. A. (1993). Reflections on quantification in the study of conversation. *Research on Language and Social Interaction, 26*(1), 99–128.

Schenkein, J. (1978). *Studies in the organization of conversational interaction*. New York: Academic Press.

Schilling, N. (2013). *Sociolinguistic fieldwork*. Cambridge: Cambridge University Press.

Schmidt, R. (1983). Interaction, acculturation and the acquisition of communicative competence. In N. Wolfson & E. Judd (Eds.), *Sociolinguistics and second language acquisition* (pp. 137–174). Rowley, MA: Newbury House.

Schmidt, R., & Frota, S. N. (1986). Developing basic conversational ability in a second language: A case study of an adult learner of Portuguese. In R. Day (Ed.), *Talking to learn* (pp. 237–326). Rowley, MA: Newbury House.

Schneider, C. E. (2015). *The censor's hand: The misregulation of human-subjects research*. Cambridge, MA: The MIT Press.

Schneider, N. (2015). Intellectual piecework: Increasingly used in research, platforms like Mechanical Turk pose new ethical dilemmas. *The Chronicle of Higher Education*. Retrieved April 19, 2005, from http://chronicle.com/article/Intellectual-Piecework/190039/?key=HW57JVw8MyFOY343MztCYW5QbnRvN05yYCRIbH17bI9VEA==.

Schütze, C. (1996). *The empirical base of linguistics: Grammaticality judgments and linguistic methodology*. Chicago, IL: University of Chicago Press.

Scollon, R. (2001). Action and text: Toward an integrated understanding of the place of text in social (inter)action. In R. Wodak & M. Meyer (Eds.), *Methods in critical discourse analysis* (pp. 139–183). London: Sage.

Shavelson, R. (1988). *Statistical reasoning for the behavioral sciences*. Boston, MA: Allyn & Bacon.

Schumann, F., & Schumann, J. (1977). Diary of a language learner: An introspective study of second language learning. In H. D. Brown, C. Yorio, & R. Crymes (Eds.), *Teaching and learning English as a Second Language: Trends in research and practice* (pp. 241–249). Washington, DC: TESOL.

Sheen, Y. (2007). The effects of corrective feedback, language aptitude, and learner attributes on the acquisition of English articles. In A. Mackey (Ed.), *Conversational interaction in second language acquisition: A collection of empirical studies* (pp. 301–322). Oxford: Oxford University Press.

Sheen, Y. (2010). Differential effects of oral and written corrective feedback in the ESL classroom. *Studies in Second Language Acquisition, 32*(2), 203–234.

Silver, C., & Lewins, A. (2014). *Using software in qualitative research*. Thousand Oaks, CA: Sage.

Silver, R. E. (1999). Input, output, and negotiation: Conditions for second language development. In B. Swierzbin, F. Morris, M. E. Anderson, C. A. Klee, & E. Tarone (Eds.), *Social and cognitive factors in second language acquisition: Selected proceedings of the 1999 Second Language Research Forum* (pp. 345–371). Somerville, MA: Cascadilla.

Sinclair, J. M., & Coulthard, R. M. (1975). *Towards an analysis of discourse: The English used by teachers and pupils*. London: Oxford University Press.

Skehan, P. (1996). A framework for implementation of task-based instruction. *Applied Linguistics*, *17*(1), 38–62.

Skehan, P. (1998). *A cognitive approach to language learning*. New York: Oxford University Press.

Skehan, P., & Foster, P. (1999). The influence of task structure and processing conditions on narrative retellings. *Language Learning*, *49*(1), 93–120.

Spada, N. (1994). Classroom interaction analysis. *TESOL Quarterly*, *28*(4), 685–688.

Spada, N., & Fröhlich, M. (1995). *The Communicative Orientation of Language Teaching (COLT) observation scheme: Coding conventions and applications*. Sydney, Australia: Macquarie University, National Centre for English Language Teaching and Research.

Spada, N., & Lightbown, P. M. (1993). Instruction and the development of questions in L2 classrooms. *Studies in Second Language Acquisition*, *15*(2), 205–224.

Staphorsius, G., & Verhelst, N. D. (1997). Indexering van de leestechniek [The development of a domain-referenced index of the decoding load of texts]. *Pedagogische Studiën*, *74*(3), 154–164.

Storch, N., & Tapper, J. (1996). Patterns of NNS student annotations in identifying areas of concern in their writing. *System*, *24*(3), 323–336.

Swain, M., & Lapkin, S. (1998). Interaction and second language learning: Two adolescent French immersion students working together. *The Modern Language Journal*, *82*(3), 320–337.

Swain, M., & Lapkin, S. (2001). Focus on form through collaborative dialogue: Exploring task effects. In M. Bygate, P. Skehan, & M. Swain (Eds.), *Researching pedagogic tasks: Second language learning and testing* (pp. 99–118). Harlow: Longman.

Systat Software. (2008). SYSTAT 13 [Computer Software]. Retrieved April 19, 2015, from www.systat.com.

Tashakkori, A., & Creswell, J. W. (2007). Editorial: The new era of mixed methods. *Journal of Mixed Methods Research*, *1*(1), 3–7.

Tashakkori, A., & Teddlie, C. (Eds.) (2010). *Handbook of mixed methods in social and behavioral research* (2nd ed.). Thousand Oaks, CA: Sage.

Tavakoli, P. (2012). Planning time. In P. Robinson (Ed.), *The Routledge encyclopedia of second language acquisition* (pp. 490–493). New York: Routledge.

Tetnowski, J., & Damico, J. (2001). A demonstration of the advantages of qualitative methodologies in stuttering research. *Journal of Fluency Disorders*, *26*(1), 17–42.

Thompson, R., & Jackson, S. (1998). Ethical dimensions of child memory research. *Applied Cognitive Psychology*, *12*(3), 218–224.

Thorndike, E., & Lorge, I. (1944). *The teacher's word book of 30,000 words*. New York: Columbia University.

Tomlin, R., & Villa, V. (1994). Attention in cognitive science and second language acquisition. *Studies in Second Language Acquisition*, *16*(2), 183–204.

Toth, P. D. (2000). The interaction of instruction and learner-internal factors in the acquisition of L2 morphosyntax. *Studies in Second Language Acquisition*, *22*(2), 169–208.

Trochim, W. M. (2006). *The research methods knowledge base* (2nd ed.). Retrieved January 25, 2015, from www.socialresearchmethods.net/kb.

Tse, L. (1996). If you lead horses to water they will drink: Introducing second language adults to books in English. *California Reader*, *29*(2), 14–17.

Tyler, A. (1992). Discourse structure and the perception of incoherence in international teaching assistants' spoken discourse. *TESOL Quarterly*, *26*(4), 713–730.

Ullman, R., & Geva, E. (1983). *Classroom observation in the L2 setting: A dimension of program evaluation*. Modern Language Centre, Ontario: Institute for Studies in Education.

Ullman, R., & Geva, E. (1985). Expanding our evaluation perspective: What can classroom observation tell us about Core French programs? *The Canadian Modern Language Review*, *42*(2), 307–323.

University of Pennsylvania (n.d.). *Institutional review boards' standard operating policies: Section 500 SC, reviews requiring special considerations* (pp. 80–93). Retrieved January 25, 2015, from www.upenn.edu/regulatoryaffairs/Documents/irb%20sop%207-1%202009.pdf.

Valdman, A. (1993). Replication study. *Studies in Second Language Acquisition*, *15*(4), 505.

Van Daalen-Kapteijns, M., Elshout-Mohr, M., & de Glopper, K. (1981). The acquisition of word meanings as a cognitive learning process. *Journal of Verbal Learning and Verbal Behavior*, *20*(4), 386–399.

VanPatten, B., & Cadierno, T. (1993). Input processing and second language acquisition: A role for instruction. *The Modern Language Journal*, *77*(1), 45–56.

van Someren, M., Barnard, Y., & Sandberg, J. (1994). *The think aloud method: A practical guide to modeling cognitive processes*. London: Academic Press.

Verburg, M., & Huijgen, M. (1994). *Van dale Juniorwoordenboek Nederlands* [*Van Dale junior dictionary of Dutch*]. Utrecht, The Netherlands: Van Dale Lexicografie.

Wallace, M. J. (1998). *Action research for language instructors*. Cambridge: Cambridge University Press.

Watson-Gegeo, K. (1988). Ethnography in ESL: Defining the essentials. *TESOL Quarterly*, *22*(4), 575–592.

Watson-Gegeo, K. (1997). Classroom ethnography. In N. H. Hornberger & D. Corson (Eds.), *Encyclopedia of language and education: Vol. 8. Research methods in language and education* (pp. 135–144). Dordrecht, The Netherlands: Kluwer.

White, L. (1985). The "Pro-drop" parameter in adult second language acquisition. *Language Learning*, *35*(1), 47–62.

White, L., & Juffs, A. (1998). Constraints on wh- movement in two different contexts of non-native language acquisition: Competence and processing. In S. Flynn, G. Martohardjono, & W. O'Neil (Eds.), *The generative study of second language acquisition* (pp. 111–129). Mahwah, NJ: Lawrence Erlbaum Associates.

White, L., Spada, N., Lightbown, P. M., & Ranta, L. (1991). Input enhancement and L2 question formation. *Applied Linguistics*, *12*(4), 416–432.

Wilkinson, L., & Task Force on Statistical Inference (1999). Statistical methods in psychology journals: Guidelines and explanations. *American Psychologist*, *54*(8), 594–604.

Willett, J. (1995). Becoming first graders in an L2: An ethnographic study of L2 socialization. *TESOL Quarterly*, *29*(3), 473–503.

Williams, J. (1999). Learner-generated attention to form. *Language Learning*, *49*(4), 583–625.

Williams, J., & Evans, J. (1998). What kind of focus and on which forms? In C. Doughty & J. Williams (Eds.), *Focus on form in classroom second language acquisition* (pp. 139–155). Cambridge: Cambridge University Press.

Winke, P., Gass, S., & Sydorenko, T. (2010). The effects of captioning videos used for foreign language listening activities. *Language Learning & Technology*, *14*(1), 65–86.

Winke, P., Gass, S., & Sydorenko, T. (2013). Factors influencing the use of captions by foreign language learners: An eye-tracking study. *The Modern Language Journal*, *97*(1), 254–275.

Woods, A., Fletcher, P., & Hughes, A. (1986). *Statistics in language studies*. Cambridge: Cambridge University Press.

World Medical Association (2000). *Declaration of Helsinki. Ethical principles for medical research involving human subjects*. Retrieved January 25, 2015, from www.wma.net/en/30publications/10policies/b3.

Wray, A. (2001). *Formulaic language and the lexicon*. Cambridge: Cambridge University Press.

Young, R. (1991). *Variation in interlanguage morphology*. New York: Peter Lang.

Young, R., & Bayley, R. (1996). VARBRUL analysis for second language research. In R. Bayley & D. Preston (Eds.), *Second language acquisition and linguistic variation* (pp. 253–306). Amsterdam: John Benjamins.

Yuan, F., & Ellis, R. (2003). The effects of pre-task planning and on-line planning on fluency, complexity and accuracy in L2 monologic oral production. *Applied Linguistics*, *24*(1), 1–27.

Zsiga, L. (2003). Articulatory timing in a second language. *Studies in Second Language Acquisition*, *25*(3), 399–432.

Subject Index